HEALTH AND HEALTH CARE IN THE NEW RUSSIA

Dedication to Nadia Davidova

We would like to dedicate this book to the memory of one of its authors, Nadia Davidova, who tragically died not long before it was completed. From the very beginning of our work and throughout all three of the projects conducted by our international research team, Nadia was not just a member of the group. She was a keen enthusiast for her work, and none of us could match her in inspiring and mobilising the whole group, uniting and rallying us towards a common goal. Without her, our extensive project would have been simply impossible; with her death at the age of only 42, the academic world has lost a serious, thoughtful scholar who still had great promise ahead of her. In her short life, Nadia managed to take part in dozens of projects, including international ones, to publish over 60 works and to become a member of the editorial committee, as well as Russia consultant and coordinator, for the three-volume *Routledge International Encyclopaedia of Social Policy* (Fitzpatrick et al., 2006). In the UK, she worked actively with Oxford Analytica, the international independent consultancy, publishing materials on their web site about the social situation in Russia; and, in Russia, she carried out commissions for major Russian Federation government bodies and expert reviews on socioeconomic issues for a number of regional administrations. We should also particularly mention her role in the creation of the Russian Sociological Data Archive.

Health and Health Care in the New Russia

Edited by

NICK MANNING
University of Nottingham, UK

NATALIYA TIKHONOVA
Higher School of Economics, Moscow, Russia

Translations by KAREN GEORGE

ASHGATE

Published by
Ashgate Publishing Limited
Wey Court East
Union Road
Farnham
Surrey, GU9 7PT
England

Ashgate Publishing Company
Suite 420
101 Cherry Street
Burlington
VT 05401-4405
USA

www.ashgate.com

British Library Cataloguing in Publication Data
Health and health care in the new Russia
    1. Public health - Russia (Federation) 2. Medical policy -
    Russia (Federation) 3. National health services - Russia
    (Federation) 4. Health attitudes - Russia (Federation)
    I. Manning, Nick P. II. Tikhonova, N. E.
    362.1'0947

Library of Congress Cataloging-in-Publication Data
Health and health care in the new Russia / [edited] by Nick Manning and Nataliya Tikhonova.
    p. cm.
    Includes bibliographical references and index.
    ISBN 978-0-7546-7427-6 (hardcover) 1. Health care reform--Russia
(Federation) 2. Medical care--Russia (Federation) 3. Health behavior--Russia
(Federation) 4. Social medicine--Russia (Federation) 5. Medical economics--Russia
(Federation) I. Manning, Nick P. II. Tikhonova, N. E.
    [DNLM: 1. Health Care Reform--economics--Russia. 2. Health Knowledge, Attitudes,
Practice--Russia. 3. Health Status--Russia. 4. Socioeconomic Factors--Russia. WA 540
GR9 H396 2008]

    RA395.R9H43 2008
    362.1'04250947--dc22

                          2008031181

ISBN 978 0 7546 7427 6

Mixed Sources
Product group from well-managed
forests and other controlled sources
www.fsc.org Cert no. SGS-COC-2482
© 1996 Forest Stewardship Council
FSC

Printed and bound in Great Britain by
TJ International Ltd, Padstow, Cornwall

Contents

List of Figures   *vii*

List of Tables   *ix*

Notes on Contributors   *xiii*

Preface   *xv*

1   Social Policy and the Health Crisis in the New Russia   1
     Nadia Davidova, Nick Manning, Hannele Palosuo
     and Meri Koivusalo

PART I   HEALTH BELIEFS IN THE NEW RUSSIA

2   Measuring the Population's Health   27
     Nataliya Tikhonova

3   Understanding Health   53
     Svetlana Goryunova and Nataliya Tikhonova

PART II   HEALTH AND SOCIAL STRUCTURE

4   Inequalities and Health   79
     Nataliya Tikhonova

5   Poverty in Post-Reform Russia   97
     Nadia Davidova

6   Poverty and Health: The Longitudinal Experience   119
     Nadia Davidova

7   Health and Employment   147
     Inna Nazarova

PART III   HEALTH AND SOCIAL ACTION

8   Access to Health Care and Self-Care   173
       Inna Nazarova

9   Health Behaviour   201
       Irina Popova

10   Gender, Health and Poverty   227
       Irina Popova

11   Life Stories of Ten Russian Households: The Sequence of
       Events over Ten Years of Reform   251
       Nadia Davidova (with linking material by *Karen George*)

Appendix: Project Methodology   273
Nadia Davidova

Bibliography   *295*
Index   *307*

List of Figures

1.1   Life expectancy by gender from birth, Russia, Finland, UK   12

2.1   Deaths according to main classifications of cause of death, 2005
(in percentages of total number of deaths)   28

2.2   Prevalence of certain chronic diseases in various age groups,
RLMS, 2005 (%)   29

2.3   Distribution of health indicators according to EQ-5D method,
respondents aged 14 and over, RLMS, 2005 (%)   32

3.1   Proportions of people with different understandings of health and
sickness, groups with different standards of education,
RLMS, 2005 (%)   71

4.1   Model of the social structure of Russia and the UK   94

5.1   Dynamics in living standards of respondents in our panel study
(1997–2005)   115

6.1   Self-rated health x changes in household's material welfare,
1997–2004 (%)   128

6.2   Health on the EQ-5D x changes in household's material welfare,
1997–2004 (%)   128

6.3   Health on the GHQ x changes in household's material welfare,
1997–2004 (%)   128

6.4   Households' social capital x level of material welfare, 2004 (%)   139

List of Tables

1.1 Official poverty levels in Russia, 1992–2006, % of population 8

1.2 Out-of-pocket spending on health as % of total health expenditure *x* household 16

2.1 Distribution of health indicators according to EQ-5D method, UK and Russia, results of national research surveys (%) 31

2.2 Distribution of health indicators according to EQ-5D method, various age groups, RLMS, 2005 (%) 33

2.3 Consistency in identifying oneself with people who have serious health problems, panel respondents grouped according to their own assessments of their health, 2005 (%) 36

2.4 Health indicators of panel respondents grouped according to various assessments of their own health, 2005 (%) 36

2.5 Distribution of panel respondents' health indicators according to EQ-5D method, 2005 (%) 40

2.6 Health standards of panel respondents grouped according to various assessments of their own health, 2005 (%) 41

2.7 Correlation of panel respondents' health indicators on the two scales used, 2005 (%) 41

2.8 General picture of Russians' health according to EQ-5D indicators reduced to a three-level scale, RLMS, 2005 (%) 41

2.9 Correlation of indicators of material welfare, panel respondents grouped by standard of health on the EQ-5D scale, 2005 (%) 44

2.10 Age structure, panel respondents grouped by standard of health according to the EQ-5D scale, 2005 (%) 45

2.11 Some particular features of respondents grouped by standard of health according to the EQ-5D scale, 2005 (%) 48

2.12 Health indicators for various occupational status groups defined according to ISCO-88 classification, RLMS, 2005 (%) 49

3.1 Russians' understanding of health and sickness, RLMS, 2005 (%) 63

3.2 Russians' understanding of health, various groups of respondents, RLMS, 2005 (%) 68

3.3 Russians' understanding of sickness, various groups of respondents, RLMS, 2005 (%) 69

3.4 Understanding of health and sickness, groups with different standards of education, RLMS, 2005 (%) 70

3.5 Understanding of health and sickness, according to self-rated position on a scale from 'indigence' to 'wealth', RLMS, 2005 (%) 72

4.1	Distribution wages by decile groups, in April 2006	80
4.2	Distribution of total income across quintile groups, selected areas, 2005	81
4.3	Per cent below the subsistence minimum, selected areas, 2000–2005	82
4.4	Distribution of per capita incomes, 2000–2005 (%)	83
4.5	Respondents' own assessments of aspects of their lives, 2006 (%)	84
4.6	Ownership of consumer durables, 2006 (%) (percentage that has none of a given consumer durable)	85
4.7	Use of fee-paying social services in the last 12 months, 2006 (%)	87
4.8	Achievements over the previous 12 months, 2006 (%)	88
4.9	Attitudes to social justice and inequalities, 2006 (%)	91
4.10	Assessments of own health, 2006 (%)	95
4.11	Assessments of own health, 2005 (%)	96
5.1	Rosstat estimated poverty rates, 1992 to 2000 (%)	98
5.2	Level and depth of poverty among households, 1992 to 2004, RLMS (%)	108
5.3	Material circumstances of respondent households, 1997 to 2005 (%)*	112
5.4	Deprivations experienced by the families of our respondents, 1997–2005 (%)	114
6.1	Employment of household respondents (%)	123
6.2	Ways of spending leave from work x levels of material welfare, 2004 (%)	126
6.3	Types of unobtainable medical care x level of material welfare, 2004 (%)	129
7.1	Average assessments of own health, in points, RLMS	150
7.2	Main sources of income, 2006 (%)	157
7.3	Additional work activities, 2006 (%)	158
8.1	Patterns of use for different health care establishments (%)	174
8.2	Frequency of visiting the doctor, 2005 (%)	175
8.3	Views on social justice, 2006 (%)	183
8.4	Paying for medical services (%)	190
8.5	Payment for medicines, syringes and dressings (%)	191
8.6	Features of fee-paying and free services, 2005	192
8.7	Responsibility for tackling social problems, 2006 (%)	194
8.8	Changes in social support during Putin's presidency, 2006 (%)	195
8.9	Opinions on changes in the health care x level of material welfare, 2006 (%)	196
8.10	Opinions on health care funding x level of material welfare, 2006 (%)	196
9.1	Attitudes to health and changes in health status (% of group)	210
10.1	Socioeconomic changes which have influenced the health of men and of women	228
10.2	Men's and women's opinions about reform difficulties	233

10.3	Men's and women's opinions about contribution to the family budget, by level of welfare, 2006 (%)	243
10.4	Health indicators of women and men, EQ-5D scale, 2005 (%)	245
10.5	Differences in attitudes to maintaining health, by gender (%)	246
A1	Number of family members in households studied (N)	277
A2	Demographic type of households studied (N)	278
A3	Socioeconomic structure of families (N)	279
A4	Socioeconomic status of heads of households (N)	280

Notes on Contributors

Nadia Davidova was a Senior Research Fellow in the Institute of Sociology of the Russian Academy of Sciences. She held a PhD in Sociology, and published around 50 works in Russia and the UK. She specialised in social policy in general, and in issues of poverty in particular.

Karen George has a BA in Russian from the University of London and is a member of the Chartered Institute of Linguists and the Institute of Translation and Interpreting. She has over 50 published translations in the social sciences, including Patrick Le Galès' *European Cities: social conflicts and governance* (Oxford University Press, 2002), which was awarded the Stein Rokkan Prize for comparative research by the International Social Science Council.

Svetlana Goryunova (MSc Economics) is a Research Fellow in the Institute of Sociology of the Russian Academy of Sciences, and a faculty member in the State University, Higher School of Economics. She has published more than ten works, devoted mainly to issues of living standards and particular behavioural features of various social groups.

Meri Koivusalo is a senior researcher in the National Research and Development Centre for Welfare and Health, Helsinki. She is a medical doctor with a PhD in epidemiology. Research experience includes domestic and international health policy. She has edited and co-authored several books and scientific articles in the area. She has been an expert advisor to the European Commission, World Health Organisation, UN/DESA and UNRISD. She is currently an editor of the journal *Global Social Policy*.

Nick Manning is Professor of Social Policy and Sociology, and Director of the Institute of Mental Health, at the University of Nottingham, UK. He has been engaged in research on social issues in Russia since 1979 (*Socialism and Social Welfare in the Soviet Union*, 1980, with Vic George), and has published more than 25 books and editions, and numerous articles and chapters. Recent work includes *Social Policy*, 2007 (with John Baldock and Sarah Vickerstaff), *International Encyclopaedia of Social Policy*, 2006 (with Tony Fitzpatrick, Huck-ju Kwon, James Midgley and Gillian Pascall), *A Culture of Enquiry*, 2006 (with Jan Lees, Diana Menzies and Nicola Morant), and *After the Fall* 2003 (with Roy Bradshaw and Stuart Thompstone). He was elected a member of the UK Academy of Social Sciences in 2007.

Inna Nazarova is a Senior Research Fellow in the Gender Issues Working Group at the Higher School of Economics, and holds a PhD in Sociology. She has published over 50 works (including *The health of the working population*, 2007, and many others), mainly devoted to the sociology of health.

Hannele Palosuo, PhD (sociology of health), is a senior researcher in the National Research and Development Centre for Welfare and Health, Helsinki, in the project on reducing inequalities in health. She has recently been an advisor in the preparation of the national action plan to reduce health inequalities in Finland. She has published on health and health behaviour in Finland, Russia and Estonia and health policy in Finland and other European countries. She has taught medical sociology at the University of Helsinki.

Irina Popova is a Research Fellow in the Institute of Sociology of the Russian Academy of Sciences. She has published over 50 works, devoted primarily to the sociology of occupational groups and to gender differences in employment behaviour.

Nataliya Tikhonova has published more than 250 works in Russia, the USA, Germany and the UK *(Social Stratification Factors during Transition to the Market Economy*, 1999; *The Phenomenon of Urban Poverty in Contemporary Russia*, 2003; *Social Stratification in Contemporary Russia: experience from an empirical analysis*, 2007; and many others). She is interested in the consequences of economic change, particularly for social structure. She is a Doctor of Science in Sociology, and a professor. She currently holds the posts of Director of the Department of Social and Economic Systems and Social Policy at the State University, Higher School of Economics and is Deputy Director of the Institute of Sociology of the Russian Academy of Sciences.

Preface

It is 15 years since this programme of work on the social consequences of change in post-communist Russia was conceived. At the time, in 1993, the shape and focus of the constituent projects were as yet unclear. However, work on grass roots political developments in the immediate post-communist days was already underway through a study of housing and environmental social movements (Lang-Pickvance, Pickvance and Manning, 1997). This study had highlighted the way in which the old social supports of the State socialist era were rapidly unravelling, but not the shape of things to come. 1993 also saw the setting up of the European Union of INTAS, the 'International Association for the promotion of cooperation with scientists from the New Independent States of the former Soviet Union'. This seemed the ideal vehicle for funding the planned programme of research, and indeed INTAS has generously funded all three of the projects that have made up the programme, of which this is the final report.

The INTAS programme was aimed not just at research projects, but also at creating regular scientific exchange between Russia and Western research staff at all levels. The current project and its predecessors have worked actively in the INTAS spirit, with regular meetings and exchanges, and the encouragement and development of the scientific careers of younger staff. More than 20 Russian colleagues have worked on and published on aspects of these projects. Six colleagues from the UK, Denmark and Finland have been closely involved. Over this period of time, again in the spirit of INTAS, we would expect Russian expertise to grow and the careers of the key staff to flourish. This has indeed been the case, with senior staff, who began as research fellows and PhD students, now at the level of full professor and reader in the best Russian State universities.

The methodological approach adopted has been unique. Rather than the design of pan-Russian questionnaires, of which there have been dozens over the last 15 years, we sought to understand in much greater depth the experiences of households and individuals struggling with the employment, income, and health consequences of rapid social change. We chose to use detailed in-depth interviews with hundreds rather than thousands of respondents, concentrated in a few cities: Moscow, St Petersburg, Voronezh, Vladikavkaz, Kazan. We were also, uniquely, able to keep a small number of households in the study covering a ten-year period (1996–2006), as detailed in the final chapter of this book. Their stories are a vivid account of the hopes, fears, and in some cases deaths, that are the real lived experience of this tragic period of change in Russian history.

The current project, reported in detail in this book, focuses on health. The previous projects showed how the 1991 abrupt change to a market economy affected the life chances of millions, precipitating most into poverty. With the return of economic growth for most countries in Eastern Europe, and the return to aggregate levels of GNP last seen in the late 1980s, it might be hoped that the years of economic privation would be over. This is not the case for many, since inequality has also grown rapidly, and the long term consequences can be seen in the deterioration in the health of poor people.

A Note on Disability

Disability as a socially constructed category represents a point at which the main themes of our trilogy – employment (Book I), poverty and social exclusion (Book II) and health (Book III) – converge. As such, attitudes towards it in present-day Russia are ambivalent. The WHO has characterised Russia as a middle-income country [that offers] just one example of how far many societies still have to go to match their good intentions to ease the plight of the disabled, with deeds. The country has a first-rate disability law guaranteeing social security assistance to people with disabilities as well as unrestricted access to public transportation, government buildings, sports activities and a free education. (WHO BLT, Vol. 83, No. 4, April 2005, pp. 241–320.)

Yet some regional and national institutions are currently engaged in projects to 'increase the numbers of disabled people enjoying independent professional and social lives' (http://ec.europa.eu/europeaid/where/neighbourhood/country-cooperation/russia/russia_en.htm), with partners ranging from an EU External Cooperation Programme to the Canadian Government, reflecting the severe social exclusion that still prevails.

Throughout this book, we have repeatedly mentioned respondents' applications for the status of disability pensioner, with its attendant social guarantees. This throws some light on the Russian version of the tendency, well-known in welfare systems throughout the developed world, towards fluid boundaries between unemployment, early retirement and formal disabled status as routes of exit from the labour market. During the 1990s, in common with many other countries, Russia made certain specific changes and additions to the conditions for receipt of benefits, etc. for the various categories of disability. Over the five years following these legislative changes, the number of disabled people increased exponentially. Over the period of our most recent surveys, 1,463,000 people were newly registered as disabled in 2004 and 1,799,000 in 2005; by 1 January 2007, the official total number of disabled people in Russia was 13,014,000 (Rosstat figures – http://www.gks.ru/bgd/regl/b07_13/ isswww.exe/Stg/d02/08-34.htm).

Yet, as the wide variations in our respondents' experiences show, the fact of 'how disabled' somebody is bears little relation to their disability status. This is not to suggest that Russians who manage to register have made 'false claims': levels of morbidity in the general population show the reverse – see Chapter 2 – and, in 2004, some 60 per cent of those newly registered were in the more serious second category, as against 30 per cent in the third, whose members retain a greater capacity to work (Rosstat). Rather, it is the case that many people who have obvious functional impairments find it prohibitively difficult to tackle the process of registering as disabled. Evidence of disability sends a patient for exhaustive investigation by a full range of specialist doctors, even if the nature of the disability is obvious (if you cannot walk at all, for example, you will still have to go to an ophthalmologist), facing the huge queues and inconvenient hours that pertain throughout Russian health services. Recent legislation to ease the situation focuses on later re-examination (to retain disabled status), but even then is largely directed at the terminally ill, though some attempt has also been made to grant permanent disability status to people with severe cardiac or respiratory diseases (Rehabilitation System – Services for the Disabled, http://www.rehabsys.ru/index.php/en/news/ 177.html). After assembling a full set of specialists' reports, the patient then goes before a committee which allocates them to one of the three disability categories. These have different rights (mostly concessions, the most important of which are subsidised housing and utilities and the right to free or part-paid medicines) and receive different amounts of disability pension (ranging roughly from £6 to £60 a month). All disability pensions are paid from one source – the State (Federal) Pension Fund. In some regions, including Moscow, there may be additional allowances paid by local offices of the Fund from local budgets. In all this, disabled people do not know who is paying them, for what or from where (hence their widespread belief that they are being cheated out of their pensions), and in practice they cannot clarify their situation because of queues and confusion at local offices of the Fund.

Looking at the overall picture, and comparing the Russian experience with that in many other countries, it becomes apparent that this situation has a complex, but nevertheless direct relationship with the issues not only of health but also of unemployment and poverty. As real incomes and employment opportunities have diminished, especially for older members of the population, Russians have consciously started to use disabled status as an economic survival strategy. Maleva asserts that the sudden growth in the number of disabled people in Russia is a distinct 'manifestation of need' among socially weak groups within the population, including those who are losing out on the labour market (see Maleva, 2000; and – for comparison with other countries – OECD, 1999).

Chapter 1
Social Policy and the Health Crisis in the New Russia

Nadia Davidova, Nick Manning, Hannele Palosuo and Meri Koivusalo

Соловья баснями не кормят
Nightingales don't feed on fairytales

Three Studies on Social Change in Russia

This is the third book in a trilogy that has set out to explore and analyse the impacts of social change in Russia since the fall of communism in 1991 (Manning, Shkaratan and Tikhonova, 2000; Manning and Tikhonova, 2004). The substantive issues covered in the first two books were respectively employment and labour markets, and poverty and social exclusion. In this book we turn to the issues of health and health care. All three books are based on extensive original data. Some of this has been gathered through representative sample surveys, but other data has come through detailed repeat interviews with a panel of households, some of whom have been interviewed six times across all three projects, since the original 1996 round. This is a unique qualitative panel of data that has been a significant methodological innovation.

In this first chapter, we will review the recent social policy context, introduce the rationale for this project, review the state of health in Russia, and summarise the main findings from the project.

SECTION ONE – SOCIAL POLICY

New Millennium: New Social Paradigm?

In the two earlier books from this team we have charted many of the twists and turns of social policy. Here we will pick up the story as it has unfolded in the new century. According to an Independent Institute of Social Policy (IISP) survey, social policy in Russia has had two stages. The first stage (from the beginning of the 1990s up to 1996–97) is characterised not by social reforms as such but a basic reaction to chronic financial deficits. Only from 1998 has the attitude to social reforms in Russia gradually changed. Before this time there was an assumption that, when financial stabilisation had been achieved, economic growth would begin by itself, and social problems would be solved. By 1997 financial stabilisation was achieved but social problems were still not being tackled. At the end of the 1990s it became clear that there was an urgent need to elaborate a concept of social reforms over the long term. A serious demographic situation, weak institutions in the social field, inadequate incomes, and other factors appeared to be an obstacle for further economic growth. The maintenance of social welfare institutions as previously practised seemed ineffective, and a poor basis for reform, and in the main they were very expensive since they were poorly targeted. At this time politicians began to discuss seriously and more pragmatically new labour legislation, pension reform, the existing system of privileges and benefits and other social issues. There was a marked appetite for serious institutional change.

What was the situation Putin inherited when Yeltsin handed over the presidential reins of government? The economic reforms of the 1990s had brought significant social costs. Russia had suffered a 50 per cent reduction in GDP, with a corresponding fall in household incomes. At the same time, the former social protection system, which – at least in theory – guaranteed social care to all citizens free of charge, much of it through the old enterprise system, had substantially disappeared without being replaced by anything comparable. This led to a decline in welfare, opportunities and quality of life for a significant part of the population. Health status, particularly the reproductive health of women and the life expectancy of men, had declined, and this was accompanied by impoverishment, increased income differentiation and social disintegration. Russian society had already paid a high price for the social policy vacuum that existed during the first decade of market reforms, and was waiting for serious efforts to deal with concrete social problems such as poverty, public health, high mortality, chronic unemployment, and so on.

The complexity of the situation arose from the transitional stage of development in Russia, moving from the Soviet system to a desirable long-term model, many parameters of which are still not clear. However we would suggest that the active development of 'human capital' is an indispensable condition for public and economic progress and social well-being. The position of the International Monetary Fund, influential for Russian policy makers, is quite clear: transition countries need to reform their social sectors to promote the welfare of their citizens and spur economic growth. This means building up and redesigning social safety nets and addressing problems in such areas as social insurance, budgetary transfers, health care and education, labour markets, and tax administration. It also requires cutting some benefits and privileges. In this sense the formation of a long-term concept of social policy appeared to be inevitable.

Since 2000 the social policy situation has undergone major change. First, serious economic growth has been achieved. Russia has largely overcome the economic crisis caused by the collapse of the Soviet Union. Putin's government was able to announce the next stage of reforms and set out to draft a ten-year plan mapping out a strategy for sweeping change under three headings: modernisation of the economy, social policy, and restructuring of the power system itself. Among the creators of this plan were ministers Gref and Kudrin (Economy and Finance ministers in all of Putin's cabinets), who had close ties to the former architect of the State privatisation programme, and Chubais, a relatively right-leaning liberal politician. 'What we're planning is not a revolution, but it's an attempt to change

the existing system of interests. We need to announce that the rules
are going to be changed' (quoted in The St Petersburg Times, 572, 30
If implemented, the plan could double the country's GDP over the ne
Doubling GDP became a top priority for the country's authorities, alt
Minister for the Economy himself later doubted that this goal could be ꞏꞏꞏꞏeved
as planned.

The positive trends in economic development, stable finances and the market
allowed the government to discuss forming a new model of social security for
Russian citizens to ensure their constitutional rights. This new model is based
on the social insurance principle, including retirement insurance, social security
insurance and obligatory medical insurance. In 2005, the President again called for
the above large-scale strategic tasks, faced by the country, to be fulfilled, in order
to retain high levels of competitiveness in the world. These tasks were thought
of as 'system-forming'. 'We need an integral vision of the prospects of Russia's
development, with very clear aims and with due account taken of the possibilities
to attain them' (RIA-Novosti, July, 2005). Putin added that Russia is unable to
tackle its strategic tasks 'without the freedom of economic activity and effective
social policy.'

The year 2005 was marked by the movement of social problems from the
political periphery to the centre of the government's socioeconomic programme
and politics. In 2005 a new Federal law (Act No. 122) came into force, kick-
starting the reform of social benefits. The task of poverty reduction came to be
seen as equal in importance to the task of doubling GDP. The president declared
four high-priority national projects: health, education, affordable and comfortable
housing, and development of the agricultural sector. In his 2006 annual message
to the Federal Assembly he announced a large-scale programme to overcome the
demographic crisis, particularly to stimulate the birth rate. Thus 2005 could be
seen as a crucial year for social policy in which Russia entered a third stage of
development following the fall of the USSR.

The economic background was favourable. Russia's GDP increased by 34.7
per cent from 2000 to 2005. Official sources reported that over the four years of
Putin's government, the Russian population's real incomes increased by 40 per
cent. By 2006 Russia's gross domestic product exceeded the level it was at when
the Soviet Union collapsed in 1991. Russia's Stabilization Fund, set up in 2004 to
accumulate surplus revenue from high world oil prices, amounted to $55.7 billion
as of March 2006, rose to $89 billion by the end of 2006 and then soared to $158
billion before it was split at the beginning of 2008 (see below). The Central Bank
reported that Russia's gold and foreign currency reserves stood at $260.4 billion
as of September 2006, leaving the country with the world's fourth largest foreign
currency reserves after China, Japan and Taiwan.

Putin insisted that 'we must not miss the opportunities now emerging in the
Russian economy ... but we can spend only as much as we earn.' The 2006 budget
was the first 'development budget' in several decades, official reports said. A
'development budget' implied primarily the implementation of national projects

and the development of science-intensive technologies. Under it, spending on education and agriculture increased by more than 30 per cent, on health care by 60 per cent, and spending on housing quadrupled.

The president proposed setting up a council to implement these priority national projects that he intended to control personally, and underlined that it was extremely important that legal institutions oversee the proper use of funds. The Stabilization Fund, where the government accumulated extra funds received from oil exports, had not been set up to tackle social issues but to maintain Russia's macroeconomic stability. It was created 'to prevent price growth, to keep inflation in check, and to make sure that we can solve social issues in these conditions'. However in September 2006 the government initiated the creation of a new 'fund for future generations', which could use up to 10 per cent of the Stabilization Fund. The money has been earmarked for education, health care and social security programmes.

The Putin Years: An Assessment

The relative success in addressing social issues under Putin's administration is due to three critical advantages over his predecessor Yeltsin: a more cooperative legislature, a growing economy with rising real incomes, and greater State capacity. However, speaking at the 10th International Economic Forum in St Petersburg in June 2006, Putin said that high inflation, sectoral monopolisation, bureaucracy and corruption are still the main problems holding back Russia's economy. The shadow economy still exceeded 40 per cent of the GDP, and net capital flight from Russia reached $9 billion in 2005. In a recent study, the Fitch international rating agency said that, despite increasing macroeconomic stability, the high level of capital flight from Russia reflected a complex business climate and a lack of confidence in State institutions and observance of property rights.

Numerous surveys indicate that a majority of the public believes that the most needy (invalids, orphans, large families, pensioners, unemployed, single parents, low-paid workers, students) should receive free or subsidised care, particularly medical care, nursery and kindergartens, housing, professional training, and municipal transport. There is also a disturbing lack of faith in the future among many sectors of society and most particularly among its poorest sections. The prospect of coming social reforms has not yet altered this pessimism.

According to the Constitution, Russia still is a 'social State'. But the social State is no more than a declaration – a declaration of intentions for an indefinite future. This inconsistency in modern Russian social policy is a result of its conceptualisation. The 'social state' is merely one particular aspect of the (neo)liberal project in Russia. The project is supported by the World Bank and implemented through the State budget. A Welfare State aspires for all to enjoy good social standards in pensions, in health services, and in education. But a (neo)liberal society guarantees only minimal standards and consequently supports

only the most vulnerable citizens. Russia has announced that it asp
social standards, but in fact the State provides only minimal guarantee
creates a basic contradiction: ambitions are great, but resources are in

The State remains, in spite of everything, the main actor for social p
is an intensified configuration of power: the strong authority of the presi̲ ̲ ̲ ̲, a one-
party (pro-president) State Duma, and local self-government dependent on the State.
The relations of State authorities and business cannot in any way achieve civilised
dialogue. The institutions of civil society (such as non-governmental organisations,
trade unions, employers' associations) because of their general weakness are not
ready to form their own constructive alternatives in the sphere of social policy. These
tendencies leave insufficient resources and space for self-organising communities
and citizens, yet on the other hand State actors propose policy changes that would
actually reduce the State's role, eliminate broad subsidies, and transfer much
responsibility for social provision to individuals and markets.

The economic growth which has been achieved in Russia since the beginning of
the century is not sufficient to reduce social problems. Privatised markets in housing,
education and public health services coexist alongside insufficient basic benefits,
low living standards and a deterioration of health. Even though the beginning of the
new century demonstrated an increasing concern with social problems in Russian
society (and not only by the public, but also the government), the conception of
'social policy as such' is still undefined and debatable. The boundaries of social
policy resources and responsibility are not outlined, either in a public, political, or
academic sense. Two approaches and ways of understanding are still mixed up:
practically any action in the economic sphere can have social consequences. At the
same time there is an urgent need for a transformation of basic institutions in the
social sphere, but these transformations in turn will be costly.

Economic growth itself has two consequences. First, the growth of incomes and
salaries is concentrated in successful economic branches, in other words the growth
is for the top 20 per cent of the Russian middle class. Second there is a growth of
State expenses and an increase of spending on social projects, indexation of pensions
and budget-sector salaries. Maleva argues that only the top and lower layers of the
population are gaining from current economic growth, but that the middle – the basic
bulk of the population – are not. Economic growth figures remain something of an
abstraction to many people in the country. Consequently the problem for Russian
social policy in the near future is to spread the positive results of economic growth to
the rest of the population. The simultaneous problem of implementing different but
very serious social reforms including housing, public health services, and education,
is a big load even for more or less affluent Russians.

The failures and successes of Russian social policy have coexisted in all the
stages of Russian reforms. For example, Russia avoided the social explosion which
was assumed to be inevitable by many Western experts in particular, because
of mass latent unemployment in the middle of the 1990s. But the price of this
success was poverty and low incomes for the population caused by the low salaries
necessary to pay for the artificially high rate of employment. But Russia in the

middle of the first decade of the new millennium is in a different place from the Russia of ten years ago. In relative terms, there is now a greater sense of political and social stability compared to the 1990s. The near future should tell whether we are witnessing a trend of growing State capacity and policy coherence in Russia.

The Situation in Different Social Areas

Demographic Situation

The authorities have acknowledged that the demographic problem is one of the most serious problems Russia has faced. In his annual 2006 address to the nation the president said that the decline in Russia's population in recent years has been 700,000 people a year. The United Nations has warned that Russia's population – which stood at roughly 145 million in a 2002 census – had fallen to 144 million by 2005 and could fall by as much as a third by 2050. On 1 January 2008, it was estimated at 142 million. The country's economic productivity and even State sovereignty could be threatened if the situation does not improve.

The population has been steadily shrinking in recent years as the death rate has greatly exceeded the birth rate. There is concern about the country's rapidly ageing population and the problem of alcoholism, which are responsible for some alarming demographic trends. Alcoholism is particularly corroding Russian provinces where the economy and infrastructure are poorly developed and there are few jobs for people. In addition to alcohol abuse, other causes of early deaths include cardiovascular diseases, road accidents, and crimes.

Tackling Russia's demographic crisis is another significant project that is connected to the country's four priority national projects. Life expectancy for men is, at 58 years, ten years less than for men in China. From the official point of view the problem could be solved in three ways: to cut the death rate from unnatural causes, to develop a clear and effective migration policy, and to encourage people to have more children (including the increase of child benefits as one way to ameliorate the situation, which is also affected by unhealthy lifestyles and poor living conditions). From 2007 the government will give women at least 250,000 roubles ($9,200) each as financial tax-free aid following the birth of a second child. The payouts will be revised annually to adjust for inflation, and can only be spent on education, invested in housing, or put into an individual pension account, and only after the child is three years old. There is a debate as to whether it is possible to solve the Russian demographic problem by allowances. The most disadvantaged and poor part of the population will react first of all to the new programme. For middle-class and affluent people higher salaries will reduce the effect of 'second-child' money. It is a substantial benefit, but it may fall short of making enough difference to a family's income. The government could go further and create conditions for parents to earn adequate wages, and for this purpose it would be necessary to change labour legislation to provide women with easier opportunities to return to the labour market after the birth of a child.

Following moves to boost birth rates by offering financial incentives to parents it is also necessary to consider children's health, which is a cause for alarm in Russia in comparison with the other developed countries. According to the Prime Minister 'it is known that a mere 30 per cent of the country's newborns can be called healthy.' There are more than 500,000 disabled children in need of various rehabilitation treatments and 730,000 children left without parental care. It is expected that the next step of Russian demographic policy will be measures to improve children's health in Russia.

Poverty

From the beginning of the Russian reforms, the issue of poverty revealed itself as very evident and severe, symbolising the social cost that the population paid in the transition from the Soviet model of welfare to the market. The economic reforms triggered a 50 per cent reduction in Russian GDP, the consequence of which was a corresponding fall in the population's incomes. Price liberalisation in the early 1990s not only provoked large price rises but also devalued the savings of most of the population – bringing about, in effect, a large-scale redistribution of wealth in Russia.

Over the final decade of the twentieth century, the worst years from the point of view of poverty were 1992–93 and 1999–2000. In 1992–93, the rise in the number of poor people was the consequence of price liberalisation and rampant inflation. In 1999, the high rate of poverty was the consequence of the 1998 financial crisis and the default on public and private debt.

In recent years the rate of poverty in Russia has seen a steady downward trend. But, despite this, there continues to be distinct variation in the scale of Russian poverty. Poverty levels varied from 8–9 per cent to 70 per cent in some areas in 2004, and according to survey data the real rates are higher than the official figures. Against the background of Russia's recent dramatic petroleum-led economic growth, an estimated 30 million Russians still live in poverty.

The monitoring of poverty conducted by the World Bank (World Bank, 2005) highlights the groups that are at high risk of impoverishment in Russia. These are: the rural population (according to survey data from the Russian Institute of Sociology in March, 2006, 30.4 per cent of them were poor, while the proportion of poor people in the urban population was 15.7 per cent); children (while the rate of poverty overall across the country was 19.6 per cent, among children under 16 it was 26.7 per cent); the unemployed (one in three unemployed people was poor, while among the whole population capable of work one in five was poor). Finally, there are workers with a low standard of education (the probability of falling below the poverty line for people with only primary education was 50 per cent higher than in the population as a whole).

Table 1.1   Official poverty levels in Russia, 1992–2006, % of population

Total below poverty line	Distribution across years							
	1992	1993	1994	1995	1996	1997	1998	1999
	33.5	31.5	22.4	24.8	22.1	20.8	23.4	29.9
	Distribution across years							
	2000	2001	2002	2003	2004	2005	2006	
	29.0	27.5	24.6	20.3	17.6	15.8	14.3	

Source: Russian Federal State Statistics Service, www.gks.ru/wps/portal.

Among the countries of the CIS, Russia occupies first place for inequality in the distribution of incomes. The share of the best-off 10 per cent of the population was 29.8 per cent of total income, while the share of the poorest 10 per cent was 2 per cent in 2004. This situation differs from the position in other industrial societies, where the difference in incomes between the decile groups at the two extremes is far less. In Russia, the Gini coefficient is closer to that of countries of the Third World (Manning, 2007).

Further growth in inequality may essentially weaken the positive influence of economic growth on the reduction of poverty, as the World Bank persistently warns: 'if the advantages of economic growth are not distributed evenly, then its influence on the poverty rate will be weakened' (World Bank, 2005). It is in this regard that most serious analysts emphasise that the goal set in 2004 to reduce poverty sharply is potentially achievable; however, it is extremely difficult.

Health Care

Reform of health care was inevitable, since it still relied in the 1990s on residual budget funding. But the question then arises as to whether the new system will be a State or a private one. Taking a purely market approach to health will simply put a sizeable section of the population outside the scope of access to the most important public services. In the majority of current Western systems, the degree of private provision of these social areas is not very large.

This question stands high on Putin's cabinet's priority list. It is acknowledged that post-Soviet Russia faced a dramatic deterioration in general physical, mental and social health. Self-reported levels of ill health in Russia are between 50 per cent and 100 per cent higher than the Western European average. Health has proved to be one more price that the Russian nation is paying for the policy of reform. However, since 2005 Russia has started to implement national projects on health, which have become a key signpost of current policy reform.

The marked polarisation of the Russian population on the basis of income levels is slicing health care into layers, with the gradual formation of a hierarchy of 'élite' and 'cheap' health-care establishments. Consequently, the chance of receiving specialist health care varies dramatically for members of different social groups.

As we show later in the book, the poorest strata of the population, showing the lowest levels of health, find it hardest to obtain access to good-quality health care, since free medical services are being gradually phased out. In interviews, experts have called the present situation with medical service in Russia 'the triumph of paid health care'. State guarantees are covering fewer free services than before, and the Ministry of Trade and Economic Development has suggested amending the Tax Code to stimulate voluntary medical insurance. The new package of social reforms seems to place on the shoulders of the population a part of the responsibility for tackling a whole range of social and health problems. It hardly needs to be said that this excludes a significant proportion of badly-off Russians from access to health care.

Apart from this, by the end of 2006 the Health and Social Development Ministry found itself under a cloud over a corruption scandal caused by a nationwide subsidised drug shortage. Officials of the compulsory health insurance fund were arrested on suspicion of receiving bribes from pharmaceutical and other companies. Subsequently there have been more corruption probes against officials subordinate to the ministry, including the Federal Health and Social Development Agency, the Pension Fund and the Social Insurance Fund.

Trying to free itself from dealing with mounting costs for health care, central government has decentralised public hospitals, passing responsibility for them to local governments. The merits of decentralisation notwithstanding, local governments were not in a better fiscal position to support these facilities – hospitals with excess bed capacity, extensive spa and recreation services, and redundant health practitioners. Their task was complicated by demands for higher wages, as workers tried to cope with inflation, and by opposition to privatisation, which many workers feared would lead to large-scale layoffs. Resources were typically channelled toward curative care, leaving little for primary health and preventive services.

SECTION TWO – HEALTH

The Russian Health Crisis – What is it, and Why has it Developed?

A significant part of the exceptionally serious demographic situation in Russia is connected with the dramatic decline in the level of public health. The international and Western literature on health has sometimes considered health problems in Russia predominantly in terms of different specific determinants of population health, rather than in the broader context of poverty or access to services. The general focus has been on the gravity of the overall Russian health crisis and especially the role of alcohol in explaining it, the concern over the upsurge or recurrence of infectious diseases such as HIV/AIDS and tuberculosis, and the general model of health services and the state of health care reforms in Russia. This book aims to deal with the Russian health crisis in its social context in that it will describe actual life situations of people experiencing health problems, using enquiries about health and health care, as well as contextualising health in the social structures where people live and act.

The Russian health crisis came to broader international attention mainly in the latter part of the 1990s (e.g. Field, 1995; Bobak and Marmot, 1996; Palosuo, 2003). The nature of the health crisis is important as, in contrast to better-known traditional health or epidemiological crises where infectious diseases and epidemics have been of crucial importance, the Russian health crisis in the 1990s emerged steeply and included the increase of both non-communicable and infectious diseases. The health crisis hit working-age men hardest, with very high mortality differences between men and women.

The origins of the Russian health crisis in the 1990s are generally traced to the developments of the 1980s, which saw sudden fluctuations in life expectancy in the first part of the decade and a downturn in life expectancy from the late 1980s. The specific nature of the Russian health crisis has been that, while certain infectious diseases such as HIV/AIDS and tuberculosis have been of broader and longer-term concern in prisons and other specific populations such as drug users, in Russia infectious diseases also rose in the general population. However, the main causes of mortality are to be found in non-communicable diseases and violence. During the economic crisis in 1992–93, considerable deterioration could be seen across many causes, with particularly sharp increases in tuberculosis and dysentery. However, in the 1990s external causes of death had the highest relative rate of growth. This was strongly related to alcohol use. However, alcohol is unlikely to be the only explanation in the substantial increase of homicides, suicides, accidental poisonings and other causes of accidents and trauma (Pridemore, 2003). The striking five-year decline in life expectancy during the four years between 1990 and 1994 is said to be beyond the peacetime experience of industrialised countries (Notzon et al., 1998).

The changes in Russian mortality can be seen in the comparison between reduction in life expectancy through death before 65 years in three countries, showing the change in trends in Russia, the United Kingdom and Finland (Figure 1.1).

Some demographers trace the long-term origins of the Russian and Eastern European health crisis to the mid-1960s. At that time the post-War increase in life expectancy slowed down or halted all over Europe. This was the time when finally the shift from infectious diseases to non-communicable diseases took place (Vallin and Meslé, 2002). From the beginning of the 1970s life expectancy increased again in all Western European countries, mainly due to a decrease in cardiovascular mortality. However, at this point Eastern Europe started to lag behind Western Europe and the East–West health divide emerged Vallin and Meslé, 2002). Yet the development of Russia has not been matched anywhere. While Russia had practically caught up many Western countries in life expectancy, including Finland, by 1965, it was the first industrialised country where life expectancy in fact started to decline, and between 1965 and 1980 life expectancy of males at birth decreased by three years (from 64.4 to 61.5 years) (Vallin and Meslé, 2002). From the early

1980s there has been an unforeseen fluctuation in trends of life expe
Russia. Life expectancy of men increased sharply for three years d
anti-alcohol campaign of 1985–87, then fell even more sharply in 199u–y+. ⸻
rise in mortality during the years around the collapse of the Soviet Union and
thereafter was concentrated on less educated men and women and was largely due
to an increase in cardiovascular diseases and violent deaths (Marmot, 2006). Life
expectancy increased again after the mid-1990s, but declined in 1999 after the
financial crisis of 1998 (Brainerd and Varavikova, 2001). During all these shifts,
women have basically followed a similar pattern of changes in life expectancy as
men, only with considerably milder fluctuations.

Economic crisis associated with social stress and health-damaging shifts in
consumption have provided an important general explanatory framework for the
Russian health decline. However, the role of other factors needs to be considered
as well. In Poland mortality from coronary heart diseases declined rapidly in
1990–94, associated with a shift in consumption of fats predominantly for
economic reasons (Zatonski et al., 1998; Zatonski and Willet, 2005). In fact none
of the Eastern European countries experienced such steep and prolonged decline
in life expectancy as Russia did in the 1990s (Brainerd and Varavikova, 2001). In
Cuba economic crisis was associated with overall lower mortality from diabetes
and cardiovascular disease. In these countries causal emphasis has been put on
broader shifts in nutrition, which were realised during or after economic crisis
due to changes in nutrition and increased mobility. The impacts and implications
of economic crisis for health are thus not necessarily straightforward and depend
on the existing health system, public health policies and prior consumption and
nutrition patterns.

The Russian health crisis may best be considered in the mixed and complex
context of social stress, broader social disruption and violence and economic
difficulties conducive to expansion of consumption of alcohol, tobacco and drugs
and unhealthy dietary practices. In view of the long-term deterioration of public
health and abrupt fluctuations in mortality connected with profound systemic
changes, the acute mortality crisis of the 1990s has also been characterised as an
'adaptation crisis' (Cornia and Paniccià, 2000), in which several negative factors
have interacted with each other.

The lack of public health focus and deficiencies of primary health care
within the health system have become further complicated by reforms fostering
inequalities in service provision and a focus on medical services (e.g. Andreev et
al., 2003). It can also be claimed that neglect of the population's health and action
on issues that determine it are Putin's historical burden

The Main Causal Factors Explaining the Russian Health Crisis

Demographers and epidemiologists have studied the Russian mortality crisis quite
extensively since the mid-1990s. The health crisis is not only a mortality crisis, but
data on morbidity and experiences of health and ill health have been less available

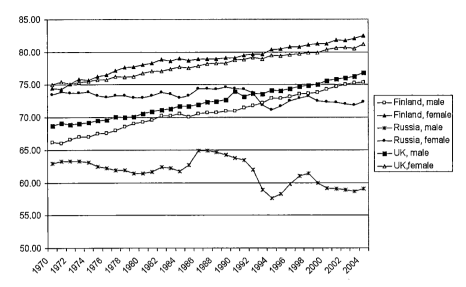

Figure 1.1   Life expectancy by gender from birth, Russia, Finland, UK

Source: Health for All database, WHO.

and also less suitable for international comparisons that have often set the standard for the Eastern European health crisis (see, e.g., Palosuo, 2003).

Several types of explanations have been given for the health crisis. The 'generation lag hypothesis', which assumed that the Russian mortality pattern is just lagging behind the development of mortality in economically more advanced societies, so that Russia will 'catch up' with the life expectancy and health levels of Western countries in a couple of decades, has not been considered convincing as a general explanation, since life expectancy in Russia was very close to that of many Western European countries as recently as the mid-1960s. One early guess put forward was based on the assumption that Russia was seeing the effects of environmental deterioration, but this has not been supported by research evidence. Other explanations deal with macroeconomic and social changes (e.g. Brainerd and Varavikova, 2001), increasing social inequality and poverty, disruption of old social networks, unhealthy lifestyles (e.g. Cockerham, 1999), psychosocial stress and the deterioration of the universal and paternalistic health care system (see Hertzman et al., 1996; Cockerham, 1999; Palosuo, 2003). The complex nature of the health crisis is often acknowledged, and most researchers tend to discuss several causes simultaneously. Obviously different explanatory models of the crisis are not necessarily mutually exclusive.

Lifestyle: The Role of Alcohol and Tobacco

The role of alcohol in the current Russian mortality crisis has been at times dominant and has sometimes even been considered almost the main explanatory variable.

Alcohol seems to be strongly connected with the fluctuations of mortality in Russia and is undoubtedly important as a proximal cause to excess mortality, particularly among men. However, it is also necessary to consider factors that explain firstly why and in what context alcohol is used and, secondly, how government policies have tried to deal with the matter. Alcohol was a major explanatory factor during the initial health crisis in the 1990s (Leon et al., 1997; McKee, 1999), and still has a major role in explaining the reason for the low life expectancy of Russian men and for large fluctuations in mortality. Researchers have drawn attention not only to the pattern of drinking, but to the high level of consumption of alcohol as well as consumption of non-beverage and illegal alcohol (Leon et al., 2007). The consumption patterns and use of alcohol is shared to some extent in other Eastern European countries and Finland. In Finland a similar rise in consumption can be seen in a context of increasing social inequalities and liberalisation of alcohol policies, since alcohol and alcohol-related causes remain the main cause of death for working age Finns of both genders (Statistics Finland, 2007). In Finland the contribution of excessive alcohol consumption to inequalities in mortality is also large (Makela et al., 1997).

The consumption of alcohol and tobacco can be influenced by pricing policies and changing access. On the other hand, drinking and smoking can also be seen as mechanisms by which people cope with stress and social crisis. In Russia the opening of the economy also further enhanced the scope for distributing tobacco and alcohol as marketable products which people could still afford (Gilmore and McKee, 2004a,b). The role of tobacco remains very important, since in other European countries the reduction in smoking has made a substantial contribution to the decline in cardiovascular diseases, in addition to reducing lung cancer mortality. For example, tobacco-related policies have explained a substantial share of the large decline in Finnish male smoking and related mortality between the 1960s and the 1990s. However smoking has been and remains highly prevalent in Russia among men, as well as a substantial percentage of women (McKee et al., 1998; Bobak et al., 2006). The opening of markets led to the marketing of tobacco, with active engagement in enhancing smoking by companies in the 1990s (Gilmore and McKee, 2004a, 2004b). This expansion was not associated with public policies or other means to reduce smoking and an international reflection of this lack of commitment is that the Russian Federation has only very recently initiated measures to join the Tobacco Framework Convention, remaining in the group of countries that have not yet signed the convention (WHO, 2008).

It is thus important to note that alongside the higher consumption of both alcohol and tobacco is central government's neglect to prioritise these public health concerns in the context of national policies. While consumption of illegal and non-beverage alcohol has been raised as a reason not to take up further policy measures, based on the experiences and complications that the Gorbachev temperance campaign created, it is not at all clear that the current emphasis on liberal policies will do anything to limit this very dangerous illegal and non-beverage consumption.

The Role of Health Care

The role of a national health system is of importance for population health in terms of health protection and promotion as well as in terms of provision of and access to health services. The Soviet health system was known to be relatively hospital-based and specialised, with lack of focus on broader public policies and measures. Soviet health care was successful in combating infectious diseases and building basic health care units and hospitals all over the vast country after the 1917 Revolution, but the system was poorly equipped and did not change in order to combat modern epidemics of non-communicable diseases, which started to predominate after the epidemiological turn of the mid-1960s. Even though primary health care was invented in the USSR (Alma Ata), it has not so far been at the core of Soviet or Russian health policies. Only about 30 per cent of Russian physicians work in outpatient settings and roughly 60 per cent of these are specialists (Tompson, 2007). The role of the health system as a whole has been addressed in a recent study on avoidable mortality, which concluded that between 1965 and 1999 the male life expectancy gap between the UK and Russia rose from 3.6 years to 15.1 years, with treatable causes becoming an increasingly important contributor to this gap and accounting for almost three years in men and two years in women by the end of the 1990s (Andreev et al., 2003).

According to a recent OECD study on Russian health care reforms, the total spending on health care remains relatively low as a percentage of GDP and was below 5 per cent in 2005. The largest share of household spending is devoted to pharmaceuticals, which account for around 30 per cent of total health care spending in Russia, as against an average of 12 per cent in OECD countries. In Russia pharmaceuticals are expensive relatively to locally supplied services and it has been estimated that a substantial proportion of the demand for medicines in Russia simply goes unmet (Tompson, 2007).

In many ways the decentralised structure of service provision coupled with insurance is likely to converge more towards an American model of health services provision than a European one. This has been due to expected gains in competition from the arrangements; however, it is unlikely that the regulatory set-up in Russia will be able to fulfil its task effectively. Furthermore it is unlikely to provide optimal support to the development of effective primary health care policies.

Considering the role of alcohol in the Russian health crisis, one of the policy changes that probably aggravated the detrimental impact of alcohol abuse was that the formerly quite strict compulsory treatment of alcoholism was removed at the same time as sales of alcohol were almost completely deregulated and the relative price of alcohol fell. This apparently led to the appearance of rough-sleeping homeless men ('bomzhy' – people of no fixed abode) in the streets of big cities. The increase in deaths of unidentified men of working age indicates the emergence of a health threat associated with homelessness and social marginalisation (Anreev et al., 2007).

The Role of Socioeconomic and Psychosocial Stress

There are relatively few studies that would have measured the stress levels of the Russian population before and during the transition years; yet most observers agree that the scale of societal changes and the uncertainty connected with it would cause stress to most people.

Psychosocial stress has, for example, been suggested as an explanation for the high mortality from cardiovascular diseases of middle-aged men (Paniccià, 1997; Cornia and Paniccià, 2002). Macroeconomic and social changes are thus believed to have caused considerable stress for a large part of the Russian population. However, stress connected with economic turmoil – such as depressions – in industrialised countries has not led to a decrease in life expectancy of the population. Therefore, it has been suggested that the unexpectedly high increase in mortality in Russia in the 1990s may partly be explained by a preceding erosion of the health stock of the population over a longer period of time, starting from the mid-1960s. Thus, the ability of the population to adapt to the radical economic reforms and other changes of the 1990s would have been heavily compromised by long-term health exhaustion (Brainerd and Varavikova, 2001). The transition in Russia has meant profound societal changes especially in 1990–94, as described earlier. Real GDP per capita decreased by a quarter; a quarter of the population found themselves trying to live on incomes below subsistence level. Prices were liberated and in 1992 there was near-hyperinflation. Unemployment and migration increased, and so did the crime rate, prostitution, and the divorce rate (Brainerd and Varavikova, 2001).

The macro-level economic changes in Russia were connected with a disruption of social cohesion, feelings of alienation and anomie. Increased criminality and suicides are indicators of disruptions affecting cohesion in society (see, e.g., Brainerd and Varavikova, 2001; Palosuo, 2003). The Russian style of binge drinking has been found to be connected with economic difficulties among men in Moscow, though not among women (Jukkala et al., 2008). During the upheaval and increase in mortality in 1989–94, the major cities of Moscow and St Petersburg suffered a greater decline in life expectancy than the rest of Russia, reflecting perhaps a faster pace of change and higher stress there. It is also important to note that between 1988 and 1994 the Russian homicide rate more than tripled, placing it amongst the highest in the world (Pridemore, 2003).

The Role of Inequality and Poverty

Social class differences were probably less marked in the Soviet Union than they were in capitalist market economies. There is, however, not much research on this concerning the Soviet period, as the topic of domestic inequality was then forbidden. The distribution of resources and rewards according to social position – the stratification process – was somewhat different in a socialist society than in market-based economies (Palosuo et al., 1998). Socioeconomic inequalities increased after the collapse of the Soviet Union and are reflected in increasing mortality differentials – by education, for example (Marmot, 2006, Shkolnikov et al., 1998). Yet the resources that people have at their disposal in Russia are still not distributed in such relatively regular patterns as are found in Western European counties. In particular, education has not been an asset and means to obtain other resources such as a high salary or secure position in work, as the results given in this book also show.

As shown above, the rate of poverty was very high during the economic crisis of the early 1990s and has fluctuated according to the macroeconomic situation in the country. Thus poverty has diminished since the beginning of this decade, when the national economy has shown considerable growth. Paniccià (2000) has suggested that poverty could impair health and increase morbidity and mortality through falling food consumption, malnutrition and immunological deficiencies. Undernourishment has generally not been a serious public health problem in Russia; yet, there have been indications of micronutrient deficiency and unhealthy eating habits among parts of the population. Another pathway for poverty could be the deteriorating health-care system. The failure of the health-care system has also resulted in insecurity and high burden-sharing by the population (Table 1.2).

Table 1.2   Out-of-pocket spending on health as % of total health expenditure x household

	Finland	Russia	United Kingdom
1998	19.4	23.6	10.9
1999	20.3	28.6	10.7
2000	20.4	31.2	10.5
2001	19.7	29.6	10.6
2002	19.4	28.7	10.8
2003	19.1	29.2	11
2004	18.4	29.7	12.6

Source: HFA database/WHO.

A third pathway concerns people who have fallen through the former social safety nets, consisting of groups such as the homeless, migrants, refugees, alcoholics and people suffering from mental health problems. There are more men than women in these new 'marginal' groups. This is reflected in recent reports of the growing number of deaths of unidentified people in Russia (Andreev et al., 2007).

The Current Project

A substantial literature thus demonstrates that issues surrounding health in Russia are more pressing than in Western European countries, and partly take a different form. The mechanisms chosen for reforming Russian society resulted in great stress and frustration generated by the destruction of accustomed value systems and fixed modes of life. In particular there was a sharp fall in the standard of living for a large majority of the people. There was an accompanying sharp deterioration in the health of the Russian population. Poverty has been revealed as a very distinct factor in evaluations of the health of working-age men, who have been at greatest risk during the period of transformation, both in Russia and in former socialist bloc countries. According to our research, it is they who, as a result of psychoemotional and social stresses, have experienced much sharper growth in stress-generated pathology, such as depression, neuroses and a whole range of psychosomatic disorders and diseases. However, the incidence of traditional socially generated diseases, primarily typical of disadvantaged social strata, has also grown – the rate of tuberculosis has doubled, and there has been an increase in the incidence of parasitic diseases.

Moreover, in the course of the transformation of Russia in the 1990s, the old health care system was nearly destroyed, and the transfer of health care to the insurance principle was poorly implemented. The ineffectiveness of the policy for financing even basic medical assistance along insurance lines and the absence of programmes to target free medical assistance to disadvantaged people led to a significant part of the population almost entirely falling out of medical services.

Health and illness are social and cultural in nature, and may be seen as universal categories only through a system of generally accepted norms. It is also the case that the range of – and boundaries between – available terms in a given language help to define a culture's understanding of health and illness. A comparison between English and Russian serves to highlight this: whereas English in all its variants provides myriad words to describe a state of good health from some angle or another ('fit', 'well', 'healthy', 'good', 'able-bodied'), Russian does the reverse. The single word *zdorovyi* has to stand for all these and more – 'sturdy', 'splendid', 'strapping', etc. The nuanced differences between 'sickness', 'illness' and 'disease' in English are not reflected by the single Russian word *bolezn'*; while the Russian for 'sick' or 'ill' (*bolnoi*) also has to stand for the noun 'patient' – literally, 'a sick person' – which can hardly help preventive care for healthy people to become established in Russian culture. (See more below about the difficulties of defining an intermediate state between health and illness.)

In the everyday Russian situation, amplified by the way in which medical certificates and invalidity benefits were not widely used in the old system, the perception of the boundary between 'health' and 'illness' was and is strongly displaced towards ill-health: feeling in a poor condition physically is not synonymous with ill-health, and this applies even more to various forms of depression and other psychological states. Even in relatively prosperous sections of the population this leads to the choice of ineffective modes of behaviour ('it'll get better on its own', trying to treat oneself, and so on).

There has been relatively little research aiming to analyse the views of the Russian population as a whole – or of separate groups or strata within it – about what health, ill-health and illness are, which models of behaviour should be used in response to a given assessment of one's own health, or what determines the practical choice of how to behave (Rusinova and Brown, 1996, 1997; Zhuravleva, 2006, Abbott et al., 2006). There is also relatively little research which would show how knowledgeable various sections of the population – in particular, the poor and socially excluded – are about possible ways of behaving following the introduction of insurance-based medicine in place of a solidaristic system of health care. There is also a lack of analysis of the views of policy makers about the views of the population on these problems, what their own attitudes towards them are, or about why real health care policy is constructed not only without taking into account real differences in the population's ability to pay, but also disregarding people's habitual health maintenance practices.

The main aims of the project reported in this book were therefore to:

- analyse the impact of the economic reforms implemented in Russia since the early 1990s on the health of various sections of the urban population, taking into account gender aspects of the consequences of the reforms;
- analyse the views of various sections of the urban Russian population about what health, ill-health and illness are, and their perceptions of health as a resource; determining the influence of these views on their own assessments of their health and on their choice of particular models for using the official health care system;
- analyse the mechanism of the interrelationship and mutual influence of poverty and social exclusion in Russian cities, on the one hand, and state of health/ill-health, on the other;
- analyse the concepts and practices involved in ensuring access of poor sections of the population to health care services and of the reasons why there is a lack of programmes directed at individuals and families with poor health and at reintegrating badly-off people in poor health into society;
- compare Russian research data with the results of research into these issues in EU countries;
- develop proposals for improving the effectiveness of current health and social policy.

Each of these six objectives was elaborated into a research strategy and methodology (presented in detail in the appendix).

SECTION THREE - SUMMARY OF FINDINGS FROM THE PROJECT

The results of the project are substantial and range over a number of areas. The results are based on several sources of data: representative population surveys conducted by the Institute of Sociology, and by the Russian Longitudinal Monitoring Survey (RLMS), and qualitative panel data consisting of interviews carried out in 2004 and 2005. This brief summary gives the reader an indication of findings elaborated in the rest of the book. (But all of these issues are complex and to fully understand the material we have gathered and analysed requires a careful reading of the relevant chapter.) The summary follows the sequence of subsequent chapters.

Part I – Health Beliefs

The health of the Russian population of all ages is characterised by high levels of widespread chronic disease and low levels of health. A comparatively new trend for Russia, judging by respondents' assessments and by the quantitative data obtained, is, however, not the increase in morbidity of the older age groups (over 60), but the sharp deterioration during the course of the reforms in the health of the over-40 age group and of children. Moreover, the most typical feature of health breakdown is the prevalence of pain (including among those who have no diagnosed chronic diseases) and anxiety or depression. There was a close connection between belonging to a certain group and prolonged stress: chronic poverty, particular features of the jobs that people with a corresponding level of health could aspire to, and a clearly-expressed age discrimination problem – especially significant in Russia, with its very profound wage inequalities. Moreover, all these problems were interconnected and created a cumulative effect for those who encountered them.

Overall, the quantitative data showed, firstly, the relatively worse quality of jobs available to respondents in poor health and, secondly, their depressed psychological state, their sense of their depreciating social status, their own lack of rights and their helplessness – all creating a state of prolonged stress. However, at the same time, no strict connection was recorded between overall health indicators – or, moreover, chronic diseases – and membership of socio-occupational groups as defined using the ISCO-88 classification. In this regard, as in the case of class defined by the ESOMAR method, the specifics of Russian conditions left their mark, distorting the classic distributions.

For example, the worst health indicators were found among professionals, and the best among skilled blue-collar workers. Within the same age groups across various types of occupational statuses, differences tended to vary in nature, but did not alter the main trend – the relatively high prevalence of chronic diseases among the more educated sections of the population employed in non-manual labour. The lowest indicators of the presence of chronic diseases were found in inhabitants of rural localities and urban-type small settlements. However diagnostic equipment in such places is much worse than in major cities and towns (where the majority of professionals and white-collar workers live), such that if there were more adequate diagnoses, indicators of chronic diseases in residents of villages and urban-type settlements, where the proportion of people in elementary occupations is relatively higher, would increase.

A broad understanding of health as not only physiological but also psychological and social, is emerging. Alongside the development of an 'internal locus of control' and the transformation of health into an intrinsic value, there is a trend towards the formation of a new understanding of health by Russians – one that is typical of developed, modern societies.

A new understanding of health is not always reflected in behaviour. For Russians' behaviour towards their own health to take a turn towards greater rationality and effectiveness, the essential thing would be a change in external conditions – overcoming profound social inequality and many types of discrimination on the labour market, raising living standards for the great mass of the population, developing a system of social guarantees, improving the work of the health care system, and so on. However, all this will not lead to the expected result if, in parallel, there is no consolidation in society of a new attitude to health as being a most important component of the quality of life, whose preservation requires efforts from the person concerned, rather than being attributable to fate from the outset.

Analysis of the understanding of health using pan-Russian data confirmed the connection – which we had established when analysing the results of our panel interviews – between understanding of health and particular features of respondents' individual life situations: this primarily meant their own real state of health, although people in the relatively less prosperous strata also had a propensity towards a traditional understanding of health. Moreover, this analysis allowed us to record a connection between a new understanding of health and the norms of urban culture and standard of education, as well as to understand the mechanism involved in this, which related to the delineation of an intermediate link between health and sickness – one for which the Russian language has not yet even formed an adequate term, so new is this formulation of the issue. The concept of 'ill-health' comes closest of all to it in meaning, defining a state of illness in which there are still no expressed signs of a specific disease, but where the beginnings of this are apparent and accompanied by impairment of one's usual capabilities.

Part II – Health and Social Structure

The connections between health and status have already been verified and long taken for granted: in particular, there is much data illustrating the thesis that the less socioeconomic inequality a society contains, the healthier it will be. In societies where the incomes of poor and rich do not differ much, the level of mortality is lower and people live longer (Wilkinson and Pickett, 2006). This is why analysis of the relationship between poverty and health is an essential antecedent to a general picture of social inequalities in contemporary Russia.

Large-scale poverty exists in Russia, affecting many millions of people. More than half the poor are people of working age, three-quarters of whom have no skills. It is precisely people in this category who are in need of active forms of employment creation, with resources needed for vocational training and retraining, and not just income support. People's health depends on: whether or not there is profound deprivation; whether or not they are experiencing stress; and their position in the social structure, including objective characteristics of this position and also their own perception of their position in the context of whether or not the social inequalities that generally exist are legitimate. The greatest perceived danger for Russians today is loss of one's own health or deterioration of the health of somebody close. This concern was expressed by 71 per cent of the population. But what is most typical is that one in three inhabitants of Russia today fears it will be impossible to obtain medical care even in case of severe need – while the poor express this fear noticeably more often than the better-off sections of the population.

The extent to which social networks, or social capital, can compensate for or reinforce these concerns has been widely debated in the literature. Our research revealed that the majority of social networks are informal in nature, which is a manifestation of the distinct lack of trust in formal state institutions by a significant proportion of Russians. We also found that social capital plays a significant role in the formation and reproduction of social inequalities and is a most important stratifying factor. The social resource of the most deprived section of society is constantly being exhausted and this inevitably leads to the increasing inaccessibility for the poor to the ways of affecting a difficult life situation that are generally accepted in the Russian community – in particular, using the possibilities of one's immediate circle, established acquaintances and contacts in tackling problems. And this situation is directly connected with their poor health, because isolation and lack of access to the resource of social networks (in other words, low social capital) hinder any change in their circumstances. Thus, the social exclusion that accompanies the life of many poor households not only has an impact on their psychological and physiological health – it also pushes them over the edge and out of the mainstream, depriving them of opportunities to reintegrate into society and tackle their problems through their own efforts.

In recent years, the progress of some negative trends has slowed. A certain positive dynamic has taken shape in people's well-being and in their behaviour. This reflects the fact that the emotional well-being of inhabitants of Russia over recent years has significantly improved: in 1994, 14 per cent of those taking part in the RLMS were completely or more or less satisfied with life; by 2005 this had risen to 37 per cent. However, very many people remained dissatisfied with life – 66 per cent in 1994 and 36 per cent in 2005. In every year of monitoring, the level of satisfaction with life seemed to be linked to self-rated health – those who assessed their own health more highly were more satisfied with life overall, and the reverse. Therefore, optimistic forecasts in relation to Russians' health are justified only if the socioeconomic situation does not change for the worse.

In addition, even the apparent trends towards a general improvement in health have in practice not reached poor sections of the population, whose health now inspires even greater concern. Judging by the way in which RLMS respondents described their work and the kind of working and employment conditions that they considered stressful, the conclusion can be drawn that there are many unattractive, low-quality jobs on the Russian labour market, which hardly enable a person to survive, are badly paid and demand heavy workloads, with consequent risks to physical and psychological health. And although in recent years a positive dynamic in risk reduction has been observed in some aspects of working conditions and employment (for example, fewer instances of compulsory leave or non-payment of wages), at the same time workloads have increased for many people, reflecting longer working hours.

Scholars, politicians and experts are calling for the main aim of social policy to be not simply material assistance to the poor, but also equalisation of the strongly differentiated social chances of various population groups, including in the interregional space of contemporary Russia. The battle must be not just with poverty and disease, but also with the growing trends of social exclusion that accompany poverty and sickness.

Part III – Health and Social Action

RLMS data reveal a real paradox: despite the deterioration in health across many indicators, during the period of reform and stabilisation in the early 2000s people began to visit the doctor more rarely, not only for preventive care, but also when they were ill or felt unwell. In 1994, 43 per cent of them had gone to a medical establishment, while ten years later the figure was only 32 per cent. In our research, we attempted to find an answer to the questions surrounding this situation.

· According to RLMS data, Russian people are increasingly paying medical staff for a visit, in money or gifts: in 1994, 5 per cent paid, but by 2005 the figure had risen to 14 per cent. The same is also true of payment for additional services (tests or procedures): in 1994, one in ten paid but, in 2005, almost one in three. By 2005, payments through official channels had increased, and under-the-counter payments had diminished. The frequency of payment at the cashier's office rose from 55 per cent in 2000 to 64 per cent in 2005, but 'cash-in-hand payments' fell from 52 per cent to 44 per cent.

It is primarily poor, sick Russians who use free State medical care. An improvement in welfare enables a person to move away from the free medical care system and into the fee-paying medical sector. So, lack of material resources and the consequent absence of essential treatment or preventive health care were given by one in three respondents as the main reason for a deterioration in health. When they are sick, the only options for people with a low level of material resources are to seek free medical care, put off a visit to the doctor, or not visit the municipal clinic at all. People who are refused help by specialists often try to treat themselves. This leads to the illness becoming worse, even chronic, and also to people more frequently seeking emergency medical assistance.

Access to resources to overcome difficult situations in the lives of poorly resourced population groups played a very significant role in improvement or deterioration in health. The most significant resources were conditions of employment and variety in sources of income, but also resources of support from social networks, including psychological support, and varieties of leisure. Aiming to ignore health problems was also very significant. In the final analysis, all this was really underpinned by membership of different classes, in which the effect of material factors mediated and intensified cultural factors, including those relating to particular features of the human capital of members of various classes and to behavioural patterns, including health behaviours. However, our research also recorded certain cultural stereotypes shared by members of all classes – primarily, the 'unseemliness' of paying a great deal of attention to one's own health and the preference for tackling health problems through 'everyday life' rather than going to see specialists – which may be connected with particular features of Russian national culture.

By contrast, any improvement in our respondents' health over the last few years has come about mainly because of a reduction in their level of anxiety – which, in its turn, has reduced the danger of stress and had a favourable effect on their somatic health. Significant factors included improvement in the quality of employment – for example, taking an active approach to raising one's skills level or improving one's working conditions. A more varied structure of sources of income, which strengthens one's position, and a variety of means of improving material circumstances also played a role. Active and varied leisure and good-quality social connections should also be noted, together with a more positive attitude towards health as a value, a factor of no small importance.

These mechanisms and models included: improving not just one's material but also one's emotional situation in the area of employment; relying on the family's material resources where one was informally employed or not employed; social inclusion in a community of people in very similar circumstances – all while simultaneously using strategies for modest preventive health care. The latter primarily meant taking measures to maintain a healthy way of life: an active approach to various aspects of life, maintaining not only the health of the body but also a good psychological mood and a wealth of emotions, with a preference for methods of health maintenance that can be applied in everyday life, such as traditional remedies, etc. People escape from the vicious circle of poverty and poor health mainly by mobilising resources in three major directions: successful employment (improving the conditions of one's work activities, on which satisfaction from employment is based); strengthening social connections, forming a stable social circle of highly compatible people; consistent modest preventive measures to care for one's health, which included a wide range of approaches (eating correctly, rejecting harmful habits, a generally active approach, and positive emotions).

Our research also revealed the characteristics of male and female behavioural models in regard to health. Women are in a relatively worse situation than men. However, particular features of existing gender roles – in which a woman, even having lost her job, has a sense of her social significance as mother, wife, grandmother, housewife, etc. – mitigate this insecurity for them. Men, on the other hand, get less upset about 'the future', but when they have real problems with work they experience especially severe stress. In addition, the prevalence of defined gender attitudes and stereotypes about one's own health limits men's concern about health and is making their situation worse.

The female model is distinguished by greater flexibility and pragmatism about one's own health, both in attitudes and stereotypes and in how people act in real situations. The male model to a greater extent reflects a code of norms prescribing that people should not worry too much about their own health. The consequence of this is that the most effective models of behaviour in relation to living standards and quality of life – which include a strategy to care for one's own health – are presented primarily by women. In our longitudinal sample, which consisted mainly of poor and badly-off households, it was precisely such strategies that had more often led to an improvement in the families' material welfare. It may be concluded that, in Russia, in situations where there are few resources and severe structural limitations, the model of health behaviour that is typical of women is more likely to offer favourable prospects for overcoming the closed circle of poverty and ill-health.

PART I
Health Beliefs in the New Russia

Chapter 2
Measuring the Population's Health

Nataliya Tikhonova

Кровь с молоком
Blood and milk, a glowing picture of health

Overall Health in Russia

Traditionally, the state of a nation's overall health may be described through the use of both statistical and sociological data. This is equally the case in regard to Russia, where the picture of overall health is much worse than in other European countries. For example, in 2005, according to data from the United Nations Economic Commission for Europe, life expectancy for men in the Russian Federation was 59 years, while in countries with a very similar standard of economic development it was much higher: in Bulgaria it had reached 69, in Estonia 67.3 years and in Poland 70.3 years. When Russia is compared with Western European countries, a still wider gap can be observed. Thus, in the UK, the corresponding indicator for 2005 was 76.9 years; in Germany, 76.2 years; in Iceland, 79.2; and in Spain, 77.4 years (UNECE).

If, in trying to obtain a more detailed picture of overall health in Russia, we use data from official statistics, then the 'most terrible scourge' of Russians is cardiovascular disease (see Figure 2.1). Moreover, causes connected with the use of alcohol do not make such a large contribution to total mortality as opinion widely holds: in 2005, 104,700 people died (The social status and living standards of the population of Russia, 2006, p. 329) from all alcohol-related causes (accidental poisonings, chronic alcoholism, alcoholic psychoses, alcohol-induced liver disease, alcohol-induced cardiomyopathy, alcohol-induced degeneration of the nervous system, chronic pancreatitis with an alcohol-related etymology) out of a total of 2,303,900 people who died from all classified causes (The social status and living standards of the population of Russia, 2006, p. 53).

Furthermore, other classified causes head the distribution of morbidity: in 2005, 39.6 per cent of cases were diseases of the respiratory system, 5.7 per cent diseases of the skin and subcutaneous tissue, 6.2 per cent diseases of the genito-urinary system, 5.0 per cent infectious and parasitic diseases, 4.7 per cent diseases of the digestive system, 4.5 per cent diseases of the eye, 4.5 per cent diseases of the musculo-skeletal system, 3.2 per cent diseases of the ear and just 3.1 per cent diseases of the circulatory system (The social status and living standards of the population of Russia, 2006, p. 318).

A sociological assessment of Russians' health standards can be obtained first and foremost from Russian Longitudinal Monitoring Survey (RLMS) data (see the appendix for details on this and other methods used). These show that, in 2005,

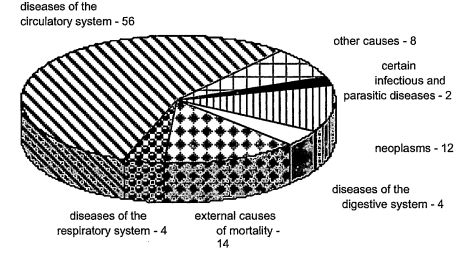

diseases of the
circulatory system - 56

other causes - 8

certain
infectious and
parasitic diseases - 2

neoplasms - 12

diseases of the
digestive system - 4

diseases of the   external causes
respiratory system - 4   of mortality -
                                  14

Figure 2.1   Deaths according to main classifications of cause of death, 2005*
(in percentages of total number of deaths)

* The social status and living standards of the population of Russia (2006), p. 329.

13 per cent of all respondents aged 14 or over had heart disease, 5 per cent lung disease, 8 per cent liver disease, 7 per cent kidney disease, 14 per cent diseases of the gastrointestinal tract, 13 per cent spinal problems, and 20 per cent other chronic diseases. Overall, 56 per cent of respondents had no diagnosed chronic diseases; however, for people aged 40 and above, this applied to less than half of them (see Figure 2.2). Moreover, 9 per cent of the group aged 41–50, 14 per cent of those aged 51–60 and 27 per cent of those aged over 60 had three or more types of the diseases listed above.[1]

There was a very stark interconnection between chronic disease and living standard: thus, of those who situated themselves on the two lowest of the nine rungs on the 'indigence–wealth' ladder, only 42 per cent did not have any chronic diseases, while among those who placed themselves on the two highest rungs, 76 per cent did not. The same trends were also recorded in the course of our panel survey.

Most respondents in our own survey were themselves also aware of the sharp deterioration in the population's health in recent years, and of the increased risk of child morbidity. They also named the factors that brought about this situation, chief among which were 'nerves', lack of money, environmental pollution, excessive workloads and, as additional factors affecting children, aggression going on

---

1 The validity of all the sociological data presented in this and subsequent chapters has been verified, using various criteria depending on the scales of the variables under investigation (chi-square test, V-Cramér coefficient, size of standard deviations, partial correlation coefficients, etc.). Only data shown to be valid have been included in the book.

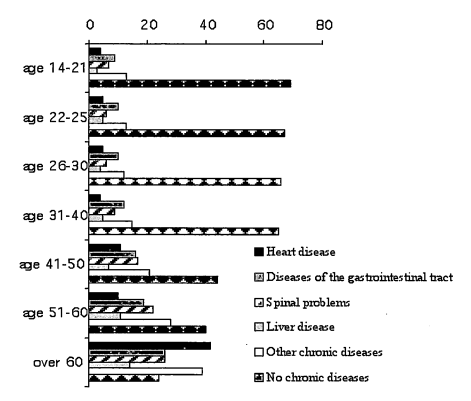

Figure 2.2 **Prevalence of certain chronic diseases in various age groups, RLMS, 2005 (%)**

around them, bottle-feeding of babies and, if a child wants to achieve something in life, an excessive workload at school:

> I think that there are no completely healthy people in our polluted environment ... On the quiet, everyone's gradually getting sicker. (Natal'ya, 39, acupressurist, Moscow; see also Chapter 11.)

> There are no healthy people now because our workloads are too heavy; everybody at work is past middle age and they all have various things wrong with them ... And some people are getting treatment, but they can't be cured. (Lev, 56, electromechanical engineer, Moscow; see also Chapter 11.)

> There are no healthy people at all now! Everyone in our family is ill – my daughter is ill, especially with that school ... She never manages to get everything done, her head is spinning, and she feels sick. She doesn't manage to eat properly, she just grabs something quick and gets on with her studies. She sits up studying until one o'clock in the morning, and there's no light at the end of the tunnel at all. (Raisa, 48, Voronezh; she herself had secondary education; over the ten years we have known her, her

occupational status had fallen from assistant retail manager through cashier to selling sweets from a kiosk.)

Children now are not as healthy as we were at their age. Because of all this pollution and bottle-feeding ... And again, it's nerves: the fact that things aren't going to work out for children in future, the material insecurity, it has an impact on children ... And, in addition to that, the attitude of teachers towards children at school, it's humiliating; they are out to swindle money; plus, there's even a kind of hatred towards the children themselves. (Lana, 44, Voronezh.)

Now there are practically no healthy children. And newborn babies aren't even born very healthy, because Mum and Dad are already pretty unhealthy. And then there's the food: people under 25 should eat properly – worthwhile food ... But here we don't even get three meals a day. (Viktor, 50, Moscow; father of five, with one disabled son; see below and also Chapter 8.)

However, chronic diseases may influence people's quality of life and life chances in differing degrees. In order to understand what state of health Russians are in (not from the point of view of whether they have certain chronic illnesses, but from the point of view of the general potential of their health as a form of physical, psychological and social well-being) we used the EQ-5D method, which helps to evaluate a person's overall quality of life as it results from his or her standard of health (see the appendix for details on this and other methods used).

As it turned out, the health standards of the population of Russia are really not high and are significantly worse, for example, than the situation in the UK (see Table 2.1).

As we can see, 65 per cent of UK citizens aged 60 and under can be considered completely healthy; as can just 37 per cent of Russians of the same age, which is almost a twofold difference. As far as respondents aged 61 and over are concerned, for them the gap is almost fivefold.

Taking into account all the above, there can hardly be any serious discussion of an increase in pension age in contemporary Russian conditions. Given the meagre size of pensions,[2] those retired people still capable of continuing to work do so, even without the pension age being raised, and, as a rule, they are to be found in a niche of low-paid jobs. (In Russia, judging by the 2005 RLMS data, 21 per cent of pensioners are working; the figure for women is 19 per cent and, for men, somewhat higher at 26 per cent; the pensioner employment indicator rose by an average of 2 per cent between 2003 and 2005).

Analysis of the structure of Russians' health problems also provides evidence of serious issues, both for the health of the population overall and in the older age cohorts. The worst indicators can be observed on the 'pain' and 'anxiety/depression' scales (see Figure 2.3).

---

2 The average size of the old age pension in 2005 was 2,761.30 roubles a month (i.e. roughly £55) (The social status and living standards of the population of Russia, 2006, p. 192).

Table 2.1   Distribution of health indicators according to EQ-5D method, UK* and Russia, results of national research surveys (%)

Health indicators	UK, 1998, n=3395		Russia, RLMS, 2005, n=10140		
	Respondents aged 60 and under	Respondents aged 61 and over	Respondents aged 60 and under	Respondents aged 61 and over	Across the sample as a whole
11111	64.9	37.1	36.5	8.2	31.0
11121	8.3	11.7	12.5	11.7	12.3
11112	7.6	3.3	11.4	1.4	9.5
11122	3.6	4.0	26.1	15.6	24.0
11221	1.5	1.6	0.3	1.2	0.5
11222	1.5	1.4	1.8	2.4	1.9
21121	1.7	6.8	0.7	3.4	1.2
21222	1.5	4.6	1.1	6.3	2.1
21122	0.9	2.9	1.8	5.2	2.5
21111	0.4	2.1	0.1	0.3	0.2
22222	0.5	1.8	0.5	7.1	1.8
22221	0.3	1.5	0.1	1.8	0.4
21211	0.4	1.3	0.0	0.1	0
21232	0.3	1.3	0.6	4.4	1.3
All others, including:**	6.6	18.6	6.5	30.9	11.3
11132			1.4	2.1	1.5
21132			0.5	1.9	0.8
21221			0.3	2.3	0.7
21233			0.1	1.2	0.3
22232			0.4	5.9	1.4
22233			0.1	2.1	0.5

* Kind et al. (1998). ** These additional items identify instances where the indicator exceeded 1 per cent in at least one of the two age groups.

However, if we review the data by age, then it becomes clear that there are two qualitative breakpoints, at which the general picture of health changes abruptly. One occurs in the 41–50 age group, when all the indicators (apart from the ability to care for oneself) start to fall fairly sharply; the second is in the over-60 age group, when most people in the group start to experience serious problems across most of the scales (see Table 2.2). If the pension age were to be raised, these breakpoints would stimulate a mass exodus from the workforce onto disability benefits.

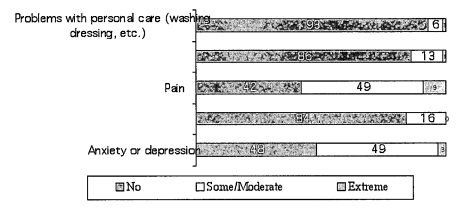

Figure 2.3   Distribution of health indicators according to EQ-5D method, respondents aged 14 and over, RLMS, 2005 (%)

The data provide evidence of the fact that, after the age of 40, 'good health' (defined as a state that allows people to lead a socially and economically active life) has ceased to be typical of the majority of members of these age cohorts. This is immediately reflected in their precarious labour market situation. Age discrimination arises as a consequence of employers' awareness of the limited nature of health resources in the relevant age groups; judging by the results of our research, it comes into play at age 35–40, and reaches its peak around the ages of 55–60. Moreover, judging by the occupational status of those who primarily encountered discrimination, the latter results from employers' understanding of the fact that capacity for work is, relatively speaking, reduced by a worse state of health rather than from the idea that it is not worthwhile investing in the human capital represented by each individual.

In insecure conditions and in material circumstances that are at best modest (and have also significantly deteriorated for the overwhelming majority of Russians over the years of reform), and given the absence of any kind of future guarantees for most of the population (because of the underdeveloped risk insurance system), fear of losing one's health, and with it also one's job, has become a genuinely mass phobia in Russia: its prevalence outstrips all other fears by a long way. Indeed, as the annual pan-Russian surveys conducted by the Institute of Sociology of the Russian Academy of Sciences show, fear of loss of health is consistently at the top of the ratings, with an indicator of over 70 per cent. At the same time, health is perceived as an instrumental value; that is, underlying the fear of losing one's health is the fear of losing one's capacity to work and, with it, losing access to work as a source of the means of existence.

Fear of losing their jobs leads people, especially the middle-aged and older generations, to try to tackle these problems by very severely exploiting the resource of their health. And, although other factors (which will be discussed more than once in subsequent chapters: particular features of national culture, lack of trust

Table 2.2 **Distribution of health indicators according to EQ-5D method, various age groups, RLMS, 2005 (%)**

Description of health indicators	Age in years				
	26–30	31–40	41–50	51–60	Over 60
Problems in walking about					
None	97	96	89	78	47
Some	3	4	11	22	51
Confined to bed	0	0	0	0	2
Problems with personal care					
None	99	99	98	95	74
Some	1	1	2	5	22
Unable to wash and dress themselves	0	0	0	0	4
Anxiety or depression					
None	56	52	43	38	34
Moderate	43	46	54	59	58
Extreme	1	2	3	3	8
Problems with usual activities					
None	97	96	91	83	55
Some	3	4	9	16	40
Unable to perform usual activities	0	0	0	1	5
Pain					
None	59	51	34	25	11
Moderate	39	46	60	63	61
Extreme	2	3	6	12	28

in doctors and their recommendations, the impossibility of obtaining good-quality treatment because of organisational problems with Russian health care, etc.) also play a part in forming this model of behaviour, it is the fear of being deprived of the means of existence that is the main determinant of behaviour, running counter to the basic instinct for self-preservation: people work even with serious diseases, using every possible means to conceal them from their superiors, a situation described by more than one of our respondents:

> People work all the same, even despite the fact that they are sick. There's one woman I know, she has breast cancer, but she works, she overcomes it, somehow she sticks at it. Because life is hard, you have to work. (Natal'ya, 46, unemployed, from Voronezh.)

If I start paying attention to myself, then I won't be able to do anything for anybody else; so I put up with it and that's that. I tried paying myself some attention; I went to Moscow and got completely checked over. And they found so many things wrong with me! But I just said to myself: 'I haven't got anything!' So I'm still alive. I know that if something happens to me, that will be the end for everyone. I simply switch off from everything that is wrong with me, and that's the only way I can save myself. (Rimma, 56, director of a printing house affiliated to the huge aircraft plant in Voronezh, with three adult males dependent on her: her disabled husband and two disabled brothers.)

Thus, statistical and sociological data provide evidence of the fact that the health status of people of all ages in Russia is characterised by high indicators of widespread chronic disease and low qualitative health indicators. However, a comparatively new trend for Russia, judging by respondents' assessments and by the quantitative data obtained, is not the increase in morbidity in older age groups (over 60), but the sharp deterioration in the health of the over-40 age group and of children during the period of reform implementation. Moreover, the most typical feature of health breakdown is the prevalence of pain (including in people who have no diagnosed chronic diseases) and anxiety or depression.

Methods of Measuring Health, with a Comparison of their Particular Features

A comparative analysis of the particular features of different methods of measuring health[3] was an original objective of our research. This analysis was initially conducted on the materials from our longitudinal panel, and then partially verified using the data of the RLMS pan-Russian research. Thus, it included several stages.

At the first stage, working with our longitudinal panel materials, all the methods used to measure health were reduced to a three-part division, which allowed us to identify a particular respondent as being, in practice, 'healthy', 'unhealthy' or 'sick'. The results obtained were then compared with one another, with most attention being given, firstly, to a comparison of people's assessments of their own health and how far they identified with sick people (adopting the sick role) and, secondly, to the correlation of GHQ and EQ-5D scale indicators. The third stage was to verify causal factors in our panel respondents' health status on the GHQ and EQ-5D scales, and the dynamic of their health over the whole period of observation, in order to assess the comparative effectiveness of these scales in Russian conditions and allow us to tackle a number of objectives. Finally, after determining the greater fitness of the EQ-5D method for the purpose of the pan-Russian survey and its practical application, the last stage was a controlled procedure for establishing the quantitative boundaries of 'health', 'ill-health' and

---

3 GHQ and EQ-5D; respondents' assessments of their own health on three- and five-level scales; how far respondents identify with people who have serious health problems; recording the presence or absence of various chronic diseases, or the presence of health problems in the 30 days preceding the survey.

'sickness', in which a large block of questions relating to the health, work and life of respondents from these groups was analysed using the pan-Russian data.

The results we obtained throughout these stages of analysis are, in part, presented in subsequent chapters of this book. The focus of this section is to look at particular aspects of reducing all the health measures used to a three-part division, allowing interpretation of data obtained within the categories 'health – ill-health – sickness', and then to compare people's assessments of their own health and their identification with sick people (adopting the sick role), to correlate GHQ and EQ-5D scale indicators and to consider causal factors in our respondents' health on the EQ-5D scale. We shall start with the reduction of all the scales to a single 'three-level' one.

In order to recode the five-level scale of self-rated health into a three-level scale, we unified the responses 'poor' and 'very poor health' into a single response of 'poor', and the responses 'good' and 'very good health' into 'good'. When we compared the data thus obtained with respondents' assessments of their own health, where they answered a question that directly offered a three-level assessment scale, it became clear that introducing a five-level scale leads to a certain loss of 'extreme' responses: 22 per cent of panel respondents rated their own health as 'good' on the five-level scale, while 16 per cent did so on the three-level scale; the corresponding figures for 'poor' assessments were 15 per cent and 14 per cent. Moreover, according to the 'Thermometer' component of the EQ-5D method (which offers the opportunity to rate one's own health on a symbolic thermometer in graphic form), those who rated their own health as 'fair' were concentrated mainly in the range from 40 to 79 out of a 100 possible 'degrees' (55 people out of 61 who thought their own health was 'fair'), those who rated their own health as 'poor' were mainly in the range below 50 'degrees' (ten people out of 12) and those who rated their own health as 'good' selected positions at 80 'degrees' or more (12 people out of 14).

Overall then, in answer to all the questions asking them to assess their own health, respondents gave fairly consistent assessments (the Pearson coefficient for self-rated health on the three-level and five-level scales was 0.795, and on the three-level scale and the 'Thermometer', –0.676). Moreover, of the questions that required subjective assessment of one's own health, the 'Thermometer' worked best of all for the groups of people in the worst health (defined according to GHQ and EQ-5D indicators); the verbal assessment of one's own health on a five-point scale worked best for the healthy, while for the group in the middle they all gave an identical picture. However, these differences were not significant.

Furthermore, in any of its variants, subjective assessment of one's own health was not a strict predictor of a respondent's readiness to adopt the sick role; so, two-thirds of people who identified themselves with the sick considered their own health to be 'fair' (see Table 2.3).

The same trend could also be traced in the pan-Russian datasets: among those who rated their own health as 'poor', according to data from the Institute of

Table 2.3   Consistency in identifying oneself with people who have serious health problems, panel respondents grouped according to their own assessments of their health, 2005 (%)

They feel they have something in common with people who have serious health problems:	People who consider their health good	People who consider their health fair	People who consider their health poor	Across the whole sample
Often	0	9 (15)	6 (50)	15 (17)
Sometimes	9 (64)	20 (33)	6 (50)	35 (40)
Practically never	5 (36)	32 (52)	0	37 (43)

Table 2.4   Health indicators of panel respondents grouped according to various assessments of their own health, 2005 (%)

Dynamic of health on GHQ scale over period of observation	People who consider their health good (n=6)	People who consider their health fair (n=49)	People who consider their health poor (n=11)	Across the whole sample (n=66)*
Health has deteriorated	1 (17%)	12 (24%)	*8 (73%)*	31 (32%)
Indicators stable (difference between first measurement and 2005 measurement in the range −4 to +4 points)	3 (50%)	18 (37%)	1 (9%)	22 (33%)
Health has improved	2 (33%)	19 (39%)	2 (18%)	23 (35%)
* Data on the health dynamic are included only for respondents from Moscow and Voronezh.				
Total number of points on GHQ scale	People who consider their health good (n=14)	People who consider their health fair (n=61)	People who consider their health poor (n=12)	Across the whole sample (n=87)
Up to and including 24	*8 (58%)*	10 (16%)	1 (8%)	19 (22%)
25–30	2 (14%)	11 (18%)	0	13 (15%)
31–35	0	12 (20%)	0	12 (14%)
36–40	2 (14%)	13 (22%)	0	15 (17%)
41–45	1 (7%)	2 (3%)	2 (17%)	5 (6%)
Over 45	1 (7%)	13 (21%)	9 (75%)	23 (26%)

Points on the physical health scale (A)				
0–9	*13 (93%)*	30 (49%)	1 (8%)	44 (51%)
10 and above	1 (7%)	31 (51%)	*11 (92%)*	43 (49%)
Points on the anxiety/depression scale (B)				
0–9	8 (57%)	21 (34%)	1 (8%)	30 (34%)
10 and above	6 (43%)	40 (66%)	*11 (92%)*	57 (66%)
Points on the social dysfunction scale (C)				
0–9	*10 (71%)*	23 (38%)	0	33 (38%)
10 and above	4 (29%)	38 (62%)	*12 (100%)*	54 (62%)
Total number of points on GHQ scale	People who consider their health good (n=14)	People who consider their health fair (n=61)	People who consider their health poor (n=12)	Across the whole sample (n=87)
Points on the severe depression scale (D)				
0–9	*14 (100%)*	56 (92%)	9 (75%)	79 (91%)
10 and above	0	5 (8%)	3 (25%)	8 (9%)
Health picture after recoding GHQ scale indicators				
Healthy (0–30 points)	*10 (72%)*	21 (34%)	1 (8%)	32 (37%)
Unhealthy (31–40 points)	2 (14%)	*25 (42%)*	0	27 (31%)
Sick (41 or more points)	2 (14%)	15 (24%)	*11 (92%)*	28 (32%)

Sociology's 2005[4] research, only 36 per cent often identified with people who had serious health problems; for 40 per cent this identification was not consistent but arose from a given situation, and 24 per cent never identified at all with people who had serious health problems.

Over the course of many years of observation of our panel respondents, we were able to record a typical mechanism for adopting the sick role. All respondents who adopted the sick role, despite relatively good indicators in the GHQ and EQ-5D tests, defined 'health' only as absence of sickness, i.e. physiologically. Although their general level of health was fairly high, it was true that they had some illnesses; and, for specific reasons, they showed a distinct tendency to give these markedly greater significance than did other respondents. There could be two such reasons: a conscious orientation towards claiming disability benefits as an attempt to tackle their material problems when rejecting a job, or an attempt to dramatise their own health situation in order not to acknowledge that they were

---

4 Data from the pan-Russian research programme 'Ownership in the life and perception of Russians', conducted by the Institute of Sociology of the Russian Academy of Sciences in 2005, with a sample of 1,751 people. (For more details of this research, see Gorshkov and Tikhonova, 2006).

rejecting employment in favour of the status of housewife (or househusband), i.e. constructing a new social status through more prestigious roles.

A typical example of the first situation was Alla, aged 57, a female respondent from Moscow, who was divorced with two children; her daughter lived with her, while her elder child, a son, lived elsewhere. Throughout the whole period of observation, the family was in persistent poverty. A former (non-academic) research assistant at a chemical and biological research institute, Alla took early retirement in the late 1990s and claimed Category II disability benefit. She did this as a conscious strategy, in order to receive a pension and concessionary benefits rather than working: with her skills, age and health she could not aspire to any kind of highly-paid job and took the view that the potential small financial gains of finding a job would not compensate her for the time and energy she would spend at work. A number of years later, despite her serious material problems, she said she was pleased with the decision she had taken at that time (see also Chapter 9).

A typical example of the second situation was Kira, aged 48, from Voronezh, who was a technician by training and had also worked at a scientific research institute during the 1990s. After the institute closed down in 1996, she registered as unemployed and then found work as a section head in a factory, where she worked for three years in total. 'The pay was very low,' she told us.

> In general, it would have been simply senseless to work for that kind of pay. But what kept me there was the fact that I needed to complete 25 years employment, and that I knew the team ... And then it just became pointless to work there ... And so, now my husband is keeping things afloat [she assessed the family's average per capita monthly income at 15,000 roubles], I am happy just to stay at home.

Although her health was not poor, Kira often identified with sick people. Of her own health, she said:

> It depends what you compare it with. If you compare how ill I am nowadays with my usual state of health before, then I feel about 75 years old. And, if you compare it with people around me, then, by comparison with a lot of girls of my age, I'm very healthy.

Overall, and in accordance with Parsons' definition of its characteristics, people adopted the sick role in order to justify freeing themselves from the necessity to work; a corollary of adopting this role was that they laid responsibility for the deterioration in their own health at the door of external factors (age, harmful working conditions in a previous job, etc.). However, because of a number of deficiencies in the Russian health care system (see Chapter 8), adopting the sick role did not involve an active approach to 'doctor–patient' relations or a willingness to follow a doctor's instructions. Moreover, these were not represented as obligatory requirements by our respondents' social circles. Thus, in Russian conditions, the socioeconomic and medical aspects of the sick role turned out to be entirely separate.

Our next objective was a comparative assessment of the heuristic possibilities of the GHQ and EQ-5D scales and the consolidation of their indicators into three-level scales. As we had already used the shortened 27-question version of the GHQ method more than once in various other projects, we had a clearer picture of this on a methodological level[5] before beginning our research, and this allowed us to move at once to describing our panel respondents' health status using the categories 'healthy – unhealthy – sick' (see Table 2.4).

When we analysed our data, the most prominent points that emerged were the notable influence of the health dynamic on people's own assessments of their health (as a rule, in the group who were inclined to describe their own health as 'poor', health measured using GHQ indicators had deteriorated over the ten years of observation). Specifically there was a distinct correspondence of people's own assessments of their health to the scale indicators of physical health and social dysfunction, the high indicators on the anxiety scale of those who rated their own health as 'poor' and the low indicators on the severe depression scale of those who rated their own health as 'good'.

Our next objective was to obtain a summarised picture of our panel respondents' health using the EQ-5D 'health – ill-health – sickness' measure, with which we had started working for the first time only in 2004–2005. Using this, the overall picture across our longitudinal sample is shown in Table 2.5.

Within this measure, 45 per cent of respondents indicated that they had problems with performing their usual activities, and 29 per cent that they had problems in walking about; 64 per cent of respondents said they were anxious or depressed.

Taking into account our respondents' own assessments of their health and the data that we had about their life stories, we were able to define distinct boundaries between good health and poor health, and thus situate the results obtained by the EQ-5D method on a three-level scale. We found that 'good' health began at the indicator 0.76, and 'poor' health at 0.69. In our sample, the interval between them was represented by only one position (0.73): 21 out of 23 respondents who had this indicator rated their health as 'fair', and two as 'good', which allowed us to

---

5 Our methods in consolidating this scale for application in Russian conditions and some of the results we obtained through its use have been described in Manning and Tikhonova (2004). So here we shall merely note that, in the UK, an indicator of 24 out of 84 possible points is usually taken as the notional boundary between normal and pathological. However, in our sample, this interpretation would mean that the overwhelming majority of respondents could not be viewed as healthy. Similar indicators were also obtained by the present author in two other local Russian research projects where this questionnaire was used. This therefore suggests the hypothesis that in Russian culture, with its readiness to complain about life in general and health in particular (connected with the predominance of an external locus of control), this boundary has become somewhat displaced. Comparing respondents' general assessments of their own health with their GHQ indicators led us to the conclusion that it was appropriate to use an indicator of 31 points as the boundary between normal and pathological for Russia. An indicator of 41 points was defined as the lower boundary of 'sickness', so indicators in the range 31–40 points corresponded to 'ill-health'. For the separate GHQ sub-scales, the boundary indicator was 9 points.

Table 2.5   Distribution of panel respondents' health indicators according to EQ-5D method, 2005 (%)

Health indicators	People who consider their health good (n=14)	People who consider their health fair (n=61)	People who consider their health poor (n=12)	Across the whole sample (n=87)
11111	6 (43%)	1 (2%)	0	7 (8%)
11121	3 (21%)	11 (18%)	0	14 (16%)
11112	1 (7%)	2 (3%)	0	3 (3%)
11122	2 (14%)	19 (31%)	0	21 (24%)
11212	0	2 (3%)	0	2 (2%)
11221	2 (14%)	1 (2%)	1 (8%)	4 (5%)
11222	0	*9 (15%)*	1 (8%)	10 (12%)
11232	0	0	1 (8%)	1 (1%)
21121	0	2 (3)	0	2 (2%)
21122	0	1 (2%)	0	1 (1%)
21221	0	2 (3%)	1 (8%)	3 (3%)
21222	0	8 (13%)	3 (26%)	11 (13%)
21223	0	0	1 (8)	1 (1%)
21231	0	1 (2%)	0	1 (1%)
21232	0	0	1 (8)	1 (1%)
21233	0	0	*2 (17%)*	2 (2%)
21332	0	0	1 (8%)	1 (1%)
22232	0	1 (2%)	0	1 (1%)
22233	0	1 (2%)	0	1 (1%)

establish it as the intermediate position for translating the EQ-5D test indicators into a three-part scale (see Table 2.6).

Furthermore, it turned out that, although indicators on the GHQ and EQ-5D scales overall were closely linked, comparing them for specific respondents showed a significant lack of correspondence between indicators on both scales. So, six people with an indicator below 0.7 on the EQ-5D scale had fewer than 30 points on the GHQ. On the other hand, three people with an indicator of 41 or more points on the GHQ scale had healthy indicators on the EQ-5D (see Table 2.7).

This prompted us to look at what was causing the differences between indicators on these scales. Our analysis revealed that the decisive role in placing members of these two groups at opposite poles was played by their qualitatively different attitudes to life in general and to their health in particular.

The first group (six people) really had serious problems with their health. Three members of the group were not working: two of these three had taken early retirement on grounds of disability, while the third was 87 years old. The other three were aged from 40 to 44, and were working as finance director of a clinic (and deputy to the senior doctor), an administrator in a university department, and a manager.

Table 2.6   Health standards of panel respondents grouped according to various assessments of their own health, 2005 (%)

EQ-5D test indicators	People who consider their health good (n=14)	People who consider their health fair (n=61)	People who consider their health poor (n=12)	Across the whole sample (n=87)
Sick (from −0.2 to 0.69)	0	23 (38%)	*11 (92%)*	34 (39%)
Unhealthy (from 0.7 to 0.75)	2 (14%)	21 (34%)	0	23 (26%)
Healthy (from 0.76 to 1)	*12 (86%)*	17 (28%)	1 (8%)	30 (35%)

Table 2.7   Correlation of panel respondents' health indicators on the two scales used, 2005 (%)

GHQ indicators (in points)	EQ-5D indicators			
	0.75 and above (healthy) (n=30)	from 0.7 to 0.75 (unhealthy) (n=23)	below 0.7 (sick) (n=34)	Across the whole sample (n=87)
0–30 (healthy)	19 (63%)	7 (30%)	<u>6</u> (18%)	32 (37%)
31–40 (unhealthy)	8 (27%)	11 (48%)	8 (23%)	27 (31%)
41 and above (sick)	<u>3</u> (10%)	5 (22%)	20 (59%)	28 (32%)

Table 2.8   General picture of Russians' health according to EQ-5D indicators reduced to a three-level scale, RLMS, 2005 (%)

Description of health	Presence of chronic diseases				
	Cardio-vascular disease	3 or more chronic diseases	No chronic diseases	Across the sample as a whole	
Healthy	21	15	73	54	
Unhealthy	23	23	21	25	
Sick	56	62	6	21	
	Age in years				
	26–30*	31–40	41–50	51–60	Over 60
Healthy	71	62	49	40	23
Unhealthy	23	30	34	32	19
Sick	6	8	17	28	57

* Four per cent of young people aged 14–21 were 'sick' (n=1520 persons), while 80 per cent were 'healthy'; in the 22–25 age group (n=804 persons), the indicators were 5 per cent and 74 per cent respectively.

One member of the group rated his own health as 'poor', the others as 'fair'. In addition, four of the six people gave health problems as among the three chief reasons why, in their view, their life was not exactly as they would wish. All six had problems with performing their usual activities; three had problems in walking about, and all complained of pain, including one who complained of extreme pain. Thus, members of this group were in such poor health that it prevented them from leading a normal life.

However, they took the view that their health problems were natural, inevitable and connected with age (to be precise, four out of the six people perceived the problem in this way), and they tried not to dramatise their situation or 'dwell on' the signs of being unwell, which they had become used to. Therefore, when answering the GHQ questions, they were inclined to make their situation seem much less severe than it really was: even on Scale A, their maximum indicator in total was 8 points, with three people scoring 6 points and two (a Category II disabled person and the 87-year-old female pensioner) 3 and 2 points respectively. Their indicators on Scale D (severe depression) were also minimal: 1 or 2 points. The latter was connected with this group's most typical attributes: a positive mood, optimism and an active approach to strategies for everyday life, which were manifested in various forms.

Firstly, whatever their level of material welfare, they generally did not complain that their material circumstances were a factor in their life not being exactly as they would wish, and they evaluated the various aspects of their life fairly optimistically.

Secondly, they all had positive reactions to the concept 'future', as did most of them (four people) to the concept 'present'. Moreover, judging by the fact that, in their open interviews, the two other respondents paid a great deal of attention to problems that are typical for Russian society as a whole today (a decline in morals, etc.), their negative associations with the concept 'present' were not connected with their own personal situation. In addition, despite their poor health, the thoughts of most members of this group were usually, according to their own assessments, focused on the future.

Thirdly, regardless of their health and age, they all tried to construct their lives themselves and not 'get carried along by the tide'. It was no accident that four of the six people had a predominantly internal locus of control, while, for the other two, the degree to which indicators of external locus of control predominated was 6 points, far fewer than in the sample as a whole.

Fourthly, five of the six people demonstrated an active model of leisure; the sixth was disabled, which limited him not only in his usual activities but also in walking about, so for him there were serious objective limitations on any kind of leisure pursuits.

The fifth and final point is that each of them had some kind of interest in life. Of those who were not working, one woman wrote poetry and moved in a related milieu; a second woman visited a 'self-help' club (which is extremely untypical of Russian pensioners); the third person was engaged in renovations and interior design for his own property. As for those who were working, all three considered their work interesting and none thought that it lacked prospects.

Thus, after we had completed our analysis, it became clear that these people, consciously or unconsciously, overstated their health indicators when replying to direct questions about specific signs of not being well, and that this was because their objective assessment of their own health was incompatible with the life they wanted and tried to lead. As one of these six respondents said:

> What does 'not ill' mean? As they say, if you wake up in the morning and nothing hurts, it means you're dead. 'Not ill' is a relative concept. (Tat'yana, 40, trained economist and deputy director of a clinic, Moscow; see also Chapter 9.)

Another echoed this: 'Illness as such is an absolutely subjective concept, of course. There is no objective concept of illness' (Anatoly, 60, retired academic biologist from Moscow). The others also expressed themselves in the same vein.

The second group (three people) was in a directly contrasting position to the first, even though in age (44 to 55), living standards (ranging from being badly-off to being averagely well-off) and employment (deputy managing director of a commercial concern; engineer in a department supplying spare parts; electrical fitter), it did not obviously differ from the first group. However, members of this group were disposed to be fairly gloomy, despite the fact that they generally did not complain of health being among the main problems spoiling their life. And, in reality, no member of this group had any problems with walking about or extreme pain.

They complained not about their health, but about their poor material circumstances. In addition, they were discontented with their work: not one of them considered their job interesting, while all, without exception, thought that it lacked prospects. 'The present' conjured up only negative associations for them, and their 'golden age' was the past; in fact, the distant past. They all thought mostly about the period 1986–1990, when, as they all said, they had belonged to the most successful sections of the population, whereas in the present they were just living 'like everyone else'.

Among other typical features of this group, we should also mention the predominance of an external locus of control, which may have been connected with the fact that they were all first-generation migrants. One came from a village and two from small towns: for comparison, in the first group, five respondents had been born or grown up in their cities, while one woman had come to study in the city immediately after leaving school and then stayed on.

Thus, it became clear that this group was formed not of people whose health was objectively poor, but of those who felt general discontent with the world as a whole and with their own lives in particular: they were ready to complain about everything, including specific signs of not being well, even strongly overstating these.

As a result of this analysis, it became clear that, given Russia's particular sociocultural features and its current social and economic situation, use of the EQ-5D scale would be methodologically more appropriate for our input into the pan-Russian survey.

Table 2.9   Correlation of indicators of material welfare, panel respondents grouped by standard of health on the EQ-5D scale, 2005 (%)

They felt helpless to influence what was happening	EQ-5D indicators			Across the whole sample
	Healthy	Unhealthy	Sick	
Often	7 (23%)	8 (36%)	24 (71%)	39 (45%)
Sometimes	11 (37%)	9 (41%)	8 (23%)	28 (33%)
Practically never	12 (40%)	5 (23%)	2 (6%)	19 (22%)
Presence of poor families in their immediate circle	EQ-5D indicators			Across the whole sample
	Healthy	Unhealthy	Sick	
Yes	10 (33%)	13 (56%)	26 (77%)	49 (56%)
No	*20 (67%)*	10 (44%)	8 (23%)	38 (44%)
Material circumstances in 2005	EQ-5D indicators			Across the whole sample
	Healthy	Unhealthy	Sick	
Poor	4 (13%)	2 (9%)	14 (41%)	20 (23%)
Badly-off	9 (30%)	9 (39%)	9 (27%)	27 (31%)
Averagely well-off and well-off	*17 (57%)*	12 (52%)	11 (32%)	40 (46%)
Own assessment of quality of food	EQ-5D indicators			Across the whole sample
	Healthy	Unhealthy	Sick	
Good	16 (54%)	6 (26%)	6 (17%)	28 (32%)
Satisfactory	13 (43%)	*16 (70%)*	23 (68%)	52 (60%)
Poor	1 (3%)	1 (4%)	5 (15%)	7 (8%)
Consumption of meat and fish products	EQ-5D indicators			Across the whole sample
	Healthy	Unhealthy	Sick	
No more than once a week	3 (10%)	2 (9%)	12 (36%)	17 (18%)
Twice a week	3 (10%)	3 (13%)	11 (32%)	17 (20%)
Three or more times a week	*24 (80%)*	18 (78%)	11 (32%)	53 (61%)

The results of applying this method in the course of the pan-Russian survey have already been briefly described above, but reducing it to a   three-part division allowed us to obtain clearer results, giving a picture of Russians' health overall and for separate age groups in particular (see Table 2.8).

We should add that 30 per cent of those who were sick according to EQ-5D indicators had a disability. However, the real indicators of disability in this group would, if the health care system worked better, obviously have been higher.[6] In any event, in the course of the 2005 RLMS survey, it was found that a third of

---

6 See the Note on Disability in the Preface.

Table 2.10   Age structure, panel respondents grouped by standard of health according to the EQ-5D scale, 2005 (%)

Age	EQ-5D indicators, 2005			Across the whole sample
	Healthy	Unhealthy	Sick	
39 and under	14 (47%)	10 (43%)	3 (9%)	27 (32%)
40–49	7 (23%)	6 (26%)	16 (47%)	30 (34%)
50 and over	9 (30%)	7 (29%)	14 (44%)	30 (34%)

those confined to bed were not registered as disabled, and nor were a third of those who were in principle unable to care for themselves (washing and dressing themselves, etc.).

Thus, our verification of how far various methods of assessing health were applicable to conditions in Russia demonstrated not only the fairly high reliability of results obtained using any of these methods, but also particular features of these results, connected in some cases with a particular feature of national culture and in others with a specific aspect of the methods themselves. Moreover, it became clear that, given the problems with the functioning of the Russian health care system (from lack of essential diagnostic equipment in many population centres to inaccessibility of doctors as a result of really very sick people having to queue for many hours to see one), discrepancies between sociological indicators of health and objective data about the presence of diagnosed chronic diseases can be explained in many cases by problems in the health care system.

Verification of EQ-5D Scale Indicators for Russia, Using Life Story and Linear Regression Methods

Given the lack of objective information about the real state of health in Russia, we undertook an additional analysis of causal factors in Russians' health, using the EQ-5D method. In subsequent chapters, these factors will be analysed from various points of view and across different datasets, but here our interest is in a general description of them, providing material for comparing our results with the results of research conducted by specialists in other countries and thus allowing us to assess the heuristic possibilities of reducing the EQ-5D scales to a three-level form.

So what does a summarised portrait of our longitudinal panel respondents who were in poor health according to EQ-5D indicators look like when reconstructed with the help of the life story method? These were mainly people who belonged to the most deprived sections of society, where it was not so much a matter of insufficient income as of real multiple deprivation. Moreover, most of them were in a difficult psychological state, part of which consisted of feeling their own helplessness to influence what was happening. And, given that almost two-thirds of them had already spent more than a year in a state of profound exclusion or were in the 'grey area' that lies between the mainstream and social exclusion,[7] it is not surprising that they were undoubtedly 'cut off' from any possibility of getting out of this situation. Their resources of assistance from other people around them were relatively small, since their social contacts were within what might be called 'their own circle'. The same trends were also to be found when we summarised the quantitative data for the panel respondents (see Table 2.9).

Most poor people were concentrated among the sick (although 22 out of the 34 people in poor health were working). By 2005, being badly off did not show such a strong link with health, although 75 per cent of those who were in the intermediate, 'ill-health' group in 2005 had been badly off in the 1990s. Thus, poverty and exclusion were strongly linked with poor health, while being badly off was connected with a genuine threat to health.

In discussing the mechanism by which this threat arises, it is necessary not only to note that being badly off (having relatively poor food and little rest, constantly struggling against a slide into poverty and with the nervous and physical overload of all this) has already in itself contributed to a deterioration in health. No less important is the fact that (in a situation where free health care has de facto disappeared from contemporary Russia, and employers are making increasingly heavy demands on workers) the deterioration in health of a significant section of the population has been part of a vicious circle. It starts with relatively declining health – which leads to failure to maintain a steady, well-paid job in conditions of deepening income inequalities – and on to poverty – not being able to continue to spend money on maintaining and rehabilitating health – further decline in health – more profound poverty and the development of social exclusion as a result of the gradual loss of any kind of steady employment and the impossibility of maintaining previous levels of social contact. The role of this vicious circle in the deterioration of Russians' health and in entrenching their poverty is all the greater because contemporary Russian social policy does not in principle see poverty and social exclusion as a consequence of the fact that individuals have health problems; neither anti-poverty strategies nor targeted Federal health care programmes contain any mechanisms for targeting assistance to people whose health has been compromised, in order to reintegrate them into society. (Programmes of assistance to people who are receiving disability benefits or war disability pensions, or have suffered from accidents at atomic power stations, etc., are the sole exception to this.)

In these conditions, one of the original objectives of our research was to verify the mechanism by which health that is relatively poor at the outset influences risk of poverty. And although subsequent chapters will devote some attention to this

---

7 The method used to identify excluded households and particular features of their circumstances in Russian conditions has been described in detail in Manning and Tikhonova (2004). Here we shall merely note that only a third of panel respondents who were in the 'sick' group in 2005 had been in the mainstream in 2000. At the same time, 77 per cent of the 2005 'healthy' group were people who had demonstrated no signs of exclusion in 2000.

problem, we would like to stress in advance that the hypothesis that initially poor health is one of the decisive factors in poverty in Russia was wholly confirmed. By 2005, half of those who had been in poor health at the time they first joined the panel were poor, while only one in five of those who had been in good health was poor by the time we completed our observations. Moreover, we observed a distinct improvement in the material circumstances of the healthiest section of the panel: among those who had been healthy at the time they joined the panel, there was an almost twofold reduction in the proportion of poor people. At the same time, the proportion of poor people among those who had been 'sick' at the outset remained almost unchanged. The difference in the opportunities available to these groups was especially evident when, in the period 2002–2005, new opportunities opened up as a result of favourable economic circumstances, and some people in Russia, especially in the major cities, were able to improve their circumstances.

Thus, poor health was a very significant limitation on opportunities to improve material circumstances: something which our respondents themselves pointed out more than once. And the main factor in this turned out to be access to a good-quality job, for which, in the overwhelming majority of cases, good health had been required at the outset. At the same time, lack of access to such a job led not only to a shortage of monetary resources, but also generated stress and a feeling that one was not needed, which contributed to further deterioration in health and served to limit labour market opportunities still more.

This is how our respondents themselves described these processes:

> The most unpleasant events that have taken place over recent years have been the change in direction by the government, and older people being made redundant. It was up in the air, whether or not they would find work. Essentially, they weren't taking older people on in jobs. That was a really bad blow to my material circumstances. But not only materially – emotionally as well. There are no opportunities to work, to feel that you are doing something useful and necessary. On the contrary, you feel that nobody needs you. (Ekaterina, 63, pensioner from Kazan.)

Valentina, who was younger (aged 42, an underground worker on the Moscow Metro; see also Chapter 11), also talked about this:

> Of course, health is everything, without it you won't achieve anything, you will vegetate. At least, you can't get into a more prestigious job anywhere; they do look at whether a person is ill or not. And if you do get a job somewhere, and if there is a glimmer of anything starting with your health – that's the end, they can simply say to you 'we don't need you any more, that's it.' And, for young people, it's also a criterion for being hired in a job.

In the group of respondents defined as 'sick' according to the EQ-5D method, work really was of less good quality: they were more likely to have complaints about it being exhausting (46 per cent) or stressful (50 per cent). It was said to be dirty, monotonous or boring, and the pay low or late (60 per cent). In addition, complaints about working under constant mental demands, in conditions with

Table 2.11   Some particular features of respondents grouped by standard of health according to the EQ-5D scale, 2005 (%)

Satisfaction with life overall	EQ-5D indicators			Across the whole sample
	Healthy	Unhealthy	Sick	
Completely satisfied/ Fairly satisfied	*49*	30	22	38
Yes and No	26	31	21	26
Less than satisfied/ Dissatisfied	25	39	*57*	36
Assessment of their own position on a 9-point scale from 'indigence' to 'wealth'	EQ-5D indicators			Across the whole sample
	Healthy	Unhealthy	Sick	
1–3 points	32	40	52	38
4–6 points	61	57	46	57
7–9 points	7	3	2	5
Assessment of their own position on a 9-point scale from 'people completely without rights' to 'people who have a lot of power'	EQ-5D indicators			Across the whole sample
	Healthy	Unhealthy	Sick	
1–3 points	40	54	67	49
4–6 points	53	42	30	46
7–9 points	7	4	3	5
General job satisfaction	EQ-5D indicators			All working respondents
	Healthy	Unhealthy	Sick	
Completely satisfied/ Fairly satisfied	*54*	39	35	48
Yes and No	22	29	28	25
Less than satisfied/ Dissatisfied	24	32	37	27
Satisfaction with working conditions	EQ-5D indicators			All working respondents
	Healthy	Unhealthy	Sick	
Completely satisfied/ Fairly satisfied	*49*	38	32	44
Yes and No	22	26	23	23
Less than satisfied/ Dissatisfied	29	36	*44*	33
Satisfaction with opportunities for professional development	EQ-5D indicators			All working respondents
	Healthy	Unhealthy	Sick	
Completely satisfied/ Fairly satisfied	37	29	24	32
Yes and No	23	23	19	23
Less than satisfied/ Dissatisfied	40	48	*57*	45

Table 2.12　Health indicators for various occupational status groups defined according to ISCO-88 classification, RLMS, 2005 (%)

Major Groups	EQ-5D indicators, 2005			Proportion of those with chronic diseases	Across the whole sample
	Healthy	Unhealthy	Sick		
Legislators, senior officials, and managers	7	7	5	46	7
Professionals	14	17	17	49	15
Technicians and associate professionals	16	19	16	47	17
Clerks	6	6	6	46	6
Service workers and shop and market sales workers	11	11	12	40	11
Skilled agricultural and fishery workers	1	0	1	35	1
Craft and related trades workers	16	12	12	41	14
Plant and machine operators and assemblers	18	16	14	41	17
Elementary occupations	12	12	17	43	12

high risk of accident, in freezing cold conditions, or working with chemicals were roughly one-and-a-half times more frequent among the sick. However, they were still afraid of losing these jobs. Practically no healthy people said that fear of losing their job prevented them taking time off work when they were not feeling well, but fully half of all working members of the 'sick' group said this did apply to them. Moreover, although half of the working sick were generally convinced that their work was detrimental to their health (contrasted with only one in six among the healthy), they continued working. The explanations they gave for this differed markedly from those offered by respondents in the healthy and borderline groups. Practically all of them referred to lack of alternatives: as a rule, because their age prevented them finding a better job.

In this connection, it is important to point out that the 'sick' group really was somewhat older than the others (see Table 2.10), although there were just eight people of pension age out of a total of 34 in this group, and another four who were in receipt of disability pension even though they had not yet reached pension age.

Even for professionals, the health factor proved, if it was intensified by additional risk factors, to be a severe structural limitation that led to poverty. A clear example of such a situation in our panel was provided by the life story of Viktor (see also Chapter 6), the head of a poor household with five children who grew to adulthood over the period of observation. Both Viktor and his wife had higher education; during the Soviet period, he had been an army officer. Having retired from the military at the end of the 1980s, he moved to Moscow to be near his parents and started work as a leading engineer at the factory attached to a scientific defence research institute; this meant that, until the start of the reforms, he received high pay and a number of concessionary benefits. However, in the 1990s, the situation fundamentally changed and, according to our index of material deprivation, his household was poor throughout the whole period of observation. 'Now, for our family to get back to its former [pre-reform] living standard,' said Viktor in 2000, 'our income would have to treble. There's no hope of improving our circumstances.'

The impossibility of obtaining a new, highly-paid job was connected to the fact that Viktor was in poor health from the very beginning of our observations: he was all of 44 years old when he joined our panel in 1999, yet his GHQ indicator was 47 points, including 14 on the somatic health scale. The impossibility of his wife being effectively employed was also connected with health, but in this case it was the health of their youngest son: she had given up work in 1997 because of his disability, and had started educating him at home. In her 2000 interview, she said:

> Any kind of expenditure is a problem. It's sometimes the case that we have nothing at all in the house to eat. There is never any money, so in those difficult situations, I send my husband – he tries to get money somehow; he's already completely in debt. If we do manage to find something, then it's for the children's clothing. I've never had anything, no nice clothes, nothing fancy … I wear whatever people give me.

By 2005, the situation in the family had not improved, despite the fact that the older children had grown up and started earning; Viktor himself, now 50, ascribed this in the first instance to health problems, since new 'defects' had been added to his old ones. In the course of his interview, he said:

> Recently it's become hard for me to do certain things. My vision is poor, so it's hard to do work that I used to manage with ease before – now I can't do it even with glasses on. And my legs ache, I'm short of breath, I have problems with my heart, lots of things … And my nervous system is fit for nothing … I'm not taking any medicines, simply because there's no money, and because I just don't trust doctors now … I'm permanently completely in debt – I owe money on the flat. I owe money for the electricity. I have to pay off everything, but I don't know how – wages aren't going up, and inflation is enormous …

As we can see, initially poor health and having a lot of children and, subsequently (when the children had grown up), new health problems conspired to completely close off any possibility of this educated, well-socialised man, who had begun with extensive social and skills capital, avoiding poverty. Another very difficult situation arose when the health problems concerned were 'visible' in nature: small stature (there was one woman with restricted growth on our panel), a stammer (two instances among our respondents), etc. For people with such physical defects, despite the presence of higher education and a very broad regional labour market (all these instances were in the Moscow section of the sample), access to any kind of secure job was closed, and their lot was ever-growing exclusion, as a rule accompanied by poverty.

Overall then, our research using the life story method demonstrated not only that we had correctly divided people into 'healthy', 'unhealthy' and 'sick' groups, with the scales from the EQ-5D method consolidated into three levels, but also that there was a very close connection between belonging to a certain group and prolonged stress, chronic poverty, particular features of the jobs that people with a corresponding level of health could aspire to, and a clearly-expressed age discrimination problem, especially significant in Russia, with its very profound wage inequalities. Moreover, all these problems are interconnected and create a synergetic, cumulative effect for those who encounter them.

The second component of our work to verify the factors most strongly connected with belonging to a certain health group was the linear regression method, which we applied to all the variables of the 2005 RLMS dataset, numbering over 700.[8] This dual verification demonstrated the close link between the EQ-5D scale and respondents' own assessments of their health (Pearson coefficient −0.590). Which of the three main health groups a respondent belonged to proved to be connected with the presence of chronic disease (Pearson coefficient −0.497), health problems in the previous 30 days (−0.358),[9] chronic diseases of the cardiovascular system (−0.383), disability (0.251) and a number of other variables recording objective health problems. In addition, standard of health was closely connected with satisfaction with life in general and in various aspects: first and foremost, work (see Table 2.11).

Overall, the quantitative data confirmed, firstly, the relatively worse quality of jobs available to respondents in poor health and, secondly, their depressed psychological state, their sense of their depreciating social status, their own lack of rights and their helplessness, all leading to prolonged stress.

However, at the same time, no strict connection was recorded between overall health indicators (or, moreover, chronic diseases) and membership of socio-occupational groups defined using the ISCO-88 classification[10] (see Table 2.12). In this regard, the realities of Russian conditions left their mark, distorting the classic distributions.

---

8 We initially used the Chaid subroutine of SPSS (Tree–Select method), and then, as a control procedure, applied the Pearson coefficient.

9 Seventy-seven per cent of 'sick' people (measured using EQ-5D) had had such problems, while 80 per cent of 'healthy' people had not.

10 For a description of this method, see International Labour Office (1990).

As we can see, the worst health indicators were found among professionals, and the best among skilled blue-collar workers. Within the same age groups across various types of occupational statuses, differences tended to vary in nature, but did not alter the main trend: the relatively high prevalence of chronic diseases among the more educated sections of the population employed in non-manual labour.

The lowest indicators of the presence of chronic diseases were found in inhabitants of rural localities and urban-type settlements. Diagnostic equipment in such places is much worse than in major cities and towns (where the majority of professionals and white-collar workers live).[11] In addition, 36 per cent of those who did not (they said) have chronic diseases complained that they felt some pain, and 2 per cent that they experienced severe pain. This led to the hypothesis that, if there were more adequate diagnoses, indicators of chronic diseases in residents of villages and urban-type settlements, where the proportion of people in elementary occupations and service workers and shop and market sales workers is relatively higher, would increase.

However, this did not explain why, also according to the EQ-5D scale, health indicators for people in non-manual work turned out to be worse than for less-educated blue-collar workers of the same age. An answer to this question can be found partly through analysing the way Russians understand health as a specific socio-cultural phenomenon; a phenomenon that allows us to look at their assessments of their health from a somewhat different point of view.

---

11 Across various types of towns, 52–55 per cent of people had no chronic diseases, while the corresponding figure for villages and urban-type settlements was 60–67 percent.

Chapter 3
Understanding Health

Svetlana Goryunova and Nataliya Tikhonova

Душа меру знает
The soul knows the right measure

As even Parsons (1958) noted, views of health and sickness are social and cultural in nature and may be seen as universal categories only via a system of generally accepted norms. However, for a long time, the international academic literature did not view the issue of a population's understanding of health and sickness as a free-standing problem; and all social policy in the area of health care was constructed with an orientation towards treating disease rather than supporting health.

Interest in this issue has arisen only in recent decades (Blaxter, 1990). One of the earliest researchers, Herzlich (1973), showed that there are several approaches to defining health and that, in particular, there are visibly 'positive' and 'negative' definitions of health. A 'negative' definition interprets health as absence of disease (experienced by the respondent, or diagnosed), while a 'positive' definition includes the qualities and characteristics that a person must possess in order to be described as healthy (energy, etc.). Different definitions and interpretations may, in their turn, lead to differing ways of supporting health and differing patterns of self-care behaviour (O'Sullivan and Stakelum, 2004). A new understanding of health also leads to changes in demands on the health care system (Walsh et al., 2000). Therefore, analysis of a population's understanding of health and of its influence on attitude to one's own health has not only theoretical, but also practical significance. However, issues of the population's understanding of health and sickness as applied to Russia have not yet been studied.

Russians' Understanding of the Phenomena of Health and Sickness

Interviews

We initially analysed the issue of how Russians perceive the phenomena of health and sickness through our interview materials, and then also using the RLMS pan-Russian survey data. In the interviews, many respondents highlighted a special intermediate state lying between health and sickness and opposed to both of them. They mentioned it several times in the open interviews; yet this state has never been defined as qualitatively special in Russian culture, and there is not even an adequate term for it in the Russian language, a fact that was also reflected in the way respondents themselves described this state.

It's hard to call him [my husband] 'sick', but sometimes something hurts. It's not that there's anything seriously wrong, but his general condition is not normal, that is – periodically he has stomach pains or his blood pressure drops; sometimes his heart races. (Ira, 39, from Voronezh, whose husband Yevgeni is a karate trainer working at a sports club.)

I think of myself as relatively healthy. But because I have an enlarged thyroid gland, there's something going wrong inside me; also, sometimes I just don't want to go rummaging around inside. (Yelena, 48, director of a social adaptation centre for homeless people, Moscow.)

Even if a person isn't sick, that doesn't mean he is 100 per cent healthy, because all the same, there will be something ... (Ol'ga, 43, chemical production operative, Kazan'.)

It also turned out that this intermediate state could be recorded quantitatively. Thus, where respondents had selected Response 1 ('No problems') on the mobility and usual activities scales in the EQ-5D test and had fewer than 10 points on the GHQ A scale (physical health), they usually rated their own health as 'good'.

They usually described their health as 'fair' if they had chosen Response 2 ('Some problems') in answering the questions about pain or discomfort and anxiety or depression on the EQ-5D scales. About 60 per cent of those who chose this response were located in the range of 25–40 points on the GHQ, while the others were distributed across the two extreme groups: 16 per cent with scores of 0–24 points and 25 per cent with 41 or more points.

Respondents who described their health as 'poor' reported that, on the EQ-5D scale, they had moderate or extreme problems in walking about and/or performing their usual activities, and also severe pain, serious depression or strong anxiety. As a rule, those who described their health as 'poor' had a total of 44 or more points on the GHQ and their indicators on Scale A (physical health) were 10 points or higher.

Thus, for them, 'health' was a state in which they experienced no limitations on their actions (walking about; performing their usual activities), while 'sickness' was a state where they were not only limited in their actions but also experienced severe pain or psychological difficulties. In their perception, there was a certain interim state between good and poor health, a border zone, where the person is not healthy but is not yet sick. This may involve minor limitations on their activities, limitations that arise from time to time, some pain, anxiety or depression: in other words, general psychological and physical discomfort, which had fairly clearly recorded quantitative boundaries on the GHQ and EQ-5D scales.

When it came to giving a verbal definition of the connection between health and the presence or absence of specific diseases, only a quarter of respondents indicated that they understood health merely as absence of disease (15 people out of the 63 who were able to give us a definition of their understanding of health in the course of their interview).

In defining what health is, 23 people said that it was, of course, the absence of disease (or 'pains'; that is, a person was healthy 'when he has nothing that hurts'); but not only that, they also focused on other aspects of the issue of health. A typical example is taken from the interview with a female respondent whom we observed for many years; over this time, she had experienced serious depression, which she had then successfully overcome.

> For me, health is made up of several aspects. It is the health of the physical body, the health of the mind and the health of the spirit. (Natal'ya, 39, an acupressurist from Moscow, interviewed as a medical worker, who joined our panel in 1996 aged 30 when she was unemployed; see also Chapter 11.)

Another 25 people, i.e. 40 per cent of the panel, did not generally mention physiological problems when defining health, concentrating solely on other aspects. Among these other aspects of health, the following were most often mentioned.

Vitality

A person is healthy if they have 'vitality', enabling them to maintain a certain way of life, and if they are 'interested in life': these signs of health were singled out by half of all those who attempted to express their understanding of health. On the other hand, a person is sick when they 'have already reached the stage of not needing anything' (Tat'yana, 40, Moscow, who had joined our panel in 1999 aged 35 when she was unemployed) or 'don't want anything' (Genady, aged 44 at interview, librarian from Voronezh).

> Being healthy is a comfortable state, while being sick is a state of discomfort. (Lev, 55, Moscow; see also Chapter 11.)

> Being healthy is being hale and hearty, not having any ailments; feeling the joy of life. Being sick is when you have no strength for anything. You have no interest in anything at all. (Ol'ga, 43, chemical production operative, Kazan'.)

> Health is most probably the very state where you aren't thinking about it and you don't notice it, when you can simply allow yourself to behave as you want. (Svetlana, 39, Voronezh, office worker in a university department.)

On the other hand, a person is sick when:

> You cannot work at full strength; that is, you're not working at the height of your powers. (Galina, 47, technician, Voronezh.)

> Being sick is when you're sluggish and not in the mood for anything. (Ludmila, 45, proprietor of a small food shop, Kazan'.)

> Giving up on life – that is, the person has already reached the stage where they don't need anything. (Lana, 44, accounts clerk from Voronezh.)

Being sick is most probably when you don't want anything – when indifference appears. (Sveta, 41, kindergarten music teacher, Voronezh.)

Stress

Twenty-four people out of 63 said that a person is healthy if they are not experiencing any stress.

The situation is such that the people's nerves are getting worn out, and your health depends totally on your nerves. Everything that's wrong with people starts from their nerves ... There isn't much money, not enough money; it's all nerves, entirely just nerves: not being able to pay for something, not being able to look in the fridge without worrying! ... People rush at one another like dogs – what's that all about?! All of it comes from that! And so everyone's sick. (Larisa, 40, saleswoman in a music shop, Voronezh.)

Our organism is constructed in such a way that it reacts to the complications, difficulties and nervous states that arise in one situation or another, and whichever organ is the weakest at that time starts to get sick. (Tat'yana, 40, Moscow, finance director and deputy director of a children's clinic.)

We don't get so sick from food – all illnesses come from the nerves. You can eat black bread with salt and be healthy; it's not that aspect. So, today there's no money for meat, but tomorrow there will be: these are the trivial things in life. (Vera, 51, housewife from Moscow; see also Chapter 11.)

In this regard, many people underlined the lack of opportunities to remove stress or to slacken the pace, which could be an important factor in loss of health.

We are living in times when you are more often faced with a stressful situation than with anything relaxing. We don't know how to slacken off. Just look at how we rest. Even when we get home from work, 'rest' for us is just lying on the sofa. Actually, of course, the best kind of relaxation is to go out, walk, talk with people close to you. And why are we like that? Because our heads are crammed with something else. I can't relax, I constantly have something in my head – either my problems that have built up, or work, or something else. For women it's generally very serious; but I won't begin to talk about men – that's an absolute catastrophe. And what is there that women can splash out on? Well, there's just retail therapy, if you've got the money [*laughs*]. Then you can allow yourself to enjoy that. And if not? For women, it's a double burden. And for men, on the whole. A woman can at least burst into tears, but men don't even have that. (Tat'yana, 40, Moscow, finance director and deputy director of a children's clinic.)

This highlighted the role of money, on which our respondents often focused, in creating positive emotions and relieving stress: overall, well-off people enjoyed better health. Our interviewees recognised that the advantages enjoyed by members of the better-off sections of society lay not only in their having enough money to gain access to medicines and doctors as such, but also in being able to afford a way of life that involved less risk of falling ill, because they had both greater security and more possibilities for relieving stress.

> When a person has got enough, he doesn't have to economise on anything. And it seems to me that such people are healthier than those who just have to keep toiling on all the time. Their mental health is better than ours, and they eat better, and they can go on holiday wherever they like, and they worry less than we do about the problems that tomorrow will bring. (Tanya, 44, a postal worker from Moscow.)

> Health ... depends, first and foremost, on material welfare. You can't afford to go to any kind of fitness classes, play sport, go on holiday, so there are constant stresses; that's where all these complications [diseases] come from. And it builds up ... (Lana, 44, accounts clerk, Voronezh.)

> If there's money, then the person is healthy: that is, if a person has enough money, then he can afford worthwhile rest and nutritious food. Yes, business may give him a headache, but he can calmly cut himself off from that and go away on holiday for a week; he can 'let off steam' somewhere else, if he has money ... That kind of person is not in a vicious circle, he always has some way out. (Tat'yana, 40, Moscow, joined panel in 1999 aged 35 when she was unemployed; now finance director and deputy director of a children's clinic and one of our more prosperous respondents.)

Attitude

Health is the reflection of a defined psychological mood. The importance of how a person perceives their health and what kind of 'attitude' they take towards it was indicated by 14 of the respondents we interviewed. At the same time, most of our interviewees revealed a predominantly stoic attitude in their general assessments of health, with the presence of certain age-related problems viewed as normal. Thus, diseases had to reach a particular 'critical mass', a point at which a person agreed to see themselves as sick; moreover, this 'breaking point' was a very individual thing, and sometimes lay far beyond the boundaries of medical diagnosis or common sense.

> I think that the less you go to the doctor, the better you feel. I remember when I fell ill and went to the doctor, she sent me somewhere else for tests, and then I felt worse still. And I decided that I simply wasn't going to think about it. (Marina, 44, manager, Voronezh.)

Those of our panel who described such a 'stoic' attitude were generally people who, because of particular features of their character and attitude to life, did not want to accept the sick role. On the other hand, willingness to accept the sick role, where there were defined, objective bases for doing so, became stronger when respondents began to feel that it was impossible for them to lead a normal life because of limitations connected with their health. For people who had previously, for all practical purposes, been in good health, the sudden and unexpected nature of this new state made them relatively more willing to accept the sick role than the gradual deterioration in health of those who had not been so healthy all their lives; the latter had been ready to accept from the outset that their health might place some limitations on the way of life they wanted and that this in itself did not mean they were metamorphosing into a sick person. A new state of health, promoting acceptance of the sick role, was normally revealed through respondents complaining that their usual activities were beginning to take them longer, that in their free time they usually 'just rested' (i.e. lay down and did nothing) and that they were suffering headaches and other signs of a general deterioration in health.

Moreover, the feeling of their growing personal incapacity in an aggressive external environment contributed to an increased sense of injustice about what was happening and of the impossibility of changing anything, as well as to a heightened focus on the family's material circumstances, which, in their turn, all generated stress that had a serious impact on health. People who were involved in white-collar work reacted especially painfully to such a weakening in their health: they had something to lose (their competitiveness on the labour market) and, as we shall see below, they were more likely to understand health as a state of general physiological, psychological and social well-being, not just as absence of serious diseases. As a result, they paid a great deal more attention to their own health, monitored it more actively with the help of diagnostic medicine, and gave more critical assessments of it, which also led to all the health indicators for people doing non-manual labour being worse than the indicators for less-educated respondents of the same age who were involved in manual labour.

Respondents in this situation usually first tried to make some alteration to it by going to doctors: they started actively visiting their local clinic. However, when it became clear that this was not bringing the expected effect, yet, for some reason or other, they could not or did not want to accept the sick role, they simply began to ignore any signs of not being well, instilling in themselves the idea that they were healthy. Frequently, for them, this was accompanied by 'modest preventive health measures': correcting their diet and taking herbal medicines or well-known 'mild' drugs (anti-fibrolytics, barbiturates, etc.) as a supporting measure.

Strange as it may seem, and despite the widely-known dangers of self-treatment and of ignoring illness, in Russia (with its distinct shortage of skilled doctors, poor-quality diagnostic medicine and frequently counterfeit drugs) this turned out to be a very effective strategy: in a number of cases, it led to improvements in health and, in even more cases, helped to stabilise it (see Chapter 9). In any event, it proved more effective for health than accepting the sick role, with its corresponding activities (running round from one doctor to another; using all prescribed medicines) and inevitable fall in living standards. (This, of course, does not relate to people who take on the sick role only formally, in order to obtain specific goods: disability pensions, concessionary benefits, etc.).

Well-being

Health is not simply absence of disease, but also overall social well-being, including first and foremost a feeling of being needed by society, as well as moral and material well-being. Thirteen people focused attention on this aspect of health.

> Being a healthy person – that's when you not only have nothing that hurts, but also when you are content with life, when you are needed ... When you have some kind of unpleasantness, that's when illnesses begin. Not being sick does not mean being healthy. For example, things can be bad for you emotionally and yet you are healthy; but, if things don't get better for you emotionally, then you will get sick. That is, if things are bad for you in your soul, then you are already sick. (Ekaterina, 63, pensioner from Kazan'.)

> Being healthy is having good genes, not abusing anything in life, knowing how to be moderate in everything, being cheerful, an optimist, a decisive person, loving life, doing good and not playing dirty tricks on people. Not humiliating yourself in front of others. Respecting yourself and others. Being sick – that's the reverse of the coin of human existence. In other words, what I've just said, but in reverse: playing dirty tricks on people, being a pessimist, i.e. destroying your personality. Physical health is connected with spiritual health. (Sergei, 35, museum administrator, Kazan'; see also Chapter 11.)

> Health is physical, mental, moral and social well-being. And ill-health is the opposite. Not being sick does not always mean that you are healthy, since a person can be healthy while, in their soul, storms may be raging – suffering and stress. (Rezeda, 35, female dentist, Kazan'.)

As we can see, the range of different understandings of health ran from absence of serious diseases to the potential to feel that one is a worthwhile member of society with an appropriate way of life. Correspondingly, the measures that people used in the battle for their own health ranged from 'running round from one doctor to another' and taking prescribed medicines to attempting to normalise their state of mind and, through that, their health.

If Natasha's travelling 300 kilometres from Moscow and then 5 kilometres through deep snow, with a complete change of circumstances, is viewed as stressful, then this example may be seen as an instance (exceptionally rare among our respondents) of the positive effect of stress. However, this is indeed the exception that proves the rule: practically all the stresses experienced by our respondents over the period of our observations were a kind of psychological trauma and, as a rule, had a negative effect on health, especially because of the way they built up and interacted. Positive changes in their lives were not usually associated with stresses.

A typical example of the latter was the life story of Natasha from Moscow, d.o.b. 1954, a member of our panel since 1996, who for a long time was the main breadwinner in a family that also included her son (d.o.b. 1978) and her husband, a driver. Only in the mid-2000s did her husband increase his earnings from work to the point where he became the family's main breadwinner.

A nurse by profession, until the early 1990s Natasha had worked first at the Vishnevsky Surgical Institute and then at the Centre for Psychological Health. With the start of the reforms came crisis in the public sector: as a result of this and because of her low pay, she left this job; she then worked for eight years at the First Aid post in a meat-processing plant.

Natasha recalled this period literally with horror.

> Now that some time has passed, I think: 'My God, did I really work there? How could I have worked there?' And then I started to get ill: very frequently, and constantly. I can't even give a definite reason why. I don't know how to explain it. I can only suggest that everything there was somehow negative ... And, whether from that negative – it's true that we didn't have any actual slaughtering section there, but all the same, all those dead bodies ... And, possibly – it's just my suggestion, maybe in reality it isn't the case – but, for some reason, a lot of people fell ill. I do have something wrong with my lungs: I had it already, but there it became infinitely worse. If you compare it – now, I feel a great deal better. Both physically and emotionally.

The respondent said that, throughout her eight years at this job, she 'felt ... very tired and just needed to rest; I was already ill; although, financially, it was easy there.'

When she left the meat plant, Natasha found work as a chambermaid in a small private hotel; however, she was soon released from there, and she became profoundly depressed. 'Apathy, wanting to do nothing ...' she said about this period.

> And you think 'What am I doing all this for?' And that's when you start digging around inside yourself; everything is so bad, black, everything is somehow gloomy. And then I got out of it – I just upped and went to our dacha in Vladimir Province. There, I had to get through 5 kilometres of deep snow, cross country, but I managed to get there anyway. And somehow people were welcoming to me there. And it's a feeling of nature, of beauty, and you think: Lord, well, why – there it is, it exists, you can live for that and be glad to be alive!

> I didn't take any kind of antidepressants, but I just had to do something – maybe just get out of this city which somehow presses in on us; we get some kind of negative experience from it. And there – the untouched field, the white snow,

the sparkling sun – and the people who live there – they simply live their lives in an ordinary way.

In this regard, it must be said that the respondent was someone with a broad understanding of health and an active concern about it. She displayed this concern in the widest sense, removing any stressful 'negatives' and making sure that she did pleasant, restful things that were also beneficial for her health: swimming, trips to the dacha and, whenever possible, to the seaside (the Crimea or Turkey). In trying to define health, she said that

> health is both your outer and your inner state – the state of your soul – being more optimistic, not giving into any kind of difficulties, trying to find some kind of compromises, you know ... Well, and also, probably, being needed by society too, however old you are – that also bears some relation to the kind of health you have.

Natasha, like many other respondents, also focused attention on the connection between health and material well-being (and her own experience confirmed this opinion):

> when, on the material level, a person can afford more – those positive emotions, when you can go somewhere, when you can see something, they also influence your health.

Moreover, again, like many other respondents, she was categorically opposed to adopting the sick role. 'Even the word "pain" – if something hurts, don't say it ... Simply don't articulate it. Just say: "Somehow I don't feel too great"', she said emphatically. Despite her serious bronchial asthma, it was natural for this respondent not to identify with sick people. Natasha said:

> Essentially I don't consider myself to be a sick person, although I know that I do have a number of diseases. Probably you just have to somehow internally position yourself, give yourself the attitude that you mustn't dwell on these diseases ... So I've given myself that attitude and that's the attitude I live with. You mustn't directly consider yourself a sick person ... you just have to live, and enjoy it.

By 2005, Natasha was working at the First Aid post at a swimming pool run by the TSKA, the Central Association of Sports Clubs; and, over our period of observation, we recorded a positive dynamic in both the respondent's health and her family's welfare.

RLMS survey

The information we obtained allowed us to devise a question about the interpretation of health, which was then included in the 2005 RLMS survey questionnaire. The available responses to this question covered the three most prevalent understandings of health mentioned by our panel in the course of the interviews (absence of serious diseases, presence of vitality, absence of stress) from which one main response had to be chosen. As we hypothesised, for the majority of the population (both here and below, the calculations refer to the population aged 18 and over) the understanding of health that was most typical was absence of disease (65 per cent); 23 per cent suggested that being healthy meant a feeling of vitality; 12 per cent suggested that being healthy primarily means not having any kind of stress. At the same time, the question touched respondents 'to the quick'; even in the pan-Russian quantitative survey, a lot of people (78 in all) added their own responses. Usually they wrote that all three markers were equally important: 'all three points are equally important – you can have chronic diseases and feel healthy; you can have no disease but be depressed', or they defined two out of the three responses as being equally significant. Also added were such variations on the definition of health as 'psychological well-being', 'being a worthwhile person in all respects', 'loving everything and everyone', 'looking after yourself, looking after your own well-being', 'being able to perform any job', 'not experiencing discomfort', 'not experiencing physical and mental problems', 'the absence of mental, social and physical disorders', and 'a state of complete physical, mental and social health'. However, on the whole, all these answers fitted into the classification constructed above on the basis of our panel respondent interviews.

For the majority of Russians, being sick meant 'having some kind of serious disease' (64 per cent); 27 per cent defined the state of 'being sick' as 'constantly feeling unwell'; another 9 per cent considered that 'being sick' means primarily 'being in a constant state of tension'. Here too, we found that people added notes when answering the question, relating to the much-vaunted 'psychological mood', of which many of our panel respondents had also spoken: 'you shouldn't think about it', 'you shouldn't think about the fact you're sick', 'you shouldn't think about diseases', 'you shouldn't mention it, you should say "I'm healthy!"'; and, in contrast, describing the state of 'being sick' as 'constantly thinking about one's own health', 'thinking that you are sick'.

However, people's understandings of the essence of health and sickness, although they were closely connected, did not strictly coincide (see Table 3.1).

Fifty-two per cent considered both that 'being healthy' meant 'not having serious diseases' and that 'being sick' meant having such diseases. Thus, the 'physiological' model of health and sickness, which does not presuppose the existence of an intermediate state between them, is still shared by half of Russians and is the dominant one in Russian culture. On the one hand, this is a general consequence of particular features of Russian culture: for centuries, feeling generally unwell was not regarded as a basis for failing to perform the work one

Table 3.1   Russians' understanding of health and sickness, RLMS, 2005 (%)

Understanding of health and sickness		Being sick means ...		
		... having serious diseases	... constantly feeling unwell	... being in a constant state of tension
Being healthy means ...	... not having serious diseases	81	42	22
	... vitality	13	**45**	33
	... not experiencing stress	6	13	**45**

was obliged to do. On the other hand, it also results from the practice of accepting as 'sick' only those people who have received a medical certificate as the basis for payment for a period of temporary incapacity for work solely because they have specific types of illnesses, which was also typical of Soviet social policy.

The specific nature of the type of locus of control that is characteristic of Russians and their perceptions of health as an instrumental and not an intrinsic value both also contribute to Russians' attitude to health as a particular sociocultural phenomenon.

Verification of locus of control is especially interesting in Russia, where huge social changes have taken place in the last two decades, beyond the control of individuals, leading many people to feel a complete loss of control over the course of their lives. At the same time, the logic of reforming health care, with its transition from the compulsory check-ups typical of the Soviet health care system to insurance-based medicine (where preventive investigation is not considered an insurable event) has presented people with the need to change quickly, taking on complete responsibility for their own health in conditions where they do not have sufficient money, time or skills to do so.

Our research recorded a distinct predominance among our respondents of the norm of an external locus of control with regard to their own health.[1] The average score for internal locus of control was 13.92 points, while the median was 13. For external locus of control, the corresponding indicators were 24.35 and 25 points respectively. Moreover, for half our panel respondents, external locus of control indicators exceeded internal ones by between 11 and 25 points. Since, with a predominantly external locus of control, people do not take responsibility for their own health, but, on the contrary, present themselves as some kind of victims of circumstances (to whom poor health gives the right to increased attention and assistance from those around them), it is not surprising that Russians love talking

---

1 It has already been noted that attempting to ascribe responsibility for one's own health mainly to external circumstances is a consistent characteristic of a mass consciousness (see Zhuravleva, 2005).

about their health and complaining about it: something that the respondents themselves also said.

> Maybe it's some kind of national mentality, but we don't consider it unseemly [to talk about health]; it's even one of the main topics: discussing your own problems, complaining to one another, sharing. (Svetlana, 39, Voronezh, office worker in a university department.)

> Conversations on public transport, in public places, these endless conversations about state of health, about what illness one person's got, about each other's illnesses. (Alyona, 39, accountant from Voronezh.)

At the same time, a person's understanding of health, identification of themselves with sick people, self-rated health status and even behaviour in regard to health were not in any way significantly linked with indicators of locus of control. This may possibly be explained by the presence of more significant causal factors; indeed, in conditions of economic and social reform (from the severe need to earn enough to feed oneself where social transfers are minimal, to the impossibility of obtaining skilled medical care where the health system is collapsing), life itself leads many Russians in practice to reconsider their attitude to health, which is characteristic of an external locus of control, even though some principles typical of it may be preserved at the level of norms. This hypothesis is favoured, for example, by the fact that agreement with the statement that one should do only what a doctor advises (typical of an external locus of control) was expressed by less than a third of respondents, reflecting a lack of trust in doctors that is characteristic of Russians nowadays.

Attitudes to health as an instrumental value (something that will be discussed again in subsequent chapters) were contradictory in nature. On the one hand, 69 per cent of respondents took the view that health is a major value in itself, and only 31 per cent that the support of good health is essential in order to work. On the other hand, in the open interviews, many respondents, especially men, said that they had to neglect their health for the sake of their work, and their life stories usually confirmed this. At the same time, there were also reverse instances, where respondents, typically women, constructed conscious, long-term strategies to change their job from one that presented a real threat to their health to one that created a state of physical, psychological and social comfort. In this regard, it should be noted that, in all age groups without exception, men had higher health indicators (measured on the EQ-5D scale and by presence of chronic diseases). Thus, for example, in the 51–60 age cohort, where there is a very high indicator of male mortality, men were exactly half the group of 'healthy' people, though their proportion in this age cohort was just 40 per cent. However, two-thirds of people in the 'unhealthy' and 'sick' groups of this age were women. A sense of paradox arose: men mostly live healthily, but they die early; women, on the other hand, experience all kinds of ailments, but live with them much longer.

In subsequent chapters, we shall analyse how gender roles typical of Russian national culture, including its understanding of masculinity, influence both the formation of this strange picture and the self-care behaviour of men and of women. In the meantime, here we have simply attempted to record this unusual feature and to emphasise that the possibility of admitting one's own weakness (including as a result of poor health), which in the context of Russian culture is available without serious loss of self-esteem and primary group status only to women, allows the latter to report any signs of not being well in themselves earlier than men (judging by the data we obtained, for the majority of Russians, such reporting 'triggers' care for one's own health) and therefore to construct a more appropriate strategy in the struggle to preserve their health. Men, on the other hand, prefer not to display 'signs of weakness' and to ignore signs of disease: as a result, these are exacerbated. It is thought that the main reason for the large-scale deterioration in men's health during the post-reform period in Russia and for their low life expectancy (much shorter than women's) lies precisely in this, rather than in the large-scale development of 'health-damaging habits' among men.

Thus, we see the dissemination of a broad understanding of health as not only physiological but also psychological and, in a number of cases, social well-being, alongside a nascent internal locus of control and, for some Russians, the transformation of health into an intrinsic value: all these provide evidence that a trend is arising towards the formation of a new understanding of health by Russians.

Of course, even for the people who demonstrate it, a new understanding of health is far from always, and certainly not immediately, reflected in behaviour. However, if no changes had taken place in the way the Russian population interprets health, then it would be senseless to expect changes in their self-care activities. For Russians' behaviour towards their own health to take a turn towards greater rationality and effectiveness, of course, the first, essential thing is a change in particular external conditions: overcoming the most profound social inequality and many types of discrimination on the labour market, raising living standards for the great mass of the population, developing a system of social guarantees, improving the work of the health care system, etc. However, all this will not lead to the expected result if there is no parallel consolidation in society of a new attitude that health is a most important component of quality of life, whose preservation requires efforts from the person concerned rather than being a part of his fate, prescribed from the outset.

In order for this new understanding to directly alter behavioural practices, time is required, with the accumulation of a particular 'critical mass' of people who are bearers of the new norms and values and whose behaviour is a reference point, if not for society as a whole, then at least, initially, for particular social strata. This is why we attempted to pinpoint the sites of a new attitude to health and of new behavioural practices towards health, as an independent objective of our research.

Specific Features of Social Groups Characterised by Different Understandings of Health

As has already been noted above, 52 per cent of Russians adhere to a purely physiological understanding of health or sickness. At the same time, about a quarter of Russians (23 per cent according to RLMS data) do not mention disease at all when determining the main marker of the states of 'being healthy' and 'being sick'. In what ways do these groups differ? What influences one or the other understanding of health and sickness? We shall try to answer these questions primarily by using the results of our decade's observation of a panel of households.

Judging by analysis of our panel respondents' situations, the primary influence on the understanding of health as absence of disease was the presence in their households of people with health-related limitations on their activities in life. In households where one member of the family had serious health-related limitations on their activities, it was three times more likely that health would be described via the presence of disease than in households where there were none. Obviously, against a background of the serious diseases of other family members, the respondent's own ailments seemed trivial, and the boundary between health and ill-health shifted sharply towards disease.

Overall, those people for whom health was primarily absence of disease were, as a rule, respondents from badly-off households, who had people with limitations on their usual activities among the family members living with them. These respondents' lives had not turned out very well: things were not going too well for them either in terms of family relationships or in that they had no favoured recreational activity. For them, leisure typically meant just passively resting at fixed times and spending their time off work at a dacha or in the country.

Those who understood ill-health primarily as lack of vitality were usually people who had reached a certain age (in our sample, the age of 50) and whose health really had markedly deteriorated. For them, a painful aspect of this experience was the fact that they were no longer in a position to maintain the way of life and carry the burdens that had previously been habitual and natural for them. In fact, they faced the necessity of taking up a way of life that was new to them. It was precisely this need to change their way of life that depressed them more than the illnesses they had, which they perceived as being natural at their age. However, those who had already passed through this stage and taken up a new way of life, usually as a result of retirement or claiming a disability pension, were more likely to perceive health in terms of somatic illnesses than as an issue of lack of vitality.

The biggest influence on the perception of health as absence of stress was being overburdened by extra employment: 14 out of the 24 respondents who highlighted the link between health and stress were working in an additional job, while 21 people said that the thing they did not like about their job was frequent overtime. The relationship between level of welfare and reference to stress in defining understanding of health was not recorded, although the main stressors may have been a drive to maintain a particular standard of living at any price (primarily through overwork) and an awareness of instability in their material circumstances. It also seemed natural that the majority of members of this group (19 people out of the 24) recorded that they themselves suffered from anxiety or depression, as measured on the EQ-5D scale.

It is also far from insignificant that understanding health via its connection with stress turned out to be closely related to defining health through vitality: almost two-thirds of respondents from this group associated absence of stress with the presence of vitality.

Finally, for those who talked about the importance of 'mood' in relation to their own health and emphasised the subjective aspect of health, the first point to note is that there was typically a positive dynamic in their life situation. At the time they first joined our panel, members of this group were distributed proportionally between the poor, badly-off and averagely well-off bands, and their GHQ health indicators were practically identical to other respondents'. However, by 2005 they were typically in relatively more favourable material circumstances and had also demonstrated health improvements as measured by GHQ indicators: in both areas, greater improvements than those whose description of the concept of health did not touch on the importance for their own behaviour of a particular psychological 'mood'. At the same time, members of this group were not distinctly different from the rest of the groups in other ways: this confirmed the conclusion that their refusal to accept the sick role and their understanding of the importance of an appropriate mood in regard to their own health together represented, in particular conditions, a very effective behavioural strategy for Russia.

As we can see, there were fairly distinct particular features in the social portrait of groups differentiated by their understanding of health, and these were primarily particular features of their individual situation in life, their personality and their state of health.

However, the limited nature of the sample in our panel research prevents us from seeing how far a given understanding of health is typical of members of different social strata and groups, and whether it is conditioned only by the situation in households and the respondent's personal experience, or whether there are external, structural factors that allow us to pinpoint the site of different types of understanding of health by Russians. In tackling this question, we made use of RLMS data.

The first thing that the data from this survey confirmed was the very close relationship between serious limitations on their usual activities for the respondents themselves or members of their household as a result of disease and an understanding of health as an absence of disease. Thus, if the respondents had no problems in walking about, personal care or performing their usual activities, then, when defining the state of 'being healthy', they were more likely to focus on the presence of vitality and the absence of stress. Those who had serious problems walking about or could not care for themselves or perform their usual activities were more likely to talk about absence of serious diseases as the main marker of health.

Table 3.2   Russians' understanding of health, various groups of respondents, RLMS, 2005 (%)

EQ-5D indicators		Being healthy means …		
		… not having serious diseases	… vitality	… not experiencing stress
Pain	None	43	41	30
	Moderate	47	52	59
	Extreme	10	7	11
Anxiety or depression	None	52	45	34
	Moderate	45	52	60
	Extreme	3	3	6
Integral indicator	Healthy	56	54	41
	Unhealthy	23	28	34
	Sick	21	18	25
Assessment of own health	People who consider their health good	36	34	24
	People who consider their health fair	49	55	64
	People who consider their health poor	15	11	12

However, it was the connection between understanding of health and the presence of pain and depression/anxiety that was most distinct (see Tables 3.2 and 3.3). Those who interpreted health primarily as absence of stress or presence of vitality were more likely to be in the borderline state where, although a person cannot yet be described as 'being sick', they can no longer be viewed as 'being healthy'. Moreover, the healthy were more likely to understand health only as absence of disease, and this is easy to comprehend: this understanding of health was, we might say, 'fed to them with their mother's milk'; it was typical of Russian culture as a whole, and nothing in their own experience led them to look more broadly at the issue.

On the other hand, different understandings of health affect people's assessments of their own health. Thus, those who thought that health was the absence of serious diseases were relatively more likely to rate their own health as 'good' or 'very good' by comparison with people for whom health was absence of stress, 'a life without nerves' (see Table 3.2). Moreover, this was typical of all age groups. All the evidence suggests that being free of stress and 'nerves' is a more serious demand to make of one's health and that, where people use this definition of health, fewer of them are able to rate their own health as 'good', so people who are inclined to interpret health not only as physical health are distinguished by their lower

Table 3.3 **Russians' understanding of sickness, various groups of respondents, RLMS, 2005 (%)**

EQ-5D indicators		Being sick means ...		
		... having serious diseases	... constantly feeling unwell	... being in a constant state of tension
Pain	None	44	36	37
	Moderate	47	54	54
	Extreme	·9	10	9
Anxiety or depression	None	52	42	40
	Moderate	45	55	53
	Extreme	3	3	7
Integral indicator	Healthy	57	49	49
	Unhealthy	23	29	29
	Sick	20	22	21
Assessment of own health	People who consider their health good	36	30	32
	People who consider their health fair	50	56	58
	People who consider their health poor	14	14	10

assessments of their own health. Thus, understanding of health partially influences people's assessments of their own health, setting criteria for defining the states of 'being sick' and 'being healthy'.

However, Table 3.2 shows that among healthy people there is also a certain proportion that perceives the category 'health' fairly broadly. What distinguishes this group, and can it be viewed as the site of a new attitude to health?

In answering this question, it is first worth noting that these differences are unconnected with age: there are no significant differences in understandings of health and sickness between different age groups, and the proportions of those who understand the states of 'being healthy' and 'being sick' via the presence of disease were practically the same in the different age groups. This means that no 'age-related', natural shift in ideas about what 'being healthy' or 'being sick' means has taken place in Russia as yet.

Of course, there are nevertheless some differences in understandings of health between people of different ages: thus, in the group who gave high ratings of their own health, middle-aged and elderly people were more likely to focus attention on the presence of vitality as a factor in health than were young people; while young people, in their turn, were more likely to note the importance of absence of stress. In the group who gave low ratings of their own health, Russians aged over 60 were

Table 3.4   Understanding of health and sickness, groups with different standards of education, RLMS, 2005 (%)

Education	Being healthy means ...		
	... not having serious diseases	... vitality	... not experiencing stress
Primary	77	15	8
Basic secondary	70	18	12
Full secondary	64	22	13
Higher education	59	31	10
Education	Being sick means ...		
	... having serious diseases	... constantly feeling unwell	... being in a constant state of tension
Primary	69	26	5
Basic secondary	63	29	8
Full secondary	65	25	10
Higher education	61	31	8

more likely to talk about health as an absence of serious diseases, while young people were more inclined to mention vitality and absence of stress. That is, for each age group, it was the aspect of health that was most current for them in their individual life situation that came top of their list.

Education was a noticeably greater influence on understanding of health than was age. As their standard of education became higher, people were less likely to talk about the absence of serious diseases as the main criterion for state of health, and more likely to focus attention on the presence of vitality (as 'being healthy') or constantly feeling unwell (when describing the state of 'being sick') (see Table 3.4).

However, one section of respondents demonstrated a consistent 'physiological' approach to both health and sickness; another, equally consistently, perceived both of them more broadly; while a third section demonstrated different intermediate combinations, giving evidence of a gradual transition from the traditional understanding of health and sickness to a new understanding of them. Therefore, it was interesting to correlate respondents in these groups to various standards of education (see Figure 3.1).

As we can see, when we delineate groups of people who took different approaches, the trend in the connection between understanding of health and standard of education becomes even more evident: the site of new views of health is the group of Russians with higher education.

These results correspond fully with conclusions obtained by other authors: as Blaxter (1990) writes,[2] research has revealed that a 'positive' definition of health

---

2 Blaxter, M. (1990) *Health and Lifestyles.*

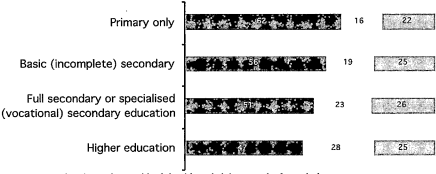

■ People who understand both health and sickness only through the
presence or absence of disease
  People with a broad understanding of both health and sickness (through
stress or vitality)
□ All others

Figure 3.1   Proportions of people with different understandings of health and sickness, groups with different standards of education, RLMS, 2005 (%)

(of which an interpretation of health as the presence of vitality is an integral part) is characteristic, in the first instance, of more educated sections of the population and, overall, of more prosperous groups in society, since it is closely linked to class membership.

In order to verify whether this last assertion applied to Russian conditions, it would have been necessary to delineate social classes within the RLMS dataset and to base this delineation primarily on socio-occupational status, standard of education, material circumstances, etc. However, as will be shown in the next chapter, in contemporary Russian society, with its most profound sectoral and regional inequalities, the traditional approach to socio-occupational classification is not very effective; furthermore, it did not demonstrate a significant relationship with the understanding of health. In all ISCO 88-defined occupational groups, interpretations of health were fairly close: however, professionals were least likely to adhere to the physiological approach (58 per cent as against 31 per cent who understood health as the presence of vitality), while industrial blue-collar workers were most likely to do so (66 per cent as against 22 per cent who understood health as the presence of vitality); service workers and shop and market sales workers were relatively more likely to mention absence of stress as a marker of health (15 per cent, as against 9 per cent of legislators, senior officials and managers, which was the lowest indicator).

The dispersion of opinions on the understanding of health across groups of people who placed themselves on various rungs of the 'indigence to wealth ladder' was also roughly in the same range (see Table 3.5).

As we can see, despite a marked dominance of the traditional norms of Russian national culture in all groups defined according to their assessments of their own material circumstances, the most prosperous sections of the population are still slightly more likely than other people to focus attention on the issue of vitality in describing health. And, in contrast, stress, as an aspect of health, is more of a worry to the least prosperous sections of the population than to other people.

Table 3.5   Understanding of health and sickness, according to self-rated position on a scale from 'indigence' to 'wealth', RLMS, 2005 (%)

	Being healthy means ...		
	... not having serious diseases	... vitality	... not experiencing stress
The two lowest 'rungs'	67	**19**	14
Rungs 3–4	66	23	11
Rungs 5–6	61	26	13
The three highest 'rungs'	64	**27**	9
	Being sick means ...		
	... having serious diseases	... constantly feeling unwell	... being in a constant state of tension
The two lowest 'rungs'	64	27	9
Rungs 3–4	64	27	9
Rungs 5–6	63	27	10
The three highest 'rungs'	70	22	8

These data tell us not only that inequality in living standards helps to define inequality in chances, including health inequality, but also that the erosion of a traditional understanding of health will take place in different ways within different sections of the population. While the most prosperous, educated Russians focus increasing attention on vitality as an aspect of health, the least prosperous sections of the population express their departure from the traditional model of the understanding of health through placing greater emphasis on stress, to which they themselves are strongly susceptible.

Since we were interested in the sociocultural aspect of the consolidation of a new understanding of health, we also deliberately delineated, within the RLMS sample, social groups that differ according to their type of culture: urban dwellers with higher education and, as the polar opposite group, people with a standard of education below secondary level, who live in villages and urban-type settlements. In the group of urban dwellers with higher education, 47 per cent interpreted both the state of 'being healthy' and the state of 'being sick' via disease, as against 55 per cent of residents of urban-type settlements and villages with a low standard of education. Definitions of health in these two groups were distributed as follows: 59 per cent of the first group and 71 per cent of the second named absence of serious diseases as the chief marker; 32 per cent and 17 per cent respectively, vitality; and 9 per cent and 12 per cent respectively, absence of stress or 'nerves'. Differences between their understandings of sickness were smaller, and this, alongside the data given above about the understanding of health and sickness in groups with various levels of material welfare, enables us to say that the erosion of traditional views of health and sickness is taking place because the most prosperous (in all regards) groups in society are quicker to recognise that health and sickness must be characterised using a three-level scale, where there is an intermediate level of 'ill-health'; while, for the undoubted majority of people in the lowest social strata, a dual scale of health/sickness still operates as before.

This trend towards consolidation of a new understanding of health using a three-level scale, where a huge role in assessing health is played not by the presence or absence of disease but by health as general physical and psychological well-being, was demonstrated still more obviously by one group of Russians: people with higher education who had been urban dwellers from birth. Within the sample, this group was fairly small in number,[3] but its understanding of health and sickness was highly exemplary. Only 40 per cent of people in this group understood both 'health' and 'sickness' via the absence or presence of disease. Practically equal numbers of respondents in this group described the state of 'being healthy' through serious diseases and through the presence of vitality (47 per cent and 45 per cent respectively). However, at the same time, the understanding of sickness in this group differed little from the one accepted throughout Russia as a whole: 63 per cent defined it in terms of the presence of serious diseases and 34 per cent in terms of constantly feeling unwell.

As we can see, factors of national culture remain very strong; however, we can talk about a trend towards the siting of a new understanding of health in a group of people who have been urban dwellers from birth and have higher education, of whom practically half already talk about vitality as being the main marker of health. Moreover, it is primarily the traditional understanding of health that is being eroded, not that of sickness: a fact that is connected with the consolidation of a new three-level scale of health instead of the old two-level one.

---

3 Numbers of townspeople and of people living in rural areas of Russia became roughly equal only about 50 years ago, and it is still the case that the majority of urban dwellers are first-generation migrants from villages and urban-type settlements, with the peasant-type culture and way of life characteristic of such areas.

Conclusion

For the majority of Russians, health and sickness are understood 'negatively' and, up to now, in terms of disease. This understanding is a cultural phenomenon, which arose in the pre-Soviet period and was officially strengthened by Soviet social policy. However, this understanding of health is gradually changing, and increasing attention is starting to be focused on other aspects of health: the presence of vitality and the absence of stress, and the requirement to feel that one is integrated into and needed by society.

Analysis of the understanding of health using pan-Russian data confirmed the connection, which we had established when analysing the results of our panel observations, between understanding of health and particular features of respondents' individual life situations: 'life situations' primarily meant their own real state of health, although it was also the case that people who were relatively less prosperous were more likely to lean towards a traditional understanding of health. Moreover, this analysis allowed us to record a connection between the consolidation of a new understanding of health and the norms of urban culture and standard of education, as well as to understand the mechanism involved in this, which related to the delineation of an intermediate link between health and sickness: one for which the Russian language does not yet even have an adequate term, so new is this formulation of the issue. Although the concept of 'ill-health' comes closest of all to it in meaning (defining a state of illness in which there are still no expressed signs of a specific disease, but where the beginnings of this are apparent and accompanied by impairment of one's usual capabilities), the phenomenon is not completely adequately described by this term, which is also why our respondents almost never used it.

The thresholds between these three states of health can be fixed with a fairly high degree of probability, using relevant methodologies as well as respondents' own integral assessments of their health. However, in interpreting any results obtained, it is essential to take into account the influence, present in both approaches, of national cultures (including the different understandings in various cultures of particular features of gender roles) and the influence of subcultures (particular features of urban and rural cultures, or the specific cultures of social strata with differing standards of education, etc.). With relevant coefficients, which could be obtained by empirical means in the course of sociological research, it becomes possible to make fairly accurate assessments of the population's general state of health and of the structure of groups with various standards of health. However, as applied to a specific individual, such an assessment will always be highly notional in character.

The use of qualitative methods alongside quantitative ones also allowed us to establish the increased probability of a broader understanding of the essence of the phenomenon of health than as purely physiological; this probability arises when the respondent's habitual way of life is under threat from a fall in their 'vitality', even apparently unaccompanied by any specific ailment, that makes it impossible to maintain their way of life. Moreover, respondents repeatedly emphasised that loss of vitality is an outcome of stress, and that concrete diseases arise as a further consequence of stress. The results of our observations confirm the special part played by stress, on which specialists working in the area of health issues (WHO, 2001), especially the connection between health and inequalities, have increasingly been focusing attention. For Russian conditions, stresses have practically always played a negative role, although individual exceptions have been encountered in which stresses have 'triggered' an improvement in health.

Among the reasons for stresses with such negative consequences arising in Russian conditions, those connected with macro factors played the decisive role. However, there were also special life situations that were equally significant: the death of a close person, especially the family breadwinner; the development of alcoholism or drug addiction in a member of the household; etc. Over the period of observation, we recorded some cases in our panel of literally catastrophic deterioration in health resulting from precisely such reasons.

Our respondents also paid a great deal of attention to the need for positive emotions in order to overcome stress and maintain vitality and, in the final analysis, also for health itself. Most of them considered this to be the most important component of self-care behaviour, and, where it was impossible to obtain positive emotions in order to remove stress, they tried to use direct auto-suggestion, or 'mood', instead. And, as our many years of observation of panel households demonstrated, they were right to do so. At the same time, social support, even purely psychological, also played a huge part. Moreover, real social capital turned out to be significant, whether using Coleman's (2000) interpretation of social capital as the resource of the social networks in which the individual is included, or Putnam's (2001) interpretation of it as a level of trust, if not in the macro community, then at least in the microenvironment in which the individual lives.

It must be said that sometimes the impression was even formed that positive emotions affect the biochemistry of the organism and cause the development of some kind of enzyme or hormone that is absolutely essential to the person's organism, the absence of which can in itself even lead to disease developing. Or that stress – the most important causes of which, in a Russian society that has experienced 'cultural trauma' (Shtompka) over recent years, are that a vast number of people feel they are cast in the new role of social outsiders, that there is rising anomie, an increasingly very aggressive external environment, a sense of helplessness and lack of rights, insecurity and hopelessness – leads to the development of some other enzyme or hormone, which in itself has a depressing effect on health, regardless of any others.

Moreover, in conditions where the impact of these factors is intense, all others (particular features of way of life, the presence of specific chronic diseases, harmful working conditions, etc.) play an incomparably smaller part than in more usual, stable conditions. People sense this, and in such an unfavourable environment, they try to save their health through the mechanisms that form positive emotions or neutralise negative ones. The presence of the means to do so free of charge helps in no small degree, while their absence hinders it. And the role of money in forming positive emotions or neutralising negative ones is at least as important as the opportunity it affords to pay for doctors' services, medicines or good-quality food.

Possibly also connected with this is the relatively worse health of people in societies with a high level of social inequalities and a low level of trust, since both of these (through the sense of one's own unfavourable position in the social formation, through unstable circumstances and, in the final analysis, through a reduced sense of security) provoke a large-scale deterioration in health, even regardless of a person's own way of life (although the part played by the latter, especially in stable conditions, is undoubtedly difficult to deny).

Overall then, the material that we obtained in the course of our research enables us to say that, both objectively and subjectively, health for Russians is not only a most important resource, with a special, growing role in conditions where abrupt structural change in Russian society is accompanied by exhaustion of other resources, but also a most important component of a worthwhile life. When it deteriorates, not only do a person's opportunities to achieve basic rights narrow sharply, even to the point of profound exclusion, but negative psychological states (a sense of helplessness, hopelessness, etc.) also develop: these sharply reduce quality of life and, in turn, lead to further deterioration in health.

Thus, each of the main sociological approaches to analysis of the phenomenon of health (behavioural and cultural explanations, the psychosocial model, the materialist model and the life-course model; Bartley, 2004) are each in their own way correct and are confirmed empirically. However, none of them alone is sufficient to describe the processes that take place in the area of health. Rather, here we can say that there is a complex chain of interactions, a complete chain of factors that define objective health and its subjective understanding, and that these include both social and biological factors. The real extent to which they are detrimental to health is always situational in nature and is defined by a number of circumstances. Depending on whether we are talking about the health of people in stable or transforming societies or about members of certain social strata and cultures, and whatever their family circumstances, the set of factors that influence health will differ, as will the comparative role of those factors, of people's understanding of the phenomenon of health, and of their practical behaviour in relation to it.

PART II
Health and Social Structure

Chapter 4
Inequalities and Health

Nataliya Tikhonova

Кому пироги да пышки, а нам желваки да шишки
Some get cakes and buns, but we get lumps and bumps

Income Inequalities

The connections between health and status have already been verified and long taken for granted: in particular, there is no small quantity of accumulated data illustrating the thesis that the less socioeconomic inequality a society contains, the healthier it will be (see, for example: Shi and Starfield, 2000, pp. 541–55; Wilkinson, 2000; Mellor and Milyo, 2002, pp. 510–39; Marmot, 2004), although discussion of the mechanism through which income inequality and health interact is ongoing. Some (Brunner and Marmot, 1999; Wilkinson and Pickett, 2004) suggest that this mechanism has its roots in the characteristics of individuals' social status and the class they belong to (the specific nature of the way of life and behaviour of a given class; chronic stress associated with a sense of being socially humiliated; loss of control over one's own life; the low level of trust felt by those lower down the class structure, etc.). Others consider the main influence to come from the direct impact of income inequality and low living standards on health, while others again do not perceive any consistent association between health and income inequality (Deaton, 2003; Lynch et al., 2004).

For Russia, the set of issues surrounding the link between population health and income inequality is especially pertinent, since income inequality in Russia has increased sharply over the last 20 years, while there has been a simultaneous sharp deterioration in the health of the population. What has been behind this: an upsurge in feelings of humiliation, a growing loss of control over one's own life, a fall in the level of trust in society – all affecting members of different classes to differing extents? Or has the real reason for the deterioration in Russians' health been first and foremost the acute impoverishment of the population, making it impossible for many people to ensure they have enough to eat and can buy essential medicines?

Many chapters of this book are devoted to seeking answers to these questions. In this chapter, the focus will be in the first instance on a general picture of social inequalities in contemporary Russia and how they are perceived by the population, alongside some particular features of life in various social strata. As both statistical and sociological data show, income inequalities in Russia are very profound. Thus, judging by the Rosstat data, in April 2006 the average wage in the top decile was more than 25 times that in the bottom decile (see Table 4.1).

Table 4.1   Distribution wages by decile groups, in April 2006

	Total amount of accrued wages, %	Average wage, in roubles
Total	100	9847
decile groups		
First	1.4	1366
Second	2.7	2631
Third	3.8	3771
Fourth	5.0	4931
Fifth	6.3	6209
Sixth	7.8	7654
Seventh	9.6	9435
Eighth	12.1	11920
Ninth	16.2	15971
Tenth	35.1	34582

Note: All amounts recorded as paid to workers, both in monetary and non-monetary forms, are included.

Source: Federal State Statistics Service (Rosstat).

The secondary distribution somewhat reduced this inequality, though not by much. Moreover, strong regional differences in the depth of social inequalities can be observed. These were also apparent in the regions where respondents from our longitudinal panel lived: the depth of inequalities in Moscow was incommensurably higher than in Voronezh (the chief city of Voronezh Province) and Kazan' (the capital of Tatarstan) (see Table 4.2). Overall, in 2005, the Gini coefficient in more than 80 regions of Russia ranged from 0.311 to 0.567.

As we can see, over the 15 years since the beginning of the reforms in Russia, polarisation of the incomes of the highest and lowest quintile groups has markedly intensified. A deterioration in circumstances has been typical, although varying in degree, of the three lowest quintile groups; the fourth quintile group has remained in practically the same situation as before; and the fifth quintile group has seen a sharp improvement. However, a part of this picture is that within the highest quintile there has typically been more differentiation than across the other four quintiles taken together: a sharp increase in level of income between 1990 and 2005 has been primarily typical of the top 5 per cent of the population, and not of the whole quintile. In addition, it was only in 2006 that Russia returned to pre-reform (1990) levels of GDP and level of average per capita incomes. This means that the drop in average per capita incomes in the lowest quintiles between 1990 and 2005 was not only relative, but also – and more – absolute in nature. In these conditions, it is not surprising that the poverty rate in Russia remains high.

In 2005 a new method of calculating the subsistence minimum was introduced, with its size now determined by the regions themselves. The regions define the subsistence minimum that is used for calculating allowances, subsidies and

Table 4.2   Distribution of total income across quintile groups, selected areas, 2005

	Proportion of monetary income of relevant population group, in percentages					Gini co-efficient	Decile co-efficient of income differentiation, times
	First (with smallest incomes)	Second	Third	Fourth	Fifth (with largest incomes)		
Russian Federation, 1990*	9.8	14.9	18.8	23.8	32.7	–	–
Russian Federation, 2005	5.5	10.2	15.2	22.7	46.4	0.405	14.8
City of Moscow	2.9	5.6	10.2	20.6	60.7	0.567	38.6
Voronezh Province	5.8	10.6	15.5	22.8	45.3	0.391	13.4
Republic of Tatarstan	5.8	10.6	15.5	22.8	45.3	0.391	13.3
Ivanovo Province (which has lowest indicators of inequality)	7.9	12.7	17.2	23.1	39.1	0.311	7.6

* Statistical Year Book of Russia (2006). In 1990, Rosstat did not calculate capital or Gini coefficients.

Source: The social status and living standards of the population of Russia (2006), p. 155.

concessions to poor households, taking as their starting-point the regional value of a Federally-established basket of goods; the region must then take this value as 60–66 per cent of the subsistence minimum (the exact figure is at its discretion). The nature of this basket of goods can be judged by the fact that, for example, under Ordinance of the Government of the Russian Federation of 12.08.2005, No. 511, defining the minimum set of food products for the main population groups, the calorific value of a minimum basket of foodstuffs is basically made up of carbohydrates – bread, processed grains and cereals, pasta products and potatoes – to a total dry weight of 281.7 kg per year for men and 200.4 kg for women. Ten per cent of the value of all non-foodstuffs (i.e. 3.4–4 per cent of the subsistence minimum) is allocated to basic necessities, including washing powder, shampoo, etc. – and medicines. In reality, this means that poor people in poor health have to go without food in order to buy medicine, something which members of our panel mentioned more than once.

This new method means in effect that there are no national level statistical data on total numbers living below the poverty line. According to regional statistics the

Table 4.3   Per cent below the subsistence minimum, selected areas, 2000–2005

	2000	2001	2002	2003	2004	2005
Russian Federation	29.0	27.5	24.6	20.3	17.6	–
City of Moscow	23.6	21.8	20.7	18.6	14.6	13.2
Voronezh Province	41.9	36.6	33.8	28.8	25.1	24.1
Republic of Tatarstan	33.2	27.3	23.6	19.2	15.8	13.5
City of St Petersburg (lowest proportion of population with incomes below subsistence minimum)	27.3	23.8	21.2	15.6	12.7	10.1
Republic of Ingushetiya (highest proportion of population with incomes below subsistence minimum)	94.3	88.0	87.4	81.4	73.3	61.3

Note: In the calculations for 2000–2001, retrospective assessments of the size of the subsistence minimum are used, based on the basket of consumer goods established in constituent areas of the Russian Federation, or on projections of this basket to the end of 2002.

Source: The social status and living standards of the population of Russia (2006), p. 161.

proportion of poor people in various regions ranges from 10.1 per cent to 61.3 per cent. Moreover, in the regions where the respondents from our longitudinal panel lived, it is high, especially in Voronezh (see Table 4.3).

Given the severity of the poverty issue for Russia, we shall attempt to evaluate the scale of the problem across the country using other methods. Application of the criterion of $2US a day (using purchasing power parity), which is accepted by the World Bank as a measure of absolute poverty, also provides evidence that absolute poverty in its most extreme forms is widespread across Russia (taking into account climatic conditions). In 2005, the proportion of the population living on less than $2 a day was 12.1 per cent, which exceeded the analogous indicator in Albania (11.8 per cent) and was close to that of Romania (12.9 per cent) (Russia and countries of the world, 2006, p. 107).

Overall, looking at income levels, the average per capita monetary income in the Russian Federation in 2005 was 8,023.20 roubles a month (about £160) (Statistical Year Book of Russia, 2006, p. 188). Moreover, if we define 'poor' on the basis of the relative approach, taking the poverty line to be 50 per cent of median incomes for the whole country, then in 2005 – according to the statistics – about 30 per cent of the population had incomes below 50 per cent of the median (see Table 4.4). Furthermore, 7.1 per cent of Russians had per capita incomes below 25 per cent of median incomes for the country: this represented about a quarter of all those people defined as poor on the basis of the relative approach.

Table 4.4   Distribution of per capita incomes, 2000–2005 (%)

Population distribution according to size of average per capita incomes, 2000–2005, in %	2000	2001	2002	2003	2004	2005
Whole population, including those with average per capita monetary incomes, in roubles per month, of:	100	100	100	100	100	100
Up to 1,000	20.4	12.5	6.8	3.3	1.9	0.8
1,000.00 – 1,500.00	19.9	15.0	10.6	6.5	4.3	2.4
1,500.10 – 2,000.00	16.4	14.4	11.8	8.5	6.1	3.9
2,000.10 – 3,000.00	20.7	21.7	21.0	17.7	14.3	10.6
3,000.10 – 4,000.00	10.4	13.4	15.2	15.1	13.7	11.7
4,000.10 – 5,000.00	5.3	8.2	10.4	11.7	11.7	11.0
5,000.10 – 7,000.00	4.4	8.2	11.9	15.4	17.0	17.8
7,000.10 – 12,000.00*	2.5	6.6	12.3	15.2	19.6	24.1
Over 12,000.00	–	–	–	6.6	11.4	17.7

* For the period 2000–2002, over 7,000.00 roubles.

Note: In commenting on this table, we should point out that the data in it have not been corrected for the purchasing power of the rouble in different years. Taking into account the inflation rate, the 2,000 rouble corresponded to roughly 50 kopecks in 2005.

Source: The social status and living standards of the population of Russia (2006), p. 138.

However, the question of whether it is correct to define the poor only on the basis of their incomes is a very problematic one, even for countries where economic development is stable. Applied to Russia, where the most profound income inequality has arisen over literally just a few years, it raises serious doubts. The picture has been made more complex by greater inequality of expenditures, depending on the composition of households and their members' standards of health – inequalities that have become deeper because of the severe crisis in all branches of the social sphere during the implementation of reforms. Finally, in this regard, we cannot fail to mention the unequal distribution of so-called 'shadow' incomes and of widespread interfamily transfers, both in money and in kind, which also make a significant contribution to de facto inequality, even where officially there is formal equality of incomes.

So, we cannot give a full picture of social inequalities in contemporary Russia unless we also describe inequalities in level of welfare and in the nature of current consumption, which create real inequalities between households in terms of living standards and quality of life. The fullest picture of these types of inequalities (and also, we should add, of the prevalence of the main forms of deprivation) is provided not by the State's statistical data, but by materials from sociological research.

This approach to describing the situation with inequalities and poverty is also particularly significant because, judging by our research data, people who

Table 4.5   Respondents' own assessments of aspects of their lives, 2006 (%)

Aspects of life	Good	Satisfactory	Poor	Don't know
Material well-being	8	59	33	0
Food	25	65	10	0
Clothing	16	66	18	0
Housing conditions	27	57	16	0
Opportunities for leisure pursuits	14	52	33	1
Opportunities to get away on holiday	12	41	37	10
Opportunities to obtain the education and knowledge they need	15	55	21	9
Position or status in society	16	66	16	2

Source: Tikhonova (2007).

themselves are in the most deprived sections of the Russian population define poverty first and foremost using signs of deprivation, and not simply as insufficient income for current needs (Manning and Tikhonova, 2004). Without dwelling in detail on this question, we shall simply note the findings from a survey conducted by the Institute for Multidisciplinary Social Studies of the Russian Academy of Sciences in March 2003 with a sample of 2,106 people representative of the population of Russia by sex, age, region lived in, and type of settlement (for more details, see Gorshkov and Tikhonova, 2004). Respondents highlighted the main signs of deprivation as relating to quality of food (85 per cent), not being able to obtain clothes and shoes (55 per cent), quality of housing (54 per cent), standard of medical service (52 per cent), not being able to obtain a good education (40 per cent), impossibility of satisfying primary needs without getting into debt (38 per cent), lack of access to leisure and holidays, because these involved extra expenditure (33 per cent), and lack of opportunity for children from poor families to attain the same in life as the majority of their peers (25 per cent). Moreover, the poor themselves, defined according to the relationship of their average per capita incomes to median incomes, gave the same answers.

Thus, among the most important consequences of income inequality, Russians single out both those that directly affect health (quality of food, quality of medical care, opportunities for leisure when on leave from work or on holiday) and the way that the limitation of life chances acts as a strong stress-inducing factor for Russians, the overwhelming majority of whom were socialised in an egalitarian society. What is the picture presented by these inequalities in life chances, whether in the area of consumption or in the life of Russians overall?

Table 4.6   Ownership of consumer durables, 2006 (%) (percentage that has none of a given consumer durable)

Consumer items	Less than a year old	From 1 to 7 years old	Over 7 years old	None
Refrigerator	4	38	55	2
Colour television	5	57	34	4
Carpet or other floor covering	2	24	67	7
Vacuum cleaner	6	38	40	15
Suite of furniture (including fitted kitchen, wall units, sitting-room suite, cupboard units, etc.)	4	26	54	16
Washing machine	6	40	37	17
Mobile phone	14	43	–	43
Video player/recorder	3	30	17	50
Microwave oven, food processor, electric grill or other domestic appliances	7	33	9	52
Electric drill, electric or petrol-driven saw, other tools	3	19	23	54
Music centre	3	25	7	65
Computer	6	21	3	71
Russian-made car	1	11	15	73
Black-and-white television	1	3	16	80
Video camera, digital camera	3	8	1	87
Motorbike or motor scooter	1	3	7	89
Freezer	1	5	4	90
Foreign-made car	1	4	2	93
Home cinema	3	2	0	95
Satellite television	1	2	0	97
Air-conditioner	0	1	0	98
Dishwasher	0	1	0	99

Note: In this table, items highlighted in bold are those most likely to have been acquired in recent years; those in italics are the ones which relate to the standard of consumption that is the social norm for Russians: absence of the latter is perceived as a distinct manifestation of deprivation. In this regard, it should be noted that, in Spring 2006, only 65 per cent of Russians actually owned all the items in this sub-group.

Source: Tikhonova (2007).

Inequalities in Living Standards and Quality of Life

Difficulties with food, clothing, acceptable housing, accessibility of essential treatment (primarily medicines) and with paying for the simplest forms of leisure etc., are typical of large-scale and widespread deprivations in Russia (see Table 4.5).

The total numbers of people who assess their opportunities to satisfy three basic requirements (food, clothing and housing) as 'poor' show that 30 per cent of Russians cannot satisfy at least one of these on an acceptable level and that 11 per cent cannot satisfy two of them, or all three. Moreover, only 29 per cent of the latter group are people who could be evaluated as 'poor' in relation to median incomes for the place they live in. (Incidentally, the number of people in Russia who assessed their own opportunities to satisfy these three basic requirements as 'good' was exactly 10 per cent of respondents – in other words, they actually equated to the top decile as defined using the deprivation approach.)

In this regard it should be noted that, in the course of our research, we made a special analysis of the effectiveness of applying the deprivation approach and the income approach to defining the people in greatest need: our results showed that it is in fact the deprivation approach that allows a more adequate definition of this group in Russian conditions. So, for example, 9 per cent of those defined as being in the lowest decile (and thus the most needy) according to the deprivation criterion could afford all the medicines and medical services they needed, whereas 13 per cent (i.e. one-and-a-half times as many) of those in the lowest decile by income could do so.

The poorer position of those who were defined as poor on the basis of the deprivation rather than the income criterion was also clearly evident in an aspect of life that is very important during transition to a market economy, with its profusion of goods: households' level of ownership of consumer durables. Across the sample as a whole, according to data from the Institute of Sociology's 2006 research, the median indicator was nine types of consumer durables, including five types acquired within the last seven years. People in the lowest income decile typically owned seven types of consumer durables out of the 23 shown on the questionnaire (see Table 4.6), of which five were acquired more than seven years ago (as a rule, even longer ago: during the Soviet period). This group's median indicator for number of types of consumer durables acquired within the last seven years was two; moreover, some of the people who had renewed their household property had obtained these items from more prosperous acquaintances and relations when the latter had replaced them with newer ones. We also encountered cases, even in our panel sample, of people giving away their property free: the kinds of things given away were furniture, computers, old cars, etc. Using the deprivation approach, we found that the median indicator for items that were seven years old or more fell to six types of consumer durables, while the indicator for new items fell to one.

As for housing provision, it was typical of the bottom deciles, as defined using either approach for establishing these, for the size of accommodation occupied to be slightly less than in the rest of the population; the bottom deciles had an average

Table 4.7   Use of fee-paying social services in the last 12 months, 2006 (%)

Kinds of services:	Lowest decile by deprivation	Lowest decile by income	Poor (no more than 50% of median income)	Across the sample as a whole
Medical services	27	21	25	31
Educational services for children	10	4	11	23
Adult education facilities	6	8	9	13
Children's health and leisure facilities	10	4	5	8
Adult health and leisure facilities	0	0	1	5
Tourist or educational trips abroad	0	0	1	4
Building or buying a house	3	2	3	4
Have not used any of these services	68	71	67	54

Note: Data on the use of adult education facilities refer to respondents who were working; data on the use of educational, health and leisure services for children – to those who had children under 18; and the other data – to the whole population.

Source: Tikhonova (2007).

of 15 square metres of total living space per person, while the median for the population as a whole was 17 square metres. However, the main inequalities were not in size but in quality of accommodation occupied. So, 63 per cent of the lowest income decile were inhabitants of rural localities, mainly those who had their own house or part of a house, and only 9 per cent of members of that decile were living in hostels, rented accommodation or communal flats. However, in the lowest decile defined according to the deprivation criterion, 19 per cent were in that position, of whom 10 per cent were living in hostels. Under current legislative provisions in Russia, hostel dwelling means not only relatively higher housing costs, but also the possibility of being evicted by the landlord of the hostel at any minute, even if the payments are being met. Five per cent were renting accommodation and 4 per cent were living in communal flats.

Fee-paying social services were practically inaccessible to the worst-off strata of the population (see Table 4.7), despite the fact that the accessibility of fee-paying social services, especially given the extremely low quality of their free counterparts, is a most important indicator of quality of life in contemporary Russia.

Thus, in principle most of the population (including the lower classes of Russian society) have no opportunities to change things in their lives for the better

Table 4.8   Achievements over the previous 12 months, 2006 (%)

	Lowest decile by deprivation	Lowest decile by income	Poor (no more than 50% of median income)	Across the sample as a whole
Achievements				
Improvement in material circumstances	2	6	7	15
Promotion at work or getting a new, more suitable job	4	4	7	11
Making expensive purchases	0	0	5	10
Improvement in standard of education and/or skills/ qualifications	4	4	4	10
Improvement in housing conditions	2	8	8	7
Improvement in health	3	4	4	4
Visiting another country	0	0	1	3
Starting one's own business	0	0	0	1
Have not achieved any of the above over the last year	88	75	74	61
Dynamic in material circumstances				
Material circumstances have deteriorated over the last year	53	40	43	26

Note: Data on those who obtained promotions and those who increased their skills/ qualifications refer to respondents who were working; and the other data to the whole population.

Source: Tikhonova (2007).

(see Table 4.8); although, as can be seen from the figures given above, their present standard of living does not guarantee that these strata of the population will be reproduced. In fact, social inequalities in contemporary Russia are manifested, even for the poorest strata of the population, not so much in income inequality as in qualitatively different life chances (both in terms of consumption and in maintaining and building up their human capital), which serve to preserve these inequalities for the future. Indeed, a mere 23 per cent of respondents across the whole sample said that their life had improved over recent years (as against 26 per cent who said it had deteriorated and 51 per cent for whom it had not changed) and also, for those with incomes no higher than 50 per cent of the median for the place they lived in, the corresponding indicators were 11 per cent, 43 per cent and 46 per cent, meaning that a much faster deterioration was observed in their lives. Many people stated that no positive changes had taken place, even in areas not directly connected with their financial situation, and this was more distinctly the case for the poor defined according to the deprivation criterion.

This provides evidence of the need to take into account, when analysing the dynamic of population health in Russia, not just income inequalities but the whole spectrum of basic social inequalities. Methodologically, this means that, in any review of the situation with poverty and health in Russia, the level of current incomes is not as important as indicators of deprivation. So, in order to clarify how standards of living in various strata of Russian society (which is fairly poor overall) differ, it is worth drawing on our 2006 data to give a short portrait of the standard of living of a typical family (which usually consists of two adults and one child) corresponding to: 1) a median standard of living, 2) being in poverty and 3) the standard of living of the highest decile in contemporary Russia:

1. The typical Russian family with a median standard of living usually lives in a two-room flat with a total area of no more than 45 square metres, and does not possess any immovable property apart from this accommodation and some savings; they own a fridge, television, vacuum cleaner, wall units and a washing machine, as well as another three or four consumer items of some kind, according to their preferences; in the last seven years, they have acquired no more than five kinds of consumer durables for the home (as a rule, these include their television, their washing machine and a mobile phone); their use of fee-paying social services over the last three years has been confined to medical services; the only leisure activity that they can afford is to go to the cinema, and they cannot go away on holiday when they are on leave from work.
2. As far as poverty is concerned, the picture differs depending on both the depth of poverty involved (indigence, poverty or being badly off[5]) and its duration. Nevertheless, in describing the situation of a typical poor urban family consisting of three people, we first note that the members of the family themselves typically assess their own food and clothing as 'poor'; that, apart from furniture, the only consumer durables they own are a television, a fridge and a carpet; and that they have practically no new household goods at all. This family does not have any kind of immovable property of their own; their accommodation provides an area of about 12 square metres per person; they do not have savings of any kind or, moreover, any opportunities to make use of fee-paying services such as medical services, going to the cinema or taking part in sporting activities. In a word, they are vegetating miserably on the edge of physical survival, facing the gradual depletion of all the resources they had built up earlier, from their ageing property to their deteriorating health, and the impossibility of giving their children anything at all that would contribute to their development.
3. For people who are situated in the middle of the highest decile, a combination of indicators such as the following is most typical: 1) the three-person family lives in a comfortable flat, 72–75 square metres in size; 2) they have

a dacha, a garage and a car; 3) there are 12 kinds of consumer durables in the household, of which ten items have been acquired for the first time, or renewed, in the last seven years (as a rule, these are a television, a fridge, a vacuum cleaner, a suite of furniture, kitchen appliances, a washing machine, a video player/recorder, a music centre, a computer and a mobile phone); 4) they have used no less than six kinds of fee-paying social services over the last three years; 5) they take part in no less than three kinds of fee-paying leisure activities (visiting theatres, concerts, cinema, museums, bars, restaurants, etc.); 6) they have savings, although these would not be sufficient for them to live on for a year or more. It goes without saying that the quality of life of the top 1–1.5 per cent of the population by income is very different again.

One particular feature typical of the system of stratification in Russia is that the specific nature of differences between regions is manifest not in the median standard of living (which is very close in the overwhelming majority of Russian regions), but a) in the proportion of those who can afford a standard of living similar to the one described above for the top decile, and b) in the proportion of poor people. In addition, in the wealthiest regions there are also sections of the population that are very rich even by international standards, while in other regions the size of such groups is statistically insignificant.

This means that, even though very profound social inequalities are typical of Russia as a whole and of the majority of its regions, and the overwhelming majority of the population has a low standard of living, in certain regions, first among which is Moscow, these inequalities are simply glaring. Superimposed on the 'cultural trauma' (as Shtompka calls it) experienced over the last two decades, they represent the strongest stress-inducing factor with a direct influence on the health of the Russian population (Alexander et al., 2004).

Perceptions of Social Inequalities

The influence of profound social inequalities, especially obvious in the wealthiest regions, on the social and psychological state of Russian society and, in the final analysis, on people's health, is not simply a result of the depth of these inequalities, but also of the attitude of the population of Russia to inequalities as such. In this regard, we must first note that the depth of income differentiation that seems normal to Russians is comparable to indicators of real social differentiation in Western European countries. In any case, according to the Institute of Sociology's 2006 data, the indicator of how far the income of a highly-skilled specialist or manager in Russia might exceed the country's average income was 4.6 times. Given that Russians, according to data from the same research, draw the poverty line roughly at a level of 50–60 per cent of average income, we reach the conclusion that Russians see a depth of inequality of 8–9 times as entirely legitimate.

Table 4.9   Attitudes to social justice and inequalities, 2006 (%)

Statements	Lowest decile by deprivation	Lowest decile by income	Poor (no more than 50% of median income)	Across the sample as a whole
When some people have more money than others, this is fair as long as they had equal opportunities to earn it	55	59	57	64
It is fair when people who can afford it give their children a better education	43	52	56	53
It is fair that people with the means to do so can buy themselves better housing than other people	36	47	48	50
It is fair that people who have higher pay will also get a bigger pension	35	39	41	43
It is fair that people with the means to do so can use higher-quality medical services than other people	25	36	33	33

Note: The respondents represented in this table are people who agreed, or more or less agreed, with these statements and therefore with the fairness of the corresponding types of inequalities. For all the statements, apart from the one about accessibility of medical services, the proportion of those who did not agree, or more or less did not agree, was smaller than the proportion who agreed. The rest were respondents who 'partly agreed, partly disagreed'.

Source: Tikhonova (2007).

Apart from those in the lowest deprivation decile, Russians are also very tolerant of concrete manifestations of social inequalities: for them, the only absolutely illegitimate inequalities are those where lack of access to medical care results from income inequality (see Table 4.9).

As we can see, Russians as a whole are fairly tolerant towards inequalities, and it is no coincidence that, even with inequalities as clearly excessive as they currently are, a quarter of all respondents agreed with the idea that a high level of income differentiation is necessary for Russia to flourish economically. We can compare this pattern with the UK through the British Social Attitudes Survey, conducted in 1999 (Jowell et al., 2000; Thomson et al., 2001). The analogous indicator for the UK was 19 per cent in total; however, at the same time, 48 per cent of UK respondents said that Britons are receiving worthwhile rewards for their intellectual abilities, skills and honest hard work; this point of view (in relation to Russians) was shared by only 18 per cent of Russian respondents. Thus, the problem lies not so much in the mythical egalitarianism of the Russian consciousness as in the lack of connection between work and incomes in contemporary Russian society; consequently, the Russian population sees the colossal social differences that exist as illegitimate.

Thus, when differentiation is actually much greater than what public opinion regards as optimal and, moreover, appears to be illegitimate, people inevitably start to have a very acute sense of profound social inequalities. In the year before the Institute of Sociology's 2006 survey, only 9 per cent of Russians had not felt that everything going on around them was unjust. Nineteen per cent said that they had often felt simultaneously that they could not go on living like this and that they were helpless to influence what was happening; only 10 per cent said they practically never experienced such feelings. Among people whose incomes were no higher than 50 per cent of the median for the place they lived in, 28 per cent habitually experienced all these different feelings, as did 30 per cent of those in the lowest income decile and 39 per cent in the lowest decile defined by the deprivation criterion.

Our longitudinal panel respondents also told us, at all stages of observation, that they were depressed not only by their own poverty, but also by the injustice of the situation that had developed. Moreover, the prevailing mood meant that people typically did not protest against the existence of the rich per se, but displayed an unwillingness to accept as normal a situation in which a very few people are free, healthy and wealthy. As Lidiya (45, from Voronezh), who had worked as a governess in a wealthy family, said 'There are lots of sick people now, but the circle of people who I've come into contact with – they're healthy. I can see that from their way of life, because of the way they work: a sick person just would not be able to do that much work.' But the overwhelming majority of the population is helpless and has no rights. 'The situation in recent years has been one of low pay, with no light at the end of the tunnel; and not everyone can cope with it: some take to drink, some degrade themselves, and family and personal relationships deteriorate,' said Sveta, 41, a music teacher in a Voronezh kindergarten.

The loss of any kind of prospects, which many respondents mentioned, generates feelings of hopelessness and apathy, which reach their apogee among poor people; many respondents drew attention to this when describing the essential nature and the markers of poverty: 'poverty means having no tomorrow' (Valentina, 42, underground worker from Moscow; see also Chapter 11); 'poverty is when debts and other problems just pile up to such an extent that you can't find any way out' (Masha, 45, manager from Voronezh).

This sense of hopelessness, starkly expressed by many, had clear links, both in our longitudinal panel and in the pan-Russian surveys, with standard of health: so, among those Russians who often felt that they could not go on living like this and that they were helpless to influence what was happening, 33 per cent of respondents to the Institute of Sociology's 2006 survey described their health as 'poor' or 'very poor', and only 12 per cent as 'good' or 'excellent'. Among those who practically never experienced such feelings, the corresponding health indicators were 11 per cent and 36 per cent, i.e. the complete reverse. Moreover, the influence of this factor could also be traced among groups at the same level of welfare or the same age. Thus, the stress that results from the impossibility of changing an unacceptable situation was a most important factor in poor health. Moreover, and according to respondents' assessments during interviews and to data from longitudinal observations (see Chapter 11), this turned out to have an even more significant effect on health than the material consequences of lack of resources (poor food, etc.).

It is natural that the most deprived sections of the population should feel the injustice of what has happened more acutely; but in the highest income decile, too, about 90 per cent of people agreed that income differentiation in Russia is now unjustifiably great. This means that the social inequalities existing in Russia today seem unjust to all sections of the population, and that protest against the excessive differentiation of incomes between Russians reflects the breach of a particular sociocultural norm in Russian society, according to which only a certain depth of social inequality has been viewed as admissible.

It is also natural for respondents to lay their main complaints about the situation that has developed at the door of the State and 'the powers that be': 'Well, I'm not against it – let them be rich. I'm not against there being any rich people, I'm against there being any poor people ...' emphasised Tat'yana, a trained economist from Moscow, who herself was certainly materially prosperous. (Aged 40 at the time of this interview, she had joined our panel at the age of 35, when she was unemployed; see also Chapter 9.) 'But if the State allows such wealth to exist alongside indigence, then it's a State that is next to worthless.'

As a consequence, there has been a total lack of trust in government bodies for many years, while lack of trust in other people has become established as a norm in interpersonal relationships. According to data from the Institute of Sociology's pan-Russian research of 2004, 17 per cent of respondents trusted nobody at all, 75 per cent trusted only their closest friends and relations, and only 8 per cent trusted someone they knew slightly. Living in an environment that they perceive as hostile, with material circumstances that deteriorated sharply in the 1990s, with a constant sense of the injustice of what is happening and a feeling that they cannot influence the situation, and without any effective mechanisms of social protection, Russians a priori have not been in a position to care for their own health. So Wilkinson (2000) is right when he says that profound social inequalities, stress and lack of trust intrinsically form a single triad.

If we want a better understanding of how the situation that has developed translates into stress for Russians, it is helpful to look at their views on their own status in society. If we reconstruct a model of the social structure of Russian society on the basis of respondents' subjective assessments of their own status, then we can conclude that the public consciousness is now dominated by a picture of the social organisation of Russian society in which most of the population is

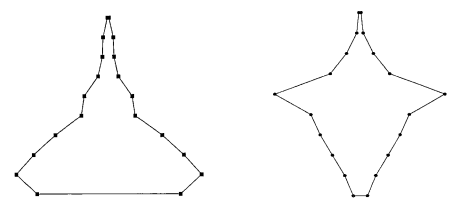

Figure 4.1   Model of the social structure of Russia and the UK

Note 1:This test, involving a vertical 10-point scale of status positions, is widely used in international research. In Russia, measurements by this method have been in use since 1992, in the context of an international research project (ISSP – International Social Survey Programme – Social Inequality II). The numerical values used to construct the model (in percentages) were:

Position 1 (highest) – 0.2   Position 6 – 7.4
Position 2 – 1.4   Position 7 – 14.6
Position 3 – 1.6   Position 8 – 20.5
Position 4 – 2.8   Position 9 – 25.3
Position 5 – 6.6   Position 10 (lowest) – 19.6

Note 2: Data from the British Social Attitudes Survey were used for this model. Numerical values used to construct the model (in percentages) were:

Position 1 (highest) – 0.4   Position 6 – 18.1
Position 2 – 1.2   Position 7 – 14.7
Position 3 – 4.9   Position 8 – 10.2
Position 4 – 10.9   Position 9 – 5.7
Position 5 – 31.4   Position 10 (lowest) – 2.6

at the very bottom of the pyramid, strong social differentiation exists and most people feel they are 'social outsiders' (Tikhonova, forthcoming in 2008; see Figure 4.1). Figure 4.1 shows clearly the qualitative differences of this from a picture reconstructed on the basis of Western European respondents' own assessments of their status, taking the UK as an example: very obviously illustrating the fact that the most important specific feature of the type of social structure that has arisen in Russia in the last two decades is that the majority of Russians typically 'depreciate' their assessments of their own social status.

These differences between Russians' and Western Europeans' ideas of their own social status have a huge influence on their health. Application of the linear regression method to the Institute of Sociology's 2006 dataset showed that, disregarding the age factor, Russians' assessments of their own health are most closely connected with their assessments of their lives overall (Pearson coefficient

Table 4.10   Assessments of own health, 2006 (%)

Assessment of own health	Groups defined on the basis of their own assessments of their material circumstances			
	Good	Satisfactory	Poor	Across the sample as a whole
Good	67	32	12	28
Fair	28	58	55	55
Poor	5	10	33	27
	Groups defined on the basis of level of per capita income			
Assessment of own health	High income (twice the median or more)	Average income (from 1 to 2 times the median)	Low income (over 50% but lower than the median)	Poor (no more than 50% of median income)
Good	39	23	9	12
Fair	54	62	61	52
Poor	7	15	30	36
	Groups defined on the basis of deprivation criterion			
Assessment of own health	Highest decile by deprivation	Deciles 2–9	Lowest decile by deprivation	
Good	63	26	11	
Fair	33	60	41	
Poor	4	14	48	
	Class defined on the basis of respondents' own assessments of their social status on a ten-point scale			
Assessment of own health	1–4 points (highest class positions)	5–6 points	7–8 points	9–10 points (lowest class positions)
Good	42	31	19	5
Fair	52	58	64	51
Poor	6	11	17	44

Source: Tikhonova (2007).

0.405) and only then with material circumstances in all their main forms (quality of food, possibility of acquiring clothing, number of consumer durables acquired in the last seven years, their own assessment of their material circumstances overall). Their assessment of their own social status comes far lower (Pearson coefficient 0.335). At the same time, the class someone belongs to, defined on the basis of occupational status and education, turned out to be less significant than position in a social hierarchy constructed on the basis of income inequality. The reason for this lies in the enormous role played by sectoral, regional and local inequalities in Russia, as a result of which the link between occupational status and standard of living has been broken. As a consequence, it is impossible to apply methods of

Table 4.11   Assessments of own health, 2005 (%)

Assessment of own health	Class defined according to ESOMAR method					
	A	B	C1	C2	D	E
Good	32	19	23	25	21	19
Fair	56	72	64	63	66	54
Poor	12	9	13	12	13	28

Note: Data from the pan-Russian research programme conducted by the Institute of Sociology of the Russian Academy of Sciences in 2005, 'Ownership in the life and perception of Russians', which had a sample of 1,751 people, constructed in an identical manner to the sample in their 2006 research.

defining class in Russia that come well recommended by their use in all Western European countries.

We can illustrate this through data obtained on the basis of class definitions of the Institute of Sociology's samples, using the ESOMAR method (European Society for Opinion and Marketing Research, 1997) (see Tables 4.10 and 4.11).

As we can see, the most distinct, practically linear dependency with people's self-rated health is demonstrated by groups defined according to the deprivation criterion, while the weakest relationship is with the ESOMAR class definition. Of course, this does not mean that class affiliation is not a causal factor in the health of the population of Russia. However, in conditions where there is a mismatch between occupational status and level of material welfare – arising from low pay levels in the public sector (where 33.7 per cent of Russians currently work; Statistical Year Book of Russia, 2006, p. 138), from very profound regional and sectoral differences in pay for work of the same quality, and also from the relatively similar lifestyles of different classes (a factor inherited from the Soviet period) – it is not easy as yet to apply conventional class-definition approaches, including use of the ESOMAR method, to Russia and achieve acceptable delineations of the main classes in Russian society. However, we were able to confirm the conclusion, already illustrated more than once in various research projects, that people's health depends on the depth of social inequalities, the mechanism of whose effect is connected primarily (although, of course, not solely) with the stress that is experienced as a result.

Chapter 5
Poverty in Post-Reform Russia

Nadia Davidova

Бьётся, как рыба об лёд
Struggling like a fish against ice

Poverty: Official Views

From the beginning of the Russian reforms, the issue of poverty revealed itself as very evident and severe, symbolising the social cost that the population would have to pay in the transition from the Soviet model of welfare to the market. However, it would be untrue to take the view that poverty did not exist in Russia in the Soviet period. In so far as poverty, in the opinion of most researchers, is the inability to maintain an acceptable standard of living, 'classic' poor families with a typical set of 'disadvantaged' socio-demographic and skills characteristics exist everywhere and at all times. It was simply that, during the Soviet era, ideological considerations meant it was not the done thing to talk about this. A simple analysis shows that if there were two children in a Soviet family and both parents were working in low-paid jobs, then this family could have been considered poor, since the minimum wage was then one-and-a-half times the subsistence minimum, and such low-paid parents could feed only one child without falling into poverty. This situation was usual when there were non-working elderly people in the family, and was especially true when these were former collective farmers (Ovcharova, 2003). According to data from the Independent Institute for Social Policy, something like 16 per cent of families of blue- and white-collar workers in Russia in 1985 had incomes below the subsistence minimum, while among collective farmers (rural dwellers) about 40 per cent were in that situation.

So what has happened in Russia because of the transition to the market? How have 'radical' economic reforms and the breakdown of the old welfare system been reflected in the living standards of the Russian population? In short, who is in poverty? Where is the fault line in contemporary Russia that represents the real scale of poverty? This chapter will attempt to find an answer to these questions.

The price liberalisation implemented in the early 1990s not only provoked a massive rise in prices but also completely wiped out the savings of the great mass of the population. Its chief results were not a positive benefit from satisfying the consumer market, but a fall in real incomes, a marked polarisation in society and the growth of poverty. The economic reforms that had been initiated triggered a 50 per cent reduction in Russian GDP, the consequence of which was a corresponding fall in people's incomes – against a background of an unstable labour market situation, growing unemployment and rampant inflation.

In these qualitatively new conditions, poverty began to be interpreted in various ways: either as a low level of income and expenditure, or as the absence of necessary resources, or as the impossibility of maintaining desired living standards, or as a certain sense of oneself in the social formation, or as a social comparison with one's previous, pre-reform status. All this led to a situation where, according to different assessments, the scale of poverty in Russia could vary from 20 per cent to 70 per cent of the population. The worst results were most often based on subjective assessments by the population, which allowed some researchers to conclude that there had been a 'societal impoverishment' of the Russian population (Standing, 1998). It was necessary to define what was, in the final analysis, to be considered 'poverty' and, further, to define this precisely at the level of the State in order to develop effective means to react to the problem.

Absolute Concept of Poverty

Russia settled on an absolute concept of poverty, presupposing a formal correspondence of incomes to the officially established minimum needed for existence (the 'subsistence minimum'). As a result, the majority of politicians, civil servants and ordinary Russians have come to interpret poverty from the point of view of disposable income, using direct comparison with the cost of a minimum basket of consumer goods, established on the basis of subsistence minimum calculations, as the indicator of whether someone falls into the category 'poor'.

According to data from Rosstat (the Russian Federal State Statistics Service), the proportion of poor people in Russia in the 1990s is detailed in Table 5.1.

Table 5.1   Rosstat estimated poverty rates, 1992 to 2000 (%)

	Distribution across years								
	1992	1993	1994	1995	1996	1997	1998	1999	2000
Percent in poverty	33.3	31.5	22.4	24.7	22.1	20.8	23.4	29.9	30.0

Source: Russian Federal State Statistics Service Analiticheskiy vestnik Soveta Federatsii FC RF (2003), p. 213.

Over the final decade of the twentieth century, the worst years for poverty in Russia were 1992–93, 1999 and 2000. In 1992–93, the rise in the number of poor people was a consequence of price liberalisation, as a result of which Russians' real incomes fell significantly. In 1999, the high rate of poverty was a consequence of the 1998 financial crisis and the default on public and private debt that accompanied it.

In later years, according to official statistics, the poverty rate in Russia has seen a steady downward trend. Thus, in 2002 the proportion of poor people in the Russian population fell to 25 per cent (35.8 million people), in 2003 – to 23.3

per cent, while in 2004 it reached 17.8 per cent. According to the most recent data published by the Ministry for Economic Development on the basis of Rosstat figures, in 2005 the proportion of the population of Russia with incomes below the established subsistence minimum was at a record low – 15.8 per cent (Federal State Statistics Service).

In this regard, we should like to focus attention on the fact that it was actually in 2005 that the official method for evaluating poverty was itself changed. Previously, calculations of the subsistence minimum and collection of information about the poor (and, correspondingly, distribution of assistance to people in need) were conducted at Federal level; now, authority for this has been transferred to the regions, which independently establish the size of the subsistence minimum, starting from local cost of living and income differentiation. Social support to people in need is also provided through regional budgets. Theoretically, in calculating the subsistence minimum, the regions are obliged to follow the Federal Law on the Subsistence Minimum. As a recommendation from central government, a method for determining who could be claimants for social assistance was also circulated to the regions. (According to this, households whose incomes are no more than 60–66 per cent of the regional subsistence minimum have a right to a means-tested benefit.) In practice, it is difficult to determine what criteria govern the territories of the Russian Federation in defining the priorities of regional policy in the area of poverty (in many ways, this depends on the socioeconomic situation of the region itself); in addition, information on scales of regional poverty and volumes of social support does not always get from the regions to Federal statistical organisations promptly. Already, therefore, a situation has arisen in which the average poverty indicator across Russia – calculated taking into account the new distribution of powers between the centre and the regions, in force since 2005 – cannot be considered absolutely objective, even within the framework of the officially accepted method.

It must be noted that, even though official statistical bodies in Russia present a picture of a relatively satisfactory dynamic of poverty, there continue to be distinct divergences between expert definitions of the scale of Russian poverty, despite every effort on the part of politicians and of experts themselves to develop an adequate method of assessment. The World Bank, for example, is oriented towards its own methodology for assessing poverty. In particular, the nature of this as applied to Russia – and also to other CIS countries – is that a person may be considered poor when they can spend no more than \$2.15 a day, recalculated according to the real buying power of the dollar in its '1989 form' in the country concerned. The section of the World Bank that deals with anti-poverty measures and economic regulation has involved both international and Russian experts in producing a continuous stream of special reports evaluating poverty in Russia.

The most recent of these, evaluating poverty in the countries of Eastern Europe and the former Soviet Union, was published by the World Bank in Autumn 2005. Despite a fairly optimistic general forecast of the situation, based on the fact that in most CIS countries economic growth has enabled significant progress in reducing absolute poverty, the World Bank experts stated that poverty remains a serious problem in this region – not just for poor people themselves but also for large groups, already at various stages of deprivation, which are vulnerable to poverty. In addition, concern was openly expressed for the first time about the non-material aspects of poverty, which cannot be measured by income level. These are the aspects of poverty that limit the access of a significant part of the population to resources for development: high-paid work, good quality education and health care services, the opportunity for successful socialisation of children and young people.

This was a reflection of a broader approach to poverty being applied to the situation in Russia: this approach presupposes that, when assessing poverty, we must take into account not only lack of money for day-to-day consumption, but must look much more broadly – at level of housing provision and property, particular features of the structure of consumption, and accumulated resource potential (social, skills, physiological). The persistent weakness of evaluations of poverty based solely on income is that they ignore a broad spectrum of available or unavailable non-economic resources that have an effect in maintaining people's material welfare.

As a result, many criticisms are continuously levelled at the official use of the subsistence minimum criterion, which itself can give different results, depending on what is meant by this. The method of calculating the subsistence minimum, on which definition of the statistical 'boundaries of poverty' in Russia is based, applies the principle that it should start from a minimum basket of consumer goods. But the fact of the matter is that, given inflationary processes and dynamic changes in the structure of consumption, the officially established standard of poverty, developed on the basis of the Federal Law of 2000, is morally and physically obsolete. Special measures are needed, directed at reviewing the method itself and, first and foremost, at rejecting the distinct trend towards underestimating the proportion of essential non-food expenditures in the composition of the minimum basket of consumer goods. In particular, the sweeping reforms of recent years in municipal housing and public utilities and other social spheres have taken their toll on the total budgets of families and the structure of their main expenditures; however, this is in no way taken into account when calculating the proportion of poor people within the Russian population.

This may be connected with the fact that the Russian government has set the objective of reducing the poverty rate by 2.5–3 per cent a year, as officially announced in August 2004. German Gref, head of the Ministry of Economic Development of the Russian Federation, announced a government programme with the aim of radically reducing the poverty rate and bringing this indicator out of double figures. Accordingly, it has been planned to bring the poverty rate in Russia down to 5 per cent by 2015. Moreover, officials have declared that the proportion of poor people within the population had already fallen to between 10.5 per cent and 12 per cent by 2007. The same figure can also be found in the above-mentioned 2005 World Bank report, which indicated that if the rate of economic growth in Russia exceeded 5 per cent annually and consumption grew by 5 per cent a year, then the scale of poverty might be reduced to 10.2 per cent by 2007 (Alam et al., 2005). However, international experts warn that, if poverty reduction is to be achieved, GDP will have to grow at faster rates than consumption; this diverges somewhat from declarations made by the Russian government, which (as has been said above) takes the view that the problem of poverty can be resolved where 'rates of growth in the population's real incomes exceed economic growth.'

Relative Concept of Poverty

However, it should be noted that, despite the significant improvement in quality of life in EU countries over recent years, there are on average 60 million poor people in the EU, or 18 per cent of the total population (La Stampa, 2003). So, meeting the objective of reducing poverty to 5 per cent would only relate to the question of calculation method; it is not in itself a means of tackling the problem of poverty. In fact, in European countries, as in most industrially developed nations in the world, another method of evaluating poverty, differing from the one that applies in Russia, has already been in use for a long time – based not on an absolute concept of poverty, but on a relative one.

On a statistical level, a method of counting the poor according to the median principle is the most sensible one. Within the framework of this concept, those whose income consists of a defined proportion of the 'average' income in a given country at a given period of time are said to be 'relatively' poor, and this enables them to claim social support. In practice, it means that the official subsistence minimum is calculated as a defined proportion of the median income that is statistically typical of living standards in a given society – and not as the cost of a minimum basket of consumer goods established on the basis of standards laid down by the State. It must be said that this approach to the study of poverty recommends itself a great deal, especially in comparative research. In particular, in Russia, it was first used by Khakhulina and Tuchek (1995) in their cross-national research into inequality in post-socialist countries.

Using this approach in Russia, it would follow that those to be counted as 'poor' are people who have no more than 50–60 per cent of the average (median) income across the country. In practice, this is what Russians are referring to when they answer questions like: 'What income, in your opinion, must a family have (calculated per family member) in order for the family to be considered as living below subsistence minimum standard?' and 'Starting from what income (calculated per person) would you think that a family is living below the poverty line?'. According to the results of large-scale pan-Russian research by the Institute of Sociology of the Russian Academy of Sciences in 2006, the views of most respondents about the sufficient subsistence minimum needed coincide to a surprising extent with the median income of respondents, and the poverty line is defined at of 50–60 per cent of the latter, which fully corresponds to the principle accepted in a number of countries for calculating the poverty line and assessing the degree of relative deprivation.

However, it must not be forgotten that Russia is a huge territorial-settlement space with various levels of socioeconomic development, depending on region and type of settlement. Substantial inter-regional and local differentiation of incomes makes it difficult to assess the situation on the basis of averaged indicators. But the main problem lies in the fact that, since the quality of regional statistics is not high, regional differences in the population's incomes are very difficult to track, against a background of differences in the volume of the shadow economy, in the calculated volume of incomes in kind from a personal plot of land, and in regional prices for goods and services. There is also yet another problem that, in principle, cannot be tackled through statistical measurements, even where these are done correctly. This is the subjective evaluation of their own incomes by inhabitants of various types of settlements. An income that seems sufficient to a village resident will be perceived by a Muscovite as representing extreme poverty, not only because prices are higher in the capital, but also because of different standards of consumption.

Following a painstaking analysis of statistical information, experts at the Independent Institute for Social Policy concluded that regional differences in income levels and poverty rates became much stronger in the 1990s. 'Loser' regions were in the first instance those oriented towards the military-industrial complex, engineering, light industry and the food industry, while the corresponding 'winner' regions were those connected with energy production. In addition, in the 1990s, mechanisms for redistributing and equalising the incomes of regions became weaker, and volumes of finance and public funding for many underdeveloped regions fell. Finally, much depended on a subjective factor: the policies of regional governments and the regions' differing levels of support for their inhabitants, whether financial or publicly funded (Independent Institute for Social Policy, 2005). As a result, the differentiation of average incomes by region in Russia, according to Rosstat, reached tenfold in September 2006. And, although monthly average per capita incomes of residents of Moscow were 29,562.50 roubles (around £600 GBP per person per month) and incomes in the oil-and-gas-producing regions (Tyumen Province, which includes the Yamalo-Nenetskiy and Khanty-Mansiyskiy Autonomous Districts) were on average no less than 20,000 roubles (£400 GBP) monthly, the incomes of inhabitants of, for example, Voronezh Province were only 6,774.50 roubles a month (£135 GBP). And, in the underdeveloped 'outsider' regions such as Tyva, Buryatiya or Kalmykiya, the level of average per capita incomes frequently failed to exceed 3,000–4,000 roubles a month per person (£60–£80 GBP) (Federal State Statistics Service). These trends are also demonstrated in the results of sociological research, where people gave their own assessments of the level of their incomes.

The economic boom that took place after the 1998 default on public and private debt obviously helped to increase levels of income from work and size of transfers, which has also led to a marked reduction in the statistical boundaries of poverty in Russia over the course of recent years. At the same time, however, the social stratification of Russians is growing stronger, and this is confirmed by both statistical data and data from numerous sociological research studies. Over the years of reform, differentiation in the population's incomes has grown continuously. Among the CIS countries, Russia occupies first place for inequality in distribution of incomes. According to Rosstat, in 2004, the total volume income share of the best-off 10 per cent of the population was 29.8 per cent, while the poorest 10 per cent's share was 2 per cent.

The situation in Russia from the point of view of income differentiation also differs markedly from the position in developed countries of the world, where the difference in incomes between the decile groups at the two extremes is 7–8 times (and in the Scandinavian countries, even less). In Russia, the Gini coefficient gives a difference of 14–15 times – and, taking into account shadow incomes, even more; so here, Russia is closer to the countries of the Third World (Manning, 2007, pp. 161–78).

However, the main problem lies not so much in the scales and the dynamics of poverty in Russia as in the inadequacy of the State's social policy measures. Official views of poverty do not take into account the fact that forms of poverty and the very socioeconomic essence of poverty are changing all the time. Numerous sociological research studies show that, over the years of reform, the structure of poverty in Russia has changed from its traditional determination by a particular set of disadvantageous sociodemographic characteristics (primarily, being of pension age, the family having several children or a disabled member, etc.). It first became closely connected with unemployment and non-payment of wages, and subsequently with insecure employment and the particular nature of this. In the last case, it is evident that many working people fall into the vice-like grip of poverty. One of the models of a typical poor family in Russia is that of working city dwellers who have children and are in receipt of low wages. Among them is a high proportion of public sector employees, whose wages hardly reach the official poverty line. They are mainly concentrated in the spheres of education, health care and the cultural sector.

As a result, the majority of poor people in Russia now are people who have education (sometimes even higher education), a family and a job. People are willing to work wherever they can, for any money, just to make ends meet. But the causes of their poverty have their roots in the specific nature of the Russian labour market. The main source of poverty is the low pay of most workers employed in the public sector of the economy, and also the large proportion of jobs that do not require any of the kinds of skills that have been preserved by the structure of the economy.

There is also another social problem connected with this: in Russia nowadays a huge number of people, although they are not poor, are teetering on the brink of poverty. The World Bank calculations already mentioned demonstrate that, each time the incomes of Russians fall by 10 per cent at the national scale, the number of poor people immediately increases by 50 per cent.

In addition, Russian poverty is more actively moving 'downwards'; that is, there is an increasing intergenerational effect. Children from less well-off families have far fewer opportunities to continue their education beyond the compulsory stage. Specialised research projects have recorded significant differences in the chances of entering a higher education establishment for children from various social strata; and this inequality is even more evident in access to prestige higher-education establishments and to vocational training that guarantees entry to a profession for which there will subsequently be demand on the labour market and a decent level of pay. Fifteen per cent of entrants to élite higher education establishments come from poor and badly-off families, as against almost 80 per cent from prosperous families (Roshchina, 2003).

This kind of situation may already be leading to the emergence .of a social pattern of reproduction of the 'true' poor, of whom there were practically none during the Soviet period. According to a statement in 2003 by the then Italian Minister of Health, Girolamo Sirchia, a large number of 'silent poor people' exist in prosperous Europe. These are not people who can be seen on the street or in social security offices; they are those who never ask for anything. They do not leave the house. Millions of old people have no possibility of paying their electricity bill. And, if the doctor prescribes medicines that are not on the concessionary 'A list', they cannot afford them (La Stampa, 2003). Such poor people (and there are many of them in Russia too) are also in severe need of help, but they have simply disappeared from the politicians' field of vision.

Further growth in inequality may essentially weaken the positive influence of economic growth on the reduction of poverty, as the same World Bank (2005) experts persistently warn. 'If the advantages of economic growth are not distributed evenly, then its influence on the poverty rate will be weakened,' their official statement asserts. In this regard, most serious analysts emphasise that the goal set in 2004 by the President of Russia, Vladimir Putin, to reduce poverty sharply is potentially achievable: however, it is extremely difficult. And not all the questions connected with particular features of the development of this social phenomenon in the Russian context can be answered by official statistics. Therefore, we shall now move on to an analysis of special research that throws more light on poverty.

Sociological Research on Poverty

The social importance of the issue of poverty in Russia is difficult to overestimate, and this encourages many researchers to try and improve methods of studying it. Specialised research studies can serve as a distinctive alternative to official statistics. The World Bank's research (1997, 2000, 2005) represents just one such project. It throws detailed light on such issues as the nature and profile of Russian poverty, and highlights groups that are at high risk of impoverishment; these are groups that will not be able to derive any advantages from a general improvement in the economy. These are, first and foremost, the rural population (representative research showed 30.4 per cent of this population to be poor, while the proportion of poor people in the urban population was 15.7 per cent); children (while the rate of poverty overall across the country was 19.6 per cent, among children under 16 it was substantially higher at 26.7 per cent); and the unemployed (one in three unemployed people was poor, while among the whole population capable of work one in five was poor). Finally, there were workers with a low standard of education: the probability of falling below the poverty line for people with only primary education was 50 per cent higher than in the population as a whole.

A separate section of the World Bank report drew attention to the regional aspect of poverty, in the aim of tracing the marked differences between regions as regards living standards and the related issue of the structure of poverty in Russia. Huge regional differences were revealed between proportions of poor people, which varied from 3.1 per cent to 55.6 per cent in 2002. Moreover, it was mainly the populations of small, remote towns that were suffering, as well as inhabitants of depressed regions.

As we shall see, the alternative quantitative assessments of the structure and extent of poverty provided by the World Bank diverge from the official ones. Using the official methodology, based on the indicator of monetary incomes, 25 per cent of the population of Russia was below the poverty line in 2002; according to the World Bank, the figure was 19.6 per cent. This may be connected with the fact that there is a higher proportion of pensioners in the officially calculated Rosstat poverty index (as well as with some other factors that do not really merit detailed explanation).

Be that as it may, there is general dissatisfaction with methods of measuring poverty. In their analyses of poverty, many researchers have therefore started to make active use of the broader base of the Rosstat microeconomic data (and previously, from Goskomstat of Russia) given by the Observations of Household Budgets (OHB). The OHB is a regular statistical investigation of tens of thousands of Russian households, which has been conducted since 1952. However, it must be stressed that it is practically impossible to rely on OHB data when analysing poverty in Russia dynamically on the basis of changes in the income levels of various population groups: over that period of time, the social and economic regime in Russia has changed, against a background of unremitting large-scale inflation accompanied by transition to the market and a number of monetary reforms, while in 1992 and 1998 a significant part of Russians' savings was wiped out. Therefore, although measurements of the dynamics of incomes over time are widely used in research into stratification and other topics (especially health) in the West (Benzeval and Judge, 2001), in Russia such calculations will inevitably suffer from lack of comparability of data.

In addition to the weakness of this and other statistical databases, until recently there was still ignorance of a broad spectrum of other available resources, not economic in nature, which have an effect on maintaining people's material welfare. One attempt to study precisely this aspect of the issue in quantitative terms was undertaken within the framework of the unique Rosstat research programme, NOBUS (National investigation of the welfare of the population and its participation in social programmes). This investigation was carried out in 2003 with the financial support of the World Bank. The size of the randomised sample was 44,500 households from 79 regions of Russia, which enabled representative evaluations to be obtained at the pan-Russian, local and regional (for 46 regions) levels. In income and expenditure characteristics, this study corresponds to the OHB and to official statistical data, which were used as control indicators in the course of the analysis. But the main feature introduced by NOBUS was the additional assessment of disposable resources, including all the household's monetary and non-monetary receipts. As a result, for example, when the data were processed, people who had a second home were not included among the poor.

The main aim of this study was to collect information on employment and on the incomes and expenditures of households. Data analysis (in which both international and Russian experts took part), combined with a review of published official statistics, allowed an analysis of the rate, profile and causes of Russian poverty. In the course of this, the effectiveness of the official index of the number of poor people in the population (which, we should recall, is defined in Russia as the proportion of the population with incomes below the subsistence minimum) was called into doubt. Experts concluded that it is far from always the case that this indicator can be considered a good measure of poverty, especially in analysing the effect of given social policies on the poor. From Ovcharova's (2005) point of view, the most informative thing on the latter subject is the per capita income deficit indicator, expressed in percentages of the subsistence minimum; however, data on this cannot be found in officially published sources.

Assessments of the scale of poverty in Russia based on analysis of NOBUS data do not coincide with assessments of the poverty rate based on other sources. NOBUS showed higher scales of poverty by comparison with official data: 26 per cent of households and 33.4 per cent of the population. Many Russian researchers have therefore come to the conclusion that it is better to rely on NOBUS data about disposable resources in order to reveal the particular features of Russian poverty. Overall, these give a more reliable assessment of real material welfare, since they take into account non-monetary sources of consumption.

So, even where only methods that assume an absolute approach to poverty are applied, attempts to measure poverty in Russia using the methods described have resulted in significant discrepancies, both in numbers of poor people and in the structure of poverty itself. However, any serious researcher in the field of poverty knows that there are not just one but at least three conceptions of how to measure poverty. These are the absolute, the subjective and the relative (or deprivation) concepts.

The application at a national level of the relative approach to assessments of poverty is statistically difficult and expensive; however, the results of specialised sociological research can be helpful here. If not only the income/expenditure aspect of Russians' lives is used in assessing poverty, but also certain indicators that are important for the relative concept of poverty – such as accumulated property potential, the structure of consumption, the dynamic of opportunities for consumption, available resources (and not just material ones) – then poverty in Russia takes on the following specific features. According to the pan-Russian representative survey 'Rich and poor in contemporary Russia', conducted in March 2003 (organised by the Institute for Multi-disciplinary Social Research of the Russian Academy of Sciences; sample size, 2,315 households), no less than 23 per cent of Russian households were living below the poverty line at the time of the survey (see Gorshkov and Tikhonova, 2004). According to assessments by the Institute of Sociology, based on its 2006 research, one in five Russian families was living in poverty, measured by lack of resources and by deprivations experienced.

The results obtained also showed that the average age of members of poor strata does not differ significantly from the age of the statistically average respondent taking part in these research studies. (Therefore, the conclusion that the poor are mainly pensioners suffering from the reforms can hardly be claimed as a true reflection of reality.) However, the poor are different from others in the demographic composition of their households. The proportion of families with a large number of children, lone-parent families and families with other types of problems (in particular, multi-generational families that include pensioners, disabled people and children at the same time) is higher than in the population as a whole. In addition, there is an obvious trend for Russian poverty to shift towards small towns and rural settlements. The part of the population which is below the poverty line differs appreciably from others in its possibilities of having even a minimal set of essential property items. Moreover, a distinct trend can be tracked in which gradual wear and tear on the main consumer durables (television, fridge, everyday items of furniture, washing machine) leaves people in a situation where it is completely impossible for them to renew these. Things were also more or less as bad with other aspects of their resources: ownership of immovable property, opportunities to accrue savings or to use fee-paying services (in the first instance, essential medical services), etc.

Thus, on the wave of criticism of traditional methods, interest has increased in Russia over the last ten years in the newest sociological approaches to understanding and measuring poverty. Here we are speaking, primarily, of the concept of relative poverty considered to have been pioneered by Peter Townsend (1993). In addition, some Russian sociologists are starting to come to the conclusion that it is possible to understand Russian poverty and investigate not just its true scale but also its essence, specific nature and prospects only through longitudinal research studies and with wide use of qualitative methods. At the same time, these approaches may help to obtain answers to many other questions connected with poverty: Who are the majority of the Russian poor? How do they live? What has been the dynamic of their living standards over the years of reform, and what should be used to define it? How meagre are their resources, and how should these be supplemented? ... and so on.

The largest longitudinal sample study of households, implemented from 1992 to the present day, is the Russian Longitudinal Monitoring Survey, or RLMS for short (Swafford, 1997). The uniqueness of this research lies not only in the

Table 5.2   Level and depth of poverty among households, 1992 to 2004, RLMS (%)

Level of poverty	Distribution across years						
	1992	1996	1998	2000	2002	2003	2004
Below 50 per cent of poverty line	3.0	18.5	15.9	9.1	5.5	5.1	3.2
From 50 per cent to 100 per cent of poverty line	8.1	16.1	22.2	17.4	9.1	8.0	6.3
Households below the poverty line	11.1	34.6	38.1	26.5	14.6	13.1	9.5

Source: Mroz, Henderson and Popkin (2005); see also Swafford, Kosolapov and Kozyreva (1999).

fact that, over the course of 15 years, it has carried out large-scale monitoring of families living at the same addresses where they originally joined the sample, but also in the fact that it may be used as a panel survey, allowing us to track the fate of specific households and individuals (children and adults) over the period from 1992 to 2005. Moreover, it covers various groups in the population and provides information about the dynamics of a wide range of economic and social indicators, which characterise the circumstances of Russian households and individuals in the conditions of a transitional economy. In addition, this study was one of the first in Russia to move from the level of the individual to the level of the household.

Taking all this into account, it is not surprising that RLMS data for the whole reform period serve as a distinctive alternative to official statistics in conditions where many of the most important statistical indicators (such as the population's health, the structure of its nutrition, the distribution of incomes and expenditures, the dynamic in its standard of welfare, etc.) have been either unobtainable or insufficiently reliable. Apart from anything else, these data have been extremely important in calculations related to defining poverty in Russia, and they are actively used in this regard. Practically all assessments of the living standards of Russians, whether carried out in Russia or abroad, are based on analysing the structure of average per capita expenditures taken from RLMS data. Although its main trends coincide with results obtained by applying other methodologies, analysis of RLMS results nevertheless differs markedly from the rest, in that it sets much lower indicators of the level of poverty (see Table 5.2).

As is evident from the above table, the scale of poverty calculated on the basis of the distribution of the population of Russia according to expenditure, based on RLMS data over recent years, in fact differs by 2½ times from the level of poverty recorded by NOBUS and by a whole range of authoritative sociological centres that rely on representative data. (In fact, it also differs by 1½ times from the official statistics, which are distinctly underestimated.) This leads to the suggestion that, despite the obvious pluses of the RLMS in analysing poverty, it clearly lacks a sufficiently well-thought-out methodology for defining the poverty line itself.

In addition, subjective assessments of their own material circumstances by people themselves (usually based on comparisons with their pre-reform status or with reference groups who in practice have other, higher standards of living) do not guarantee complete reliability of data. Right up to the year 2000, more than half of Russians considered that they were materially badly off (that is, in fact, poor), and although in recent years this indicator has fallen to one-third, it nevertheless differs significantly from poverty indicators calculated using other methods. In reality, no direct relationship can be observed between subjective self-assessments and people's actual standard of welfare. The relationship is more in the nature of a trend, as has been shown more than once by Zaslavskaya (1996) and a number of other researchers looking at the socio-economic situation. So, according to the pan-Russian representative survey 'Rich and poor in contemporary Russia' (2003), 37 per cent of Russians considered that they were poor, while only 21 per cent of respondents could really be acknowledged as poor on the basis of their incomes (that is, they had incomes of no more than 60 per cent of the median) (see Gorshkov and Tikhonova, 2004).

It was precisely the inadequacy and the contradictory nature of interpretations of data for understanding the specific and characteristic features of Russian poverty that prompted our research team to continue its series of joint research projects. The main feature of these has been their particular accent on the use of primarily qualitative methods in trying to assess and verify phenomena and trends revealed by statistical data and pan-Russian quantitative surveys.

Analysing Poverty Through Qualitative Methods

As has already been mentioned above, all our research into poverty, conducted jointly with Western colleagues and using qualitative methods, has taken as its basis the concept of relative poverty proposed and developed by Peter Townsend. It is this concept that, as we had already established (Manning and Tikhonova, 2004), corresponds most closely with Russians' own views of what poverty is.

The aim of the research we undertook, described in Chapter 1, was to reveal fully the main features and the specific nature of poverty in Russia. In the course of market reforms, which population groups were more susceptible to risk of impoverishment than others? What was the dynamic of their poverty, and what factors, in the final analysis, meant that some remained stuck in poverty, while others managed to get out of it?

We chose to base our research on a multivariate approach to assessing poverty and the dynamics of the overall situation in the households we tracked: that is, a concept of multiple deprivation. This was, in the first instance, because our main aim was to gain an understanding of the essence of the phenomenon, not to measure it precisely. The research group started from the point of view that an in-depth analysis of deprivation and the limits on social participation should primarily articulate the 'threshold', below which need grows abruptly to the point where it may be putting the household on the edge of social exclusion; that is, de facto exclusion from the activities of normal life in a Russian community. This related to Townsend's (1987) hypothesis that, where the degree of measured deprivation remains above a certain 'deprivation threshold', the household's material circumstances then deteriorate more slowly and less obviously, so the dynamic of change is less of an 'avalanche'. The issue of poverty within the framework of this approach is simultaneously both process and result: the growth of deprivation and restrictions on the generally accepted set of essential goods and types of activity, which is linked with lack of resources, is evidence of the dynamic of a falling standard of living; and poverty as a deep, self-generating state – from which, once you have entered it, it is extremely difficult or practically impossible to escape – is connected with crossing a certain qualitative threshold in the experience of deprivation.

Our main difficulties in applying this approach lay primarily in the fact that there had been no experience in Russia of conducting this type of research. In addition, the application of this approach presupposed that three main methodological objectives would be tackled: 1) how to define indicators of deprivation; 2) to what extent they provide evidence of a reduction in the generally accepted standard of living for a given community; 3) how to define, as applied to Russian conditions, the qualitative 'deprivation thresholds' that enable us to make an assessment of the living standards of a given household. However, all these objectives in some way or another had already been tackled in previous (non-Russian) research studies; the deprivation approach has already undergone scientific appraisal in many countries of Europe and has proved its theoretical and heuristic significance. In this case, invaluable help was provided by our Western colleagues who took part in the joint projects: Peter Abrahamson (1998) and John Veit-Wilson (1999) (see also Mack and Lansley, 1985; Townsend, Gordon and Gosschack, 1996).

In our first two projects, we were able to study particular features of Russian unemployment in the post-reform period. The chief one was the fact that unemployment was in large part hidden. This in many ways predetermined the impoverishment of people affected by it, since they were outside the boundaries of state guardianship. We were also able, using a combination of expert and survey methods, to explore with poor people themselves the 'absences' that they most associated with extreme poverty, in order to define indicators of deprivation that are typical of poverty in Russia. From our conversations with respondents, it also became clear that their impoverishment had various depths and causes. For some, it was connected with the negative consequences of the recent reforms; for others, poverty was persistent in nature and had grown from roots put down in the Soviet era. (These people, as a rule, had a whole set of disadvantageous sociodemographic characteristics traditionally associated with poverty: a low level of skills, a large number of children, harmful habits, etc.) It became clear that the differentiation that has arisen among the poor themselves, who may be 'old' or 'new', 'stuck' in poverty or 'drifting' into it, should be taken into account in any well-designed social policy measures to combat poverty.

A separate problem that we encountered in carrying out our first two research projects was the phenomenon of social exclusion, which has also been very little studied in Russia. Our data directly showed that social exclusion, in reproducing poverty again and again, exhausted not only people's material but also their social resources. Employment crisis and prolonged loss of any connection with a workplace led to the destruction of social ties, change in the model of social participation, deformation of the social environment and social isolation, which in turn all start to have a serious impact on people's prospects of getting out of their difficult situation. People experience the destruction of their habitual social bonds, and so access to additional resources for survival becomes narrower. As a consequence of this, deprivation starts to grow swiftly; multiple deprivations come into play, affecting all aspects of life.

The idea for our most recent project arose because, on the one hand, in the course of the previous research projects, we had established that poor health often generates poverty and the growth of exclusion, and, on the other hand, we needed to investigate what had really happened with Russian poverty over the intervening period – in particular, in the households we were studying. As has been shown above, the statistical situation with poverty had significantly improved over the whole period of reform implementation; the Russian authorities have recently been inclined to connect this with steady growth in the economy over many years. According to World Bank data from 1999 to 2002, about 30 million Russians have exited poverty, which in percentage terms means a twofold reduction in the poverty rate (according to the World Bank, 2005, method): from 41.5 per cent in 1999 to 19.6 per cent in 2002.

We should point out that something in the order of two-thirds of our sample already consisted of people who were deprived according to the results of our first research project. A quarter of those surveyed were actually poor: i.e. living below the poverty line. The second research project had revealed that it was precisely those who had already been living below the poverty line during the first project who were affected by a negative dynamic: that is, five years after the first survey, many households were 'entrenched' in poverty.

This research, our third project, has shown that it was precisely those who were previously living in poverty who were again affected to the greatest degree by a further fall in living standards: that is, their deprivation continued to grow over the course of time – in fact, over a full ten years of observation. Moreover, according to data from all three research projects, there was only an insignificant reduction in the actual proportion of poor people, defined on the basis of the deprivation method, despite the improvement in Russia's economic situation (see Table 5.3).

To this we should add that one in three households (29 per cent) in our most recent survey expressed extreme dissatisfaction with their material circumstances. One-third of respondents also confirmed that, over the three years preceding the 2005 survey, they had experienced a serious reduction in living standards. Moreover,

Table 5.3   Material circumstances of respondent households, 1997 to 2005 (%)*

Standard of material welfare	1997	2000	2005
Poor	31	32	25
Badly-off	34	45	31
Averagely well-off	35	23	44

* The index of multiple deprivation, which we used to assess the level of welfare of participants in our research, was calculated on the basis of a unified method at all points in the longitudinal survey. For more details, see Davidova (2004), as well as the appendix to the present volume.

the town in which they lived did not play any special part here, and it should be noted that Voronezh nowadays does not number among Russia's depressed or disadvantaged regions – and Moscow could hardly be described as such! – so the problem is clearly not linked with the regional labour market situation.

In the method we adopted, our respondents' standard of material welfare was defined according to the presence in their families of significant deprivations. Moreover, the results of our previous projects confirmed that a qualitative 'welfare threshold' really exists, and this in turn led to one of our most important conclusions: in any approach to assessing poverty on the basis of deprivation, both the quantitative and the qualitative aspects of deprivation must be defined. There is no doubt that the less widespread a particular deprivation in everyday life, the greater its weight as 'actual proof' of poverty, where poverty is a state of marked deviation from generally accepted living standards. At the same time, as it moves farther away from real poverty, deprivation starts to become mainly social, rather than material, in nature. Some types of deprivations are seen by the overwhelming majority of people as undoubted signs of poverty and therefore their presence means the most profound need: extreme deprivation, or 'crossing the threshold'. Other indicators are less distinctly associated with (especially, extreme) poverty, moving through a middle position and then a gradation of those that are less significant from the point of view of describing poverty precisely, towards those that reflect some restrictions on an average way of life in a given community, rather than poverty.

It was important for us to understand how far, over these years, the actual structure of the deprivations experienced by the poor has changed, what restrictions they have to suffer now and in what direction their further impoverishment (if any) is moving. In other words: what is the portrait of Russian poverty in our 1997–2005 sample? What features and phenomena were typical of it then, and are now? Surely the fact that, over these years, the socioeconomic situation in Russia has in many ways normalised – with the majority of average statistical indicators demonstrating growth in economic activity, incomes and consumption – must somehow also be reflected in the circumstances of the poor? That is, from the point of view of a relative approach to the analysis of poverty, the set of deprivations that makes it impossible to achieve a generally accepted way of life in a given society must change along with an increase in living standards and quality of life for the rest of the population.

We also tried to verify how far this hypothesis was true and what the real situation of the poor in Russia has been in the time dimension, using the results of our observations over many years. We should add that the advantages of qualitative longitudinal methods for tackling such research objectives became especially evident.

If we review the situation in a typical poor Russian family in the late 1990s, then it is easy to see that, in the main, there were not enough resources for adequate food, and that economies were made in this area even where there were children in the family. This did not mean that Russians went hungry (although our research did record some such cases), but we can say with complete accuracy that in practice the poor had no fresh meat or fish; their consumption of fresh fruit and vegetables, juices and even treats for children was restricted. Many complained about lack of clothing and shoes; they found it difficult to keep their home in good repair, or acquire enough simple everyday furniture (quite apart from the fact that it was even difficult to renew everyday household appliances). It was their social life that sustained extreme restrictions due to poverty: people were forced to deny themselves the traditional Russian styles of social contact such as inviting people round and going visiting. Having worthwhile rest and recreation did not even come into the picture. Finally (and this is very important for us in the light of the objectives of our third project), the Russian poor in the late 1990s often could not afford vital medicines and medical appliances, and sometimes even personal hygiene products, because of their severe lack of monetary resources.

The Persistence of Poverty

So what is the picture of Russian poverty today? What has changed over the intervening years? Firstly, it must be noted that the situation with clothing and hygiene products has not been as severe. Poor families were economising on food and children's requirements to a lesser extent than in 1997. Although previously one-third of the poor could not afford fresh meat or fish more often than once every week or two (compared to only one in ten of the badly-off), the data from our most recent research shows that only three poor families out of 24 were still in this situation. Nevertheless, the quality of nutrition for the poor remains low, including a large proportion of processed foods, carbohydrates and tinned foods. It is enough to state that, in 2005, as before, over half of those surveyed were having fresh protein foods less often than twice a week, while up to 70 per cent of the poor had fresh fruit and juices only rarely (four out of 24 poor families in 2005 said that they could not afford them at all). Naturally, this situation is not typical of the quality of nutrition in the other groups that we established on the basis of their standard of welfare.

Table 5.4   Deprivations experienced by the families of our respondents, 1997–2005 (%)

Cannot afford:	Poor		Badly-off		Averagely well-off	
	1997	2005	1997	2005	1997	2005
To buy clothing and shoes	84	50	28	9	5	7
To renew consumer durables	78	75	60	26	19	7
To visit or invite people round	73	50	31	17	7	0
To use fee-paying services	84	71	66	26	27	15

However, the main thing that must be noted in the dynamic of living standards and the structure of deprivations of the Russian poor today is that it is practically impossible for them to renew or improve their own living environment. It was the poor who were absolutely unable to renew household appliances or buy consumer durables, and problems even frequently arose for them with the purchase of clothing and shoes – all because of chronic lack of monetary resources.

Although it would have been the case that living standards in the 1990s did not allow the majority of Russians to satisfy even the most pressing requirements for their family (since this was a time of prolonged economic crisis, with large-scale wage and pension delays), Table 5.4 shows that, by 2005, the situation had changed somewhat. The need to restrict themselves absolutely and the impossibility of affording any additional expenditures, apart from the most pressing, remain primarily the preserve of the poor, whereas in the late 1990s it was not only they but also the badly-off, and even some averagely well-off Russians, who had to face these problems. Moreover, the typical portrait of a poor Russian in those years would also have to mention their loss of hope of doing anything to change their own life for the better, the degradation of their property and living environment and the housing they occupied, the increasing inaccessibility of medical and educational services (see Chapter 8), and many other non-material aspects of poverty, not least the inaccessibility to the majority of Russians of varied leisure pursuits and worthwhile rest.

So, over the last few years, Russian poverty has acquired some new features and become a more complex, varied phenomenon, since improvements in some areas of life have been accompanied by deterioration in others. This is especially typical of those who are in persistent poverty.

In this connection, we need to understand precisely what proportion of poor households are in persistent poverty. Judging by the households we studied, no less than half of poor households are in this situation. In fact, in the cities where our research was carried out, things were slightly better than across Russia as a whole, offering a few more possibilities of escaping poverty; but, even so, half our

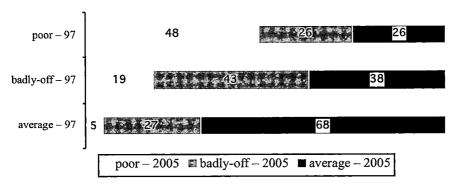

Figure 5.1   Dynamics in living standards of respondents in our panel study (1997–2005)

panel respondents were living in persistent poverty (see Figure 5.1). This is also confirmed by the fact that, in the Institute of Sociology's 2006 research, half the poor said that their position over the last few years had remained unchanged, and 45 per cent even said that it was relatively worse.

As can be seen from Figure 5.1, about half the members of each group defined by standard of material welfare can be said to have been in a relatively stable position. This allows us to speak with some certainty of the formation of large-scale persistent poverty, even in big cities, which are relatively prosperous compared to Russia as a whole. This trend can also be observed among those 2005 respondents who had not participated in the 1997 research into unemployment, but had joined the panel for the 1999 investigation of poverty (whose situation, therefore, could not be shown in Figure 5.1). There were 18 such respondents in our sample (n=87), and all of them were from Moscow or Voronezh. At the time of the most recent survey, the standard of material welfare remained unchanged for about half of those who were badly off in 1999 and for two-thirds of those who were averagely well off. As for the 1999 poor, their situation was even worse than that of the 2005 sample as a whole, with 90 per cent of them continuing to live in poverty.

How then do our long-term respondents interpret the dynamic of their own lives? Let us give a few examples.

From the 1980s to the 1990s you might say that I prospered both emotionally and materially, and lived completely respectably. And then perestroika began, with a complete shift in what the state did, and as a result everything 'went over the side' for us. The most unpleasant events that have taken place over recent years have been the change in direction by the government, and older people being made redundant. It was up in the air, whether or not they would find work. Essentially, they weren't taking older people on in jobs. That was a really bad blow to my material circumstances. But not only materially – emotionally as well. (Ekaterina, aged 63 at interview, a pensioner from Kazan' who joined our panel in 1997 aged 56.)

In Chechnya in 1995 we were in a really difficult position, absolutely catastrophic. In the most difficult year, because of that – because of the war, we lost everything. When I went down to Chechnya, I saw that nobody was working: you know what it means to go hungry. And then here in Moscow it's turned out to be very difficult, the years have been unlucky. You start to do something, the deal is taking shape, but everything falls through because of some muddle. In 1998, there was a crisis, everyone lost a lot then; it was hard for everyone, not just me, with values dropping by almost half. And now prices are increasing and they ask for dollars. It's being done deliberately. (Abukhasan, a small trader/entrepreneur in Moscow, who joined our panel in 1999; see also the second book in our trilogy and Chapter 11 of this book.)

The reforms brought a sharp alteration in our social status. We lost stability, inflation 'ate up' our wages; we live in a situation where we constantly have to restrict ourselves. All this has an impact on the microclimate in the family. It's because of a particular kind of tiredness from problems related to survival. Because in principle a person must get on with his job at work – that is, carry out duties of some kind and carry them out properly – while at home he is busy with the family, trying to get some kind of break for everyone. And when that doesn't come about, when, as it were, at work you're thinking only about how to earn money and at home only about that ... the general psychological atmosphere is difficult – and it's just the material problems of recent years that underlie everything. (Viktor, aged 50, leading engineer at a defence industry institute, Moscow; father of five, with one son disabled; he suffered continually deteriorating health; see also the second book in our trilogy.)

This is the picture that our respondents gave of their life situations. They themselves partially defined the causes of their material disorders as being independent of the restrictions on their chances to overcome them. Moreover, our research projects together show that the state's social policy has practically no influence on the situation. Over the ten years during which we have observed these people, no measures of social or any other kind of policy have helped the most deprived. The data provided marked evidence of the fact that they have remained in poverty.

Thus, whatever the method used to establish who is poor, it is obvious not only that there is large-scale poverty in Russia, but also that large-scale persistent poverty, affecting many millions of people, really exists there and is being reproduced – a situation which cannot be put to rights, given its profile and the factors involved, by the methods that the government is currently proposing. However, given the mass nature of this phenomenon, it is essential to take a differentiated approach to different groups of poor people. Each group needs its own strategy for overcoming poverty. In any case, it must be borne in mind that more than half of the poor are people of working age, three-quarters of whom have no skills resources. It is precisely people in this category who are in need of active forms of employment creation, with resource allocations needed for vocational training and retraining, and not just income support (Tikhonova, 2003).

In the last few years, a new 'package' of social reforms has come into force in Russia, initiated by the government (see Chapter 1). In brief, its essence and intention seem to be that it plans to place on the shoulders of the population itself at least part of the responsibility for tackling a whole range of social problems (primarily those connected with health, education and housing). It hardly needs to be said that this almost completely excludes a significant proportion of Russians from access to any means of satisfying pressing vital requirements and from access to growth in overall living standards. There is already a marked gap between the initial opportunities of poor and non-poor Russians, in addition to which the majority of poor people have specific characteristics of social disadvantage. All this is likely to further deepen social inequality in the very near future and, in the end, preserve it.

Thus, first and foremost, politicians, experts and ordinary Russians must refrain from creating myths around issues as serious as the scales of poverty in Russia and the outlook for the poor: this merely hinders understanding of the problems and reduces the effectiveness of social policy in combating poverty. And, although the Russian political elite has recently been trying to move society towards the belief that large-scale poverty in Russia can really be eradicated in just a few years, we must remember that it is impossible to avoid seeing its true scale and severity or to overcome it just by manipulating figures.

Chapter 6
Poverty and Health: The Longitudinal Experience

Nadia Davidova

Без друзей да без связи – как доктор без мази
Being without friends and connections is like being a doctor without ointment

The Intersection of Health and Poverty

In the previous chapter, we examined how the situation with poverty in Russia has changed over the course of time, using examples drawn from people's real lives, and looked briefly at the reasons for a reduction in the living standards of a particular section of the population over the last two decades. However, there remains one major question: why some households get 'stuck' in poverty and their deprivation becomes more profound, while others, in contrast, cope with their difficulties and get out of poverty. It must be said that, in recent years, quite a lot of specialised research has been devoted to tackling this issue. In particular, we would like to refer to the results of two pieces of research that looked especially at the factors involved in entry to persistent poverty. The authors of these have concluded that prolonged poverty is strongly correlated with family size, with the presence of children and pensioners in the family, with certain characteristics of the head of the family, with place of residence and also whether any family members are unemployed (Spryskov, 2000; Poduzov and Kukushkin, 2002). In this regard, we would like to draw attention to one factor which our respondents constantly mentioned, but which for some reason is never reflected in the Russian sociological literature on causes of poverty: the influence of a person's state of health on their entry into persistent poverty. Moreover, the link between poverty and health has long been established – and repeatedly confirmed – through research conducted in various countries (Oppenheim and Harker, 1996; Bartley, 2004). Thus, for example, it has been noted that when people move into a lower social class they have fewer opportunities to use medical care than if they still had a higher standard of living. In addition, income inequality and insecurity in life cause persistent psychosocial stress, which over time leads to destruction of health and to high mortality (Wilkinson, 1997).

In Russia, the situation is exacerbated firstly by the fact that, as a result of many years of stresses arising from the economic reforms (which have caused not only large-scale impoverishment but also a qualitative shift in the whole habitual lifestyle of the Russian population), the health of the population started to deteriorate especially quickly. According to data from the Centre for Demography and Human Ecology of the Institute for Economic Forecasting (Russian Academy of Sciences), many Russians face difficulties in their struggle just to exist: in recent decades, over 70 per cent of them have been in a state of 'prolonged psychological, emotional and social stress' (see Andreyev et al., 2000). And, secondly, in parallel with the economic reforms, social reforms – including reform of health care – were initiated, and these have made access to good-quality medical care even more difficult for the most restricted social strata.

These circumstances were also confirmed in the course of our research. Thus, the 2004 survey of our longitudinal panel showed (as in all previous stages of the research) that, in practice, if a family remained in poverty, this meant that the health of its members would become worse, both according to objective indicators of their physical, psychological and emotional state, and according to people's own assessments of their health. Practically 40 per cent of poor respondents (ten out of 24) said that they were in poor health. By comparison, in groups with a higher level of material welfare, three respondents out of 63 gave the same assessment. Even despite the fact that the poor people taking part in our survey were somewhat older than the rest (their average age was 50, while respondents from the non-poor families were on average 44 to 45 years old), differences in their own assessments of their health were more than perceptible. It must be said that not only the health of the respondents themselves but also the health of their families provided stark evidence of a lack of well-being and the presence of specific, disturbing trends. Thus, our research established that half of poor households had at least one disabled member, as against only in one in four of the badly-off households and one in five of the averagely well-off households.

In addition, the use of the EuroQol scale for people to assess their own health, which we pioneered in Russia, also demonstrated that even if health does not determine poverty, then it most probably accompanies it. The average current health status score of the poorest group was 0.49, compared to an average of 0.72–0.75 in the better-off groups.

It should be pointed out that, in answer to the direct question as to how their health had changed over the years of reform, two-thirds of respondents said that it had deteriorated. Naturally, this reflects all the factors particular to Russia mentioned in the previous chapter, in our review of the costs and social consequences of the reforms for the population as a whole. However, poor people mention the loss of their health significantly more often (in practically 90 per cent of cases). Here are a few quotations from our interviews with members of the respondent households, which shed light on how they felt in their post-reform circumstances.

> What should I say? Recently I've been living so that I have to choose: either you buy medicines, or you buy food. Of course, you buy food, and you don't buy medicines. You're hardly going to let yourself starve. Probably I'm not healthy, since I've lived through so many unpleasant things in life over all these years: I've lost my job, I've worked where I didn't want to, my daughter's gone abroad, I don't have enough money. I'm constantly going through painful experiences. (Nina, aged 54, nurse at a district clinic in Kazan'.)

A lot of things have influenced my health in the last ten years. That is, it is impossible to travel where you want, even to walk where you want; it is impossible even to meet your friends when you want. That is, there are no opportunities to restore your health, to rest, only to work in order to feed yourself and your family. The situation in recent years has been one of low pay, with no light at the end of the tunnel; and not everyone can cope with it – some take to drink, some degrade themselves, and family and personal relationships deteriorate. (Sveta, 41, kindergarten music teacher, Voronezh.)

A lot of people I know have scarcely enough to sustain themselves; this is true of my relations and other people of the older generation; they're all pensioners, and if they don't find some additional earnings, they become poor; it is also difficult for people working in the public sector. My mum cut back and now she's given herself anaemia – the reason for it is nutritional, and hers is not an isolated case. It's hard to say whether there have been any periods more difficult than this one: we had a lot of difficulties before as well, but times like that were just episodes – you could get through them. Now we just have the feeling that there's no way out. (Alla, 57, a disability benefit claimant from Moscow; divorced, living with her mother and her non-working daughter – see also Chapters 2 and 9.)

While many participants in our research said that their own health had deteriorated – connecting this to a certain degree with the difficulties of transition to the market in Russia, with insecurity and with 'nerves' – it was the poorest members of our longitudinal panel who were more likely than others to say that difficult material circumstances in the family and the absence of necessary treatment (or preventive measures to care for their health), resulting from lack of resources, were the main reasons for their currently feeling unwell. Half our poor respondents talked about this (as opposed to one in ten of the averagely well-off respondents). Apart from this, a quarter of poor respondents complained about poor (meaning poor-quality) food, harmful habits and an unhealthy lifestyle, all of which had had a negative effect on their health in recent years.

Alcohol

We would now like to go into more detail about this last factor. Frequently, it was the alcohol or drug dependency of one member of the family (most often the male breadwinner) that had caused the family's impoverishment and their slide over the poverty line, and had then made it impossible for them to get out of the situation. There is an obvious feedback effect here, in which a way of life that consciously undermines health leads in the end to the exhaustion of resources and then to the growth of deprivation, and consequently predetermines the family's persistently indigent existence. Many sociologists studying persistent poverty and the health of the Russian population indicate the presence of this problem, especially Finnish academics who have investigated alcoholism in Russia (Simpura and Levin, 1997).

Turning to the data we obtained, we should first mention that, over the period of observation, some respondents from households taking part in our panel study died. In two cases, these were elderly people (a man and a woman born in 1929 and 1933 respectively); in two further cases, the cause of death of the man and the woman concerned was cardiovascular disease (both born in 1948, and both just over 50 years old at the time of death); finally, two further deaths turned out to be directly connected with alcohol dependency – and, at the same time, with profound poverty in the households of these people. These were two men born in 1972 and 1956. As we shall see, even this small, sad statistic is evidence of the fact that, in Russia, alcohol and other harmful habits are frequently – directly or indirectly – the cause of deterioration in health and in standard of living. Moreover, although well-off respondents were also susceptible to individual harmful habits (for example, smoking), the problem of alcoholism was concentrated in the groups with low living standards. And, although one in four families who were maintaining an average standard of living stated that one of their members had a problem with alcoholism, in the poorest families this was a serious problem for almost half – 11 households out of 24. This tendency manifested itself especially starkly in Kazan', where five out of six of the poorest households told us there were problems of alcohol abuse; Voronezh and Moscow were far behind, with three out of nine families in each of these cities.

However, it would be absolutely untrue to ascribe all the misfortunes and disorders of the poor solely to the respondents themselves. The fact was that their deprivation had reached such a level that they had practically no opportunities for worthwhile recreation or to recoup their energies. In addition, it is worth drawing attention to the fact that one in three poor households had a working family member who at some time had suffered an industrial injury, while up to 80 per cent of respondents from poor households who were capable of work were convinced that their work was detrimental to their health. By comparison, in better-off households, up to 80 per cent of people had never had an industrial injury, and they were significantly less likely to consider their own job harmful (this was especially notable in the averagely well-off group, where respondents were employed in more skilled posts that did not involve physical labour). When asked why they did not change their job if they were certain that it was harmful to their health, the poorest replied that 'I have to earn a crust' or 'there simply are no other jobs'.

Employment

In this regard, it is essential to take into account that half our respondents were the main breadwinner in the family, and in some cases the sole breadwinner: in one out of three poor families, there were no other working people (this was true for three out of 24 badly-off families, and for just one out of 39 averagely well-off families). In other words, poor people were much more likely than others to find themselves in a situation where they had no one they could really count on. Moreover, in 15 cases out of 24 (i.e. two-thirds) poor households were headed by women (the gender distribution in other families was 50:50 – in other words, there was an equal probability that the household would be headed by a man or by a woman). Half of heads of households that were in poverty had no spouse (five of them were widowed, three divorced and another five never married), so for them it was extremely difficult to count on any additional material or psychological support. Again, we should note that this situation was characteristic of only one in three of our better-off respondent households.

So, given the difficult situation they were in, people stuck to any job they had, in order to feed themselves and their family – even if this job was, in their opinion, detrimental to their health. So what kinds of jobs were these? (See Table 6.1.)

Table 6.1   Employment of household respondents (%)

Nature of employment	Poor	Badly-off	Averagely well-off
Specialists and skilled white-collar workers	25	33	59
Auxiliary and service staff	18	13	8
Skilled blue-collar workers	12	16	5
Ancillary blue-collar workers; unskilled labourers	12	4	0
Self-employed; sporadically employed; engaged in unregistered employment	4	13	10
Unemployed	8	13	2
Pensioners	21	8	8
Non-employed; housewives/husbands	0	0	8

As we can see, in the 'poor' group there was a higher proportion of people employed in heavy manual, service or ancillary work. Yet they could not really aspire to any other kind, since their standard of education was significantly lower than that of the other members of our panel. Over half our respondents who were more successful materially had higher education, and only 10 per cent of respondents from families with an average standard of living had failed to continue their education beyond secondary level (and in half such cases, a higher standard of education was recorded for other family members, who were the main breadwinners). The situation of poor respondents was quite different: a third of them had no special vocational education, and only six out of 24 (that is, a quarter) had higher education and a specialist degree.

These highly-educated poor respondents mainly worked in specialist posts, but as a rule they were employed in low-paid branches of the public sector, including education, culture and State medicine. Moreover, many of them were in a difficult family situation: two families had a large number of children; in another, the woman was the only working person and had two adults dependent on her – her brother, who was disabled, and her disabled husband; our sample also contained a lone father who, over the whole ten years of our observation, was forced to maintain two sons under 18 and his dying, paralysed mother; and so on. These people really were in the poverty trap, from which even the fact that they had skilled paid employment could not save them. In order to make ends meet, other poor respondents were frequently forced to continue working at their old job (or find additional unregistered employment) even after they had started drawing their pension; they worked as hospital orderlies, janitors, cleaners – that is, they took on fairly heavy unskilled manual work. This could not fail to have an impact on their psychological state and on their health. Here is what they themselves said about their life and work.

> I know some people who are working in four places, just in order to survive somehow. They grab at any job. Single women run around grabbing these bits and pieces, in order to get through life somehow. (Yuliya, 56, organiser of the Centre for Psychological Support at Kazan' University, with the rank of deputy director.)

> People work all the same, even despite the fact that they are sick. There's one woman I know, she has breast cancer, but she works, she overcomes it, somehow she sticks at it. Because life is hard, you have to work. (Natal'ya, 46, unemployed, Voronezh.)

> A lot of people work now with a great deal of difficulty; they're forced to, since they have to live. You know, among people of my age, almost everyone is sick. One of my friends came to see me not long ago. Now she's just working until she is worn out, in two places at once, without any days off at all. And so she came to me in a complete state: I took her blood pressure, and it was 170 over 110. And she's frightened of everything – especially if she were suddenly to lose her job, then she would simply have no way of paying for her flat. (Lyuba, 49, unemployed, Voronezh.)

The outlook for the health of the poor holds a danger of future deterioration because they are not in a position to restore the strength they have expended on hard physical work; and no less than 40 per cent of our poor respondents thought their work was physically hard – twice as many as among other people; another 57 per cent think that it was exhausting, as against one in five other respondents who saw their job in that light. In addition, their job frequently does not bring them satisfaction, which has an impact on their psychological state and intensifies their accumulated stresses. Only two working poor people considered their job interesting and only four were sure that it was secure, although practically half our remaining respondents (including the badly-off) valued their job precisely because it had these qualities. Thus, poor people's jobs can be characterised as generally of very low quality.

In this regard, it must be said that the problem of the working poor in Russia is extremely acute, and its essence, as applied to health, lies in the fact that increased workload and dissatisfaction with the results and nature of one's work frequently cause a further deterioration in health, which, in turn, reduces poor people's potential for work. It is possible to form a judgement about the mechanism and consequences of these mutual effects on the basis of the life stories of some of our working respondents, whose living standards fell constantly over the whole period of observation.

Take, for example, Dmitri, aged 39, from Moscow, who had joined our panel in 1996 at the age of 31 after being released from a building organisation when it went into voluntary liquidation. His usual occupation was a skilled one (technician and mechanic, which meant he had vocational secondary education), but throughout the whole period of reform he had to work in various other blue-collar posts, including doing unskilled heavy labour. Private firms, in which he was mainly employed, quite frequently went through crises or collapsed, and he often had to change his place of work. After a spell of unemployment in 1996–97, when he became disillusioned with the possibilities offered by the Employment Service, he retrained as a carpenter, on the advice of a friend – who also subsequently helped him find a job. However, until the late 1990s, his employment remained insecure (all depending on his employers' order books) and this had a marked effect on his family's material circumstances, which gradually deteriorated. For the whole period of observation, he was married with two children under 18. His wife also worked (as a cashier in a grocery shop). From 2000, the respondent understood that it was necessary to seek some kind of permanent job that would not be dependent on orders, and he found work at Spetselektrod, a privatised industrial enterprise, first as a porter ('because there were no other jobs any more') and then as a forklift driver in their large Moscow warehouse. He was still working there when we interviewed him again in 2005.

> At present, there's nothing that can improve our health. There is no security. If there were some kind of security – if prices were fixed, even just for a year – perhaps we would be able to plan our life. This insecurity keeps you in a constant state of tension. With life as it is now, there are no healthy people, I would say. People are always sick with something. Well, they are working, but all the same they have some kind of illnesses; it's just that they don't have the time to be sick. Up to a certain point in time, illnesses just lie dormant. But if there is some kind of stress, some kind of disagreement at work or in the family – then immediately, for some reason, some kind of illness appears. And then you don't want anything at all, you're in that state where you don't want to work, or to see or hear anyone. A decline in strength – that's what I'm describing. It goes on for a certain period of time – the stress, the burdens have an impact on you. There isn't enough money – all these things just accumulate. You have to find some kind of way to earn something, to feed your family and all that kind of thing. We don't get any sick pay now. Here, it's one of two things – either you're sick or you work. There's no third option. So, I know I've got a chronic illness – a stomach ulcer. It gets worse according to the seasons, but I don't go to the doctor, though now I have started taking the medicines that were prescribed for me five years ago. And if I do go to the doctor, well then – she says to me – 'You need time off sick, I'm signing you off for a month.' But I went back to work after a week, when it seemed as if things had quietened down, because they don't give us any sick pay and you have to earn money.

It is obvious that the respondent sees a connection between the deterioration in his health and the constant need to try and support his family, with resultant stresses and exacerbation of chronic disease. He does not like his job, primarily because it fails to maintain an acceptable standard of living for the family, which at the time of the last survey was poised on the boundary between being badly-off and poor (see also Chapter 7).

Rest

Returning to the question of poor people finding it impossible to afford worthwhile rest, it should be noted that only one poor family out of the 24 we surveyed said that the whole family could regularly travel outside the city. A few travelled outside the city on rare occasions, but essentially the majority of poor households never went away anywhere. Practically none of the poor respondents on our panel was able to afford to go on holiday to resorts; moreover, half the poor families had so narrowed their requirements that they rejected this completely, saying that they did not need to go. Here it should be noted that, in Russia nowadays, holidays at health resorts or other holiday centres, or at guesthouses, let alone tourist travel as such, are accessible to – and in reality taken by – only the middle strata of the population, and even then not always, since they are fairly expensive. As our research showed, the badly-off did little better than the poor in terms of worthwhile rest (see Table 6.2).

Table 6.2   Ways of spending leave from work x levels of material welfare, 2004 (%)

How leave was spent	Poor	Badly-off	Averagely well-off	Total
At home	50	25	18	29
At a dacha or staying with relations	29	34	28	30
At a health resort, guest house or holiday home	8	8	15	11
On a tourist trip	0	8	26	14
Had to work	13	25	13	16

The data in the table demonstrate that half our poor respondents spent their leave at home. Only two poor households had their own dacha (as levels of welfare increased, the figure for people who had acquired a dacha rose to one in three); for the other five who said that they went to a dacha or stayed with relations, this meant specifically a trip to visit relations in the country.

Pathways into Health

Thus, the conditions in which the poor exist, their living environment, their real opportunities and particular features of their behaviour all significantly predetermine the course of their life and also undoubtedly influence how they feel both physically and psychologically. We can look at this problem from the point of view of various pathways towards an understanding of the interrelationship of poverty and health. Whether these pathways are cultural and behavioural, psychosocial or materialist (see Bartley, 2004), clearly there is one obvious thing – the negative effect of poverty on the health of those people who are permanently in it. The results of our many years of observation confirm this; however, we have not yet obtained a distinct answer to the major question voiced at the very beginning of this analysis: to what degree is poor health a factor that keeps people in poverty and narrows their prospects for getting out of it?

We shall attempt to review the situation dynamically, using the example of the concrete life stories of our respondents and their families. Naturally, over the years of observation, the circumstances of each of our respondent families changed both for the better and for the worse, but here we are particularly interested in the stories of those families who were consistently 'stuck' in poverty, and in the link between persistent poverty and a deterioration in people's health.

In our research, we used various methodological approaches to determining state of health (see the appendix) but here, in the aim of comparing one method with another, each is reduced to a consolidated three-point assessment scale that records 'good' health, 'fair' health (with separate markers of ill-health) and sickness or 'poor' health. Where a five-point self-rating scale had originally been used, the health of those who rated their health as very good or good was now taken to be good, and as fair, satisfactory, while bad and very bad corresponded to poor health. Where the EQ-5D scale had been used, individual health indices, calculated in accordance with the methodology recommended by the EuroQol Group (Brooks with EuroQol Group, 1996) were consolidated on the principle that an index value of -0.18 to $+0.7$ was considered to represent poor health, a value of $+0.7$ to $+0.75$, satisfactory health and a value exceeding $+0.75$ was evidence of good health. Finally, the abbreviated standard version of the GHQ, which measures health across four scales, was analysed through consolidation of an aggregated index on the following principle: respondents who had up to 30 points (inclusive) were considered healthy; with 31–40 points, unhealthy; and those with 41 or over, sick. Figures 6.1–6.3 show the results we obtained.

The results we obtained show that persistent poverty is very strongly correlated with poor health and that people whose living standards are starting to decline are among those at risk of deterioration in health. And, although results obtained using different methods for assessing health differ (and quite significantly), examination of the close mutual relationship between chronic poverty, low living standards and deteriorating health reveals a clear negative trend. The use of differing methods only serves to supplement this picture: people's assessments are somewhat gentler when they give their view of their own overall health; when they assess their health on the EQ-5D scale, which is more specific and consequently more objective, they reveal a more severe picture of their actual psychological and physical state. (Respondents assess their potential for mobility, their ability to take care of themselves and perform their everyday tasks and duties without any problems,

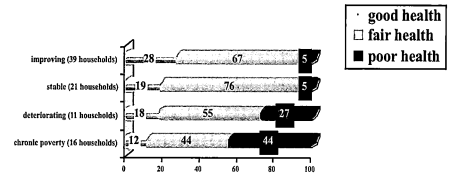

Figure 6.1 Self-rated health *x* changes in household's material welfare, 1997 to 2004 (%)

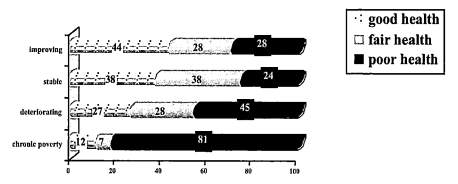

Figure 6.2 Health on the EQ-5D *x* changes in household's material welfare, 1997 to 2004 (%)

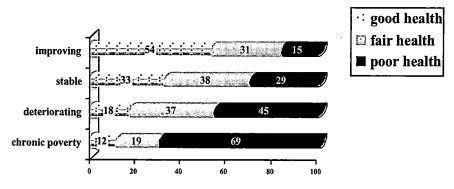

Figure 6.3 Health on the GHQ *x* changes in household's material welfare, 1997 to 2004 (%)

and also whether they are suffering pain, discomfort, anxiety or depression.) The results of applying this scale provide evidence that poverty is accompanied by a high level of social dysfunction, induces stress and entails depression, apathy and, in the end, exclusion.

The analysis we carried out showed that a distinctive vicious circle is formed: poverty in all its negative manifestations (the disordered nature of life, poor nutrition, the absence of elementary opportunities to properly regain one's strength, the constant worry about one's daily bread) leads to a deterioration in health, while poor health in itself prevents one from overcoming this situation, takes away the hope of changing anything or attaining success, and thus becomes one of the number of very important factors that influence the formation and reproduction of persistent poverty.

Access to Healthcare

In this regard, it is important to understand what chances the Russian State still offers the poor to access health care or to pursue any concern to preserve their own health. Unfortunately, the data from our research provide evidence that these chances are slim and that lack of money severely restricts an individual's access to medical services.

Here it is necessary to add the proviso that, formally, health care in Russia remains free of charge and universally accessible. However, much specialised research has emphasised that lack of access to good-quality health care is a serious problem for the poor, who characteristically also have lower health indicators. Most worrying of all is the fact that the burden of payment for obtaining care from a doctor is growing (see Higher School of Economics, Moscow State University, 2004; Besstremyannaya and Shishkin, 2005). According to calculations initiated by the World Bank, between 30 per cent and 50 per cent of total expenditures on health care in 2004 were private expenditures. Moreover, payments for medical care from people's own pockets represent a disproportionately high element of consumption, particularly for the poor (World Bank, 2005).

Table 6.3   Types of unobtainable medical care *x* level of material welfare, 2004 (%)

Unobtainable over the year preceding the survey	Poor	Badly-off	Averagely well-off	Total
Clinic treatment	23	13	0	10
In-patient treatment	27	4	0	8
Dental treatment	41	17	4	22
Essential medicines	41	8	5	16
This did not happen: they had the resources	27	42	60	46
No one in the family needed medical care	0	25	22	17

We shall give just one example from our longitudinal panel, which more than obviously illustrates this difficult situation. The situation in this household was so bad that it was first outlined in the second book of our trilogy and has been discussed again by our research team in other chapters of this book. The household in question represents a typical example of persistent poverty that has arisen not from inadequate lifestyle choices, but from the extremely difficult consequences of the socioeconomic reforms for a particular section of the population. The head of the family, Viktor (aged 50), was a former army officer who, as a result of the reforms, had been forced to leave the army and take a job as a leading engineer at a scientific defence research institute. This change in social status left the family increasingly vulnerable to the problems associated with public-sector employment; in just one year – between their joining our panel in 1999 and our second interview with them in 2000 – their standard of living fell sharply and they crossed the threshold into indigence. We should also note that this Moscow family belonged to the category of those with a lot of children: they had five. The respondent's wife (a teacher by profession) had for a large part of her life not worked but instead looked after the children and the home. In the Soviet period, the family had received numerous concessionary benefits, and they continued to get some of these right up to recent times; however, as a result of the current social policy reforms in Russia, many of their social concessions had now been lost. At the time of our most recent survey, the two daughters of the family, aged 18 and 20, were working, having been forced to give up the idea of continuing their education because of constant material difficulties, and the 16-year-old son was earning extra on a regular basis, combining a job with studying. Viktor himself, however, suffered greatly from their ever-deepening poverty, and experienced a deterioration in his own health, complaining of chronic fatigue. The younger children were sick (one with an allergy, the other disabled), and had problems with studying at their general secondary school. The family had petitioned to be allowed to educate the two youngest children at home, but had been refused. In Victor's opinion, it would have been a better arrangement, not only because of the children's health but also because they would not have had to spend anything on school clothing or food at school. This is how the respondent himself describes the situation in his family.

> A lot of people I know are almost on the poverty line. Old friends, neighbours, acquaintances – everyone I meet. A lot of my wife's relations. It's hard to define poverty in two words; you can only define it by comparison. People use or consume just what's necessary, what is directly required for life. Going to visit our relatives outside Moscow is already tough: it means getting into debt. In the past, it wasn't an issue, even though I was earning less (in relation to the dollar exchange rate). Or medicines: I've been getting subsidies for a little while now, but all the same we can't afford medicines even though the treatment is free. We can't afford to pay doctors' fees, even for essential dentistry. We haven't got any kind of savings or reserves; everything goes on just keeping alive. Every price increase tells on our budget, and a lot of illnesses arise from that. Being on the poverty line means you can't really live – just survive. Poor people can't consume

anything extra, only what's necessary. Take us, for example: we live on what I earn. Our youngest child is ill, but I'm forced to buy the kind of foods I can afford, rather than the ones needed. If I buy what he needs, the other children will go hungry. It was essential to buy my youngest son two medicines, his cerebral circulation is compromised – but even such a simple natural medicine as extract of chestnut, made from the fruits, even that is very expensive. No, well, we bought them, of course, but at the cost of what other economies! ... So, if all of a sudden money for medicines becomes necessary, then it is a complete catastrophe, since we can't put off spending on that. Medicines, treatment and funerals – they simply can't be postponed, and that's that. Our health is getting worse. Both mine and my wife's. Plus also our food is poor, we get no holidays and we're under constant stress; obviously, this all affects our health. (Viktor, aged 44 when this interview took place in 1999 – see also the second book in our trilogy and Chapter 2 of this book.)

The impression is formed that in essence the poorest section of Russia's population is gradually being dragged away from life's most important human right – the right to protect one's health and receive essential medical care; in fact, if health is to be preserved, the highest priority should be to improve the population's quality of life, not just to reform the medical sector. Social policy directed at improving the health of disadvantaged and vulnerable social groups must take into account the fact that, without adequate nutrition and proper conditions in life, no medical measures are likely in themselves to halt the negative dynamic of deterioration in the health of the poor – in other words, the primary issue is the struggle against poverty. In its document 'Bridging the gaps' (1995), the World Health Organisation says: 'The world's most ruthless killer and the greatest cause of suffering on earth is ... extreme poverty.' This statement (like the conclusions of Peter Townsend's 'Black Report', Whitehead et al., 1992; and a number of European Commission documents relating to the problem of social exclusion) again emphasises the significance of poverty as a factor that has an extremely unfavourable influence on health.

On the other hand, to interpret health simply as a product of medical services (accessible or inaccessible to a given social stratum) would be inaccurate. It is also an issue of individual responsibility – and an issue of serious control over the development of policies in all spheres that might have an influence on the factors that determine health (lifestyle, education, working conditions, housing conditions, and so on). This is precisely why it is so important, in developing a strategy for the reform of health care, to strive to observe the principle of justice in the provision of medical care, making it accessible for all groups in the population, and, in particular, for the most vulnerable. However, in Russia, there are at least three objective limitations on attaining this goal: financial, geographical and bureaucratic, the latter dictated by the parochial interests of particular political groups.

The Soviet model of health care was in its essence egalitarian. It offered State medical care to all citizens in a volume calculated on the basic requirements for a basic set of medical services and not on the ability to pay for them. Now, Russia has rejected the principle of universality, trying to place part of the responsibility and expenditures for the population's health onto the shoulders of people themselves.

Inequalities of a new kind have arisen, which were absolutely unknown to those who had spent the greater part of their lives under the Soviet regime. Although there has always been poverty, it is still the case that inequality in access to basic medical services – with the possibility that medical care might not be obtainable, even in case of severe need – represents an extremely unaccustomed 'risk' for Russians, who increasingly fear finding themselves in such a situation. According to data from the Institute of Sociology's 2006 research, which has already been mentioned, the thing Russians now fear most is loss of their own health or deterioration of the health of somebody close – a concern expressed by 71 per cent of the population. But what is most typical is that one in three inhabitants of Russia today fears it will be impossible to obtain medical care even in case of severe need, while the poor express this fear noticeably more often than the better-off sections of the population. This raises the question of whether there are alternative resources for people to tackle their own problems – first and foremost, the important resource of social capital?

Social Capital and Health

Research into resources and forms of capital is comparatively new and contentious, both in the theoretical and in the methodological senses. However, despite differences between conceptual approaches, the majority of researchers see social capital as a special component of resource potential – a component that can have an active influence on processes of socioeconomic differentiation and stability in society. In this regard, an analysis of social capital may throw additional light on the issue of the interrelationship of poverty and health.

The most difficult methodological issues in analysing everything connected with social capital are, firstly, understanding it and, secondly, measuring it. Social capital may be seen as a group resource of social cohesion and solidarity, a resource which is able to help further consolidate social organisations and local communities, on the basis of voluntary cooperation and in the aim of attaining shared advantages. At the basis of this conception by Putnam (1993; World Bank, 2000) and his adherents lies the principle of trust in the basic institutions of democratic civil society. Apart from this, social capital may be seen through the key concept of previously formed social networks, whose decisive significance lies in their very existence – and in the individual's inclusion in them (Coleman, 1999). The possibility of the individual deriving advantage from taking part in the activities of social networks and tackling various problems through these networks enlarges volumes of individual social capital. In both instances, the issue of social capital is contained in the nature and quality of the interaction between the public and the private (see Twigg and Schecter, 2003), and also in the broader context of social stratification.

In addition, many researchers are increasingly inclined to understand social capital as an initial principle of the social behaviour of individuals in combination with the social context of the society in which they live, seeing it as a culturally generated category. This approach seems very promising, since it is widely known that Russians traditionally ascribe a great deal of significance to inclusion in social networks of interfamily support, which makes the process of overcoming many everyday difficulties and problems significantly easier for them. In conditions where it is becoming harder to count on the State, this most important additional resource (informal contacts and the mutual assistance of friends, neighbours, relations and all those around you) helps many people to overcome poverty, stress and illness.

The interrelationship of social capital and health, as a rule, is viewed in the context of behavioural and cultural or psychosocial approaches to understanding health (Bartley, 2004), which emphasise that health depends on the type of self-care behaviour practised in a given social environment. Behaviour that is potentially detrimental to health (alcoholism, smoking, neglect of preventive measures to care for one's health) may be typical of the lifestyle of the particular social group in which a given family mixes. As a rule, the choices people make depend strongly on status and material circumstances: at least, in our panel, one-third of poor and badly-off households said that there were no rich people in their close circle (while only one in five averagely well-off families had no wealthy acquaintances). Moreover, poor families were more likely to be in a closed circle of people like themselves: only eight poor families out of 24 said that there was nobody within their close circle whom they would describe as living below the poverty line. All this cannot fail to be reflected in the quality of their social capital and the way it functions, including as it applies to their health behaviour.

As far as the psychosocial approach to understanding health is concerned, we have already spoken above about the role of stress in the life of contemporary Russians. Negative emotions connected with disorder in one's life, with insecurity, with material difficulties or with accumulated problems not only provoke particular behaviour (for example, smoking), but sometimes lead to the edge of social exclusion, to alienation from society. Moreover, not only is social participation reduced and social apathy increased – but the desire to socialise and have contact with other people disappears. Thus, established social connections are broken, social networks gradually disintegrate, and all this together leads to the exhaustion of social capital. The results of our previous study of poverty demonstrated that maintaining existing networks in an unchanged state is not only the key to potential help in case of need, but also a guarantor of welfare at a particular level (Davidova, 2004), while the data from our ten-year observation of a panel of households confirmed that this applies not only to welfare, but also to health. Many Western researchers have also concluded that where relationships between people are intensively maintained at a good level and there is a stronger sense of support from outside, then people's health may improve independently of their level of income (Lang and Hornburg, 1998).

On the other hand, it has been proved that people who are forced to manage their problems on their own are more likely to become ill and die than those who are living in a harmonious family (Armstrong, 2003). Apart from this, it should not be forgotten that many problems in Russia, including problems associated with the medical sector and medical treatment, were tackled in the Soviet period and are still tackled now through people's connections. Accordingly, the presence of significant connections (knowing a doctor or officials in the medical sector and elsewhere: people who are able to offer professional consultations or valuable advice) can have a significant effect on a household's opportunities to obtain skilled medical care – and, moreover, it will be free of charge.

Thus, the social capital of Russian households, seen through the prism of pre-existing social networks, can at once be connected with health, through certain factors. These factors are the volume of social connections, the intensity of contacts, the way social networks function (expressed in the types of support given), the presence of a close social circle (in which the family plays a special part) and the particular way of life that determines membership of a given social stratum. Many Western researchers studying social capital as applied to health have come to similar conclusions (for example, Richard Rose's research project, 'Coping with Organisations: Networks of Russian Social Capital', 2003; as well as research by the Institute for Social and Economic Research at the University of Essex, undertaken for the Health Development Agency – Pevalin and Rase, 2004) It is true that one clarification is necessary, relating directly to Russia. At the moment, unfortunately, most mutual exchanges of social capital are informal, because of the underdeveloped nature of the institutions of civil society and the absence of a tradition of active participation in the activities of formal organisations at the level of clubs, associations, the voluntary sector and local communities – practices that are not typical of contemporary Russia.

Connections to the Mainstream

Taking into account everything that has been said above, our project looked at our respondent households' social capital from two angles: 1) as a sign of being 'in the mainstream', when a family lives with a sense of inclusion in an extensive system of interpersonal and interfamily contacts and relationships – that is, possesses a developed social resource; and 2) as a system of significant connections – that is, the types of social networks which are in shortest supply and which can be used to most effectively tackle difficult problems in life (specifically relating to health).

Let us start from the fact that, for our respondents, being 'in the mainstream' meant a life that included a sense of satisfaction with their opportunities for social contact and with the certainty of potential support from people close to them if they needed it ('when there is someone to rely on'), and a state of psychological comfort, with no sense of loneliness. It is not for nothing that, in Russian society, family discord and lack of support from relations and friends are perceived as factors that, against the background of economic difficulties, may not only make a person feel worse in themselves, but also lead them to the threshold of real poverty. Data from the Institute of Sociology's 2006 pan-Russian research, which has already been mentioned several times, provide evidence of this: in total, one-third of Russians surveyed said that they knew of such things happening among poor people in their own immediate circle (Gorshkov and Tikhonova, 2007).

According to data from the same research, over 80 per cent of the population of Russia are 'in the mainstream' – that is, they live with a sense of satisfaction at the intensity of their own social contacts. Only 17 per cent of those surveyed said that they had not succeeded in finding any reliable friends in life; just 7 per cent considered their opportunities for social contact with friends and relations to be poor, while 6 per cent suffered from lack of social contact with relations, and 4 per cent from loneliness. If we look at the results of our many years of observation of the members of our respondent panel, then it becomes clear that over 80 per cent of them are also in the mainstream: however, this only applies to those who have not crossed the poverty line.

In poor families, trends of growth in social exclusion, loss of traditional social connections with relations and friends, and a feeling of loneliness and helplessness are much more marked. Eleven poor households out of 24 had in some way or another dropped out of the mainstream, and three of them were at the stage of the most profound social exclusion. One in three poor respondents was not sure that there was a person in their close circle whose help they could count on at a difficult time (and this despite the rich, well-established Russian traditions of mutual assistance between families), while 40 per cent considered that they had not succeeded in finding any reliable friends in life (this applied to no more than 15 per cent of other respondents). Finally, half of poor households stated that they had not succeeded in creating a happy family and were hardly likely to do so in future; and one in four respondents from poor households assessed their own family situation as 'bad', as against only two out of the other 63 respondents. Moreover, the data from our research show that it was precisely those respondents in whose households social exclusion was manifest who much more often complained about their own health: a third of our respondents from households that showed signs of social exclusion assessed their own health as 'poor', and use of the EuroQol and GHQ scales significantly aggravated this worrying trend, with 70–75 per cent of those who had dropped out of the mainstream being 'sick'.

The most clearly obvious trend of a link between deteriorating health and dropping out of the community's generally accepted way of life manifested itself against the background of low standards of living. The data confirm that, of those people who are dissatisfied with the quality of their social interactions or alienated from the community for some reason, one in four (assessed on the EuroQol and GHQ scales) suffers from poor health, even if their material resources enable them to avoid poverty. Moreover, a full 90 per cent of the people we studied who were poor and also worst-off in terms of support from friends and family were sick.

Our research also revealed as fairly prevalent the situation where relations, friends, colleagues and acquaintances advise one another on how to cope with a particular minor illness without going to the doctor, how to care better for their own health and how to behave properly in order to preserve it. Such contacts are very important, since the views of these significant people help someone not only to get through an illness more easily, but also to choose a particular strategy of self-care behaviour. In 60 of the households we studied, people said that they often – or at least, when necessary – asked advice from people close to them about their own health concerns (for the rest, either they did not need to, or they preferred the advice of a specialist). As we can see, this is the overwhelming majority – in fact, two-thirds of respondents – so we can describe this as a generally accepted, widespread practice. It is noteworthy that, among people whose self-rated health was 'good', over 70 per cent were accustomed to taking advice from those close to them, while among those whose self-rated health was 'poor' the figure was no more than 50 per cent. In this regard, seven households out of 24 in the group of poor people could not rely on anyone's help and advice (among the averagely well-off, only one respondent out of 39 told us that this was the situation). Thus, it is obvious that the possibility of using this additional resource of concern for one's own health, directly connected with social capital, is frequently simply unavailable to the poor.

It is also of no small importance that 14 respondents from poor households answered the question: 'If you or your relations had to have a fee-paying operation or expensive treatment, where would you get the money for this?' with complete bewilderment and despair, saying that they could not even imagine what they would do in this situation. By comparison, only five averagely well-off households out of 39 were really worried about the possibility of such a situation and did not know how they would begin to cope with it. A third of the averagely well-off would get by with their own resources, while only one poor family was counting on this; the other two-thirds would turn to relations and friends for help – in contrast, fewer than half of our poor respondents felt they could rely on others.

As far as formal channels for tackling such problems were concerned, just a few individuals felt ready to resort to them. So, only one in ten of the households we studied was counting on the assistance of relevant State organisations in a critical situation where the health of any member of their family would require fee-paying treatment, and just three families were counting on support from the voluntary sector.

However, no less than half of poor people are counting on the resources of their immediate circle: in analysing the interrelationship of poverty and health, it is not possible to find any other component of social capital that is more important, and it is precisely the role of connections that ensure the well-being of a given household. Many researchers who have studied the way networks of interfamily support and mutual assistance function have devoted attention to the significance of tackling various types of problems through 'who you know' or 'string-pulling', which in Russia has a particularly long tradition and a broad sociocultural dimension (see Shlapentokh, 1989; Rose, 1993; Ledeneva, 1998). The use of connections and existing social networks can operate in various ways: there are fairly fixed relationships with 'the people you need', or methods of obtaining protections, guarantees and recommendations through networks, all of which ensure access to the person who will be pivotal in solving a given problem or to a free consultation at home from someone who is a professional in the given aspect of life. At the same time, it is important to play an integral part in mutual actions within the informal social network.

As a result of an analysis of interfamily exchanges of assistance, services and connections, carried out in the context of the Institute of Sociology's 2006 pan-Russian research, we can form a judgement about the way pre-existing informal support networks function actively in the everyday life of Russians. The research data demonstrate that two-thirds of Russian families (67 per cent) are receiving various types of help from their immediate circle. However, if we also take into account those respondents who, although they are not using the support of those close to them, are themselves supporting others, then we can state that up to 80 per cent of the population of Russia participates in mutual exchanges of assistance involving relations and friends. Thus, it is correct to refer to the large-scale involvement of Russians in private informal support networks as being a feature of the generally accepted Russian way of life and as evidence of being in the mainstream.

Moreover, it should be noted that the data also record the following trend: relations within informal private networks are almost always arranged on a mutual basis and, although no one calculates the equivalence of such exchanges, equivalence in relationships between Russian families does exist at an invisible level. People participating in mutual exchanges of social capital not only receive but also offer help, services and connections. On average across Russia, there are not actually many people who purely receive or purely give (15 per cent of each), while 70 per cent of social exchanges take place on a mutual basis (Gorshkov and Tikhonova, 2007). In this regard, we shall now look at the particular features of the functioning of social networks in our longitudinal panel households.

The Function of Networks

A quarter of respondents said that not only were they not receiving any help from relations, acquaintances or friends, but also they had not used connections or services in their immediate circle over the three years preceding the survey. Furthermore, as we have already pointed out, the degree of social participation in the activities of formal organisations and voluntary associations in Russia is in general extremely low (a total of 15 families out of the 87 we studied participated in some way or other, but they included those with regular involvement in sports groups) – and the above-mentioned quarter of respondents absolutely never did. This may be interpreted as a second indicator of the fact that one in four of the households we studied had no social capital at all, or at least could not make use of social capital that functioned at the level of social networks.

At the same time, the proportion of poor people who had no support and were not using connections was significantly higher than the proportion of better-off people: a zero level of social capital was recorded in ten poor households out of

24, yet in only 11 of the remaining 63 households. It is obvious that the additional possibilities offered by one's immediate circle are greater for people who are more prosperous and successful. The data from our research also demonstrate that those poor people who nevertheless succeeded in making use of the social resource of informal networks could, as a rule, count only on simple household support, small everyday services or sympathy, but in no way on money or connections that would help them solve difficult problems, particularly health-related ones. Judging by our respondents' answers, an active approach to using connections as the equivalent of money was least prevalent in the group of the poorest people, with only three households telling us about this. It reached its peak in the group of badly-off people: as a result of lack of money, one in three of them was actively trying to maintain their social networks and would activate their connections when tackling problems. It then fell somewhat in the group of averagely well-off people, who preferred to tackle many problems on a paying basis and had more possibilities of doing so – only one prosperous household in five had used connections in their pure form to tackle problems.

The most important social network resource in helping to look after and improve one's health is knowing a doctor to whom one can go in case of need. As a rule, such connections, which develop over years and are stable in nature, are a significant component of the social capital of households in a context where the situation in post-reform Russian health care is not yet completely clear. Opportunities to use such connections can obviously have a positive influence on the health of family members, and they bring additional chances of access to resources that are in short supply (in-patient treatment without joining a waiting list, referral to a health resort, freedom from confusion and queuing when visiting a medical service, skilled recommendations for correct choice of medicines and methods of treatment, etc.). A person who has such connections and acquaintances essentially receives additional guarantees of good-quality contacts with the health care system. Half of our respondent families who were materially prosperous knew a doctor (and we should remember that their health was also significantly better than other people's), but as we went down the 'welfare ladder', the lack of connections of this kind became more marked. Again, worst of all was the situation that had arisen for the poor – only seven households out of 24 could count on their connections. It is not surprising that half of the respondents who rated their own health as 'good' or 'fair' had medical staff in their circle of acquaintances, while this was true of only three out of 13 respondents in 'poor' (self-rated) health.

So, what is the distribution of amounts of overall social capital – whose inter-relationship with health can hardly be called into doubt, given our data – according to our respondent families' level of material welfare? Figure 6.4 helps to answer this question.

This figure clearly shows that poor people have a lower amount of social capital than all others, although some of them receive certain kinds of support and are included in major interfamily contacts and interactions. However, they frequently lack access to connections and to complex multifunctional support, which is an

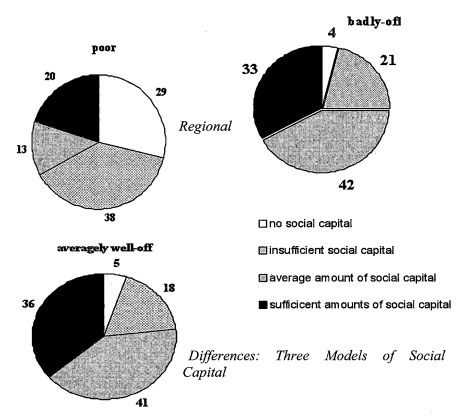

poor

badly-off

averagely well-off

Regional

□ no social capital

▨ insufficient social capital

▥ average amount of social capital

■ sufficicent amounts of social capital

Differences: Three Models of Social Capital

Figure 6.4   Households' social capital *x* level of material welfare, 2004 (%)

extremely important component of the potential of informal networks, in the first instance acting to overcome difficult situations. This means that poor sections of the population suffer not only from chronic lack of income, but also from a shortage of other resources that are important in life and, first and foremost, from an absence of social capital – a situation which, in its turn, preserves their position in poverty and has a negative impact on their health.

Furthermore, it is necessary to take into account that a particular feature of our longitudinal panel was the inclusion of people who were fairly well socialised and well educated – not marginal but typical members of the urban population of Russia, who had had to face difficulties of inevitable adaptation to reforms. Looking at Russia as a whole (through Institute of Sociology data from 2006), the position of the poorest section of the population with regard to social capital is more worrying still. Fifty-five per cent of poor people lack the social networks resource (they do not receive any kind of help), and 70 per cent possess absolutely no connections or ways of influencing their circumstances. A trend has been noted throughout Russia towards steady exclusion of the poor from the most significant, multifunctional inter-family exchanges involving social capital, with a displacement towards the receipt of simpler types of help in the way support networks function among the most deprived.

Regional

Differences: Three Models of Social Capital

Turning to particular regional features of the functioning of social capital, which are closely connected with way of life and traditions in local communities, it can be asserted that, in the broader territorial and regional space of Russia, social capital is formed and 'works' in different ways (and manifests itself differently as applied to various social strata), and this factor is yet another very important dimension that is difficult to ignore. In addition, this again allows us to focus attention on the comparative sociocultural context, a framework which researchers increasingly frequently use to examine social capital (see Scheepers, Te Grotenhuis and Gelissen, 2002).

As the reader already knows, we studied households from three Russian cities: Moscow, Voronezh and Kazan', and each of these regions had its own particular features of the use of social capital in general and as applied to health problems in particular. The qualitative material we obtained from our interviews with respondents, as well as certain trends that are manifest from inter-regional comparative analysis of the data we obtained, allows us to define at least three models of established social interactions. Firstly, there is a model that is modern in form, in many ways connected with the development of market relations and their penetration into various areas of social life. The word 'modern' is not used randomly in this regard, since this model is very far from the picture of Russians' lives – widely current in the West – in which informality and 'string-pulling' play a central part. In conditions of partial privatisation of health care and a high level of mistrust in existing State institutions, the main point of this model is precisely to obtain access to high-quality medical care through the social capital that one has. And this means not so much an exchange of money for connections in order to tackle problems with one's health, as access to the necessary information about who to pay and how much, whether formally or informally, in order to be more effective. This functional model of social capital is most prevalent at points of faster market growth, where people have fairly high average per capita incomes. In our case, it most obviously manifested itself in Moscow, although we also encountered it in households from other cities (as a rule, such households were averagely well-off).

Let us look at the modern model of how social capital functions, using the example of the life story of Katya, from Moscow, who was 31 at the time of the interview reproduced below. She was a social worker by profession, helping homeless people in a social rehabilitation centre to get into employment – in other words, she worked in the public sector. Her husband was an alcoholic, but by the time we first met her in 1999 she had separated from him and was living with her small daughter, her parents – both pensioners – and her sister, who was under 18. Before the reforms, her family had never had to face any material difficulties. Later, Katya married again, so now there were more working people in the family: her father had some earnings from time to time, in addition to his pension, because he was a skilled electrician; her sister had started work; her husband was working. Material circumstances in the family had improved: however, just at the time of the last survey, the respondent was in hospital with suspected cancer and she had to have a serious operation and lengthy treatment. Here is how she herself described this period in her life.

I had an attack. I felt absolutely fine that day – absolutely well. I was sitting at home at 11 o'clock in the evening – and suddenly my blood pressure just fell dramatically. So what did I do then? At one time my sister worked as a cleaner in a hospital, and so from there she knew how to give an injection. She gave me the injection herself. And the medicine was one that had been recommended to me at work: at the night shelter for the homeless, we have very highly-qualified medical staff, with a doctor who treats our clients. And if you call an ambulance – then it takes a very long time to get to the hospital. There's no sense in waiting. And going to our district clinic to sit in the queue for a doctor – that's a very long time. But after that attack, I finally decided to go into hospital for an operation.

What can I say about my tumour, which was operated on not long ago? I saw that myself too, in 2000, so I've known about it for a long time. But I didn't go to the doctor straightaway. Again, first of all I went to the doctor who treats the clients at my workplace. I showed her this tumour. And she told me that it was a benign tumour, a kind that people live with for 30 or 40 years, that if it didn't bother me and didn't grow, then it wasn't anything terrible, I could live with it. But it would be better to see specialists and have some tests done. I went to Hospital Number 40, which was the one she recommended me to go to. Actually, at first, I spent a long time looking for a good clinic myself. Through someone I knew. Someone who knew some surgeons. And I went round and round in circles, because it turned out that my old friend's mother had been operated on by a surgeon from exactly that hospital 15 years ago and was still being monitored there. And so, having gone round in a circle, I went to Hospital Number 40, which is really a specialist oncology unit, with very high standards. And the doctor I went to see was the same doctor who had done my friend's mum's operation ...

Of course, I had to show my gratitude to the doctor and the nurses. Nobody asked me specially about doing that. You just have to thank someone for taking something like that away. And the nurses: well, it's simply essential – really young girls are working there, their wages there are tiny, and all of them are working there day and night: equivalent to time and a half. So it's just to say 'thank you'.

Interviewer – Hmm ... and so this 'thank-you' was in the form of ...?

In the form of money. Before that, when I went there, when I agreed with them that I would go into the ward directly under that doctor, and he would operate on me, then

I gave them some gifts as a thank-you. But after the operation I did thank them with money.

The second model of how social capital functions is more traditional for Russia, and we found that this was also based mainly on the informal use of connections as an equivalent for money in obtaining services. This is apparent in the fact that a person who attends a medical establishment 'not from outside', but through people he knows, receives more attention and has his problems tackled without waiting in a queue, or else has the opportunity for the most effective possible interaction with State medicine, receiving free of charge services that others are offered on a fee-paying basis. In this model, the presence of a permanent circle of relations, neighbours and long-standing acquaintances, who give relevant recommendations and assistance in the matter concerned (including even caring for the sick person in hospital or at home) is very important. This system is close to the version that was known as 'blat' – string-pulling – under the Soviet regime. As a rule, the strongest traditions of mutual rescue and mutual assistance are closely connected with a rural culture, and they manifest themselves not in the highly-developed market-based regions, but in the poor agrarian regions of South and Central Russia, where people do not have such high incomes. Such a region was represented in our research: Voronezh.

Meeting respondents from this region allowed us to conclude that the traditional spirit of collectivism, the preservation and maintenance of wide social contacts and an altruistic willingness to help people who are close to you seem to be more active here than in post-industrial, individualised Moscow. Suffice it to say that even the poor here were not, as a rule, excluded from the mainstream – that is, 80 per cent of them were not among the people whom we found to be worst off in terms of concern from friends and family: in Moscow this was true of only one-third of the poor, and in Kazan', of half.

Let us introduce an example of just such a traditional use of social capital in Voronezh. Sergei, a 50-year-old participant in all our research surveys, had faced unemployment several times during the period when reforms were being implemented in Russia. His circumstances were further exacerbated by his being forced to bring up his two sons, both under 18, alone (their mother had been deprived of her parental rights and had spent the last few years in a psychiatric clinic), and because, for most of our period of observation, he was also caring for his paralysed mother (she died early in 2004). He was the sole breadwinner, and at the time of the 2004 survey, he was working as a repair fitter in a factory producing agricultural machinery. The situation of this business was not very secure, Sergei's pay was not high, and throughout all our years of observation the family in fact existed on the borderline of indigence. Sergei felt that he was sick and so it was difficult for him to work, yet he was forced to do so. Here is what he himself said about this.

At the factory, we have a planned, statutory occupational medical examination: without it, they don't allow you to work. But my chances of passing it were practically nil – my stomach, my heart, and all this constant stress. Indeed, you won't find anybody at our factory who is healthy. They carried out the last occupational medical examination recently, and 50–60 per cent of the workers at our factory should have been retired completely on ill-health grounds. But for the kind of money they pay, those are the only people who'll stay. And there's nowhere to go. Why would a private enterprise need a sick worker!? I was lucky: the doctor who did my medical examination was our local doctor; she knows me and she knows the situation in my family: when Mum was ill in bed she used to come to us every month to examine her. But if it had been another doctor, then perhaps I would have been released because of my health, too. Or they would have offered me a different job, with lower pay, as a general labourer: 'If you want to – work, but if you don't want to – go ...' So knowing that doctor really rescued me then: I didn't even ask her, but I just dropped a hint – I said, 'The kids have got to be fed.' (See also the second book in our trilogy and Chapters 10 and 11.)

Local traditions of using social capital are closely connected not only with the type of settlement and the degree of market development in a region, but also with the national and faith affiliations of the people who live in the region. It is no secret that the religious factor has a strong influence on the inter-relationships of people who are members of the same faith. In our longitudinal panel, there were people whose Islamic culture meant that they interpreted the role of social connections, informal inter-relationships and support in their own life somewhat differently from our other respondents. The majority of Muslim respondents lived in Kazan'; however, there were also individual Muslim households in the other cities. While remaining primarily traditional, their perception of the role of social capital had certain specific features.

> Obviously, in Islamic culture, it is considered a great sin to harm yourself, your health, or the health of those close to you or your neighbours. And it is also said: 'If you are rich today and somebody beside you is poor and hungry, then you must not leave that person hungry tonight, but must go and make sure he goes to sleep full.' (Abukhasan, 70, a small trader/entrepreneur in Moscow, of Chechen origin – see also the second book in our trilogy and Chapter 11 of this book.)

> Generally, when you go to see the doctor, you always have to take a present with you, just to put him in a good mood, just so that he will be attentive towards you. (Linar, 34, small businessman in Kazan'.)

> Services at the clinic in the area where I live are kind of free of charge, but we all understand that if you go there empty handed, then the service you get will be a response to those empty hands. You have to take something with you. And, recently, we have come to understand that it has to be not a gift, but money. (Logman, 44, small businessman/commercial trader in Kazan'.)

As we can see, traditional models of social capital, functioning through all its various interconnections, are closely interwoven not only with the way of life of local communities of different kinds, but also with the new situation in Russia. Medicine really is becoming to a large degree fee-paying. Nevertheless, free State medicine remains a central key element of the existing system of Russian health care, and working within the system means a significant increase in social capital, not only for the employees themselves but also for all those who are part of the social network that has grown up around each of them. So, the third discernible model of how social capital 'works' in the contemporary Russian context is the model of loyalty to a particular occupational group. Many public sector medical workers adhere to this model, despite their low pay and the fact that transferring to the private medical sector could significantly improve their own material circumstances. Here is how a dentist from Kazan' who took part in our research described this.

> I work as deputy to the senior doctor at a State medical centre. For the time being, I am not planning to change my place of work, although several times I have been offered a transfer to work in the commercial medical sector. I don't tell anyone what I earn – it is so little, it's simply shameful: 4,000 roubles [£80 GBP]. But at least I'm not ashamed to talk about what I do. And then, you still don't know how everything is going to turn out with fee-paying medicine: there could even be insecurity there, and improper behaviour by the management – they could just let you go without explaining why. What keeps me here is the fact that, within the Ministry of Health system, I can tackle any health-related problems. Everything that my relations need. I'm responsible for the health of the whole of a large family. I phone all the specialists in any of the medical establishments in the city to tackle all our problems. I can even phone any establishment and talk with the senior doctor, or else with somebody I've never even seen; I only have to introduce myself and tell them what I need. Professional solidarity gets to work, and of course they help me. I have an awful lot of connections across the city and also a lot of possibilities in the particular centre where I work. Various specialists also work with us here, to whom I can send people who need consultations, and so I can solve their health problems. Then they also help me out with something. Our senior doctor has said to me that there is prestige in working in the Ministry of Health system. These days, patients have more trust in doctors who work in the State medical system. It stands for a certain sign of quality. If you go to a commercial centre, who are you? You will lose your connections, because there will not be the kind of solidarity that there is now. The attitudes that both patients and doctors who have stayed in the Ministry of Health system take towards you will change. (Rezeda, 35, interviewed in her capacity as a medical worker.)

So this is what our research revealed about particular features of the social capital of Russians and of the interconnection of social capital with standard of living, poverty and health. We can see that the majority of social networks are informal in nature, which is a manifestation of the distinct lack of trust in formal State institutions by a significant proportion of Russians. We can also see that social capital plays a huge part in the formation and reproduction of social inequalities and is a most important stratifying factor. The social resource of the most deprived section of society is constantly being depleted and this inevitably means that the ways of influencing a difficult life situation that are generally accepted in a Russian community – in particular, using the possibilities of one's immediate circle, established acquaintances and contacts in tackling problems – are increasingly inaccessible to the poor. And this situation is directly connected with their poor health, because isolation and lack of access to the resource of social networks (in other words, low social capital) hinder any change in their circumstances. Thus, the social exclusion that accompanies the life of many poor households not only has an impact on their psychological and physiological state – it also pushes them over the edge and out of the mainstream, depriving them of opportunities to reintegrate into society and tackle their problems through their own efforts.

Obviously, those academics, politicians and experts who are calling for the main aim of social policy to be not simply material assistance to the poor but also equalisation of the strongly differentiated social chances of various population groups, including in the inter-regional space of contemporary Russia, are right. The battle must be not just with poverty and disease, but also with the growing trends of social exclusion that accompany poverty and sickness.

Chapter 7
Health and Employment

Inna Nazarova

Без труда не вынешь и рыбку из пруда
Without labour you won't get the fish out of the pond

Trends in Health Over the Years of Social and Economic Reform

The reform of all areas of life in Russian society caused a shock wave of increased psychological, emotional and social stresses, depression, neuroses and other psychosomatic disorders and illnesses in the population. The number of deaths from various types of illness has grown, and cases of suicide have become more frequent.

At the same time, the health care system has been essentially unable to cope with the upsurge in problems – indeed, a breakdown of the system itself has begun. Given a lack of proper organisation and financial provision, the first hasty attempts to introduce market elements into the system of providing medical care, the acceptance of the innovation of medical insurance (compulsory and voluntary) and the development of private medicine have all merely led to a deterioration in the situation. The unstable administration and functioning of health care has been intensified by the fact that, over the ten years from 1990, the Ministry was headed by eight different people.

Attempts to reform the sector have also continued in recent years, and in 2004 there was a merger between the Ministry of Social Protection and the Ministry of Healthcare. This means that the Ministry for Health and Social Development of the Russian Federation is now in charge of practically all issues in the social sphere, apart from education. Suffice it to say that it coordinates and monitors the activities of bodies as different as the Federal Inspectorate for Consumer Protection and Personal Well-Being, the Federal Inspectorate for Health Care and Social Development, the Federal Service for Labour and Employment, the Federal Agency for Health Care and Social Development, and the Federal Medical and Biological Agency – all of which fall within its structure. The Ministry also coordinates the activities of the Pension Fund of the Russian Federation, the Social Insurance Fund of the Russian Federation and the Federal Fund for Compulsory Medical Insurance (Ordinance of the Government of the Russian Federation, 2004).

Constant changes in the administrative structure of the health care system and under-funding of the sector have weighed heavily on the function of providing medical care to the population of Russia. The consequences have been especially serious where they have been superimposed on the results of a simultaneous sharp fall in the living standards of the overwhelming majority of the population and increased stress because of changes in all areas of life.

The conversion of service benefits into the form of money (i.e. the replacement of services for people in various social categories by cash payments), which took place in 2005, has also played its own small part in making these consequences worse. In the course of this conversion, for instance, free medicines were in some cases replaced by monetary payments that, on average, did not cover the costs of the necessary combination and amount of medical products. But, because they often do not even have enough money for food, poor sections of the population – which include especially many people in poor health – prefer monetary compensation.

Taking all this into account, it is not surprising that the initiation of economic reforms meant a sharp deterioration in the health of the Russian population. Thus, total mortality per thousand people in 1989 was 10.7, but by 1994 this indicator had gradually climbed (Minister of Health Care and Social Development of the Russian Federation). From 1995 to 1998, some health indicators improved a little, beginning to return to their pre-perestroika levels. However, in 1999, following the 1998 macroeconomic crisis, the demographic situation in Russia again deteriorated, and mortality rose to 14.7 per thousand. As a result, by the turn of the twenty-first century, Russia had one of the highest rates of natural population decline in the world. In the early 2000s, the number of those who died per 100,000 of the population, from various categories of causes, continued to grow (1361.1 in 1998; 1636.5 in 2003) (Rosstat, 2004). In 2003, mortality per 100,000 of population according to the standard classification was:

1. from diseases of the circulatory system – 927.5 (in 1998 – 748.8[1]);
2. from accidents, poisonings and traumas – 233.6 (in 1998 – 187.5);
3. from neoplasms – 202.5 (in 1998 – 202.5);
4. from diseases of the respiratory organs – 70.5 (in 1998 – 57.2);
5. from diseases of the digestive organs – 56.8 (in 1998 – 38.1);
6. from certain infectious and parasitic diseases – 25.9 (in 1998 – 19.0), including all forms of tuberculosis – 201.9 (in 1998 – 15.4).

Thus, from the 1990s, Russia entered a phase of severe demographic crisis, which has been characterised by increased natural population decline, low life expectancy, a significant gap in longevity between men and women, high indicators of general mortality, and excess mortality among men of working age. The main causes of death at working age have been external – accidents, poisonings and traumas, including suicides. The relationship between the suicide rate and certain social and economic conditions (such as the level of the population's per capita GDP, or the unemployment rate) in former Soviet republics has been noted in the literature (Shkolnikov, Cornia and Leon, 1998; Brainerd, 2001). Male mortality

---

1 On the mortality situation, see for example Averina, Nilssen, Brenn, Brox, Kalinin and Arkhipovsky (2003).

has been significantly higher than that of women, not only from external causes, but also from infectious and parasitic diseases, diseases of the respiratory organs and diseases of the circulatory system, and this has created a gap in average life expectancy between men and women of more than ten years.

Furthermore, the overall morbidity rate, according to data based on Russians' attendance at health care establishments, has shown a trend towards growth among practically all age groups and across the majority of classes of disease. Moreover, the greatest proportion comprised socially generated diseases. Thus, in the early 1990s, Russia was the scene of a deteriorating situation in the epidemiology of tuberculosis, with morbidity increasing 2.2 times. Despite the fact that the increase in cases of tuberculosis has been less marked in recent years, the problem remains extremely disturbing, with growth recorded in cases of tuberculosis among men, especially aged 20 to 40.

The figure for birth defects is growing, as is the number of children born disabled or sick (with a body mass index of 1,000 grams or more – i.e. not just with an extremely low birth weight) (Goskomstat Rossiyi, 1997). In the classificatory structure of infant mortality, the main causes remain those closely connected with maternal health: illnesses and conditions originating in the perinatal period (over 40 per cent of deaths) and congenital malformations (about 25 per cent).

Thus, in the 1990s, a trend began towards reduced health status of the whole population, including children – 40 per cent of children are born with some defect, and in practice only 10–14 per cent are healthy when they start school at the age of six (Rimashevskaya, 1995).

The results of sociological research conducted throughout the Russian Federation in the post-Soviet period confirm negative trends connected with demographic indicators such as health, morbidity, mortality, and so on. Experts note the negative influence of the reforms on the health of various categories of the population (Rimashevskaya, 2003). They link high mortality with cardinal changes in all aspects of life in Russian society: 'The total socio-demographic cost of radical reforms has been 650 million years of human life' (Zaslavskaya, 1997). Every subsequent generation has a lower health status than the previous one, and the unnatural situation has arisen where health problems that used to be associated with the elderly are found in children and young people (Rimashevskaya and Korkhova, 2001).

Quite apart from the stresses it has caused, the reform period has led to the impoverishment of a significant part of the population. Poverty is in turn connected with negative lifestyle phenomena, inadequate nutrition and harmful behaviours (see, for example, Watson, 1995; Palosuo, Zhuravleva, Uutela, Lakomova and Shilova, 1995; Klugman, 1997; Brainerd, 2001; Palosuo, 2003), which – in their turn – influence health. On the basis of census data from 1987 to 1997 and demographic data from 1991 to 1993, William Cockerham has concluded that, apart from lifestyle, there are two major causes of high mortality in Russia and several other Eastern European countries: Soviet health policy and social stress. Poor health is closely linked to lifestyles involving a high level of alcohol consumption, smoking, insufficient exercise and a high-fat diet (Cockerham, 1997). The same author, on the basis of calculations carried out using RLMS (Russian Longitudinal Monitoring Survey) data from 1995, has shown that lifestyle risk factors such as frequent alcohol use and high consumption of fats are especially characteristic of employed middle-aged men who live in urban areas and have relatively high incomes and some higher education. The least educated people in this group smoke as well, and significantly more than the rest (Cockerham, 2000). Finally, Cockerham's examination of the relationship between socialist ideology (for example, membership of the Communist Party) and the negative health lifestyles of the Russian population shows that his pro-socialist respondents demonstrated less activity towards achieving good health than anti-socialists, although both were practising similar lifestyles (Cockerham, Snead, Dewaal and Derek, 2002).

Data from the RLMS, which monitors economic position and health in Russia, offer the main source of empirical sociological material enabling us to assess the dynamic of health in the Russian population. These data provide marked evidence that the population's health was in a very sorry plight during the early 1990s – the first years after the start of reforms – and (differing somewhat from official statistical data) they demonstrate that poor people's self-rated health has deteriorated still further in the 2000s, despite the latter being a period of general stabilisation and growth in the economy (Table 7.1). For example, in the period from 1994 to 2003, although 27 per cent of inhabitants of Russia rated their own health as having improved, 58 per cent said that it had remained unchanged and 15 per cent, that it had deteriorated.

In addition, although in 1994 23 per cent of respondents rated their own health as 'poor or very poor', in 1998 – 27 per cent, in 2001 – 26 per cent, and in 2005 – 15 per cent, Russians' self-rated health is poorer than that of people living in Western countries (Bobak, Pikhart, Hertzman, Rose and Marmot, 1998). The influence of gender also played a significant part in people's own assessments of

Table 7.1   Average assessments of own health, in points, RLMS

Year	N	Total	Men	Women
1994	8305	3.01	3.20	2.87
1995	7844	3.07	3.25	2.94
1996	7756	3.06	3.23	2.93
1998	7975	3.07	3.26	2.93
2000	8313	3.07	3.22	2.96
2001	9297	3.08	3.25	2.96
2002	9647	3.09	3.24	2.98
2003	9789	3.10	3.26	2.99
2004	7072	3.10	3.25	2.99
2005	9555	3.16	3.30	3.05

Note: (minimum: 1 – 'very poor health', maximum: 5 – 'very good health').

their health (see Table 7.1): men had a tendency to give more positive assessments of their health by comparison with objective data about it.

Both one-off effects – for example, trauma or distress – and cumulative negative factors – prolonged unemployment, poverty, long-term health-adverse behaviour (use of alcohol, smoking, chronic lack of sleep, not taking part in any physical activity or sport) – have an influence on health and on people's own assessments of it (Nazarova, 2003).

Judging by the RLMS data, the number of people who had had health problems in the 30 days preceding the survey fell from 48 per cent in 1994 to 38 per cent in 2005. Being slightly unwell was mentioned more rarely – in 2001, 34 per cent of those surveyed said this applied to them (the question was asked for the first time in 2001), while in 2005 only 19 per cent said that it did. Meanwhile, for example, it must be noted that, in 1994, 25 per cent of the third decile group defined by level of income said they suffered from 'poor' or 'very poor' health, while only 16 per cent of the eighth group said this. In 2005, these indicators were 25 per cent and 9 per cent respectively. Thus, among relatively well-off people, not only were there fewer low assessments of their own health, but their health situation had changed for the better over recent years – so it was they who generated the overall dynamic of indicators of improvement in health across the country as a whole.

As far as future health prospects are concerned, it is necessary to take into account not only the reduction in the part played by stress as the population gradually adapts to new living conditions, but also their readiness to accept healthy lifestyle norms. Thus, the main conclusions to a report monitoring the state of health of the population of the Russian Federation (1992 to 2005), which looked at the harmful habits of Russians aged 14 and over, stated that the extent of consumption of spirits among adult men was falling significantly, and that by 2005 the prevalence of smoking among men had also dropped. However, in the period from 1998 to 2004, the extent of consumption of spirits among women had grown steadily (from 43 per cent to 47 per cent). The prevalence of smoking among women has also continued to grow: it increased from 7 per cent in 1992 to 15 per cent in 2005 (Monitoring the health of the population of the Russian Federation (1992–2005), 2006).

RLMS data also demonstrate a reduction in the level of daily physical activity – for example, people have started to walk less (to work and back, to the shops or for other things): in 1995, people walked 3.6 hours a day on average, but ten years later (2005), just 2.6 hours. In both 1995 and 2005, 82 per cent of RLMS respondents did not take any physical exercise at all. As far as eating habits are concerned, from 1992 to 1998, the proportion of fats in energy consumption fell steadily and constantly among all adult groups. In recent years, however, it has begun to increase. Among elderly people, the proportion suffering from obesity has increased constantly: in 2005, it was 59 per cent higher than in 1992, while the corresponding figure for middle-aged people was 29 per cent (Monitoring the health of the population of the Russian Federation (1992–2005), 2006). This was due to a shift to a 'carbohydrate diet' as a result of an increase in the price of protein foods.

Thus, in recent years, the progress of some negative trends has slowed. A certain positive dynamic has taken shape in people's well-being and in their behaviour. However, the potential future impact of these trends is very limited. In addition, even the already apparent trends towards a general improvement in health have in practice not reached poor sections of the population, whose health now inspires even greater alarm.

Respondents' Views on the Reforms and Health

As has already been said above, researchers see distress – alongside a fall in living standards and a deterioration in the health care system – as one of the main causes of changes in indicators of mortality and health in Russia (see, for example, Shapiro, 1995; Cockerham, 1997). In this context, it is interesting to see how Russians themselves assess the situation in this area, and what precisely they think about the influence of the reforms on the health of the nation.

Most of those from our panel whom we interviewed in depth took the view that their health over the years of reform (1989 onwards) had deteriorated. Their interview responses were ranged along a scale from 'The reforms have had no specific influence' to 'The reforms have had a specific influence on health'.

1. 'The reforms have had no specific influence'. Those who held this position took the view that there were other objective reasons for the deterioration of Russians' health during these years. Answers were often accompanied by comments in which the idea was put forward that people should take responsibility for their own health: 'I think that the thing influencing your health is how you look after it yourself' (Lena, 42, research associate from Kazan').

2. 'The reforms have had little influence'. Respondents in this group usually indicated the mediated nature of the influence of the reforms, or pointed to other factors. Thus, Raisa, aged 48, a sales assistant for a Voronezh sweet factory, said 'It isn't because of the reforms. There are simply a lot of problems. And we work hard, physically: for instance, I work in a kiosk, where we are constantly lifting boxes – it's tough.' Over the years of reform, Raisa had changed her job several times: she was educated to secondary school standard and from 1985 to 1990 had worked as assistant manager of a shop; in 1996 she was a cashier in the same place, but by 2004 she was a kiosk sales assistant. As she moved from one job to another, her occupational status fell. She describes her recent job and her state of health: 'You work and work, and you just can't bear it. By the time I get home, I've put my back out, I'm dying. My head aches, I'm simply dying, but I have to go to work – what else can I do! You have to earn something.' However,

Raisa was already in a position where she could not raise her status. Apart from her employment problems, she also listed a number of others:

> You're ill, and no medicines help. Maybe there is already such an atmosphere around, or maybe it's because of something else again. One thing just piles on top of another all the time, and because of all this there is no such thing as health. Money is tight, then there are difficulties with the children, then there's some other kind of problem, then work – it's just one thing on top of another!

3. A contradictory position, where people said in the same sentence that the reforms had no influence on health and then that they did have an influence.

> It seems to me that they have not had any influence at all, absolutely, the reforms don't come into it here. It is connected with the whole situation ... all these price rises, everything getting dearer. There isn't enough money – all these things just accumulate. You have to find some kind of way to earn something, to feed your family and all that kind of thing. (Dmitri, a Muscovite aged 39 with special vocational education but working as a fork-lift driver; see also Chapter 7)

Dmitri did not realise that the difficult situation in Russia is actually a result of the reforms. When it came to talking about his wife, he considered that her health too had deteriorated: 'The years, and her job, and all kinds of stresses have accumulated. At present, there's nothing that can improve our health.' He also mentioned changes in the organisation of working conditions, such as not getting sick pay even with a certificate, which would have been exceptional during the pre-reform period.

> The doctor says – you've got to be off sick for a month, but I went back after a week because they don't give us any sick pay. I went back after being ill and on a diet, I couldn't work, I was shivering, my head was spinning ... Every half-hour or hour, I had to go and eat some gruel. And I wasn't doing any work.

Frequent changes of job, lack of holidays, non-payment or intermittent payment of wages: Dmitri, like many others, had encountered all these problems during the post-Soviet period. Meanwhile, he has a daughter who – thanks to new economic opportunities and despite her youth – has already achieved a high wage, supports the family, has had repairs done and bought everything that her parents needed for the flat. However, Dmitri himself has still not chosen to give up work and go onto an invalidity pension: it is very important to him to have a proper job, even though he cannot find one with decent conditions.

4. The reforms have had some influence on health: 'Maybe health has also changed over recent years. Now the situation is not so easy.' As a distinct example of this position, we can look at Valentina from Moscow, aged 42 (see also the second book in our trilogy and Chapter 11 of this book). In 1996 she was working as a crane operator, then became unemployed and went to the

Employment Service to get information about vacancies. A year later she had found work in the drainage division of the Moscow Metro; she got this job herself, without registering as officially unemployed. This is how she describes her period of unemployment.

> Unemployment had an effect on my whole situation, on my health. The factory closed, and my children were small, and my whole nervous system was overtaxed. And, although I used to react to things calmly, now a lot of things annoy me; I would like things to be calmer. I live constantly on my nerves, so my health is being undermined too.

The health of many people who held this point of view had deteriorated over the period of reform implementation in Russia, and people gave concrete reasons for this. Thus, Nadezhda, a resident of Voronezh, aged 36, now a university lecturer, had had to change her job several times:

> almost from the mid-1990s right up to now, when I've finally managed to get work in a University department, I've worked as a tutor, I've written reports, coursework and once even a final-year dissertation for money. ... we've had to live through hard times, the last few years have all been difficult. And difficult in various ways. There've been problems with money, with work – not just with work, but with finding a job in my own field, which I love and didn't want to lose. Everything is strained, unhappy, irritating; and it creates the impression that everything is not OK with people's health.

5. The reforms have had a specific influence on health. Ol'ga, aged 43, from Kazan', who had special vocational education but was working as a chemical production operative (see also Chapters 3 and 10), said:

> Health has deteriorated over recent years because of the reforms. Things have become worse materially. I work at one of the biggest and most important factories in the city. There was a period when they were cutting staff, when they didn't pay wages, but were delaying them. They cut everybody who was over 35. I was 36 or 37 then. So, still young: I worked and worked ... On the other hand, they were cutting everyone, not only at our factory, but all over the city. And that was not even the first wave of staff cuts. They said we must sign on at the labour exchange, register as unemployed. I got retrained there. And now I work as a machine operator at my old factory. The work is heavy – shift work. And it's a health hazard, because it's chemical production. But after you've been made unemployed, you're overjoyed even to get that. And also, they pay extra, both for night work and for the risk involved. In general, I can't imagine, if I were left without a job again, where I would find one or what it would be. But, of course, everything was not so simple as my memories suggest and I've just been telling you. In fact, I was unemployed for seven or eight months. Just surviving each day. At the same time, I had two daughters who had to be set on their feet, and I had to try and keep a normal atmosphere in the family.

People also linked falling health standards with a reduction in the family's standard of living, which might have been a consequence of losing a permanent paid job (because wages were too low, or as a result of redundancies or closures), or of retirement, including early retirement. Thus, the reforms had an adverse effect on various aspects of people's lives (problems for people close to them, at work, etc.). Overall lifestyle has changed: food has become worse, as has the organisation of rest and recreation. People also said that negative information in the media had an adverse impact: it was a factor in stress, 'weighing on' a person and making their psychological health worse.

However, at the same time, more than half of those taking part in our in-depth interviews (of whom the youngest was 34) took the view that the main factor in deteriorating health was age:

> when you're young, you are probably also healthy. But then, once age has entered the frame, people are rarely healthy. I've practically never met any healthy people over 40. It's rare for a person not to complain about their health. (Alla, 57, a disability benefit claimant from Moscow – see also Chapters 2, 6 and 9)

On the other hand, none of the respondents gave age as the sole reason for deteriorating health. Some indicated up to seven possible causal factors: a third of panel respondents connected a deterioration in health with the absence of essential treatment or preventive health care, resulting from material difficulties, while a fifth ascribed it to harmful habits or an unhealthy lifestyle, and another fifth to conflicts and unfavourable circumstances in the family. A quarter connected it with heavy workloads or adverse working conditions, and a fifth with difficult material circumstances, which also depended on work: having work or not, and the level of pay. Women were three times more likely to name working conditions as a negative influence on health during the period of the reforms. Mentioned more rarely were poor (i.e. poor-quality) food, incorrect treatment during illness, traumas, serious infectious diseases, the presence of a large number of dependants or family members needing care, chronic diseases, poor housing conditions, poor heredity, and also reasons leading to stress, such as the death of someone close to them ('I've had health problems for a long time. And now it has got worse, because of my age, plus such unhappiness because I'm alone, I've lost my husband') and the security problem ('attempts on one's life').

Thus people saw a connection not only between all these factors and deteriorating health, but with the introduction of the reforms. However, in our panel research, we also met people whose health had improved over the reform period. Regression analysis showed that, in the first instance, changes for the better in people's own assessments of their health had an objective link with changes in work activity. On the other hand, respondents themselves put their own efforts at the top of the list of reasons why their health had improved: healthy lifestyles (four out of ten), including giving up smoking; normalisation of family relationships; going to the doctor promptly when they needed medical care; getting the correct course of treatment. In some individual cases, positive factors listed included improvements in housing conditions or moving to a locality where the climate was more favourable to their health.

At the same time, it is interesting that some respondents thought that, although the reforms had had a negative influence on health, there had recently been some improvements. Thus, in his 2004 interview, Abukhasan, 70, a pensioner and small trader/entrepreneur in Moscow said:

> Nevertheless, in the last two or three years you can see the trend stabilising, and an improvement in people's health, everyday life and the way they behave to one another. However, I would say that the government has also started to pay more attention to the population's health in the last two or three years. I feel there's been an improvement in the clinics and hospitals. (See also the second book in our trilogy and Chapter 11 of this book)

As a rule, in these interviews, negative information about certain periods of life alternated with positive. The majority of respondents in our in-depth interviews connected health with 'mood' or emotional well-being, which in its turn was linked to how satisfied a person felt with their life as a whole and its various aspects. In 1999, two-thirds of respondents felt the injustice of everything happening around them and, in 2005, fewer than half. In 1999, more than half our respondents felt that they could not go on living like this and that it was impossible for them to influence what was happening around them; by 2005 the figure had fallen to one-third.

This reflects the fact that the emotional well-being of people living in Russia has significantly improved over recent years: in 1994, 14 per cent of those taking part in the RLMS were completely or more or less satisfied with life, but by 2005 the figure had increased to 37 per cent. However, very many people remained dissatisfied with life – 66 per cent in 1994 and 36 per cent in 2005. In every year of monitoring, level of satisfaction with life seemed to be linked to people's own assessments of their health – those who assessed their own health more highly were more satisfied with life overall, and the reverse. Therefore, optimistic forecasts about the health of Russians are justified only if the socio-economic situation does not change for the worse – although health improvement is not an unlimited resource and anyway has not as yet reached poor sections of the population.

Employment and Health

In some way or other, all those taking part in our in-depth interviews touched on the theme of work and employment, linking it both to changes in well-being and to the effects of the reforms. The most prominent themes in the interviews were losing, changing or seeking a job, non-payment of wages and low pay, lack of social protection, uncertainty about the immediate future, and lack of prospects. All these problems were a source of stress for the respondents themselves and for those close to them.

In reality, job-related distress occupies a special place in terms of its influence on a working person's well-being, and depends on the situation in their particular sector (including its unemployment rate). Stress is also engendered directly at work and results partly from the working person's psychological well-being, which in its turn depends on both the difficulty of the work and the elements of creativity and job satisfaction (see Reynolds, 1997).

Research into work-related stresses and working conditions has determined the factors that explain the appearance or intensification of stress. It is generally the case that distress at work is more likely to be encountered in low-status socio-economic groups, a fact reflected in the types of morbidity and causes of mid-life mortality that are typical of these groups (Siegrist, 2002). Lower levels of distress are connected with occupational prestige, or with the high socio-economic status of a person's employment (Fuhrer, Stansfeld, Chemali, Shipley, 1999).

The onset of psychological problems relates not only to working conditions, employment status and the organisation of work, but is also influenced by certain physical and psychological demands of work activities. According to data from the Institute of Sociology's research programme 'Social reforms: expectations and reality' (2006), the main source of income of the majority of the population is wages from their main workplace, while half rely more on pensions, benefits, grants and other types of assistance received from the State (see Table 7.2). Practically a third work on a smallholding, a plot of land at a dacha or a private plot adjoining their home, generating an income that they view as their main one. One in four has additional (sometimes unregistered) earnings. Thus, Russians receive their main income from work, whether they are involved in the formal labour market or work on a private plot of land.

Table 7.2   Main sources of income, 2006 (%)

Sources of income	%
Wages from main job	79
Pensions, benefits, grants and other types of assistance received from the State	48
Smallholding, dacha, private plot of land	27
Additional, unregistered earnings; earnings from casual work	23
Additional job	8
Maintenance; assistance received from relations, friends, etc.	4
Own business	3
Income from property, renting out possessions, interest on investments	2

Note: respondents could indicate up to three main sources of income, in order of importance.

In total, more than half of respondents are involved in secondary employment (see Table 7.3) – but despite this, in Spring 2006, according to their own evaluations, a third of them had an income of under 3,500 roubles (£70 sterling) a month per

Table 7.3   Additional work activities, 2006 (%)

Type of activity	%
Working on a private plot of land, providing themselves with some foodstuffs	41
Additional, unregistered earnings from casual and temporary work	31
Overtime working or additional job at main workplace	20
Additional jobs in several places on a permanent basis	15
Not doing anything – they say nothing can help them	13
Selling excess produce that they have grown themselves and/or selling other objects that they have made themselves	8
Receiving help from relations, friends and acquaintances	8
Retraining or reskilling in order to change job or increase pay	7
Forced to borrow money	6
Not doing anything because there is no need	6
Renting out living accommodation, a garage, a dacha, a car, etc.	2
Earnings from seasonal work	1
Selling off belongings	1

Note: respondents could mark all the responses that related to their situation, which are ranked here according to the proportion of people who selected the particular response.

person. Only 6 per cent said they had no need to do anything to improve their material circumstances.

Given such a broad spread of formal and informal secondary employment, it is not surprising that one in four of those taking part in our in-depth interviews thought that their health had deteriorated over the period when reforms were being implemented, as a result of heavy workloads and adverse working conditions. What then are the features of work and working conditions, or other closely-related factors, that were said by those taking part in our in-depth interviews to be the main influences on their health during the years of reform? In trying to answer this question, we shall look at the situation through the eyes of our respondents, and use their own descriptions.

Job Loss

This was a problem affecting an extraordinarily large number of people in the 1990s, and it continues to be a current problem in Russia, although, according to the 2002 population census, only 0.8 per cent of the population was in receipt of unemployment benefit (1,171,309 people) (Results of the 2002 All-Russian Population Census, 2004). However, this is only the tip of the iceberg: in 2000, the total unemployment rate, measured using the ILO method, was 10.5 per cent of the economically active population, and in 2005 it was 7.7 per cent, yet the percentage of these actually unemployed people who were officially registered as unemployed was only 13.9 per cent in 2000 and 33.4 per cent in 2005 (Ministry for Health and Social Development of the Russian Federation). Unemployment – including hidden unemployment – and low wage levels contribute to widespread poverty. However, as became clear from our interviews, the influence of unemployment on health was connected not only with a fall in incomes, but also with stress – especially given the fact that, in principle, there was no unemployment in the Soviet Union, and Russians were psychologically completely unprepared for it.

Here are some typical quotations from the interviews with our respondents about job loss and its influence on health:

> The deterioration in my wife's health was connected with losing her job, I can say that unequivocally.

> The reforms, which lasted many years, undermined both my health and my wife's: endless cuts at work, enterprises being wound up, long-term unemployment.

> I had always been healthy, but in the last two years there have been cuts at work; at first, closure of the enterprise undermined my emotional health, and then my physical health, because I began to have financial difficulties.

Moreover, over the years of reform, many people had encountered not one stressful situation, but several simultaneously, so they had not stood up for their rights – they were simply bewildered. There were cases not just of job loss because of closure of an enterprise or workforce cuts but – in the period when private businesses were being established – of working in breach of labour legislation and/or being fired in breach of employment rights:

> I was sacked from my job and my health deteriorated. We worked – we were standing up for 12 to 14 hours (she had worked as a sales assistant). I left that shop, and they didn't even pay me any redundancy. They made me write out a statement that I 'left voluntarily'. And, because of being let go like that, of course, my health suffered a lot. I didn't go to court. I'd written the statement that I'd left voluntarily, so I thought, 'I don't want anything to do with it,' and that it would do even more damage to my health. (Galya, 36, market stall holder, Voronezh)

Being Unemployed (once or several times)

Those who had experience of being unemployed said it was precisely their lack of a job that was the main stress factor, and felt it was in this period that their physical health had deteriorated: 'Of course, unemployment had an influence [on my health]. I didn't work for a long time, and I suffered all the time because of that,' said Valentina from Voronezh, interviewed in 2004. She had worked as an engineer at a thermal power station for many years, but left her job in 1995 because her wages were not being paid. The Employment Service helped her to get retrained, after which she found a job as a cashier/bookkeeper in a shop; but she did not stay long because she did not like the job. In the late 1990s, she found casual work as a self-employed canvasser and interviewer on the campaign staff of the candidate for governor; by the time of her last interview, she had returned to engineering (see also the second book in our trilogy).

Being Forced to Change Job (in some cases, several times)

Respondents noted several changes of job over the period since 1989. Vitali, a 53-year-old Muscovite, was unemployed at the time of his last interview in 2005, and said: 'I have already changed my job about six times over the past ten years. And it isn't because I'm difficult to get on with, but simply because those are the circumstances we are in nowadays.' Almost all respondents perceived a forced change of job as a tragedy, since the main reasons for changing job were closure of the enterprise, non-payment of wages, or low pay. People defined it as 'being forced to change their job' when they had to take work that was not in their usual occupation, which they were not interested in, or which did not have decent pay.

Jobseeking (prolonged, unsuccessful, etc.)

Apart from being unemployed, which 'weighed' psychologically on our respondents, the process of jobseeking had also unsettled them. It was not just the unemployed who actively sought work, but also those who had been forced to take work that did not suit them after their previous enterprise had been wound up. Pensioners who were not able to manage on their pensions also had problems finding work. Thus, Nikolai (aged 60, from Kazan', a pensioner but still working in the building trade), who attributed the loss of his job and his health to the reforms, said:

> In general, because of all these reforms, I have had to change my job several times, starting in 1991: I've been a bricklayer, a general labourer, and a watchman. I had to take on any work; since the enterprises were closing, they were letting people go. Building firms were changing before your very eyes: one day they were State-owned, and the next day the boss was closing them and creating a new company, even a private one. And from then on he did everything just as he wanted. So they're opening, closing, taking people on, letting them go. And we're looking round for somewhere to go next. These privatised enterprises and private firms either didn't pay wages for several months (three to six months), or they didn't pay full wages.

But there were also respondents who saw no problem in the fact that they had been forced to seek work several times.

In all the years of monitoring, mobility between occupations without changing place of work and movement from one organisation to another while maintaining one's occupational status were much rarer phenomena than a single change of job and occupation, which reflected the restructuring undergone by the Russian economy. Judging by the RLMS data, in the period from 1998 to 2005, a significant number of inhabitants of Russia changed their workplace and (or) occupation. For example, in 1998, 17 per cent of respondents changed both their place of work and their occupation; in 2005, the figure was 8 per cent. In both 1998 and 2005, 3 per cent of respondents changed their occupation but stayed at the same workplace. In 1998, 9 per cent of respondents changed their place of work but did not change their occupation, and in 2005, 7 per cent. Simultaneous change of workplace and type of work led to loss of identification both with people working in the same organisation and with occupational group, i.e. to a loss of continuity in working life. In some years, up to a third of respondents changed workplace and (or) occupation. And, although there was some stabilisation after 2001, a ten-year period of instability (from 1992 – the start of large-scale economic reforms – to 2001) had already had a significant impact on the population's health.

However, during the period of stabilisation (2001 to 2005), the influence of change of job began to make a different mark on health. A positive dynamic of satisfaction with life ('completely satisfied' or 'more or less satisfied') was noted both in the population as a whole and in people who had changed their job and occupation. In 1998, most of those who had changed their place of work and occupation were 'dissatisfied' or 'more or less dissatisfied' with life. As time went on, a change of job was increasingly likely to be accompanied by positive emotions; moreover, this was more noticeable in men who were working in two jobs and had changed their place of work and (or) occupation. It was also the case that a positive dynamic of satisfaction with life became more noticeable for men when they changed job.

In the period before 2000, people who considered their health to be 'poor' or 'very poor' changed job less frequently than those who considered their health to be 'good' or 'very good' (a difference that was also connected with age). In contrast, by 2004, working people who noted that their health was 'good' were those who had not changed their workplace and occupation. Thus, strong health facilitated upward mobility even in an economically unstable period, while for people with weaker health instability generated additional problems in finding work. One of these was the fact that, for many of them, a change of job entailed taking one without official status – that is, it would not be registered on their work record – or with no contract of employment or other agreement – which meant additional risks of lack of social protection for the worker. In 1998, 2 per cent of RLMS respondents aged 18 and over were working under such conditions in their main job, while by 2003 the figure had risen to 5 per cent.

Lack of Employment Protection and Prospects

Job insecurity means that people cannot be sure that they will not lose their jobs or that, if they do, they will be able to find another and provide themselves with all they need: 'I used to be content, I knew that I would always have two secure jobs with high pay' (Kamil', male respondent aged 62, senior professional, Kazan'); 'This insecurity keeps you in a constant state of tension' (Dmitri, 39, forklift driver, Moscow); 'people have become dependent on employers. You can't show you are dissatisfied with anything – they might sack you' (Ol'ga, 43, chemical production operative, Kazan').

According to RLMS data, the number of people who have been put on forced unpaid leave by their employer has fallen significantly since 1998. Nevertheless, insecurity of employment remains a problem for Russians – in each recent year of monitoring, 2–3 per cent of working Russians (i.e. about 1.5 million people) have found themselves in this situation. So the high level of workers' anxiety about whether they may lose or keep their job is no coincidence. Records of this anxiety peaked in 1998, when about half of those employed were very afraid of losing their job, but even in recent years one in four workers has been very anxious about this prospect. In 1994, 37 per cent were very anxious about possible job loss, while in 2005 the figure was 25 per cent. In 1994, one in three (34 per cent) of those taking part in the RLMS were not certain that they would be able to find a job on a par with their current one; the 2005 figure was one in five. In 1994, 14 per cent were absolutely certain that they would be able to find a job as good as their present one; in 2005 – 13 per cent. In 1994, 13 per cent were more or less certain of this; in 2005 – 24 per cent. According to data from the Institute of Sociology's 2006 research, a third of respondents listed the danger of losing their job among the main fears they were experiencing.

Fear of job loss sometimes led to multiple employment and high workloads, so that people were working longer even though they did not actually need to earn more.

Being Forced to Take Informal, Temporary or Casual Employment

For a worker to move into the sphere of informal employment during the period of reform implementation was often an enforced measure and, despite the fact that 'shadow employment' has allowed a significant section of the population to survive, involvement in it is fraught with stresses and other problems than can affect health. A 60-year-old resident of Kazan' told us about his experience of working unofficially.

> In recent years something incomprehensible has started to happen; it's as if there are no laws and no protection. A building firm offered us work; we had to decorate an office block. They said that if we did it quickly and well, then they'd pay us well and give us a bonus. On the day when they were supposed to settle up, a bunch of young thugs with automatic weapons turned up. They herded us into the building, gave us 500 roubles each, told us to buy ourselves a drink and clear out, to forget the whole thing and never mention it if we wanted to stay alive. (Nikolai, 60, Kazan', pensioner still working in the building trade)

Low Pay

From the beginning of the reforms, specialists began to note the appearance in Russia of a new deprived group – the working poor. From 1995 to 1998, they represented around half of those in work (RLMS). According to data from the Ministry for Health and Social Development, in 2000, 41 per cent of workers were being paid at the level of the subsistence minimum or below, while the figure for 2005 was 22 per cent (Ministry for Health and Social Development of the Russian Federation).

However, as the data from our longitudinal survey show, this improvement is to some extent illusory. Let us give just one example. Sergei, who was a family breadwinner, worked as a project manager in a private building firm; his household lived mainly above the poverty line and was not deprived, but on more than one occasion had been affected by temporary difficulties, and so things had deteriorated. It was significant that there was a certain degree of increased circumstantial deprivation in the household at various times (difficulties with work; the respondent's illness following an accident; his wife Vera's unemployment in 1995–56); on the other hand, there were times when the situation markedly improved (periods of success for the business where the husband worked; receipt of an inheritance in 1999). In 2001, Sergei himself described their situation as follows: 'I would evaluate our family's standard of living as below average at present. This is because we have not received any pay at work for the last three months.'

According to official methods based on the subsistence minimum, Sergei's family did not fall into the category of the working poor; however, because of the insecurity of his situation, they lived under a constant regime of strict economies. In 2005, he said:

> My wife is sensible; I'd even go so far as to say she is a very sensible person. She is ready to forget about herself, but she is always working out what we need and what is important for us. Well, she doesn't buy clothes; it's rather the case that you would be able to buy something a bit nicer in a shop, but she always says: 'Let's go to the market, things are cheaper there.' (Sergei, from Moscow, is the husband of Vera, whose life story appears in the second book in our trilogy and in Chapter 11 of this book)

It is precisely this problem of the working poor, still current in Russia today, which, judging by data from the Institute of Sociology's 2006 research, has led 16 per cent of those for whom pay from their main workplace is the main source of income to accumulate small debts.

Workloads and Increased Length of Working Time

Many respondents considered that the only way out of their situation of poverty was not simply to have a job, but to increase the number of jobs or the length of time they worked. And they had chosen just such strategies. In her interview in 2005, 35-year-old Lilya – a lecturer at the Kazan' Conservatoire – compared her situation with a parallel one before the reforms:

> When my mum was teaching at the Conservatoire, the workload was smaller. And now I'm working there, my workload is significantly greater. About three times more.

> Twelve hours a day, sometimes more. Twelve or 14 hours. In future, maybe we will be able to live like they did, and better – I could scarcely work any more than I am now.

In this regard, it should be pointed out that, according to Russian legislation, the length of the working week should not exceed 40 hours. Overtime working is in addition to this, but must not exceed four hours over two consecutive days, or 120 hours a year.[2] In accordance with International Labour Organisation (ILO) standards, too, the working week in one job must not exceed 40 hours a week and, where a person has more than one job, 56 hours a week.

However, these standards are far from always observed. We have already mentioned our respondent who was working 12 to 14 hours a day. Moreover, judging by RLMS data, the number of people whose working day lasted more than eight hours increased between 1994 and 2003: from 30 per cent of men in 1994 to 43 per cent in 2003, and from 22 per cent of women in 1994 to 32 per cent in 2003. From 1994 to 2003, the number of men working 220 hours a month or more rose from 17 per cent to 27 per cent and the number of women, from 8 per cent to 13 per cent.

The situation was different with the length of the working day in additional jobs, where no commensurate increase was observed. However, over the period reviewed, there was some increase in working time at additional jobs: in 1994, 6 per cent of men employed for over 220 hours a month increased their hours, but 17 per cent of such men did so in 2003; the figures for women went from 5 per cent to 12 per cent. At the same time, there was a reduction in the proportion of women employed in a supplementary job – from 16 per cent in 1998 and 18 per cent in 2001 to 13 per cent in 2003.

Moreover, people who worked eight hours a day rated their standard of health lower than those who were working ten hours a day, were less satisfied with life and less certain that in a year's time they would be living better. But with a 12-hour working day, all these indicators fell again; and for those who worked 14 hours a day, they were lower still. Thus, over-employment has its limits: the first hours of extra work above the norm may pay greater dividends, while subsequent hours may entail more negative results – or are evidence not so much of having a particular interest in the additional job as of being denied workers' rights.

RLMS data indicate that, in 1995, 18 per cent of men and 4 per cent of women were doing heavy physical work and standing up or moving about for more than six hours a day – for example, porters, construction workers and those engaged in heavy agricultural labour and similar activities. In 2002, this applied to 10 per cent of men and 3 per cent of women.

---

2 Articles 91 and 95. Law on Employment of the Population in the Russian Federation, in the version of Federal Laws of 10 January 2003, No. 15-FL.

Multiple Employment (additional job or secondary employment)

Since, as a rule, pay was low and there was not enough money even for the essentials, statements like the following were typical:

> It's partly the case that the reforms have had an influence on health. Because my husband has had to work a great deal, including in an extra job, in order to maintain the family and pay for our daughter's higher education. (Tamara, 57, Moscow, deputy director of a department)

The proportion of people who had an additional or casual job, both on our panel and in the RLMS research, remained practically unchanged from year to year, varying within the boundaries of 1–2 per cent. However, men moved in and out of secondary employment more frequently than women. Although very few in number, women were more likely than men to have a second job for two years running (in 1995–96, 1 per cent of men and 2 per cent of women; in 2000–2001, 2 per cent of men and 2 per cent of women; and in both 2001–2002 and 2002–2003, 2 per cent of men and 3 per cent of women). At the same time, men were more likely to have to take casual work (varying from 9 per cent to 12 per cent in different years) than to find a secure additional job.

The assessments of their own health given by people employed in one job were fairly constant across the whole period of our research, while those given by people who had a second job 'jumped around' from year to year. In 1994, people who had a second job gave higher assessments of their own health than those who had only one job, perhaps because, in their insecure situation, this gave them a sense of greater certainty. However, from 1998 onwards, those employed in two jobs began to give lower assessments of their own health than those who had one job. By 2003, an even wider gulf had appeared: men employed in one job were 10 per cent more likely to say that their health was 'good' or 'very good' than those with two jobs, and the difference was even greater for women. However, we should note that women who had found a second job had increased their level of satisfaction with life, which was more important to them than preserving their health: where people had one job, there was an insignificant difference between men and women in dissatisfaction with life, but a second job increased the gender gap by several times.

Thus, a second job meant greater physical and, to some extent, psychological burdens. However, there were also mitigating psychological factors, since a second job brought both additional income and certainty about the immediate future. Most men employed in an additional job did not worry at all, or did not worry very much, about whether they would be able to provide themselves with what they needed in the coming 12 months. However, there was not one year over the whole period of research where such certainty was felt by women who had two jobs.

Delays and Non-Payment of Wages

Given that the majority of Russians, as has been noted above, live mainly on wages, other problems connected with pay gave rise to serious stresses. Among stress factors related to pay, respondents listed first and foremost delays in paying wages, non-payment of wages and low pay: 'They paid our wages twice a month, then once a month, and then they had a crisis and started to pay half wages, with the rest later' (Vitali, 53, unemployed, Moscow). Respondents saw a connection between wage delays and not just deteriorating health but even death:

> In 1994–96 my husband was working, but he didn't receive any money, he suffered greatly, fell ill and died in 1997. His death also had an impact on my health. (Lida, 55, operative at Moscow's No. 2 Reinforced Concrete Construction Factory, Moscow)

In recent years, one in five employees has been owed some amount of money by their employer, which has not been paid on time for various reasons. In the 1990s, the situation with unpaid and delayed wages was significantly more serious. In all the years reviewed, men were in a less advantageous position than women, since a higher proportion of women work in the public sector, where wages are low but secure.

From 2000 onwards, the proportion of employees who had taken a pay cut in the previous 12 months at the request of their employer, or had reduced their working hours despite not wishing to do so, remained at a steady 6–7 per cent – considerably lower than in the 1990s.

Difficult Working Conditions

'It's not that the reforms have had an influence on my wife's health, it's simply that her work is heavy, her working conditions are difficult, that's all' (Vasili, unemployed, 48, Voronezh). In our respondents' opinions, working conditions have an effect on people of all ages.

> There are no healthy people now, because the workload in any job is too big. The deterioration in the population's health is because of their working conditions. (Irina, 53, Moscow, disabled, not working – see also the second book in our trilogy and Chapters 8, 10 and 11 of this book)

Respondents most often gave material factors – earning more money – as their motive for doing a job in adverse working conditions. For men, it was also important to build a career. In contrast, the results of a 1980 research study showed that the chief motive in those days was the desire to obtain a flat more quickly, followed by earning a bigger pension – in other words, motives related to plans for long-term prospects (Zhuravleva, Shilova, Lakomova and Borzunova, 1993). In a period of instability, however, it is risky to make long-term plans, so people need to earn more now. But what has not changed over the last 25 years is the attitude of Russians to health as an instrumental value.

The social benefits granted to employees in harmful and hazardous industries by the State or by their employer, to compensate them for difficult conditions, are also a serious motive for working in such an unfavourable setting. Social and economic support is available not only to employees, but also to members of their families – for example, organised summer holidays for children. Since harmful and hazardous industries are more likely to be State-owned than other businesses, many people see them as more attractive when compared to other Russian employers, from the point of view of securing basic social guarantees. For example, judging by RLMS data, employees in harmful industries were 10 per cent more likely to get regular paid leave, and even more likely to get sick pay or maternity leave, than in other industries. One employee in two could obtain free treatment at a workplace medical establishment or full or partial payment for treatment at other medical establishments, and paid visits to a health resort, holiday home or hotel or a children's summer camp (as opposed to one in five and one in four respectively in safer industries). More often still, they were provided with free places for children at workplace pre-school establishments, and full or partial payment for children at other pre-school establishments.

At the same time, there are a number of bonuses which are more often granted by employers not involved in harmful industries: free food, food at preferential rates or food payments, transport subsidies, payment for travel, sponsored study, provision of loans, credit, rent or other housing payments.

Employees were more likely to leave a job with harmful and hazardous working conditions because their employer owed them money (the average amount of which was likely to be high), which remained unpaid for a variety of reasons, or had cut wages or working hours against the employee's wishes. The average sum of money earned in harmful industries was higher than in other businesses, but the hours worked were also longer.

Participants in our in-depth interviews who had listed a number of harmful factors present in their job (chemicals, night work, shift work, noise, dust, danger of accidents, nervous strain, frequent changes in temperature, constant mental strain) were asked the question: 'If you think that your work is damaging your health, why don't you change your job?' It turned out that the attitude of the majority of people to a change of workplace was that this brought its own risks. This was especially the case when employees had no-one else to offer them material support, and where not only their own personal well-being but also the lives of other family members depended on their wages.

Many of our respondents provided clear examples of this situation. Let us give just one, typical in that it concerns a person who had not only worked all his life in a harmful industry, but continued to do so even though he was drawing his pension and was ill. Vladimir, aged 65, from Voronezh (whose life story is told in more detail in the second book in our trilogy) was a working pensioner, a skilled electric and gas welder. He had a fairly high income and had always been the family breadwinner. He said that his work involved risk of accident and frequent changes in temperature. In 1996, he was on unpaid leave, since the enterprise where he had worked for a long time was then in the process of becoming a shareholder company. In this period of insecure employment, he was actively earning through unregistered work, using his connections at the workplace to obtain orders, including from former colleagues who had started their own business. However, he did not change his job, since he was accustomed to his own factory, had a long work record at a single workplace and was due to take early retirement. After starting to draw his pension, he continued to work for the same company. He believed that people whose health standards were poor continued to work in State enterprises because private businesses did not need sick people; and that people whose health had been destroyed in a harmful industry would continue that work, since they were not fit for any other.

Among RLMS respondents who were employed in a harmful industry, only 57 per cent were healthy, measured on the EQ-5D scale. These people were asked about what they were planning to do after they had completed the specific length of service that would give them the right to early retirement. Thirty-four per cent of the sick respondents, 42 per cent of the unhealthy and 58 per cent of the healthy were intending to continue working in the same harmful industry – i.e. the higher their standard of health, the more likely they were to exploit this.

Absence of Career/Professional Development

One in four of those taking part in the Institute of Sociology's 2006 research thought that one of the main reasons for a person falling below the poverty line was having poor education and low skills. However, only 7 per cent of those taking part in the research were retraining or reskilling in order to improve their own material circumstances. Judging by data from the same research, over the previous year, only 9 per cent of respondents (or members of their families) had succeeded in obtaining a promotion at work or finding a new, more suitable job, and only 8 per cent in raising their standard of education and/or skills. This was connected both with lack of the necessary resources and with particular features of the way retraining is organised. Thus, another Vladimir, a fairly young man (aged 42 at interview in 1996), who worked as a measuring equipment adjuster in a Moscow factory, said: 'my health has deteriorated because of lack of money, and high costs. I am forced to go without everything. I can't work like a young man. And retraining is only for the young' (see also Chapter 9).

Other Shortcomings of Work

Those taking part in our in-depth interviews, talking about what they liked and did not like about their job, were usually not happy with their pay, but the main mitigating factor was the element of security. Also mentioned were stress factors: a stressful job, a job without prospects, chronically high workloads, exhausting work. At the top of the list of positive factors came elements of creativity at work – that is, varied or interesting work. In addition, a convenient schedule and fixed working hours (without overtime) were important to our respondents.

Attractive characteristics of work could serve as a motive for employment in jobs with some unattractive features. For example, a job might not be interesting, but many people did not reject it, since they had formed good relationships with management, there was a pleasant team atmosphere, and the working hours were fixed. Even for a job without future prospects, attractive features might be a convenient schedule and fixed working hours. People who considered their job to be prestigious might agree to do frequent overtime. Insecure work is 'good' – our respondents said – because, as a rule, it offers a convenient schedule and also a relatively light workload.

People with differing health standards were equally likely to be employed in jobs with attractive or unattractive features.

Lack of Worthwhile Rest

According to data from the Institute of Sociology's 2006 research, 37 per cent of respondents assessed their opportunities to rest when on leave from work as 'poor', and 33 per cent applied this description to their leisure time. Some people cannot organise a holiday even once every two years, let alone rest on a weekly or daily basis: 'I've been working for seven years in a limited company, but I've never had a holiday. After working for 25 years in a place were I always got leave – getting none at all now is very hard' (Ivan, 55, builder, Kazan'). People involved in informal employment were especially likely to get no leave, because their employer does not have a responsibility to provide employees with basic social guarantees such as regular paid holidays, days off, a working day lasting no more than eight hours, and paid leave when they are incapable of work.

Only 9 per cent of those taking part in the 2006 research said that they spent any spare cash on recreation or travel. Moreover, a third did not have sufficient income even for their general day-to-day expenditure, and another third, although they did have enough resources for day-to-day expenditure, had no money to spare. In this situation, it is not surprising that, over the previous year, 17 per cent of respondents had not had the opportunity to spend their leisure time as they would have liked, and 6 per cent had not had the opportunity to visit relations and friends.

Build-up and Interaction of Various Factors

As a rule, factors that have an unfavourable influence on health are found in a variety of combinations, and each intensifies the adverse effects of the others. Lack of a secure job, working in a business with no prospects, frequent forced changes of workplace, being unemployed and unable to find a new occupation or raise one's level of skills all limit the probability of upward occupational mobility, leading to stress, especially in the younger working generation.

Many of the factors that relate to work, job and employment, which people thought had an influence on their health, were combined with breaches of their rights as workers. The results of the pan-Russian sociological monitoring survey 'Values and interests in today's Russia' show that the right to work, while it is one of the most important values for Russians, is also one of the most compromised: it was the second most likely to be breached, out of a list of 11. People also say they are less likely to be successful in standing up for this right than many others: they put their success in defending workers' rights in seventh place on the list (Lapin, 2003).

Moreover, as many years of observation of our household panel has shown, respondents have constructed a hierarchy of values connected with work and job, depending on the situation in the country, the labour market and their personal life. Stabilisation of the labour market situation in recent years has also changed respondents' attitudes to work, shifting their career aspirations from 'ready to take any job in order to survive' to 'find work with higher pay', 'get better working conditions', 'increase my occupational and job status'. From priorities with a material element, people have moved to demanding a broad spectrum of qualitative characteristics from work and employment. It was no coincidence that the majority of those taking part in our in-depth interviews who had succeeded in changing their working conditions for more favourable ones had also improved their health.

In discussing the implementation of reforms and their lives, people said that success in life was based on job, work and career – and that success at work was based on health. One-third of those taking part in our in-depth interviews took the view that it is vital to maintain good health in order to be successful at work. Success is an important emotional component in people's lives, one which inspires them to attain new heights.

> First and foremost, health affects your ability to work. And your ability to work affects your success. But there is a reverse connection – when you have some kind of success, then that helps because the state of your nervous system is a very important factor in your health. (Alla, 57, a disability benefit claimant from Moscow; a trained biologist, she had an interest in herbal medicine – see also Chapters 2, 6 and 9)

People also expressed the view that failure, as the opposite of success, can lead to illness.

Judging by how RLMS respondents described their work and the kind of working and employment conditions that they considered stressful, the conclusion can be drawn that there are many unattractive, low-quality jobs on the Russian labour market, which hardly enable a person to survive, are badly paid and demand heavy workloads, with consequent risks to physical and psychological health. And although in recent years a positive dynamic in risk reduction has been observed in some aspects of working conditions and employment (for example, fewer instances of compulsory leave or non-payment of wages), at the same time workloads have increased for many people, reflecting longer working hours.

PART III
Health and Social Action

Chapter 8
Access to Health Care and Self-Care

Inna Nazarova

Всем сестрам по серьгам
Earrings to all the sisters

In Russia, throughout a period viewed as a time of change and reform, including in the health care system, indicators of morbidity in the population have grown or remained at the same high rates. Consequently, the number of people who are potentially patients in need of skilled medical care must also have increased. In a situation where most of the population is poor, where it is impossible to care for one's health naturally (through adequate nutrition, worthwhile rest, taking part in sport, living in comfortable and environmentally clean conditions), and where there are many stressors (loss or forced change of job, delays in payment of wages, low pay), the accessibility of health care and medical assistance is a particularly live issue.

Seeking Medical Care

RLMS data reveal a real paradox: despite the deterioration in health across many indicators, during the period of reform and stabilisation in the early 2000s, people began to visit the doctor more rarely, not only for preventive care, but also when they were ill or felt unwell. Moreover, in each year of monitoring, precautionary health care behaviour was more characteristic of women. From 1994 to 2005, about 40 per cent of women and a third to a quarter of men aged 18 and over taking part in the RLMS surveys said that in the previous 30 days they had had some kind of problem with their health. However, in 1994, 43 per cent of them had gone to a medical establishment, while ten years later the figure was only 32 per cent. In our research, we attempted to find an answer to the questions surrounding this situation.

The data from our project enabled us to analyse people's subjective assessments of the accessibility and quality of medical care during the period of transition and entry to the market economy (1989 onwards), and to gain an understanding of the boundary between an accessible health care system and the area of self-care. As has already been explained, in the course of our research we undertook in-depth, partially pre-coded interviews with 87 residents of three Russian cities. In parallel, 43 medical personnel – representing various specialisms – were interviewed about their opinions on problems in the health care system. In this chapter, the information obtained from these in-depth interviews will be compared with data from quantitative research projects, in particular the RLMS.

The majority of people taking part in our in-depth interviews said that they or people close to them had needed skilled medical care, since one in three had problems with their own health and half with the health of people close to them. However, only half of our in-depth interviewees – or members of their families – had sought either medical care or emergency treatment in the previous three years, mainly at municipal clinics in the area where they lived – that is, from State structures which have always been accessible and habitually used by the majority of people living in Russia. The leading role of State clinics is also evidenced by the RLMS data (see Table 8.1).

Table 8.1   Patterns of use for different health care establishments (%)

Medical establishment	1994	1995	1996	1998	2000
District, city, workplace, village clinic	86	84	85	86	83
District, city, workplace, village hospital	9	11	11	9	10
Fee-paying clinic	3	3	2	3	4
Fee-paying hospital	1	1	1	1	1
Private hospital or doctor	1	1	1	1	2
Medical establishment	2001	2002	2003	2004	2005
District, city, workplace, village clinic	84	83	84	84	85
District, city, workplace, village hospital	9	9	7	8	8
Fee-paying clinic	4	5	6	5	5
Fee-paying hospital	1	1	1	1	1
Private hospital or doctor	2	2	2	2	1

Source: RLMS (various years).

Of people defined as 'sick' according to the EQ-5D method, 87 per cent of respondents went to a municipal clinic, as did 85 per cent of the 'unhealthy' and 82 per cent of the 'healthy', while 2 per cent, 5 per cent and 7 per cent respectively went to a fee-paying clinic, i.e. free medical care is more often used by sick people, and fee-paying medical care by the healthy. Five per cent of respondents had been in hospital in the previous three months. Among the sick, 10 per cent had been in hospital; among the unhealthy, 5 per cent; and among the healthy, 3 per cent.

The worse someone's health, the more often they visited the doctor (see Table 8.2). One in three sick people visited the clinic 2–3 times a year, as did one in three unhealthy people – but only one in four healthy people. At the same time, people who displayed a passive attitude towards taking up exercise or sport, or drank alcohol more often, also visited the clinic less often.

Table 8.2   Frequency of visiting the doctor, 2005 (%)

Frequency of visiting doctor in the course of a year	Health measured using the EQ-5D method			
	Healthy N=2022	Unhealthy N=2413	Sick N=4683	Total N=9118
Several times a month	1	2	9	3
Once a month	4	7	17	8
2–3 times a year	25	35	36	30
Once a year	27	24	14	23
Less than once a year	43	32	25	36

Source: RLMS.

The same picture emerged from our in-depth interviews. For example, among those who described their health as 'poor' or 'very poor', two-thirds had visited the clinic in the previous year and one-third had not. The details of the survey show that the latter are generally more sanguine, and manifest less concern for their health, not only by not going to the doctor when they are ill or feel unwell, but also for preventive care. They less often stick to diets, do not observe a routine and rarely give up harmful habits. They gave as reasons for their relative absence of concern about their health not that they had no money (like those who had been to the clinic), but that they were not in a situation that allowed them to be concerned, and that they did not know what they needed to do in order to maintain their own health.

A quarter of in-depth interviewees who had visited the clinic were people in poor health according to the EQ-5D method (sick people). In some cases, if it was simply that the patients themselves thought they were unhealthy (according to their own assessment of their health), they might not go to the clinic. But if they were in poor health objectively (according to the EQ-5D method), then they would visit the clinic. Consequently, a subjective assessment of one's own health as 'poor' may sometimes be insufficient to generate an active approach and make the person feel concern about their own health – there also have to be objective reasons. A corollary of this is that rating one's own health as better than it really is can be dangerous, since it may prevent people from seeking prompt medical care.

According to RLMS data, about half of sick people (44 per cent) go for advice to the doctor when they have a health problem, but only 28 per cent each in the case of the unhealthy and the healthy. Relatively well-off patients are the most active: one in three people in the two highest decile groups by income visited the clinic when they had a health problem, compared with 41 per cent of Group 6, 29 per cent of Group 9 and 29 per cent of Group 10. The same applies to preventive investigations. Better-off people went for these slightly more often: among those whose income was above the median, 19 per cent went to see medical personnel for preventive check-ups rather than because they were sick, while this applied to 14 per cent of those with incomes below the median.

A more detailed survey of the respondents who took part in our in-depth interviews confirms the quantitative data and allows us to define the main characteristics of individuals who seek medical care, whether at free or fee-paying health care establishments. Among these are:

- a relatively high level of income;
- serious health problems (a sharp deterioration in health, a worsening disease);
- a high level of self-care activity.

Respondents who, in the course of the year before the interview, had a specific illness or trauma or needed prolonged treatment for chronic illness were more likely to have visited a district clinic or undergone a complete check-up in recent years. In cases of severe need (disease, trauma), the behaviour of patients who described their own health as 'good' largely coincided with the behaviour of those who gave a low assessment of their health (according to the five-point scale on which people rated their own health). However, people with average incomes visited the clinic not only when they needed to but also for preventive care, while the poor, as a rule, went only in case of trauma or chronic illness.

Most people who had visited a municipal clinic had encountered some kind of organisational difficulties: problems in making appointments with doctors or specialists; waiting a long time to be seen; having to get to the clinic long before opening time just to get a place in the queue. Frequently, people who really are in very poor health simply cannot put up with all these difficulties:

> I need to see a doctor, but they are the ones you most especially can't get to see now. I've already made an appointment three times, but I haven't got to see a doctor once – so then you can't be bothered any more, and you don't go. (Natal'ya, 46, from Voronezh, unemployed)

Results from other research projects also provide evidence of this (World Bank, 2002).

Reasons given for not visiting the clinic also included lack of time, which in its turn was the consequence of a heavy workload, either at work or at home, in the family. The family burden may involve the problems of those close to the respondent ('my husband had an operation and needed constant care', 'my daughter was starting university'). Judging from the respondents' answers, they also put their health in second place when they were looking for work. On the one hand, it meant they had no time, and, on the other hand, their psychological mood was not one of concern for their health but of maintaining or changing their social status and obtaining the means to exist.

Complete Check-up

A quarter of respondents taking part in our in-depth interviews had undergone a full health investigation not very long before, in 2003 or 2004 – that is, a year or two before the survey. Some individuals could remember undergoing this kind of health check before 1989 when it was a distinctive feature of the old health system. A third of respondents could not answer the question at all. The rest had had a complete check-up during the period 1989 to 2002.

Respondents who had never undergone a complete check-up were those who:

- took the view that everything was fine with their health and that there was no need to have one;
- objectively, had no possibility of getting one (they lacked social and material capital);
- had no time for one;
- were passive and, although they knew they ought to check their state of health and then obtain treatment, did not visit a medical establishment – 'you simply don't pay any special attention to it, that's all' (Natal'ya, 46, from Voronezh, unemployed).

Moreover, there were both healthy and sick people who had not undergone a full health investigation – as there also were among those who had.

Among those who had undergone a complete check-up, there was a greater proportion of people who had also been to the clinic for other reasons. Like those who go to the clinic generally, they either had more health problems or were more active in regard to their health. Those who considered their health to be poor and yet had not undergone a complete check-up at all were mainly people who were not simply poor or whose material circumstances had become worse over recent years (i.e. they had moved from the 'badly-off' to the 'poor' category), but were poor and had other problems apart from material ones. For example, frequent job losses and job seeking, death, illness of someone close to them (spouse, child), a child leaving school and going into higher education. These problems intensified the situation with their personal health and took up all the respondent's time and attention. Thus, for poor people and, to some extent, for the badly-off, concern about one's personal health usually takes second place if the person has a complex of problems of another type. In contrast, better-off people in secure employment found the opportunity to check their state of health even when people close to them had problems.

In the main, people who described their health as 'poor' or 'very poor' and who could be classed as living in persistent poverty had undergone a complete check-up in the pre-perestroika period, before 1990 (including planned check-ups at the workplace, which large enterprises used to carry out in those days). Since their complete check-up had been a very long time ago, these people might as well be categorised among those who had not undergone a full health check at all.

However, others in poor health and persistent poverty had undergone a complete check-up in recent years (2003–2004): these were people suffering from serious illness or those whose health problems had become a lot worse – leading to their being sent for full investigation – or patients with a disability or a combination of chronic diseases.

Difficult Life Situations

The passivity of some respondents towards their own health should not be viewed as absolutely subjective. Someone most probably becomes passive because one problem follows hard on the heels of another, so that it becomes impossible to tackle them and the person loses faith in being able to change their life through their own efforts. As a rule, optimism is lost when the person gets into a difficult long-term life situation and one problem piles up on top of another: loss of job, lack of money, growing debts, illness, and so on.

Sometimes people feel completely helpless in the face of the need to do something to obtain a diagnosis so that their health can be restored:

> a person can be ill for a very long time, but he doesn't go to get checked out. Then one fine day he simply has to face the facts. And decide who to go to, and which doctors to trust, and whether to take that step and pay ... My husband has been Category II disabled for a long time now, and he had to go into hospital, and when he'd been there two weeks they asked me for 14 thousand roubles [£280 – two month's wages]. (Rimma, aged 56, Voronezh – see also Chapter 2)

When a person has a serious illness, consultations are required with various specialists, who sometimes do not work at the district clinic at all, making it necessary to go to a specialised medical centre. However, at these centres, medical services are also not always free of charge: 'At the Multiple Sclerosis Centre you have to pay for consultations. Sometimes there are no medicines, you have to buy them yourself' (Tat'yana, disabled, from Moscow – see Chapter 11).

According to data from the pan-Russian research programme 'Social reforms: expectations and reality', carried out by the Institute of Sociology of the Russian Academy of Sciences in 2006, if a respondent or a relation needed a fee-paying operation or expensive treatment, then – if they could not manage with their own resources (only 14 per cent thought that they would be able to tackle the problem themselves) – their first recourse would be to turn to relations or friends for help. Forty-one per cent could not even imagine how they would cope in this situation, while a small proportion (10 per cent) would try to go to various institutions for help (public social protection bodies, the governor of their province, the Ministry of Health, the City Health Care Authority, banks, the Veterans' Committee, the Red Cross). Employees who felt that they could count on help from their workplace planned to go either to management or to the trade union committee.

In practice, only a few individuals referred to any attempt to increase their income, since, if people had such an opportunity, they had already made use of it. The data from our interviews also provided evidence of this – there too, people who were both sick and poor were less likely to rely on their own resources when they needed to spend a lot on their health, and more likely to turn to the State. More prosperous people were willing to sell something (car, garage, dacha) if they needed to. The poor often made extreme statements like: 'We would have nothing left but to die, because we have no money, and we are not going to beg or humiliate ourselves – we value our dignity above everything!' (Sergei, 50, single parent from Voronezh; a skilled worker now employed as a repairman – see also Chapters 7, 10 and 11).

Using credit to pay for health care is as yet still a new phenomenon in Russia and has not become widespread. Only 3 per cent of participants in the Institute of Sociology's 2006 research had already used credit, or planned to use credit in the course of the coming year, to tackle problems connected with health (an operation, obtaining a prosthesis, visiting a sanatorium or health resort, and so on).

Meanwhile, among those taking part in our in-depth interviews, some had had to pay a doctor for their operation, but none had had to refuse surgical intervention on financial grounds. According to RLMS data, 19 per cent of those who had had an operation had paid for this medical service. However, this does not mean that every Russian citizen who needed in-patient care could obtain it. We shall show below precisely what types of medical care were inaccessible to people because they lacked the means to pay for them, and how often this was the case.

Types of Patients

People structure their interactions with medical establishments according to their state of health, material circumstances and attitudes to self-care. As a result, we can divide them into several notional groups on the basis of their possibilities and preferences for approaching the health care system to obtain medical care – groups which could be fairly clearly distinguished in our in-depth interview materials.

Group 1

This group consists of patients who, in the last three years, have used only the services of the district clinic. The majority of them belong to the 'poor' category, and are especially likely to be living in persistent poverty, while somewhat fewer are in the 'averagely well-off' stratum – but practically all of them are classified as 'sick' according to the EQ-5D method. It may be hypothesised that it is primarily people who are poor and sick who go to the district (or municipal) clinic, because they have no choice, along with those who have connections in the clinic and are therefore certain that they will receive high-quality medical care. Yet in this group there are also conscientious patients who have been accustomed to going to the doctor as a first resort when they feel ill, and then complying with medical instructions, despite the fact that they may encounter difficulties when visiting the district clinic.

Group 2

As a rule, these respondents do not go to the district clinic for assistance, but to private clinics, including dentists' (or doctors') surgeries, or to clinics where they are registered for payment by their supplementary medical insurance. If they have also had to visit a district clinic, this was only when it was simply impossible to manage without the services of the State health care system because of legislative restrictions.

Patients in this group said they encountered a number of problems when visiting the district clinic: waiting a long time to be seen; problems in making appointments with doctors; having to get to the clinic long before opening time (to get a place in the queue); having to pay for services that were nominally free of charge. Therefore, they had consciously rejected free State medical services and moved into the private medical sector. They include members of all the various health groups measured according to the EQ-5D, and are also in a variety of groups as far as their Index of Multiple Deprivation is concerned. There are people who are 'well-off' or 'averagely well-off', as well as those who used to be 'well-off' – in 1997, for example – and have now moved into the 'badly-off' group, but continue to use fee-paying medical care.

Group 3

These people habitually seek medical care from both the district clinic and the private medical sector simultaneously. They include both sick people and healthy people; all had improved their welfare over recent years. It is possible that this group is transitional: as their position in the category of 'well-off' or 'averagely well-off' people stabilises, they will make increasing use of private medical services.

Group 4

These patients do not use either private or State medical care, since they are able to obtain medical services at their workplace or visit a clinic affiliated to it. They cannot picture how the district clinic works and are not in a position to evaluate it. The group is very diverse as far as health standards and economic circumstances are concerned. They have just one thing in common – the opportunity to obtain medical care at their workplace. We can hypothesise that, if the workplace medical establishment closed down or if they changed (or lost) their job, some of the better-off among them might go over to the private medical sector, while others would use the free district clinic. This would depend on the respondent's level of welfare, self-care activity and experience of seeking medical care from different health care establishments.

Group 5

This is the high-risk group. Patients do not use the services of a clinic doctor, but seek medical assistance only in case of extreme need, when they call an ambulance and go to an in-patient medical establishment. There is no clearly defined portrait of a typical member of this group: there are people with various health standards, whose material status has fluctuated since 1997. Generally, they all have very heavy workloads, both at their job and/or domestically. They do not have time to worry about their health – yet there is also an element of passivity:

> I absolutely don't take care of myself, I just go to the clinic 'on automatic pilot'. Now I'm not working, it's like I really should go and get a check-up, though when I remember what long queues there are there, then any desire to go completely disappears, although really of course I ought to go. (Vitali, 53, unemployed, Moscow)

Group 6

People in this group make consistent use of services at clinics where they are registered for payment by their supplementary medical insurance. These are mainly well-off people, or those with an average income, and primarily those whom we classified as 'sick'. Almost all of them have a permanent doctor or know a doctor to whom they can go in case of need. If the respondent or a relation had to have a fee-paying operation, then members of this group would manage on their own or would turn to relations or those close to them for help: they have sufficient economic and social capital to tackle health-related problems. In addition, practically all of them are working.

Group 7

These are respondents who themselves work in the State health care system and have connections (acquaintances) that help them to tackle problems connected with their health or the health of those close to them.

Accessibility of the Health Care System

Inaccessibility of Medical Care because of Lack of Means

Over the year before the Institute of Sociology's 2006 research survey, one-third of respondents had been unable to tackle some kind of problem connected with medical care, including those who:

could not buy medicine – 21 per cent;
could not obtain dental care – 16 per cent;
could not obtain in-patient treatment at a hospital, military hospital or clinic – 11 per cent;
could not obtain out-patient or clinic treatment – 6 per cent.

At the same time, 40 per cent said that no member of their family had needed fee-paying medical care over the previous year, and 23 per cent replied that they had always found the means to pay for treatment. Problems connected with lack of material resources for medical care were, naturally, encountered primarily among poor and badly-off people. The results of analysing our in-depth interviews also provide evidence of this.

Good dental services are as expensive in Russia as in the rest of the world. As a rule, patients give very low assessments of the free care available at the dental clinics where they are registered for payment under their insurance policy. Our respondents were not any more likely to be able to obtain dental care than any other type of medical care; moreover, this problem affected not only the poor, but also the relatively well-off, who often simply took the attitude that they were not willing to pay for the services of specialists in private practice.

In Kazan' in 1998, 21 per cent of respondents said that they had been refused some kind of medical care, while approximately one in three had been refused expensive medicines or medical supplies (Nazarova, 1999). Our 2005 survey of the same sample showed that respondents had a number of concessions entitling them to various types of medical services. However, not all patients were able to exercise their rights to receive this social support. First and foremost, this affected the provision of medicines. Respondents could not get their essential drugs free or at a special price, and were very worried by the decision to replace their concessionary medicines with cash payments. Our last survey was carried out during a period of social reform, when concessions were being replaced by financial allowances, and people who were entitled to concessions did not have reliable information about how things would turn out in the social sphere and what to expect in this regard. For example, Tanya, 44, a postal worker from Moscow, said:

> now they are altering the concessions, people will have to pay. They are trying to prove something. They go to the social security to find out. There's very little information, it should be explained to people more somehow, so that they have a solid understanding of it. And now everybody's asking one another about it, and nobody knows anything definite. And they simply get worried that it'll all be taken out of their purses yet again.

Respondents also said that it was easier to go to the clinic at their workplace, when there was one, rather than to the clinic in the district where they lived, since it was impossible to get to an ordinary clinic during working hours – it would be viewed as absenteeism. It was often at a workplace clinic that the first symptoms of their illness had been discovered.

Thus, it is not only the case that a person sometimes has not enough money, or no money at all, to pay for medical services directly, but also not enough to organise care in the optimum way: to obtain the good-quality medicines they need, in the amount that is essential for them, through the system of concessions they are entitled to; to be able to get to see a doctor when they need to; to get an appointment with a specialist in an uncommon condition at a specialised centre in another city (despite the fact that someone from the regions can get a consultation free of charge in Moscow, sick people in the regions often do not have the money to travel).

In this regard, it should also be noted that people have started to spend money more often on expenses connected with organising treatment – for example, on travel to and from a medical establishment: in 1994, 23 per cent had this type of expenditure, in 1998 – 24 per cent, in 2005 – 35 per cent. Judging by the sums that people spent, in some cases this meant a return journey equivalent to half the length of Russia. Moreover, the 2005 RLMS data show that 32 per cent of people who were 'sick' according to the EQ-5D method, 40 per cent of unhealthy people and 37 per cent of the healthy spent money on travelling for treatment or diagnosis. This may say something about the greater chances of obtaining help at big medical centres if the patient is willing to travel to a specialised centre in a major city.

Table 8.3   Views on social justice, 2006 (%)

Statements	Agree	More or less agree	Partly agree, partly disagree	More or less disagree	Don't agree	Don't know
When some people have more money than others, this is fair as long as they had equal opportunities to earn it	42	22	19	8	8	1
It is fair when people who can afford it give their children a better education	31	21	23	13	11	1
It is fair that people with the means to do so can use higher-quality medical services than other people	16	17	22	19	25	1
It is fair that people with the means to do so can buy themselves better housing than other people	26	23	25	13	12	1
It is fair that people who have higher pay will also get a bigger pension	24	28	25	17	14	2

Source: Institute of Sociology of the Russian Academy of Sciences (2006).

Meanwhile, in response to a question about the fairness of receiving various social goods, one in four participants in the Institute of Sociology's 2006 research took the view that it was unjust for people with the means to do so to be able to use medical services of a higher quality, while another one in five thought it was somewhat unjust for well-off people to have such possibilities (see Table 8.3). Thus, 44 per cent of Russians consider that all categories of the population, regardless of income, should have the right to high-quality medical care, with 33 per cent agreeing it is fair that money should make a difference. This belief in the need for access to high-quality medical care regardless of the presence of monetary resources was stronger than the responses about wages, access to education, receipt of pensions or obtaining housing, and it was predominant across all income, age and educational groups.

Organisational Problems in Gaining Access to Doctors

As has already been noted above, our respondents said that there were often not enough specialists at their local district clinics; in addition, if a doctor is away ill or on a continuing professional development course, then there is no one to stand in.

Shortage or complete absence of specialists leads to a situation in which patients sometimes have to wait several months for a diagnosis or consultation. For example, the patient may have to wait a month or two after their appointment for a free ultrasound examination – although they can get one immediately if they pay. So, clearly, badly-off people get a diagnosis much later than those who can pay. On the other hand, it should be pointed out that many types of medical care that used not to be available (even in return for payment) can now be obtained – primarily those that involve expensive diagnostic equipment. Here is what the manager of one Moscow clinic said on this topic.

> You should see the equipment! Before, in the children's clinic we could only do an ECG (electrocardiogram) – now we can also do ultrasound of the abdominal cavity and of the heart. You can investigate fully – from head to toe. And with an echocardiogram, it can reveal not just disease in the child at the early stages, but also any kind of heart valve defect or something like that. Before, there was none of this kind of equipment in clinics. You only used to see it in one particular medical centre, but, you know, it was very difficult to get in there. (Another Tat'yana – see also Chapter 9)

In some new districts of Moscow, doctors are even being provided with housing on condition that they work at the municipal clinic. However, in a large city, doctors have a choice of jobs: apart from clinics, they can work in pharmaceutical companies or in the fee-paying medical sector. Doctors may work in a district clinic, carrying out free consultations, and also consult in another medical establishment on a fee-paying basis. In the district clinic, they sort out the clientele, and then for some people they make appointments for fee-paying consultations, which are available at any time.

District clinics are also experiencing difficulties with a flow of new, young, trained staff.

> Very few young people work in district clinics. They only come so that they can get a reference saying they've done a stint here. In the time I've been working here (four years), not one student has stayed on to work here ... They all leave either to go into the commercial sector or to medical centres where there is an opportunity for high earnings. Or they leave completely, to go into firms where they work as pharmacologists. They have a purely commercial attitude to medicine. (Tat'yana, 40, unemployed on first joining our panel in 1999, now finance director of a children's clinic in Moscow and one of our more prosperous respondents – see also Chapter 9)

Queuing at clinics is yet another problem in gaining access to a doctor.

> Sometimes a person can't get to the doctor's because they are so busy at work; you have to earn money. And then it's difficult to get in to see a doctor at our clinic – there are queues. It can even be a problem just to get the numbered chit that allows you to queue. (Lyubov', 52, cashier in a shop, Moscow)

Possibilities of Obtaining Medicinal Products

In Kazan', in 1998, 38 per cent of respondents said that they would take all the medicines that the doctor prescribed them; 32 per cent said they would be selective, and take only the main ones; 27 per cent were only prepared to take their 'usual' ones – meaning those they had taken before; 10 per cent would take those prescribed by the doctor, but only inexpensive ones, while 4 per cent would take only expensive ones (Nazarova, 1999). Practically every in-depth interview contained some mention of problems connected with obtaining medicines: 'I try to treat myself with herbs. And I try to treat those close to me with herbs. Otherwise everything would just be spent on tablets' (Rosa, 63, storeroom operative, Kazan').

The RLMS data show that, over the last ten years, it has become slightly less likely that a doctor will recommend a patient to take a particular medicinal product: in 1994, the survey found that, in the course of the previous 30 days, a doctor or other specialist at a medical establishment – hospital or clinic – had prescribed or advised 22 per cent of respondents to take particular medicines, while by 2005 the figure had fallen to 17 per cent. At the same time, the possibilities of patients purchasing or finding essential medicines increased from year to year: in 2004, 84 per cent were able to find or buy some of the recommended medicines, while by 2005 the figure had reached 94 per cent. However, although the majority of patients who needed medical supplies were able to purchase the necessary ones that the doctor had prescribed, since 1994 the number of people who could not buy them because they did not have enough money, rather than because the pharmacy did not have them, had increased significantly: in 1994 the figure was 23 per cent, but by 2005 it had practically doubled – to 53 per cent. It was not only poor

Russians who had problems with money, but even the well-off: 79 per cent of the lowest decile group, 40 per cent of the middle group and 15 per cent of the highest group could not afford to buy medicines.

People said that in some cases they had access to a consultation with a doctor, but then no treatment was available:

> as a rule, if you go for help or advice to the doctor (where I work), they explain, they tell you how to treat yourself, what medicines it's best to take. But what's the use? There's no money for medicines! (Nina, 54, nurse in district clinic, Kazan')

In other cases they said that a consultation with a specialist was just as inaccessible as medicines:

> I'm not taking any medicines, simply because there's no money, and because I don't trust doctors now. And, in order to start taking any kind of drugs, you'd have to go to a competent doctor, who would establish the diagnosis correctly. But, as they say, it's kill or cure – and you might get either! (Vitali, 53, unemployed, Moscow)

Or

> I would like to get an appointment at a specialist clinic, have a full check-up, get recommendations from specialists. But that too is only available if you have money. So that's how you live: you don't know whether everything is in order, how to treat yourself, what to use to treat yourself or where to get the money for treatment! (Nina)

Problems purchasing medicinal products primarily affected disabled people, or middle-aged and elderly people on low incomes who were caring for dependants. In such cases, every kopeck counted:

> There are going to be changes to concessions, but for the moment we haven't felt any effects. Well, they wouldn't take our travel concessions away from us. But my mum needs the concessions on medicines. Everything should be looked at point by point: I'm young, I need travel concessions, but my mother doesn't travel anywhere now – the money is better for her, 150 or 200 roubles. She needs medicine for her eyes that costs 107 roubles; her bowels don't work too well, so she also needs medicine for that. About 800 roubles a month is going out on medicines. (Rosa, 63, storeroom operative, Kazan')

> My wage as a cleaner and cloakroom attendant is three thousand a month. But you can't imagine how much of that goes on medicines! The ones I need are not on the list of medicines you can get a concession on. (Tat'yana, from Moscow, aged 50 when interviewed here in 2000; registered disabled, she suffers from multiple sclerosis – see also Chapter 11)

Alarm about the replacement of concessions by cash is understandable, since a large number of Russians have always received concessions on medicinal products: in 1994, discount on medicine was available to 38 per cent of the population, and in 2005, to 36 per cent. Of those who were eligible for concessions in 1994, the discount was applicable at 100 per cent for 68 per cent of them, and in 2005, for 80 per cent of them; a 50 per cent discount was applicable to one in three people in 1994 and one in ten in 2005; a discount of up to 20 per cent was applicable to 1 per cent of people in 1994, and to 10 per cent in 2005. However, this discount applied only to a limited list of medicines.

There were some positive changes in terms of access to medicines between 1994 and 2005, in that people living in Russia were more likely to be able to find a medicinal product they needed, either because of the sharp increase in imported pharmaceutical products or through doctors working as consultants to pharmaceutical companies or as a result of commercial pharmacies opening on a large scale. However, since 2003, the number of people who could not find a necessary medicine at the pharmacy has begun to increase: one in three could not obtain the medicine they needed, despite the fact that the range of pharmaceutical products has become significantly wider recently. This may be connected with the absence of cheap, ordinary Russian medicines or, on the other hand, of the newest imported medicines.

In 1994, 78 per cent of respondents obtained medicines at a State pharmacy, and in 2005 the figure was 76 per cent. The figures for non-State pharmacies were one in ten and one in three in those years respectively. In 1994, one in ten bought medicines at the doctor's surgery and, in 2005, just 4 per cent. In 1994, 6 per cent bought medicines from illicit sources; in 2005, the figure was only half a percent.

This last decrease may result from lack of confidence in the quality of medicines being produced. Respondents often spoke of poor-quality, counterfeit medicinal products. For example, Vitali, 53, unemployed, from Moscow, said that medicines were not always accessible because of their high cost, but also that medicinal products were not to be trusted: 'the quality of treatment and of the drugs themselves leaves much to be desired. Medicines are expensive, but don't always help, because they are not always good quality.'

This is another reason why, alongside ordinary medicines, herbs are a widely-used form of treatment. In the Russian tradition, the use of herbs in everyday life is a common phenomenon: 'I got it from my grandmother: she used to gather some kind of herbs and believed that this would help certain diseases, so I use them, that's what I stick to' (Rosa, 63, storeroom operative, Kazan'). Pharmacies offer a wide choice of herbs; and badly-off patients often use herbs in place of diets or expensive treatments.

Specialised homoeopathic centres are also now available to individuals:

and you can be treated with herbs, and with acupuncture, and with honey bee products. In order to be treated with herbs you have to go to herbalists. I used to go at one time, but I don't now. Firstly, it's very expensive, and the herbs are expensive – both the treatment itself, and the consultation with the doctors. Consultations cost 500 roubles. [Homoeopathic] medicines are expensive. And now I'm on a pension – two thousand a month: on two thousand, how can I do it? (Tat'yana, disabled, Moscow, aged 55 when interviewed in 2005 and no longer working – see also Chapter 11)

Paying for 'Health'

One in three respondents in the Institute of Sociology's 2006 research said that, over the previous year, they or a member of their family had used their own resources for fee-paying medical services. State (district) clinics, as has already been noted above, can also not be viewed as unequivocally free medical care, since nowadays many services have to be paid for. People at all income levels had paid (in money or in gifts) for services that were officially free of charge. Even badly-off and poor patients understood that there is no such thing as absolutely free medical care, and found the means to show their gratitude to the medical staff. A fairly large proportion of those taking part in the research (48 per cent) took the view that people themselves should pay, at least in part, for medical services. However, willingness to do so depended both on their standard of health and their level of welfare: among those who rated their own health as 'good or very good', 59 per cent agreed with this, as against 22 per cent of those who rated it as 'poor or very poor'; 77 per cent of wealthy people agreed, as against 31 per cent of the poor.

According to RLMS data, Russian patients are increasingly frequently paying medical staff for a visit, in money or gifts: in 1994, 5 per cent paid, but by 2005 the figure had risen to 14 per cent (see Table 8.4). The same is also true of payment for additional services (tests or procedures): in 1994, one in ten patients paid but, in 2005, almost one in three. In 2000, half of patients paid for a visit to the doctor officially at the clinic cashier's office *and* directly to the medical staff in money or gifts. By 2005, payments through official channels had increased, and under-the-counter payments had diminished. The frequency of payment at the cashier's office rose from 55 per cent in 2000 to 64 per cent in 2005, but 'cash-in-hand payments' fell from 52 per cent to 44 per cent. A similar process also took place in the area of additional medical services. In 2000, 70 per cent paid officially for additional tests or procedures, while in 2005 the figure was 75 per cent; in contrast, the figures for payments made directly to staff in those years were 39 per cent and 31 per cent. Healthy people were more likely to pay, whether officially or directly to staff: 10 per cent of sick people, 17 per cent of unhealthy people and 20 per cent of healthy people paid for their visits in 2005. The same is also true of payments for additional tests and procedures (25 per cent, 32 per cent and 29 per cent respectively). People in the second decile by income paid for 12 per cent of visits; in the ninth decile group, for 24 per cent; and in the highest income decile, for 28 per cent, with payment for additional services in 29 per cent, 46 per cent and 32 per cent of cases respectively.

It has also become even more frequent to pay for a stay in hospital. In 2000, 14 per cent paid for this in money or gifts and, in 2005, 19 per cent. At the same time, in the course of the three months preceding the survey, approximately half the patients every year had paid for treatment and hospital care officially at the hospital cashier's office, not counting payments for medicine. In addition, unlike the situation in clinics, the level of direct payments to doctors and other medical staff in hospitals, whether in money or gifts, is growing: from 54 per cent in 2000 to 67 per cent in 2005. Thus we see differing attitudes to payment for a consultation and payment for performing an operation. In the second instance, 'under-the-counter' payments are not just continuing, but are actually tending to grow.

Every year, patients in Russia were less likely to have to pay for the medicines, syringes and dressings needed for their treatment in hospital. In 2000, 19 per cent received everything they needed free; by 2005, the figure had risen to 56 per cent (see Table 8.5).

In 2000, during a stay in hospital, one in ten patients had to make direct payments for medicines, syringes and dressings to doctors or other medical staff, in the form of money or gifts; in 2003 this figure fell to 6 per cent, but by 2005 it had grown again, to 9 per cent. In 2000, half the patients paid for medical and other vital supplies officially at the cashier's office or the pharmacy of the hospital they were in; by 2005, this figure had fallen to 29 per cent.

Despite the fact that an increasing number of patients received essential medicinal products and other materials free of charge, frequency of expenditure for medical purposes outside hospital grew. In 2000, 60 per cent of respondents who had been in hospital had themselves bought everything they needed at pharmacies not affiliated to the hospital they were in, or their families had done so at the patient's request; in 2005, the figure was 76 per cent. This may be explained by the fact that the necessary medical supplies were out of stock in the hospital where treatment was being carried out, or that the hospital never sold these items at all, or that patients were seeking a more suitably priced offer elsewhere.

Patients also paid for preventive investigations; moreover, the frequency of such 'gratitude' doubled over the period under study (1994–2005): in 1994 it was 11 per cent, and in 2005, 22 per cent. In 2000, 77 per cent paid officially and, in 2005, 91 per cent – obvious evidence of a shift of medical services into fee-paying channels. Yet patients also continue to pay the doctor or other medical staff directly, in the form of money or gifts: in 2000, one in three patients paid and, in 2005, one in ten. On the one hand, the fact that payment for preventive medical services is coming out of the shadows into the light can be seen as positive. But, on the other hand, we could hypothesise that it is precisely these preventive measures that are becoming more inaccessible to badly-off Russians, who will cut back on visits to the clinic for preventive care.

We undertook interviews with users of medical services and with medical staff. Both discussed the same themes and explained the current health care situation, sometimes agreeing with one another, sometimes taking opposed points of view (see Table 8.6). For example, patients complain about lack of access to medical services; doctors agree that patients are really suffering, but medical staff have objective reasons preventing them from carrying out their duties to a good standard. Doctors and patients give their own accounts of what is happening in the area of informal payment for medical services, how payment takes place and how the price for various types of services is established. Both take as their starting point the fact that the quality of medical care is lost if the doctor does not receive a decent reward for fee-paying services. Managers of medical establishments say

Table 8.4   Paying for medical services (%)

Payment by patients	1994	1995	1996	1998	2000
For a visit (with money or gifts), including those who paid:	5	5	6	7	11
officially at the cashier's office of the medical establishment for a visit to the doctor					55
money or gifts directly to medical staff for a visit					52
For additional tests or procedures, including those who paid:	9	7	9	18	18
when having additional tests or procedures, officially at the cashier's office of the medical establishment					70
when having additional tests or other procedures, money or gifts directly to the medical staff who performed them					39
For a stay in hospital, medical care or treatment, not counting payments for medicine, syringes and dressings, whether with money or gifts, including those who paid:					14
in the last three months for treatment and hospital care, not counting payments for medicine, officially at the hospital cashier's office					49
in the last three months for treatment and hospital care, not counting payments for medicine, directly to doctors and other medical staff with money or gifts					54
For a visit (with money or gifts), including those who paid:	12	13	15	14	14
officially at the cashier's office of the medical establishment for a visit to the doctor	52	62	56	57	64
money or gifts directly to medical staff for a visit	54	41	50	53	44
For additional tests or procedures, including those who paid:	23	23	26	25	28
when having additional tests or procedures, officially at the cashier's office of the medical establishment	75	65	74	76	75
when having additional tests or other procedures, money or gifts directly to the medical staff who performed them	29	40	31	31	31
For a stay in hospital, medical care or treatment, not counting payments for medicine, syringes and dressings, whether with money or gifts, including those who paid:	16	15	16	13	19

in the last three months for treatment and hospital care, not counting payments for medicine, officially at the hospital cashier's office	69	51	55	47	49
in the last three months for treatment and hospital care, not counting payments for medicine, directly to doctors and other medical staff with money or gifts	48	68	61	73	67

Source: RLMS (various years).

Table 8.5   Payment for medicines, syringes and dressings (%)

Payment by patients	2000	2001	2002	2003	2004	2005
Received free of charge	19	47	44	51	54	56
Some were received free of charge, some they paid for	39	30	34	30	31	30
Paid for all medicines	42	23	21	20	15	14
Officially at the cashier's office or pharmacy of the hospital they were in	50	43	38	44	40	29
Paid money or gave gifts directly to the doctors or other medical staff of the hospital they were in	11	9	9	6	11	9
They, or their families at the patient's request, bought them at a pharmacy not affiliated to the hospital they were in	66	73	70	66	66	76

Source: RLMS (various years).

that in some cases it just does not pay, doctors do not want to work in the fee-paying sector and this reflects on patients. When they try to enhance their skills or obtain a high-status job, medical staff are just as likely to get into a situation where informal rules apply as are patients at the clinic or, indeed, at their own workplaces. Medical staff often have to make official payments or give bribes in order to take part in training courses to enhance their skills.

Overall, the situation in the fee-paying medical sector is such that in many cases it is not advantageous for either the producers or the consumers of these services to come out of the shadows and move away from illicit payments.

Participants in the Institute of Sociology's 2006 research were fearful of any expansion in fee-paying services. In answer to the question about a person's attitude to these reforms in the social sphere – implementation of which has

**Table 8.6		Features of fee-paying and free services, 2005**

Patients' opinions	Doctors' opinions
'The doctor ordered an ultrasound because he suspected I had kidney stones, but out of two ultrasound doctors working in that particular clinic, one was sick and the other had upgraded his skills and came to work at the clinic extremely rarely. My appointment with him was for a month ahead. In that case, I could wait over a month for the opportunity of a free ultrasound, or I could pay and get a diagnosis straightaway. I waited 36 days.' (Patient at a district clinic)	'I might get seven non-paying people a day at my surgery, the rest are paying. It's profitable for the clinic to get as many paying patients as possible, so the clinic doesn't limit their number. For those who come to get a free consultation, there is no chance; but if a person agrees to pay, then he is given an appointment and no-one remembers that my working day will be longer, or tries to take into account how much time it takes me to see everyone. I can't manage to see everyone over the working day, so I stay late every time. But I cut down the length of each appointment so that I won't have to stay at the clinic all night. There can be 60 people – not every day, but 40 is a completely realistic figure. When you work so hard – that's no use to the doctor or the patient. It's utterly routine, like a conveyor belt. Each patient wants to hear something individual, but you don't have the energy or the time for that, and you're not in the mood to work. We have two specialists in the clinic, but now my colleague is doing training to enhance his skills, so in two months' time I'll be taking on the work of two people.' (Ultrasound doctor, district clinic)
'Medical care should be free. But if something serious happens, then we try to pay. Because they are just bringing the free service to its knees, that's all! You can't get any tests done free, and sometimes even the doctors aren't free of charge. Even your annual review by the Disability Commission isn't completely free of charge.' (Irina, 53, disabled, not working, Moscow – see also the second book in our trilogy and Chapter 11 of this book)	'There are specialists in State clinics who know their own price, and if you go for an appointment with them, they immediately say "that costs such-and-such." They have to get by, too. They've brought their scale of charges into line with their experience of the work. The doctor is going to keep hold of paying patients, he'll spend day and night with them. He all but takes them around in a wheelchair himself. He'll keep everything under his own control. Because that's what they're paying him for. Because he understands that this is how he will be able to fill up his car, buy a television, build himself a dacha. He'll be able to give his children an education. So every kopeck counts.' (Senior doctor in a commercial medical centre)

'The doctor ordered a head x-ray for me. I went to the cashier's office to pay for the service, but they recommended me to drop in and see the radiologist first. I went in to see the radiologist and he said that I could pay him a much lower amount than what they wanted at the cashier's office. I agreed.' (Patient at district clinic)	'Doctors don't want to leave to go into legitimate fee-paying medical services: there the doctor will come up against the fact that a large sum goes into their coffers and he gets the small change. There is no advantage in it. The senior doctor can be driving about in a Mercedes, while the ordinary doctor is earning kopecks. So the clinic doctor will drop a hint that they should pay him, not pay at the cashier's office. It's to the advantage of both doctor and patient. It's true that there are doctors who are afraid of taking money and don't want to have anything to do with it.' (Head of the Medical Sociology Research Section at the Tatar Republican Centre for Medical, Social and Economic Research)

Source: In-depth interviews.

already begun or may soon begin – taking as an example their attitude to the reform of medicine and health care (with restrictions envisaged on the list of cases in which medical care will remain free, while all other medical services will become fee-paying), the majority (60 per cent) said that they considered this wrong, and harmful in its consequences for them and their family. Sixty-four per cent of the poor held this opinion, 65 per cent of the badly-off, 55 per cent of the middle strata, and 47 per cent of the top 5 per cent of the population. Nineteen per cent of the sample took the view that this change was right overall, but at the same time they were afraid that their own situation would only deteriorate because of it. Most people (74 per cent) in poor or very poor health also considered that the introduction of a limited list of cases in which medical care remained free would be wrong. People in good or very good health regarded this possibility more optimistically (49 per cent). Only 5 per cent took the view that it was right, and might improve their own and their family's situation. Thus, it was not only the poor and sick who were fearful of fundamental changes that would shift medical services into a fee-paying channel, but also a significant section of wealthy and healthy people. The elderly and middle-aged were especially fearful of restrictions on free medical services.

As a rule, people who had had to seek medical assistance in a strange town when they became ill suddenly were happy with fee-paying services. If a person fell ill while on holiday or away on business, then fee-paying services were a convenient choice. Despite the fact that, under compulsory medical insurance, a Russian citizen should be able to obtain medical assistance in any population centre in the country, in practice this is always problematic, whereas one can rely on obtaining the care one needs in practically any medical establishment in return for a fee.

Table 8.7   Responsibility for tackling social problems, 2006 (%)

Problems	The central State	Regional authorities	Local authorities	People themselves	Entre-preneurs	Trade unions	Don't know
Pension provision	85	6	6	1	0	1	1
Anti-poverty strategies	74	10	9	4	1	1	1
Medical care	67	12	17	1	0	1	1
Opportunity to receive higher education	64	8	6	21	0	0	1
Opportunity to receive secondary education	64	9	11	15	0	0	1
Fair distribution of material goods	59	14	17	4	1	4	1
Fair pay	49	16	19	1	10	5	0
Assistance to families and children	48	17	24	7	0	1	3
Personal safety	44	9	26	19	0	0	2
Housing provision	37	23	33	6	0	0	1
Favourable environmental conditions	35	30	28	5	1	0	1
Safeguarding jobs	28	19	38	8	5	1	1
Pre-school provision	27	25	45	1	0	1	1

Source: Institute of Sociology of the Russian Academy of Sciences (2006).

Table 8.8   Changes in social support during Putin's presidency, 2006 (%)

Aspects of life:	Situation has improved	Situation has remained the same	Situation has deteriorated	Don't know
Supporting families and the birth rate	34	46	19	1
Pre-school provision	13	54	31	2
Secondary education	14	69	16	1
Higher education	13	52	34	1
Health care	13	43	43	1
Pension provision	29	46	24	1
The population's standard of living	20	48	32	0

Source: Institute of Sociology of the Russian Academy of Sciences (2006).

Ways of Improving the Accessibility of the Health Care System

Attitudes to reforms in Russian society are, in many cases, defined by views about the justice of what is happening in the country and about the role of the State in the social support of citizens. A significant part (77 per cent) of respondents to the Institute of Sociology's 2006 research took the view that the majority of Russians would simply not be able to survive without the constant concern and guardianship of the State. This explains why opinions like 'People must solve their own problems themselves, and not rely on the State' were held by only 4 per cent of respondents. The great mass of other people (50 per cent) took the view that the State should in some measure or other support various categories of the population, primarily all those who were in need. Only one respondent in four took the view that the State should target assistance solely at population groups who were in a difficult situation because of some specific reason (the unemployed, poor families with children, and so on). Fifteen per cent were of the opinion that the State should protect only those who were incapable of work (the aged, disabled people, orphans). However, the list of high-priority problems that the State should assume responsibility for was headed by pension provision, anti-poverty strategies and medical care (see Table 8.7).

One in ten of those taking part in the Institute of Sociology's 2006 research took the view that the health care situation had somewhat improved in recent years (see Table 8.8). However, by comparison with the institution of education, for example, health care looked distinctly weaker. A fairly large proportion of Russians took the view that the health care situation had even deteriorated (43 per cent).

It was primarily for better-off people that the situation in the health care system had changed for the better. In the first instance, this was because in the past it was not always possible to get a consultation at a prestige medical centre or use expensive medical equipment in return for a fee, and now this possibility has

Table 8.9   Opinions on changes in the health care *x* level of material welfare, 2006 (%)

Situation	Poor	Badly-off	Averagely well-off	Well-off
Situation has improved	8	11	15	30
Situation has remained the same	43	42	46	41
Situation has deteriorated	49	47	39	29

Source: Institute of Sociology of the Russian Academy of Sciences (2006).

Table 8.10   Opinions on health care funding *x* level of material welfare, 2006 (%)

Respondents' opinions	Poor	Badly-off	Averagely well-off	Well-off
The State should provide a full medical service, with increased taxes on ordinary citizens to pay for this	33	31	26	30
Personally, I am willing to pay higher taxes in order to provide free medical care to all Russian citizens who need it	17	23	29	37
People themselves should pay, at least in part, for medical services	31	42	61	77

Source: Institute of Sociology of the Russian Academy of Sciences (2006).

opened up. And not only are the opportunities of obtaining essential services for payment being extended, but also medicine has moved forward a great deal over recent years. Advances in medical care that are made in any country in the world quickly spread to other countries, including Russia, which has become part of the global world and open to innovation. However, for the poor, the badly-off and even for people with an average standard of living, the situation in the health care system has changed for the worse (see Table 8.9).

Ways of Improving the Quality of Medical Care

Almost a third (30 per cent) of Russians questioned in 2006 took the view that the State should provide a full medical service, increasing taxes on ordinary citizens to pay for it: the poor were more likely to agree with this (33 per cent) and members of the middle strata of the population, less likely (26 per cent) (see Table 8.10). A still smaller number (25 per cent) would be ready to pay higher taxes personally in order to provide free medical care to all Russian citizens who need it. Among the better-off, 37 per cent expressed such a willingness, but among the poor – only 17 per cent. The better-off supported the idea that people themselves should pay, at least in part, for medical services (77 per cent), but the poorer the group to which the respondent belonged, the less likely that this idea would be supported.

In our in-depth interviews, respondents also talked about other measures, apart from the purely physical, which would be essential in the first instance if the quality of medical care at their district clinic were to be improved, although a third of those taking part in the interviews – primarily those who had not visited a clinic – were not able to answer this question.

The responses we received can be divided into seven basic notional types (in order of popularity):

1. *Increasing pay for medical staff.* One in ten of those taking part in our in-depth interviews thought that the pay of medical staff should be raised: 'bring doctors' pay up, so that they have a better attitude to work, get doctors more interested', 'raise pay for medical staff to a human standard of living', 'so that doctors wouldn't have to make profits out of the patient's illness, they wouldn't be caught up in the business net'. Patients understood doctors' difficulties and were sympathetic towards them: they wanted the situation in the health care system to improve, and also to raise living standards for medical staff.

    Meanwhile, it should be noted that respondents, although they considered this measure essential, understood that in itself it would not change the situation. It is no coincidence that in the Institute of Sociology's 2006 research, 73 per cent said directly that increasing wages for public-sector staff would not lead to any improvement in the educational system or the health care system.

2. *Improving the technical resources of clinics and the skills profiles of medical staff.* One in ten of those questioned took the view that improving the quality of medical care was only possible if there were improvements in:

    *   the technical features of medical establishments: 'installing up-to-date diagnostic equipment and equipment for treating chronic illnesses', 'our clinic needs to move into better premises, the doctors in themselves are fine';
    *   the skills profiles of medical staff: 'we need more skilled specialists who love what they are doing'.

3. *Increasing the number of doctors.* One in eight took the view that it is essential to increase the number of doctors: 'there are not enough young medical staff, not enough doctors in the various specialisms'. Patients very

often indicated that there were no doctors with narrow specialisations. Patients took the view that 'to be healthy means to be investigated, to have information that you are healthy, that a specialist has come to this conclusion. You need all the doctors to check you over; you need to have all the tests. Otherwise you don't know whether you're sick or healthy'.

4. *Improving the organisation of medical care (reducing queuing, and so on)*. One in 20 of our respondents said it was important to improve the organisation of the service: 'At the clinic the doctors don't show any especial interest in treating the patient: they write a prescription and suggest you come back after treatment if your health alters', 'you have to get there at seven o'clock in the morning, and it is especially difficult to get to see specialists', 'they should get rid of the queues'.

5. *Optimisation of the doctor-patient relationship (medical staff should pay more attention to patients)*. Medical staff and patients noted changes in the attitude of the population towards doctors, which also affected the quality of the medical care provided:

> The attitude to the professions of doctor and teacher is changing. These professions are now service staff. But in fact it is a question of the health of a generation. For example, the doctor rings: 'Let me in, it's the local doctor' – and mum says to her through the entry phone: 'My child's asleep, come back in three hours.' We ourselves are to blame for this. We have, as it were, let life cross these professions off the list completely. (Finance Director, deputy to the senior doctor at a Moscow district clinic)

6. *Providing access to (free) medical care*. One in 20 said that medical care was inaccessible: 'doctors don't want to work with all patients', 'develop a programme to combat corruption', 'a system of extortions and additional payments developed a long time ago in hospitals'.

7. *Nothing needs to be changed, happy with everything*. Some individuals were content with the medical service at their district clinic: 'good specialists, conscientious and attentive examinations, good medical staff', 'I would say that the government has started to pay more attention to the health of the population in the last two or three years. I feel there's been an improvement in the clinics and hospitals'.

8. *Patients who had the most pessimistic outlook* took the view that: 'nothing will help, everything is neglected and ruined' or that what would help is 'the return of Soviet power'.

Thus, it is primarily poor, sick Russians who use free State medical care. An improvement in welfare enables a person to move away from the free medical care system and into the fee-paying medical sector. So, lack of material resources and the consequent absence of essential treatment or preventive health care were given by one in three respondents as the main reason for a deterioration in health.

The organisation of medical care within the framework of municipal clinics is not productive, since it is not convenient for the working population (queues, lack of specialists). This leads to a redistribution of the patient load, with those who need preventive types of care turning to extreme measures (calling ambulances, attending inpatient facilities). When they are sick, the only options for people with a low level of material resources are to seek free medical care, put off a visit to the doctor, or not visit the municipal clinic at all. People who are refused help by specialists often try to treat themselves. This leads to the illness becoming worse, even chronic, and also to people more frequently seeking emergency medical assistance.

Difficulties when visiting the district clinic are experienced by all population groups. However, well-off people have already found, or in future will try to find, more comfortable conditions to obtain medical care, through additional payments or taking out voluntary medical insurance. Badly-off people will most probably use only the possibilities offered by the clinic in the place where they live. However, it is not only the poor and the badly-off but also Russians with average means who, in the main, do not support, and are unlikely to support in the near future, reforms directed at cutting the proportion of State involvement in the social sphere, including in health care – a view which, objectively, is based on their lack of means to pay independently for medical services.

It is also probable that both the well-off and the poor will avoid visiting a clinic, because they do not want to face the problems that arise when they try to obtain medical care. It is no accident that, among those who have not visited the clinic, there is a fairly large proportion of people with serious health problems (half of those who were 'sick', as defined by the EQ-5D method, had not visited a clinic in the year preceding the survey). Consequently, people often do not visit a clinic even when they need to. Moreover, we can hypothesise that well-off Russians will use strategies different from the strategies adopted by the poor in these circumstances. People with the means to do so will most probably seek refuge in fee-paying medical services, turn to doctors in private practice, use their connections, or go straight to a specialist for help, paying for their consultations either legally or illegally. In any case, we can see them already starting to do that.

Chapter 9
Health Behaviour

Irina Popova

Узнают птицу по полёту
A bird is known by its flight

World Health Organisation research has recognised that poverty and ill-health form a vicious circle – and that poverty is not only a major determinant of poor health, but also a potential consequence of it (The European Health Report, 2002, p. 70). The World Bank's research into issues of poverty and inequality in Eastern European countries and former Soviet republics, in their recent stage of a return to economic growth, has shown that inequality of access to health care remains high and that its quality is low as a result of under-funding, non-rational use of resources and failure of resources to keep pace with needs (Growth, poverty and inequality. Eastern Europe and the former Soviet Union, 2005, pp. 28–31). As a result, the major burden of responsibility for their own health falls on people themselves, on their abilities to adapt and on their mobilising resources to maintain their own health in the face of structural limitations. There is a corresponding growth in the role of a self-care culture (Shilova, 1999) – in other words, in adapting to a new system of social norms and actions that define attitude to health at the level of society and of social groups (Zhuravleva, 2004).

In these conditions, research into the complex of factors involved in the dynamic of health that results from change in welfare at the micro level (individuals, households) acquires particular currency. What are the possibilities that people mobilise to overcome the well-known 'vicious circle' of poverty and poor health, each of which intensifies the other? Which factors facilitate this and which hinder it? And, finally, what are the feasible limits on the use of people's own possibilities at the micro level – what might be called the 'human dimension' – that must be defined and taken into account in forming social policy?

Both Western and Russian sociology have developed approaches to researching these problems. A well-known typology of models of the interrelationship of social inequality and health is the one put forward by Mel Bartley (2004). She identifies the following explanatory models: material (income, which determines quality of diet, housing, environment and safety at work), cultural/behavioural (differences in beliefs, norms and values, which are social determinants of various forms of health behaviour), psychosocial (status, control, social support at work or at home, balance between effort and reward influence health through their impact on body functions), life course (events and processes starting before birth and during childhood may influence both physical health and ability to maintain health; health and social circumstances influence each other over time); political economy (political processes and distribution of power affect the provision of services, quality of the physical environment and social relationships).

In considering models of the interrelationship of social inequality and health, researchers most often identify an opposition between the behavioural/cultural on the one hand and the material on the other, and they tend to investigate factors influencing health within that space. These factors have also been widely studied by Russian sociologists of health (see, for example, Nazarova, 2003; Zhuravleva, 2005).

At the same time, the interrelationship of the role of these two groups of factors in health remains insufficiently studied: it is not clear which has the decisive influence on health improvements in contemporary Russian society – material or behavioural/cultural factors. The same problems also exist in many other post-Soviet societies – for example, in Ukraine (Abbott, Turmov and Wallace, 2006). In this connection, one of the chief hypotheses of our research was that behavioural factors may be decisive in a positive health dynamic, but they do not act independently of or outside the socio-economic context of people's daily lives, and therefore they cannot carry the whole responsibility for the health of Russians. In conceiving social policy for health, it is essential to take into account both these components – creating the conditions for good-quality health care while trying to stimulate effective health strategies among the Russian population.

In this chapter, we shall review the major factors and particular features of models of health behaviour – with the emphasis on a positive health dynamic – of members of households which, in the 1990s, did not possess significant material resources and whose health dynamic has been simultaneously both a consequence of and a factor in implementing strategies for overcoming poverty and for reintegration into society. The chapter is based on a qualitative analysis of data from our longitudinal survey of members of households in Moscow and Voronezh, which took place over a number of years (1996–2005). The special value of these data for the set of issues analysed here derives from the inclusion in our pre-coded questionnaire, at all stages of this survey, of questions from the General Health Questionnaire (GHQ); this allowed us to track changes in the health of separate individuals over a number of years. The second method of diagnosing health, used in our 2005 survey, was through the EQ-5D scale developed by the EuroQol group. In addition to indicators on the GHQ and EQ-5D scales, we also looked at indicators of respondents' subjective feelings about changes in their health. Finally, we analysed our respondents' life stories, various aspects of which were explained to us over a number of rounds of our survey.

All this allowed us to review instances of a positive health dynamic – defined by the difference between our respondents' GHQ test values from the first longitudinal survey and those from the 2005 survey – and then to look at our interviews with respondents in order to find behavioural factors that had favoured this dynamic. One of the hypotheses being tested in our research was that a positive health dynamic and success in overcoming the 'vicious circle of poverty and sickness' in conditions of prolonged material restrictions are determined by the effect of a whole number of factors, the basis of which is to be found in a mechanism of mobilising a rational attitude to one's health in specific individual life situations.

In order to test this hypothesis through our longitudinal research materials, the following objectives were tackled: we first identified and described groups of people according to the dynamics of their health, as revealed by the GHQ; we then reviewed possible ways of looking at these in combination with the household's welfare dynamic; finally, we analysed behavioural models that were typical of the various groups of respondents who combined certain health dynamics and levels of material welfare. We paid special attention to models that involved positive shifts in both material welfare and health.

The first step in this analysis, therefore, was to define groups of respondents with various health dynamics. The data we obtained enable us to state that, for a fairly large proportion (about half our respondents), changes in health across the summarised GHQ scale may be rated as positive. These changes were defined primarily by changes on two subscales – somatic health and anxiety/insomnia. More detailed analysis allowed us to identify groups of respondents according to the nature and strength of their health dynamics. Two groups contrasted sharply: in one of them, we noted a general improvement in respondents' health, evidenced not only by a big jump in the overall GHQ indicator from the level we had obtained when they first joined our sample, but also by positive dynamics across all the GHQ sub-scales. In the other group, there was a general deterioration in health, with a large fall from the level of their first result accompanied by negative dynamics across all the GHQ sub-scales. Further analysis will focus on these two groups, since the blurred and indistinct nature of trends in other respondents' health dynamics does not allow us to describe them as such distinctly delineated types; they can be notionally classified into a third, intermediate group.

Groups Differentiated by their Health Dynamics

The 'Generally Better Health' Group

Those who had made stable improvements in their health were people who had a fairly significant positive gap between overall GHQ indicators in the most recent survey and those from the survey carried out when they first joined our panel (mainly ranging from nine to 20 points), with indicators of health improvements across all four scales. This group was fairly numerous: 16 people; in it, an intensive improvement in health was connected with a reduction in anxiety, which largely entailed improvements in somatic symptoms and in overall state of health.

This group had improved its material welfare to a fairly marked extent as the years had passed, and consisted mainly of averagely well-off people. At the same time, the respondents themselves assessed different aspects of their material circumstances in a contradictory way and were not confident that they would see an improvement in these circumstances in the next three years. This instability can be to a certain extent explained by the structure of their incomes, in which there was a relatively high proportion of allowances, benefits and assistance – not surprising, when we take into account that about half the group was not working. A large proportion also had income from property or renting out possessions. In general, the group was differentiated by a higher rate of good or satisfactory assessments of various aspects of their lives than those given by other respondents.

The health standards of people in this group were fairly high – about half were healthy according to the EQ-5D scale (over 0.75), although there was a similar number whose health indicators on this scale were low. Moreover, their behaviour in relation to health was distinguished by comparative large expenditures: by comparison with other groups, they were more likely to use fee-paying services – private clinics, doctors' surgeries, fee-paying dental clinics, supplementary medical insurance – and more likely to visit medics whom they already knew. But, despite their high level of attention to health maintenance by comparison with other groups, only one person here said that people around them thought he was behaving in the right way in regard to his health and was doing everything he could to maintain it. This may be connected with the fact that smoking was widespread in this group, although there were fewer responses relating to alcohol abuse in the family than in other groups. This group was also distinguished by the fact that its members showed concern for the quality of their food – about half of them, which was markedly more than in other groups.

In regard to particular features of their employment, this group was distinguished, firstly, by the fairly active occupational strategies of those who were working and, secondly, by a variety of forms of non-employment (non-employed people in this group included pensioners, housewives, unemployed people and people who were not working temporarily because of their health or for other reasons). At the same time, the burden of dependency borne by members of this group can hardly be described as advantageous, since two-thirds of them viewed themselves as their family's main breadwinner. The occupational status of members of this group who were working varied, as did the types of post they held, but they were mainly skilled specialists and white-collar workers (book-keepers, managers, a secretary, an economist), with some skilled blue-collar workers. In their own opinions, members of this group had been comparatively effective in adapting to the changes of the 1990s: they had often made use of the new opportunities that had opened up during the course of the reforms, and were much less likely than others to have had to give up the way of life they were used to – although a quarter of them acknowledged that they had to grab at anything that would provide them with a tolerable life. People in this group (about half) were much more likely than others to have additional unregistered earnings and markedly more likely to have mastered new occupations or acquired new vocational skills.

Other distinguishing features of this group were a greater variety of kinds of leisure and a greater orientation towards social contact with people. A further important feature was the higher quality of their social connections, which allowed them to obtain active support if they needed it.

Another thing that was very typical of a significant proportion of respondents in this group was that they considered their health to be good – sometimes contrary to objective indicators. Zinaida, aged 54, from Moscow, provides a graphic example. Replying to the question about her own health, she 'called on fate':

I am healthy, I am healthy ... You know – they took me away in an ambulance ... And one of the nurses – I always seem to see her – looked at me as if it was a catastrophe ... So I say – 'I'm healthy!' 'Really? Honestly?' 'I'm healthy!' I say.

Zinaida's life story is also an example of constant energy in trying to overcome difficulties. In the early 1990s, she voluntarily left the scientific research institute where she had a very successful career as an engineer, to go into a small business: shuttle trading – that is, small-scale independent trading of goods purchased in other cities or countries. Through this, she was able to significantly restore her material circumstances and buy a flat; but then, when the situation changed and there was severe pressure on shuttle traders from criminal organisations, she decided to go into more secure, well-paid work – as a trolleybus driver. This enabled her to live completely free of material poverty and to feel independent and prosperous.

A contrasting example is that of 58-year-old Aleksandr from Moscow, who, at the time of the 2005 survey, was working as chief executive of a market gardening partnership. The 1990s' reforms had dealt a fairly strong blow to his health and prosperity (and his social well-being). As a result, he was very critical of what was happening in Russia, which, to him, was the genesis of his difficult experiences and stress. His own assessment of his health reflected a paradox that was very widespread in our sample – a subjective sense that his health had deteriorated, even though our use of the GHQ method recorded an improvement. Nevertheless, Aleksandr too was trying 'not to give diseases a chance', 'not to take any notice' of them:

I sometimes feel lousy. I just haven't got time to bother about it. I've got up and gone on with things. If I've had the urge to go to the doctor, I've gone ... But there's no time to be bothered with all this [treatment]. And so my body thinks there's no sense in provoking me, because I won't be spending any time on it anyway [*laughs*].

This kind of health strategy was one of the most typical for population groups with poor or average resources. They simply 'take no notice' of their deteriorating health circumstances, which gives them a chance to overcome their difficulties in life despite their state of health. In conditions of severe structural limitations, health becomes a major resource for improving the situation, because assessments of one's own health are somewhat elastic and can be manipulated on the psychological level. Striving to present one's health as good despite everything – not only to others around you, but first and foremost in your own eyes – becomes an active resource for overcoming a difficult socio-economic situation. Moreover, how real this improvement in health actually is, is a question that requires additional, deeper and more specialised research; however, judging by the GHQ data for our panel, it may not be rare to encounter a deterioration in health as a result of trying to overcome difficulties and of the stress thus caused.

The 'Generally Worse Health' Group

Those who had seen a steady deterioration in their health (14 people) were respondents whose negative values on the overall GHQ scale were quite big, and for whom a negative dynamic was observed across all four scales, especially the somatic health scale. In composition, this was the group with the lowest level of welfare: poor people made up more than a third of this group, and as many were badly-off. People in this group were more likely than others to say that their level of welfare had deteriorated, and more likely (half of them) to assess it as worse than the welfare of others around them.

The proportion of those who were 'sick' according to EQ-5D indicators was half the group, although the proportion of those who were 'healthy' was also fairly high (about a quarter). The remaining respondents belonged to the 'unhealthy' group. This group sought official medical care more rarely than others, or did not seek any at all, and were also less likely to have acquaintances working in medical institutions.

Their employment rate was not high, and there were no people at all in this group who were engaged in entrepreneurial activities or self-employment on a casual or personal basis. The occupational composition of the group was predominantly technical white-collar workers and blue-collar workers. At the same time, there were some individuals who were specialists with higher education. In general, though, according to many characteristics – in particular, their lack of an active approach to their occupation – this group can be directly contrasted with the 'generally better health' group.

Finally, their leisure was the least varied. Practically no-one in this group visited sports clubs, community organisations or study groups; instead, they were more likely to spend their leisure time at home – housekeeping, with their children or at a dacha.

One example from this group was Vladimir, a blue-collar worker in a Moscow factory, who had been in our sample since 1996 (see also Chapter 7). His most recent interview, at the age of 51, found him in a state of profound social exclusion. He had lost his family and, in practice, his home: since he was not officially divorced, he lived in his sister's and mother's flat. His job did not suit him, and he was seeking a new one, although not actively. One overall problem complicated his health, which was, according to his own assessment, poor: alcoholism. And what had led to this can be formulated in terms of an even greater general problem – fatalism and a passive attitude to his health and his situation in life.

> You just lose heart ... You look – and you can't do anything. You arrive at a state of indifference, powerlessness. You just have to live out your time and that's all ... Because I haven't been able to change anything. Younger people can tackle it.

Many people fell into this group because of worsening chronic illnesses. Thus, Tat'yana, from Moscow, aged 55, had been on disability benefit since the 1990s because she suffered from multiple sclerosis. Her situation in life was very difficult: she had lost the capacity to work; her husband had died suddenly, which had exacerbated the course of her illness; her pension was small. Tat'yana linked the misfortune that had befallen her husband directly with the reforms.

> When this perestroika began, he was working in a defence installation, and all those enterprises started to fall apart. He found work in a factory, as a press operator. But before that he had worked as a leading engineer in a scientific research institute. So there were all those stresses, too. And then he had an accident to his right hand, leaving him with only one little finger. Also there were all kinds of inadequate safety techniques. ... Then all kinds of stressful situations ... He went back to the factory ..., there were some kinds of little jobs, orders, he was getting kopecks. Then he generally started working three times a week – there wasn't any work. And against the background of this, of course, utter depression ... his heart ...

Tat'yana assessed her current situation negatively and did not see any prospects for getting treatment – because of the high costs involved and the absence of effective methods in the current state of medicine, and also because of the difficulties she would have with walking to the clinic and standing in the queue to see the doctor.

On the basis of analysing these and other data from our longitudinal survey and interviews, we can draw the preliminary conclusions that the differences between these groups had formed as a result of a combination of material and cultural factors, reflecting particular features of the respondents' previous social situation and the resources related to that, and of their personal world view and behavioural characteristics. Thus, in the first group – the most successful one in terms of health dynamic – some part was played by greater diversity of resources supporting the material aspect of their existence and some by psychological attitudes that can be defined as a distinctive culture of 'not taking any notice of illness' (although some people took preventive measures rather than seeking extreme treatments for diseases that had already worsened). This culture differentiated the group, but there is no doubt that the major difference lay in the greater durability of their material resources and their opportunities and abilities to strengthen these. Therefore, for the most successful group, even retirement or disability often did not lead to deterioration in material status and health, but was a calculated, planned step towards improving their situation, including their health.

Material and Cultural Factors

The next step in our analysis was to highlight groups of respondents according to the nature of the relationship between overall changes in their state of health and changes in the household's level of material welfare. Our approach here was based on a picture of the close interaction of material and cultural factors in any possibilities for overcoming the closed circle of poverty and sickness.

This interrelationship is shown, for example, by Scambler and Blane, when they take issue with Bartley's opinion that it is predominantly material factors which determine health. They show that the general basis of material and cultural models is the determination of health by social class, and that, accordingly, any differences are manifested in various aspects of this general factor, which is viewed as the fundamental one (Scambler and Blane, 2003). We too observed this pattern more than once when analysing the dynamics of health; the results of our analysis have been described in the first section of this chapter.

Turning to possible interpretations of this interrelationship, we looked at the following variants of a combination of health and welfare: a) better health and better material circumstances; b) better health but unchanged material circumstances, or unstable circumstances – i.e. changes in various directions over the course of all our surveys; c) better health and worse material circumstances; d) worse health and better material circumstances; e) worse health and unchanged or unstable material circumstances; f) worse health and worse material circumstances.

The following four groups were most represented:

a) *Better health and better material circumstances*   Ten respondents in our longitudinal study had improved both their health and their material circumstances. They could be referred to as 'successful people': the greater proportion of them were at the average level of material welfare, while the rest were well-off. Most of them were residents of Moscow, the capital city.

b) *Better health but unchanged material circumstances (or unstable material circumstances)*   There were 19 people in this situation. Three of them remained poor throughout all rounds of our survey and five remained averagely well-off, while approximately half remained badly-off. The others were typically in an unstable situation – moving from poverty to being badly-off (or even to an average level) and back again. This indicates that, on the one hand, there is potential for their circumstances to change for the better, but that, on the other hand, there are significant restrictions on their opportunities to realise this potential.

d) *Worse health and better material circumstances* (eight people)   People in this group, in the main, had typically seen a modest change in their material circumstances – moving from being badly-off to being averagely well-off – and had predominantly seen overall, rather than particular, improvements in their health.

e) *Worse health and unchanged or unstable material circumstances*   There were 19 people in this group. Among those who had maintained the same level in their material circumstances over the course of a number of years, there were roughly equal numbers of people who had remained poor and people who had remained in average circumstances. However, the largest subgroup here consisted of people who had 'drifted in and out of poverty' (i.e. between being poor and being badly-off). This group also had the lowest level of health resources and displayed a negative health dynamic.

The smallest groups from a numerical point of view were (c) those who were in better health but worse material circumstances (three people), and (f) those in worse health and worse material circumstances (five people). Typically, the latter had 'slipped' from an average level to being badly-off, while the deterioration in their health was, in the majority of cases, not too serious.

We shall now look in more detail at factors that influenced improvements in health and level of welfare for these people, and also at models of health behaviours that might genuinely help to maintain or restore their health and integrate them into society.

Factors in Health Dynamics

Analysis of our interviews allowed us to highlight factors which in some measure influenced changes in the health and level of welfare of our various groups of respondents. We grouped these factors together according to material circumstances, behavioural practices, conditions of occupational activity, and stress.

Material Circumstances

The connection between improvement in material circumstances and improvement in health was tracked across a number of indicators. Thus, according to people's own assessments, those who had improved their health had seen more favourable changes in their material circumstances over the previous three years. We observed that degree of improvement in health was specifically dependent on variety of sources of income. The generally better health group had more varied and, probably, more lasting sources of income: they received comparatively more from concessionary benefits and assistance, and a higher proportion of their incomes came from an extra job or additional unregistered work or from renting out property.

In the group of those who were in both better health and better material circumstances, there were more people who – in their own opinion – had succeeded in making use of new opportunities and achieving successes in life, while there were absolutely no respondents who had failed to adapt to life as it is now and to the changes that have taken place. In contrast, the group of people who were in worse health but unchanged material circumstances included more people who were passive in terms of adapting to the changes that have taken place: they had either got used to the deprivation or simply increased their workload in order to provide themselves with a tolerable life. Those who were in better health but unchanged material circumstances in many ways repeated these characteristics.

Help and support from neighbours, relations, friends and acquaintances who were not part of the respondent's household was another factor in changing

Table 9.1   Attitudes to health and changes in health status (% of group)

Statements	The generally better health group	The generally worse health group
1. I have to economise on health costs because there are other, more urgent needs	5 (31)	7 (54)
2. In no circumstances should you economise on health costs	11 (69)	5 (46)
3. Maintaining good health is vital in order to be successful at work	6 (37)	8 (62)
4. Health is a major value in itself	10 (63)	5 (38)
5. Anyone who is too concerned with their own health stands out from the crowd too much	5 (31)	1 (8)
6. Consistent concern about one's own health is an indicator of a modern outlook	11 (69)	12 (92)
7. Constant concern with your own health shows you are egotistical	3 (19)	2 (15)
8. Constant concern about your own health is vital in the interests of those close to you	13 (81)	11 (85)
9. I have no time to worry about my health, I have too much else to do	6 (37)	5 (38)
10. I am forced to worry about my health in order to cope with everything I have to do	10 (63)	8 (62)

material circumstances across our various health dynamics groups. The generally better health group was most likely to receive the kinds of help that signalled the presence of significant network resources. These (material support, professional consultations and services, including treatment or home tuition) weighed in heavily to improve their circumstances; in the generally worse health group, this type of help was not mentioned at all. The resource of assistance in gaining access to people and bodies in authority who can help to solve problems is a very important one in contemporary Russia; this was also noted relatively often in our sample, and in the generally better health group it was far from insignificant. Finally, twice as many respondents in the generally better health group were receiving psychological support, participatory assistance and assistance coupled with good advice as in the generally worse health group.

Behavioural Practices and Attitudes Towards One's Own Health were distinguished by a great variety of types and forms, and also by the degree of their influence on the respondents' health dynamics.

Particular contrasts can be found in the differences between behavioural attitudes in the generally better health group and the generally worse health group (Table 9.1). In the first group, people more often shared the idea that health was a value in itself. The generally worse health group took a more instrumental view of its value (health as a resource allowing one to work and to earn more).

At the same time, some attitudes were shared by the majority of people in absolutely all the groups. Thus, respondents in the different groups were almost equally inclined to take the view that they were not doing enough for their health, and the most general explanations of this were: not enough willpower; no amount of concern can guarantee good health; no time, or their time just doesn't stretch to it. The opinion that those close to them do not approve of the respondent's behaviour in maintaining his/her own health – even directly telling him/her off for not paying enough attention to it – was almost equally predominant in all our health dynamics groups.

It is curious that even in the generally better health group, where ideas about health as an intrinsic value were fairly strong, one-third of respondents agreed with the opinion that anyone who is too concerned with their own health stands out from the crowd too much. The same thing was also observed in groups with differing relationships between dynamics of health and welfare.

These and a number of other observations made from our interview materials provide a basis for the hypothesis that Russians have a fairly strong cultural stereotype prescribing that worrying too much about one's health (usually expressed as 'chasing round from one doctor to another') is not entirely respectable.

The effect of this stereotype may be demonstrated in particular features of various kinds of health-related behavioural practices. Overall, it is possible to divide these into practices relating to the official health care system (visiting doctors, taking medicines, etc.), which arouse a degree of scepticism from respondents, and those connected with people's experience of taking preventive measures in everyday life, which overall are rather more acceptable in the context of the established cultural stereotype. We now look at each of these types of practice.

Behavioural Practices Relating to the Official Health Care System

According to the results of our research, when it came to the official health care system, there were not any great differences between the behaviours of people in the better health group and of people in the worse health group, nor between respondents in the various groups established according to relationships between changes in health and material circumstances. Those in worse health seemed to be more 'law-abiding' in terms of their orientation towards carrying out doctors' instructions and taking medicines. Differences tended rather to relate to material possibilities – for example, the generally worse health group was less likely to go to private clinics or to use supplementary medical insurance, but more likely to make use of free medical services. However, it was true that reasons for going to the doctor differed somewhat: those in the generally worse health group were more likely to go because they were actually ill or to obtain medical certificates, while the generally better health group tended to go for preventive care.

When it came to the steps that they took when feeling unwell, there were also slightly nuanced differences between the different health dynamics groups. Reactions in each group to the suggested situation of feeling ill in some unfamiliar way were fairly similar – roughly a third of people in all health dynamics groups said that they would prefer to treat themselves, and roughly a third that they would go to the doctor. At the same time, our enquiry about any specific instance of ill-health that had recently taken place in their family showed that, when there is a real, severe deterioration in health, respondents from various health dynamics groups behave somewhat differently. In a situation where someone had been feeling very ill, those in the generally better health group had called an ambulance twice as often as in the generally worse health group.

The differences we observed between the explanations given by respondents of their behaviour in these cases were that those in the worse health group said that, first and foremost, they were afraid of losing the capacity to work, while those in the better health group said that they had simply followed their usual practice of looking after their own health – in other words, these differences were determined by their particular attitudes to health as a value, already mentioned above.

Everyday Behavioural Practices is another group of practices directed at regular, conscious preventive health measures in everyday life – in other words, maintaining a healthy way of life. This group of factors was more significant than practices that related to formal health care, both for better health and worse health respondents.

Judging by responses to our questionnaire, preventive health measures were connected primarily with dietary regime, the nature of rest, and rejecting (or restricting) certain harmful habits. People whose health had improved, especially those in the better health and better material circumstances group, were relatively more likely to avoid harmful habits and to stick to diets. People in improved health were more likely to say that they ate well, while no-one in the generally worse health group said this.

One fairly significant factor influencing the health dynamic was opportunities to rest or take a holiday away from home during leave from work. People in the generally better health group were comparatively more likely to give a good assessment of their opportunities to take a holiday in the summer period – twice as likely, in fact, as people in the generally worse health group. However, overall, the ways they were able to spend their leave were fairly limited for all groups.

We also observed some contrasts between the different health dynamics groups in regard to how they spent their free time. Analysis showed that those in the better health group had more variety in their lives – through their outlook, social contacts with like-minded people, involvement in sports, and so on. Those in the worse health group were more likely to practise domestic types of leisure, 'closed in' at home, and consequently they did not experience new stimuli or strengthen their social connections.

Harmful habits (smoking and use of alcohol) represented one of the most important factors put forward by respondents asked to rate causes of deterioration in health: they most often put this factor at the top of their list, particularly respondents in the generally worse health group. At the same time, judging from our research data, this factor was not clearly decisive in health deterioration. It is possible that one explanation for this is that, in Russia, factors linked with a wide range of characteristics in people's social circumstances have played a more significant role in health dynamics.

Thus, analysis of various factors in everyday behavioural practices confirms the significance of a more expedient, rational attitude to health – which, drawing on the interviews, we might call sensible, modest preventive measures – in influencing the improvement in our respondents' health. However, the analysis also showed that, in themselves, these practices were more similar than different across the various groups; so, in most instances, they cannot explain the health dynamics.

Occupational Activities

The next group of factors we analysed was connected with occupational activities. First of all, we should note the higher standard of education of those who were in the generally better health group and in the better health and better material circumstances group. Among the 29 respondents with higher education, more than a third were in the generally better health group, and only four people were in the generally worse health group. In groups with a positive health dynamic, we also noticed a more active approach in building up all types of resources, especially human capital. Thus, people in these groups were markedly more likely to be actively strengthening their knowledge in new fields.

Employment in itself was not the decisive factor in health dynamics. Among waged blue-collar workers, who constituted most of the employed people (39 respondents), there were in fact equal numbers of people in better health and in worse health. Taking this as a starting-point, it could be hypothesised that the chief influence of employment on health dynamics lay not in the fact of employment itself, but in its nature and particular features. (We shall review below the results of testing this hypothesis through analysis of our in-depth interviews)

We also need to note the specific features of the occupation and type of post held by members of these groups. We were able to trace distinctly the specific way that the level of their job – and the potential power this gave them – influenced the nature of changes in their health and material circumstances. Thus, in the better health group there were more managers at various levels than in the generally worse health group. Among managers, there were more people in better health and better material circumstances and more people in better health but unchanged material circumstances. (Although it is also true that the proportion of managers in worse health and better material circumstances was fairly large)

Characteristics of working conditions and the nature of the work itself turned out to be fairly significant in explaining improvement and deterioration in health. The work of people in the worse health group displayed a greater concentration of negative characteristics: it was less skilled, performed in worse conditions, and lacked social prospects. For people in this group, it was fairly often also the case that work did not bring them satisfaction at the level of human relationships. People in the generally worse health group contrasted sharply with the generally better health group, complaining more often about low pay and/or late payment of wages.

Responses relating to the positive aspects of their jobs showed that the quality of jobs – in the sense of content, working conditions and prospects – was markedly higher in the groups with positive health dynamics. Thus, contrasting evaluations of how interesting they found their work were given by people in the generally better health group and the generally worse health group: in the former, more than half of respondents said their work was interesting, as against a fifth of the latter. To a somewhat lesser extent, people in the better health group said that their work gave them opportunities to build a career, while in the generally worse health group no-one at all marked this response.

The limitations of the regime that prevailed in a workplace also had a significant influence. The harshness of the regime laid down at work and fear of losing their job were additional factors of no small importance in the deterioration of health. In many cases, the detriment to their health involved respondents going to work even when they were not feeling very well – a fairly widespread practice in all the health dynamics groups. It was true that workers in the worse health group more often did this so as not to lose wages or out of fear of losing their job. In the most successful group, going to work when they were not feeling very well more often appeared to be simply a matter of habit.

As for significant features of working conditions such as chronically high workload, these were distributed in a similar pattern across all our health dynamics groups. However, taking into account the occupational composition of the groups, it can be hypothesised that people in the better health group were chronically overloaded by the 'mental strain' typical of their work (it was indeed more prevalent in these groups), while in the generally worse health group it was by the physical discomfort of their working conditions and the lack of prospects in their job.

Thus, in the sphere of occupational activities, the quality of respondents' employment (meaning actual jobs held) and the quality of their human capital had the greatest influence on changes in health – an influence which indirectly manifested itself in the respondents' ability or inability to influence decision-making in the enterprise. According to all these indicators, the situation was especially bad for the generally worse health group.

Stress

Finally, yet another important factor affecting health dynamics was stress. In this connection, it should be noted that stress was a general thread running through the health dynamic of the Russian population in the 1990s. In practically all our interviews, we in some way or other encountered indicators of stress as both a source of and a major factor in disease and deterioration of health. Here are just a few quotations from the interviews:

our food is poor, we get no holidays and we're under constant stress; obviously, this all affects our health. (Viktor, 50, leading engineer in a defence research institute, Moscow – see also the second book in our trilogy and Chapters 2 and 5 of this book)

We are living in times when you are more often faced with a stressful situation than with anything relaxing. (Tat'yana, 40, finance director and deputy director of a children's clinic, Moscow – see more below)

Constant stresses, that's where all these complications [diseases] come from ... Of course, it's all nerves, and all illnesses originate from the nerves. (Svetlana, 39, office worker in a university department, Voronezh)

I've spent the last 15 years of my life in need, under stress, in a state of the jitters ... (Nikolai, 60, working pensioner/builder, Kazan')

The radical political changes of the early 1990s had a major, powerful, stressful impact – in the words of one of our respondents, 'political perestroika ... was one of the major factors. That was when something huge, stress-generating and radical started up.' It led to a multitude of types of stresses, resulting from falling living standards, breakdown in social status, general disruption and instability in people's lives, loss of job or job security, changes in circumstances, in income levels and in roles within the household, which in turn caused tensions in the family. In trying to cope with the burdens that had placed increasing demands on them, people intensified their efforts, expending all their strength, which led them to exhaust their reserves of health and exacerbate any health problems.

Thus, analysis of our interview data allowed us to highlight models and factors that have played a part in the health dynamics of the Russian population during the years of reform. It showed that behavioural factors and particular features of the mobilisation of various kinds of resources to overcome difficult situations in the lives of poorly resourced population groups played a very significant role in improvement or deterioration in health. The most significant resources were conditions of employment and variety in sources of income, but also resources of support from social networks, including psychological support, and varieties of leisure. Aiming to ignore health problems was also very significant. In the final analysis, all this was really underpinned by membership of different classes, in which the effect of material factors mediated and intensified cultural factors, including those relating to particular features of the human capital of members of various classes and to behavioural patterns, including health behaviours. However, our research also recorded certain cultural stereotypes shared by members of all classes – primarily, the 'unseemliness' of paying a great deal of attention to one's own health and the preference for tackling health problems through 'everyday life' rather than going to see specialists – which may be connected with particular features of Russian national culture.

Models of Health Behaviour

One of the conclusions that can be drawn from a general review of factors influencing health is that analysing them separately makes it impossible to get a complete picture of their significance and of particular aspects of the way they really influence approaches to improving health and well-being. The whole picture of the influence of these factors can be gained through the point of view we have already mentioned: that there is a close interaction between the effects of material (structural) and behavioural/ cultural factors. Thus, Scambler and Blane (2003) point out that behavioural/cultural explanations involve class differences in behaviours that are health-damaging or health-promoting, and which, at least in principle, remain an object of individual choice.

Russian sociologists, who are dealing with an 'embryonic' class structure, are usually inclined to look at the totality of interrelated material and behavioural factors, without any strict class ties. Thus, in Zhuravleva's opinion, derived from her research into health attitudes categorised by way of life, behaviour mediates the effect of all the major groups of health factors; the leading part played by behaviour in the multifactoral causality of health can be explained by a change in the structure of causes of mortality and morbidity over recent decades, which has, in significant measure, resulted from people's types of behaviour (Zhuravleva, 2005).

However, our research demonstrated that, for a more adequate understanding of the essence of the processes that have been unfolding in the area of health, we should not be discussing separate factors or types of behaviour, but models of behaviour that are prevalent in different classes to varying degrees. Our respondents' life stories, based on their interviews, give an in-depth picture of these basic models of successful behaviour and the elements that comprise them. Among the latter are multi-faceted improvement in employment situation, successful social inclusion and modest preventive health measures in regard to a wide range of aspects of health. On the basis of various combinations of these, there are three basic models of behaviour that provided our respondents with health improvements and, in a number of cases, with improvements in both health and material welfare.

Successful Employment and Modest Preventive Measures for One's Own Health

As has been noted above, the simple fact of being employed did not in itself play a decisive role in improving health and material circumstances, but being able to work was very significant for satisfying a respondent's requirements and purposes, creating the conditions for social comfort. Through our interviews, we were able to track the way that better health standards and material welfare depended on real, conscious steps towards changing one's job, which were predictors not only of growth in income but also of making a job more comfortable psychologically.

This was especially clearly demonstrated in the life story of Tat'yana, 40, from Moscow, who had moved from being badly-off to being averagely well-off and at the same time had improved her health. Her life story was one of a 'fall' in the mid-1990s, in both occupational status and income – and then of a confident, carefully planned 'rise' from this fall.

> [Until 1991] I had a fantastic life and felt I was a normal, adequate person; when I said 'I' out loud, I felt it meant something. I had an excellent job, I was a senior economist – the highest grade – in the State Supply Office. What I did was a very particular kind of work, and it gave me not only money but also satisfaction and contact with people; and I can't say that a person's age or sex made any difference there. ... I'd already reached the highest grade by the time I was about 22. ... I felt I was a free person, both in terms of holidays and in my everyday life; of course, there were none of the kind of difficulties that there are now.

In 1991, she went on maternity leave and, when she returned in 1993, she (like many other people in Russia) was faced with the fact that the State organisation where she worked – part of a system that had formerly seemed to offer lasting employment – had collapsed, and she was 'flung out into the street' along with many of her colleagues. By then, Tat'yana had separated from her husband, and she got into a very difficult situation – she was bringing up her little boy alone, at a time when everything was starting all over again.

> I'm a person with a higher education in economics, and by the time it got to 1995 I couldn't find any work in my usual occupation. ... For a woman with children on her hands, just to find a job nowadays is very difficult. And I had to get work anywhere I could, just to get money and keep my child. So, even though I've got higher education, I was doing a manual job.

Like many women at that time, she took on any job she could find – she worked as a sales assistant in a shop and then as a street trader, and then became a goods manager in a mechanised bakery. Despite the fact that this job gave the respondent a certain degree of security, it did not suit her, first and foremost because of the inconvenient night work involved.

> At a certain point, I realised that, if I didn't change my job, I might as well say goodbye to my health, and so on, for good, because for women those hours are out of synch ... You just become a zombie, like the walking dead.

But her sense of a drop in social status was even more significant. She had moved into an environment that was entirely alien to her, both in terms of social class and in the new form of working relations, where employers were arbitrary and workers had no rights – relations which dominated such businesses during the 1990s.

This period continued for five to six years, and Tat'yana became aware that she was losing her professional skills, her health and her self-respect. She made a firm decision to change her job. In seeking a new direction, she relied on her own willpower and energy – because she understood that her specialist skills were being degraded – and also on assistance from people she knew.

> But I knew really … what I was capable of. I've always said that I'm a work horse, so I can move mountains. And there's no need for anyone to pay me more money for what I do, it's just that I'm ashamed of doing a job badly. So when I went somewhere in answer to a job advert or just to put myself forward, I said: 'Yes, it's true that I've been working outside my usual occupation for a long time … But I can make up for that just because I'm not afraid of work …'

Faith in her own strengths, along with her vigorous attempts to find a job that matched her aptitudes, helped Tat'yana to overcome her difficult situation: in 2000, she found a job that allowed her to put her training as an economist to use as finance director of a children's clinic, where she later also became deputy director – that is, she essentially regained, and even improved on, the social position she had lost. It should be noted that, as she herself put it, she had succeeded in doing this thanks to people she knew: until the early 1990s, she had belonged to a completely successful section of the population, and she had basically managed to preserve her social capital throughout the years of her trials. In addition, health care – as a publicly funded and, consequently, low-paid sector – was not a prestige place of employment at that time. The broader Moscow labour market picture also played a part: nevertheless, it was Tat'yana's energetic, goal-oriented attitude and actions that helped her to use these advantages to break in. She began 'bit-by-bit' to restore her lost social status. Here is her description of how she fulfilled her life plan and how her priorities shifted as a consequence:

> At that time [when she changed her job], of course, I still had a financial problem, but it was comparatively not so severe, and it was more important to get out of that job, that nightmare, so that I wouldn't actually suffer physically. When there was a problem with work … generally it would be solved, then what came next on my agenda was somehow or other to raise my material status. And that is more or less what happened. And now what comes next on my agenda is the major thing – let's call it the aspect of morale. Now, I don't just want to earn more money, but somehow to feel I am significant, a worthwhile person in general.

At the stage when her last interview took place, Tat'yana was full of new plans for further advancement: she was guided by her need to realise her schemes, by her energy, and also by her need to transform her situation 'under her own steam' and, accordingly, find a better place to apply her aptitudes.

Here, we need only note the enthusiasm and depth of involvement with which she set out (largely without any prompting from us) a general picture of the situation in the health care sector. And it sounded like a concrete programme for her own actions. The attractive thing about this programme was her active approach, her attitude not of 'implementation' but of initiative – surmounting the confusion that notably surrounds reform in the sphere of health care, at least as far as her own possibilities were concerned.

> We are not getting carried along by the tide. We are trying to draw what we need out of this situation. To make use of something even if it's in a corrupt or distorted form

– we will take it for ourselves. We'll make it live! In our hands, this monster is going to survive! If you give it to someone else – it's going to perish, it will not be able to live, it will become an invalid. But we're going to do things that will make it into a worthwhile person. Put all this in the hands of those people who are vitally interested in all of it. No-one can decide for us what we need and what we don't need.

At the end of the interview, she let us in on her plan – to leave the clinic for a new place of work, in order to join her former manager in developing new plans and new approaches to business (he had suggested to her that she transfer with him to this new job).

I want to put up this building myself ... I've been given what you might call carte blanche. ... I think that in about three years I'll be busy building something up [*laughs*].

Thus, Tat'yana revived her sense of the integrity and intelligence of her career, which had been destroyed during the years of reform, and this obviously created a base for a feeling of success and a worthwhile existence.

Another respondent from this group was Natasha, a nurse, aged 51, from Moscow (see also Chapter 3), who behaved in a generally similar way in relation to her employment and health. In 1997, she was badly-off and in an insecure situation on the labour market, yet, over the years of our research, she succeeded in becoming well-off, stabilising her labour market situation and improving her health. The key to her success, in her own assessment, lay in a smooth change of workplace, with an improvement in both her material circumstances and the emotional satisfaction she derived from her situation at work.

Somehow it's turned out that, throughout my life, my next job has always been better than the one before. That is, I've been able to improve things for myself all the time, [my circumstances] have got better and better, both materially and emotionally ...

This change took place primarily because of the advent of the reforms in the 1990s, when Natasha was forced to leave public sector nursing and seek a job with higher pay in order to maintain her family, since her husband's wages had fallen and there were dependants in the household – her mother, grandmother and son. So she found a job at the first aid post in a meat processing plant, which held particular advantages in terms of income and because it was located near her home. However, in her opinion, this job led her health to deteriorate, primarily because of the emotional discomfort and unhealthy working conditions she experienced there. After being released from this plant, Natasha found work in a hotel; however, doing a job that was not in her true profession turned out to be a heavier burden for her than low-paid work had been.

My incentive was the wages. ... but the work in itself was very boring. Well, having devoted my whole life to one occupation, I couldn't cross over to something different.

The jobs she found next – as a nurse in a nursery school and then at a swimming pool – improved her circumstances and brought her a sense of comfort and social significance because she was working in her own occupational field and social environment. Natasha emphasised that health is dependent on success in life, in which satisfaction gained from work plays no small part: 'I think that the more I succeeded, the better my health became.'

She presented an extensive, multifaceted programme of 'modest preventive measures' to care for her health, in which, in accordance with a fairly broad understanding of what it means to be healthy, she included a generally active approach, physical exercise, the creation of a positive attitude and positive emotions and impressions through travel, going to the theatre, etc., social contact and even memory training – as well as her own inner mood.

> Of course, it is probable that your inner state – being more optimistic, not giving into any kind of difficulties, trying to find some kind of compromises, you know ... Well, and also, probably, being needed by society too, however old you are – that also bears some relation to the kind of health you have.

Natasha also declared that she took the attitude that she would not view herself as a sick person, which helped her 'take no notice' of her illnesses. She saw all this as an alternative to visiting medical establishments or doctors, and to taking medicines.

> Although I'm a medic myself, nevertheless I can't say I love going to the doctor. Because I know what they will find. They can find an awful lot of diseases in a person. And even though I won't be dwelling on it, nevertheless, somewhere in my innermost mind, it will still be there – what I've got, and how I'll live with it.

From this point of view, her detailed description of how she found a way out of a difficult situation in her life, when she experienced depression after losing her job in the late 1990s, is interesting. She achieved this by taking active steps to overcome her state of mind – through a change of scene, social contact with people, interest in her life and new types of activity.

> And then I got out of it [her state of depression] – I just upped and went to our dacha in Vladimir Province. There, I had to get through 5 kilometres of deep snow, cross country, but I managed to get there anyway. And somehow people were welcoming to me there. And it's a feeling of nature, of beauty ... you can live for that and be glad to be alive! I didn't take any kind of antidepressants, but I just had to do something.

It should be noted that Natasha was a person to whom good human relations and mutual assistance meant a great deal – in our terms, establishing and maintaining social connections. In her interview, she contrasted this attitude with the situation of her husband, whose health had deteriorated. She connected this both with stress at work and with her husband's reserved nature.

Unfortunately, his [her husband's] health is not improving. And he's not like me – I keep healthy somehow, get away somewhere, maybe I've got more positive emotions, I can go out to the theatre – I think that I somehow live a better inner life ... But he ... is rather reserved ... He – is all inside himself, he doesn't really have any friends, you might say. He's pushed everyone away ... But you shouldn't do that – no man is an island!

Another side to the deterioration in Natasha's husband's health was his unwillingness to take preventive measures to maintain it; he tried to remain on his feet throughout any illness, even though the regime enforced at his workplace was not a very strict one.

We should note that the level of welfare in Natasha's household had improved significantly, not only because of an improvement in her employment situation, but also as a result of 'external' resources – the family had inherited a flat, which they began to rent out.

This mechanism – successful employment coupled with modest concern for one's own health, mainly in the form of basic preventive health measures – distinguishes many of the employed respondents in the successful 'better health and better material circumstances' group. In the final analysis, the effect of this kind of mechanism also formed the basis of health improvements among the non-employed: for them, a necessary sense of their own value and a feeling of social comfort are not created by a particular socio-occupational status, but derive from consistent and conscious inclusion in a particular community of people close to them (relations or like-minded people).

Non-Employment, Informal Employment and Support from Working Family Members

A modification of this model of successful health maintenance was when respondents who had been badly-off and had lost their employment were able to improve their material circumstances by relying on support from relatives. Thus, Rina, 55, a housewife from Moscow, who had lost her job – a fairly high-level post – when the business where she worked was wound up in the mid-1990s, had not succeeded in finding another suitable one. The loss of a job that was steady, very respectable and meant a lot to her, was stressful.

I worked in an experimental development factory ... As head of the labour and wages section. Our whole factory was wound up, it was sold off at auction ... I really liked it there, it was great. And when it fell to pieces in no time at all, and they pushed us all out one after another – of course it was stressful ...

Rina's alternative became 'employment' in the family and her son's business (looking after her grandson, running errands for the firm that her son had set up), which allowed her to improve her material circumstances from badly-off to averagely well-off. Her employment situation did not entirely suit her, but circumstances had led her to come to terms with it.

> I don't like it, but I've got used to it. It's not me at all, but that's how things have turned out. I would happily go out to work in a job that [suited] me ... But now I just can't do that, because there would be nobody to take care of the child. His parents are working. I just can't allow myself to do that. Maybe I would find something, but there's no need.

Perhaps this contradictory situation in the area of employment was the basis of her 'contradictory' state of health. On the one hand, Rina belonged to the 'generally better health' group, meaning that her health had improved across all indicators (although, in her case, by only a small margin); on the other hand, subjectively, she felt that her health had deteriorated. Rina's health maintenance behaviour came down to an active way of life, in line with her understanding of what health was – this meant, firstly, active participation in the lives of her family and relatives, and secondly, active and varied holidays. At the same time, she did practically nothing about the 'medical side' of health maintenance:

> *Interviewer*:   And what do you do about treatment?
> *Rina*:   As a rule, I don't have any treatment.
> *Interviewer*:   And where do you get information about how best to look after your health?
> *Rina*:   I do hardly anything to look after it.

Something close to this model was also displayed by Kira, a 48-year-old housewife from Voronezh (see also Chapter 2), who, over the years of our longitudinal study, moved from being badly-off to being well-off. It is true that this move came about because of her husband's income – he was 'keeping things afloat'. This allowed her to give up her job as manager of a factory production training centre, where changes had been made that she felt did not suit her. The vocational retraining courses she had taken also had no particular aims other than personal interest.

> I did retrain; and if I were to intend to do something, then it would only be for myself, because I was interested in it. And so, now my husband is keeping things afloat, everything's turned out well for him. So now I am happy just to stay at home. Our situation allows me to do it, for the time being I like it, I've got an open mind about it.

Kira's general satisfaction included the fact that she was 'entirely happy with her health', and her good health was also confirmed by the relevant survey indicators. As with Rina, the greatest changes for Kira were positive ones on the anxiety scale.

Non-Employment, Social Inclusion and Modest Preventive Health Measures

Another fairly noteworthy situation was that of people who were in unchanged material circumstances and were not employed, yet had still managed to improve their health indicators. Here the most significant factors were creating one's own community or social circle and realising alternative life aims unrelated to work. One instructive example was the life story of Alla (see also Chapter 2), aged 57, a former scientist in Moscow, who remained poor throughout all rounds of our survey, and yet improved her health. Alla was head of a household which also included her non-working adult daughter and her mother. She had separated from her husband soon after her daughter's birth. Her older child, a son, lived separately and helped his mother financially from time to time.

When she lost her job because of the collapse of her institute and cuts in the laboratory where she worked, Alla first of all put into action a strategy of claiming disability pension, giving her a minimum but guaranteed income. This was not a step that she had taken because it was really necessary for her health. Rather, it was a way out of a situation that was a dead end in a social sense – a route towards a life that she felt she would find worthwhile.

> I went onto disability pension because a close friend said to me: 'Listen, you should claim disability pension quickly, and you'll ... be as free as the wind.' I did understand that there [in the institute], I wasn't doing anything useful any more. I was the only one left in the laboratory; by the end I was spending my time typing out my own poetry. And I agreed. She also said to me – 'You'll be able to get concessions and all sorts of other things ...'

This gave Alla the freedom to realise herself within a community of amateur poets: she played a very active role in a number of literary groupings, she was an editor of and a contributor to several almanacs for self-published writers, and she went to Moscow literary meetings to read her poetry. In addition, although already middle-aged, she turned to the Russian Orthodox faith, started reading religious literature, and played a part in the life of her church community. Her life story demonstrated an especially marked connection between health and a psychological sense of social comfort and success – a connection that Alla herself clearly understood – even though she had a low level of material welfare and a dependent family.

> *Alla*: First and foremost, health affects your ability to work. And your ability to work affects your success. But there is a reverse connection – when you have some kind of success, then that helps because the state of your nervous system is a very important factor in your health. And you have to start from that ... That is, the factor of mental effect is very important.
>
> *Interviewer*: So, would you describe yourself as successful?
>
> *Alla*: At this stage, at the present time, I'm happy that perhaps eight almanacs have already come out with some of my poetry. And, not only that, I'm also mixing with such wonderful people ...

Remaining poor throughout all the years of our survey from 1997 onwards, over this time Alla also saw steady improvements in her health across all indicators, including her somatic health. In her case, another important aspect of this model of behaviour in overcoming problems was the fact that she took constant preventive measures in regard to her health, using fairly inexpensive means: following folk medicine, obtaining advice about it from the media, taking medicinal herbs. (She was assisted in this by her professional knowledge in the area of plant physiology)

> As a biologist, I use herbs to maintain my health, and I try to treat my mum too – she has high blood pressure. That is, I help the doctors who have treated her, in the treatment ... I've got a complete collection [of herbs] – I boil them up with tea, I add them to tea. I've noticed that since I started doing that – for what must be ten years now – we haven't had flu. Neither my daughter nor I. ... I try to take a preventive approach to my illnesses. That is, I take measures that help me. Herbs – because pharmaceuticals are just dangerous now ...

It could be said that Alla's life story showed how an improvement in health can result from a conscious model of behaviour relating to 'both body and soul'.

Conclusions

Thus, in our analysis of the dynamics of health in Russia, we focused our attention on instances of positive health dynamics, and this revealed a range of factors that contribute to the formation of real models and social mechanisms of behaviour in overcoming ill-health and sickness.

First and foremost, our research data established that any improvement in our respondents' health over the last few years has come about mainly because of a reduction in their level of anxiety – which, in its turn, has reduced the danger of stress and had a favourable effect on their somatic health. This confirms our hypothesis of the connection between changes in health and the stresses that have accumulated as a result of profound social change.

Behavioural models that led to health improvements involved a complex of factors, which together determined the improvement in qualitative characteristics of various aspects of life. This complex was based primarily on the close interconnection of material and cultural factors, and it habitually formed a mechanism that acted on people in conditions of structural restrictions and material deprivations – a mechanism directed at overcoming these, relying on defined norms, values and attitudes towards one's own health.

Analysis of our interview data shows the major directions of these effects. Most significant were improvement in quality of employment – for example, taking an active approach to raising one's skills level or improving one's working conditions. A more varied structure of sources of income, which strengthens one's position, and a variety of means of improving material circumstances also played a part. Active and varied recreation/leisure, and good-quality social connections should also be noted. Attitudes towards health as a value were also a factor of no small importance.

One of the most elastic cultural resources that people used in adapting to and overcoming a difficult situation was the attitude that one should think of one's own health as good. Analysis of many interviews with people who had improved their health indicators showed that this attitude tended to be directed towards 'taking no notice' of poor health. It was fairly widely supported by the social norms accepted among the majority of respondents, which prescribed that they should not worry too much about their own health; however, we must also recognise that, even though this attitude can have a positive effect, it may sometimes also play an objectively negative role in regard to health, since it offers an excuse for exploitation of health as a resource. However, overall, the plus points of using it in difficult conditions of social change far outweighed the minuses.

Our attempt to use material from our interviews to reconstruct social mechanisms and models of health improvement in situations where there were few resources resulted from a need to understand the whole picture they create. These mechanisms and models included improving not just one's material but also one's emotional situation in the area of employment; relying on the family's material resources where one was informally employed or not employed; social inclusion in a community of people in very similar circumstances – all while simultaneously using strategies for modest preventive health care. The latter primarily meant taking measures to maintain a healthy way of life: an active approach to various aspects of life, maintaining not only the health of the body but also a good psychological mood and a wealth of emotions, with a preference for methods of health maintenance that can be applied in everyday life, such as traditional remedies, and so on.

Thus, when there was a lack of material resources to improve health, other resources were mobilised – primarily, human and social capital, which often helped to noticeably improve not only health but also economic position. One specifically Russian feature may be the attitude of ignoring health problems in conditions where there is limited access to good-quality medical services – an attitude which has acquired the character of a cultural norm and found support in prevalent stereotypes of health behaviour. Accordingly, on the basis of our data analysis, a preliminary conclusion can be drawn that people escape from the vicious circle of poverty and poor health mainly by mobilising resources in three major directions: successful employment (improving the conditions of one's work activities, on which satisfaction from employment is based); strengthening social connections, forming a stable social circle of highly compatible people; consistent modest preventive measures to care for one's health, which included a wide range of approaches (eating correctly, rejecting certain harmful habits, a generally active approach, positive emotions and varied impressions, etc.). The consequence of implementing these models was that people overcame a difficult life situation and reintegrated into social life. Thus, one important objective of social policy in regard to the health of the Russian population should be the creation of conditions that support people's active approaches to employment and increase their effectiveness.

Chapter 10
Gender, Health and Poverty

Irina Popova

В чужую душу не влезешь
You can't climb into someone else's soul

Approaches to Studying Gender, Health and Poverty

The intensification of gender differences in Russians' standards of health and risk of becoming poor is one of the notable consequences of the 1990s' reforms. It became apparent during that period, firstly, that Russian social policy seemed incapable of taking gender into account in the provision of health care and, secondly, that gender was a factor in socioeconomic inequalities and in the growth of poverty. So how has the 'gender factor' in Russia helped to strengthen – or weaken – the closed circle of poverty and sickness, which are mutually determined and at the same time mutually consequential? What possibilities are there for tackling this severe social problem? One strand of our research involved seeking answers to these questions.

Research looking at the mutual influence of gender, health and material welfare has been based on the view that inequality in health standards between men and women can be defined through the inequalities in their socioeconomic positions. Thus, Annette Scambler notes the importance of understanding the connection between gender and health when researching the relative social positions of men and women in contemporary society, since 'we live in a social environment where gender plays a significant part in social status and in access to material resources, health and well-being, and where roles, responsibilities and power are not shared equally between males and females' (Scambler, 2003).

There is a striking gap in life expectancy between men and women in Russia – the largest for any country in the world that publishes mortality statistics: in 2004 it was 13.4 years, which is almost twice the indicator in the majority of industrially developed countries. The indicator for Russia deteriorated progressively during the 1990s; however, it should be noted that the scale of the problem dates from a fairly long time ago – thus, in 1958–59, the life expectancy of women was 71 years and of men, 63 (Men and women in Russia, 2004). But by international standards the life expectancy of women in Russia is not high. It differs a great deal from the indicators for European countries, the USA and Japan, a fact which also provides evidence of its relationship to a country's socioeconomic situation.

There are also differences between men and women in causes of death: across practically all classifications of causes, relative indicators show that the position of men is much worse than the position of women. Two classifications of cause of death in particular stand out, from the point of view of their contribution to overall

Table 10.1   Socioeconomic changes which have influenced the health of men and of women

Areas in which main factors operate (divided between men and women)	Factors in macro-level context (economic conditions, social policy)	Factors in micro-level context (social norms, attitudes, stereotypes, etc.)
Men		
Employment	Forced change in field of work; increased workloads, growth in competition; unfavourable (even harmful) working conditions, etc.	Impossibility of realising aspirations in a situation where sociooccupational status and career have become highly significant.
Household	Drop in income from work, fewer opportunities to be chief contributor to maintaining the family.	Impossibility of fulfilling traditional social role as head of the family and household breadwinner.
Health	Stronger influence on health of work-related stresses, of the unsettled nature of life; resulting increase in harmful habits. Appearance on the market of large quantities of cheap substitutes for alcohol, tobacco, etc.	Weak culture of self-care behaviour; tendency to an instrumental, offhand approach – neglecting one's health as a gendered social norm.
Areas in which main factors operate (divided between men and women)	Factors in macro-level context (economic conditions, social policy)	Factors in micro-level context (social norms, attitudes, stereotypes, etc.)
Women		
Employment	Lower position in employment and strengthening of secondary labour market position (less highly-paid or prestigious), leading to lower income and fewer opportunities for access to various resources.	Norms connected with flexibility of women's work, their own orientation towards secondary roles at work, their 'executant' position in the division of labour, etc. Norms connected with the need to combine the roles of 'working woman' on the one hand, and housewife, wife and mother on the other.

Household	The continuing burden of struggling with a difficult work-life balance (established in the Soviet era); worsening position in the household because responsibility for keeping the family increasingly often falls on women, especially in poor households where there are many lone-parent families or where men are not the main breadwinners.	Responsibility for running the house, which generates responsibility for the family's prosperity, the need to feed the family even when there are no means to do so, which in turn leads to stress and to women taking on additional employment.
Health	Fewer opportunities to be concerned about one's own health because of increased household burden and drop in income.	Greater sense of responsibility for one's own health by comparison with men. Stronger culture of self-care behaviour.

mortality and morbidity in the Russian population – diseases of the circulatory system and external causes: accidents, poisonings and traumas. Sharp fluctuations in life expectancy between 1985 and 1994, especially an extraordinary fall in 1992–94, related to these causes.

This situation has led to a more up-to-date approach to the issue of gender inequalities in health (see, for example, Shilova, 2000; Grigor'eva and Chubarova, 2001; Ivanova, 2005), although Russian research on the topic remains somewhat fragmentary. The issue can be conceptualised by defining a gender approach to research in the sociology of health (or of medicine) and by researching gender inequality in the areas of self-care behaviour, the socioeconomic situation of households, and so on.

In researching gender differences in health care, two main approaches can be distinguished – one focuses attention on differences in morbidity and mortality and on the underlying physiology of women and men, while the other looks at differences formed as a result of the effect of social norms and structures in society. In studying the latter, two aspects are important – behavioural, which relates to people's norms and practices of behaviour in regard to their own health, and material, which relates to inequality of access to various kinds of resources. In addition, lack of gender bias in methodology is important, as is an understanding of the fact that 'no explanation, whether on the biological or the sociocultural level, will be sufficient in itself' (Din, 2000).

It is no accident that, in practice, it is very difficult – sometimes, impossible – to separate these two approaches: any differences tend to relate to the emphases placed on their mutual influence. The emphasis of our research was on the connection between the formation and deepening of gender inequalities in the area of health care and the processes by which greater gender inequalities and restrictions on access to material resources lead to poverty.

Russian research into the gender dimension of poverty has taken as its starting-points the fact that poverty is formed as a consequence of inequality in access to material and non-material goods – an inequality that can be objectively shown to exist, since 'the greater probability of women becoming poor can be observed in any gender breakdown of indicators of poverty' (Ovcharova, 2002); and the fact that a particular way of life has formed that creates additional deprivation factors for women in poor families (Tikhonova, 2003). This is to a great extent connected with inequalities on the labour market, the 'dual employment' of women (work and housekeeping), the greater vulnerability to material difficulties of lone-parent families headed by women, etc.

Two social problems can be highlighted in this regard. One of them lies in the fact that the inherited system of gender roles in society preserves the conditions that reproduce poverty among women (stimulating the structural conditions of poverty). The other arises from the absence of appropriate social policy to regulate gender relations in society, which leads to an exacerbation of gender inequalities: the problems of poor families and of women living alone are growing, and the opportunities for women to have a career or any professional development are diminishing, while the risk factors in working conditions that influence excess mortality among men continue as before; and so on. It should be stated that, according to both statistical data and academic research, female poverty is global in nature and that reducing it depends in many ways on the direction of social policy and whether this has a gender aspect. Thus, according to data given by Yaroshenko in his comparison of the level of feminisation of poverty in various countries, 'strong social and gender policy has significantly reduced and continues to reduce the risk of women falling into poverty, while gender-neutral policy and the free market increase it' (Yaroshenko, 2005).

Failure to tackle these problems has an intensifying effect on social inequalities in Russian society overall. However, despite the great significance of the problems listed above, we naturally did not try to analyse them all in our research. We should point out that one of the main hypotheses of our research in regard to the interrelationship of poverty and health in the gender dimension in Russia arose from the proposition that different groups of factors affect the health of men and of women. In the course of our research, this hypothesis was confirmed, and our research materials (along with others on this issue) enabled us to highlight the chief among these factors.

Thus, in researching the social causes of formation of gender inequalities, the primary thing that needs to be taken into account is the influence of the overall social context and of the socioeconomic status of individuals and households. Researchers link the growth in mortality in Russia directly with the consequences of socioeconomic changes in the 1990s, with the large-scale impoverishment of the population and with widespread stresses resulting from the unstable economic situation (Shapiro, 1995). They go on to explain gender differences in mortality through variations in the degree of influence of macroeconomic stress on women and on men, resulting from differences in their social roles.

> Men are more characteristically involved in the political and economic sphere, where disappointment and a sense of loss of control over one's own fate may predominate. Women, who for economic reasons are also involved in the sphere of public employment, habitually have a range of traditional concerns: housework, family, children, husband, parents. These introduce a sense of meaning and a sense of responsibility into their lives, which to a certain extent serve as a defence from social stress and may compensate for its consequences. (Inequality and mortality in Russia ... p. 23; see also World Bank Report, 2005)

Statistical data indicate a number of social factors that have an effect in reducing gender differences in mortality – standard of education, place of residence and nature of work (Inequality and mortality in Russia ..., p. 23).

On the other hand, when researching health differences between men and women, it is important to consider differences in their social circumstances – and how much deeper the differences are between social groups than the differences between men and women taken overall. Thus, Bartley says that solely comparing morbidity rates in 'men' versus 'women' does not produce valid results, since men and women occupy such different combinations of social roles. When men and women who are in similar social and economic situations are compared, gender differences in health become much smaller or even disappear (Bartley, 2004). Research into the associations between social class and health shows that death and sickness are socially structured and vary according to differences in living standards (Scambler and Blane, 2003).

In looking at the causes of gender inequality, two main explanatory directions, which have already been mentioned above, must be taken into account. One of them focuses on material reasons connected with inequality in socioeconomic positions, and the other on cultural (behavioural) reasons: norms, values and beliefs that condition mechanisms of behaviour (Bartley, 2004). These two explanations may be conceptually unified by seeing behavioural/cultural factors as an expression (or manifestation) of social and class positions – that is, when explanations of behaviour in the area of health take into account the social and class context of this behaviour (Scambler and Blane, 2003).

The question of which explanatory models of the interrelationship of gender, health and material circumstances should take precedence in Russian society remains open. 'Economic' explanations of this phenomenon – general reasons connected with the economic crisis, fall in wage levels, and so on – are the most widespread. Yet a view is taking shape that the general cause of the feminisation of poverty lies in the systematic advantage that men have over women, which introduces a patriarchal gender order into all institutions (on the labour market, in social policy, in the family) (Yaroshenko, 2001).

However, research on gender inequalities in relation to health often prefers the behavioural explanation. Thus, the authors of the World Bank report 'Dying Too Young – Addressing Premature Mortality and Ill Health Due To Non-Communicable Diseases and Injuries in the Russian Federation' (2005) suggest that the great difference between men and women in life expectancy, for example, points to the presence of particular behavioural factors, and not to any particular features of the external environment or to the inadequacy of the health care system in Russia – since the latter affect men and women in practically equal degree. The broad spectrum of gender differences in people's health behaviours, which has been observed in research, also confirms the significance of behavioural factors in explaining gender inequalities in health. Many foreign researchers looking at causes of high mortality in Russia emphasise the particular lifestyle of Russian men, connected mainly with alcohol consumption, as a factor in excess mortality (primarily of middle-aged, working-class men) (see Cockerham, 2000; Shkolnikov, McKee and Leon, 2001; Abbott, Turmov and Wallace, 2006). Men consume alcohol more (in 2004, according to RLMS data, 70 per cent of men drank, as opposed to 47 per cent of women), and smoke more; Russia has one of the highest indicators in the world for male smoking (according to RLMS data, 61 per cent in 2004), although the proportion of women who smoke is increasing (from 7.3 per cent in 1992 to 15 per cent in 2004). Men are also more likely to sustain injuries, commit suicide, and so on (Dying Too Young, pp .9–11).

But, whatever explanatory model we use, the contrasting nature of statistically recorded differences shows that biological and social factors, in combination and under the influence of socio-economic changes in Russia, have had an especially strong effect, intensifying one another. So a multi-aspect analysis of their mutual influence acquires particular current relevance. It is important to take into account the fact that gender differences are formed and strengthened on the institutional level, through the effect of the values and norms that are woven into organisational structures in different areas of life in society – economic, political and legal, cultural and religious. This process strengthens the various kinds of gender inequalities, including in health, by restricting access to resources or to the choice of certain behavioural strategies in employment, the economic sphere, and so on. At the same time, some research has underlined the significance of socioeconomic conditions in the variations between men's health and women's health (Nicholson, Bobak, Murphy, Rosec and Marmot, 2005).

Our research also aimed to reveal the influence of these norms and structures on the behaviour of men and of women in relation to health and socioeconomic status (in the context of the main hypothesis formulated above). Since that is the case, let us now turn to an analysis of the data from our longitudinal survey, which offers the opportunity to track the dynamic of change in material circumstances, state of health and particular features of men's and women's behavioural practices in relation to their own health – men and women who, in the mid-1990s, were living in similar socio-economic conditions and belonged to practically the same social class. At the same time, since combining qualitative and quantitative data allows a

Table 10.2   Men's and women's opinions about reform difficulties

More difficult for women	More difficult for men	The same
In the opinion of men		
- Struggling with a difficult work-life balance (mentioned four times) - Loneliness, men not taking responsibility (mentioned twice) - Low status in society (mentioned once) - Discrimination at work (mentioned once)	- Overburdened psychologically (mentioned once) - Economic difficulties (mentioned once)	- Things have been equally difficult for men and women (mentioned four times)
Total: 8	Total: 2	Total: 4
In the opinion of women		
- Moral and emotional responsibility for the family (mentioned twice) - Loneliness, men not taking responsibility (mentioned once) - Combining a large number of tasks (mentioned once) - Poor material circumstances (mentioned once) - Low status in society (mentioned once)		- Things have been equally difficult for men and women (mentioned ten times)
Total: 6	Total: None	Total: 10

deeper understanding of the interaction of macro and micro factors in the mutual relationship of gender, poverty and health, we also review the general trends of this phenomenon in Russian society, as revealed in our interviews and through the data from a representative survey conducted by the Institute of Sociology of the Russian Academy of Sciences in 2006.

The first thing that should be noted in this connection is that the large-scale economic crisis of the 1990s must be viewed as the general macro-level factor that defined the socioeconomic context of the changing circumstances of men and of women. In 2002, respondents in our longitudinal sample expressed their opinions about the influence of the 1990s' reforms on the circumstances of men and of women (for more details about this research, see Tikhonova, 2003). These opinions give a picture of the main 'sore points' in the situation of men and of women in the most difficult years of reform, when, in essence, new types of gender inequality were formed and old ones deepened.

When asked to assess the influence of things that have happened in Russia over the last ten years of reform from the point of view of their consequences for men and for women, respondents of each sex described them in different ways. Men were more likely to acknowledge that things had been more difficult for women, while women were more likely to take the view that both sexes had 'caught it' to the same extent.

Analysis of our interviews reveals the most prevalent opinion to be that the causes of women's being in greater poverty lie at the level of the household:

while the distribution of roles in the household remains traditional, it has been undermined by the loss of appropriate support from men.

> The reforms have had a heavier impact on women; I mean that in ordinary families the weight of material problems and of all kinds of everyday problems and of bringing up kids falls on them. ... Maybe it's the way they've been brought up, and men make use of this. It's often the case that a woman has to slog, because a lot of women are divorced or single, and [these households] already undoubtedly have that kind of problem. And I think nervous stress affects women more, even though men also suffer from it. And illness is simply increasing because of it. (Sveta, kindergarten music teacher, Voronezh, interviewed in 2002 aged 38)

Our respondents also connected another difficult aspect of women's situation with its equally traditional 'social context' – the lower status of women in society and the labour market discrimination that arises from their family circumstances, preventing them from occupying better-paid and more secure jobs.

> ... To a certain extent, it's the woman who has borne the full brunt of all these difficulties. Everyday life, feeding the family – all that falls to them. ... Things have turned out in such a way that women and children are suffering more. Unemployment has mainly affected women. A lot of them have gone back to work, but at another level. Out of all the women I know, all of them are now either low-grade white-collar workers, or have had to take some kind of lower [-status] job, or are not working at all. (Sergei, Moscow, project manager in a private construction firm, interviewed in 2002; he is Vera's husband – see also the second book in our trilogy and Chapters 6 and 11 of this book)

Difficulties in men's circumstances when reforms were being implemented were usually seen as connected with their being less able to adapt to changes, especially in their social status. Differences between women's and men's adaptive abilities were mentioned fairly frequently. The dual nature of these was also discussed: on the one hand, they had a 'biological basis' and, on the other, there was a social causation to men's and women's abilities to adapt to difficulties.

> Men are more static; if something doesn't go well for them, it's simpler for them just to lie on the sofa – to take the situation lying down! But a woman looks for a way out – and, naturally, what someone seeks, they find. Women have more responsibility for the family – for the children and for the husband himself; when there's no money, she's the one who feels it more acutely. (Tat'yana, economist, Moscow, quoted in 2002 aged 37; a single parent, she had joined our panel in 1999 aged 35 – see also Chapter 8)

Data from the 2006 representative survey reveal variations in the ways men and women from different social strata perceive what has happened in society. These variations reflect differing sources of stress rooted in social change – one of the main reasons for the Russian population's falling health standards. These sources are primarily fears: fear of losing one's job, the impossibility of influencing how a situation is developing, a sense of injustice, a feeling that life is a dead end, etc. The structure of these fears was largely similar for men and women. However, women were more likely than men to have an inherent sense of their own helplessness to influence what was going on around them – 38 per cent of women said they felt this, as against 29 per cent of men. Moreover, women from sections of the population that included the poor and the badly-off characteristically experienced this feeling to a greater degree than men.

Thus, the materials from our respondent interviews enabled us to define the main areas in which gender inequalities are becoming deeper – these are the employment sphere, the distribution of all types of burdens within the household, and differences in adaptive potential and practices.

Men and Women, Employment and Health

Changes in the area of employment were the drivers of all the main changes in the socioeconomic position of women and of men, as well as of gender differences between their positions. However, the data from our longitudinal sample give a general picture of gender differences in models of adaptation to these changed circumstances, with men tending to take a more active approach to the labour market and women tending to minimise their requirements. Analysis of the interviews enables us to obtain a more detailed picture of the specific nature of the behaviour of men and of women in this area.

Men

In our sample, we distinguished a number of types and subtypes of situations in the area of employment; these may explain the reasons why men's health has deteriorated, depending on their active approach or their lack of activity in relation to employment.

An active approach in the area of employment was, as a rule, directed to the search for a more highly-paid job. The overwhelming majority of life stories from the three-city sample in our longitudinal research fell into this category.

It is possible to distinguish a number of subtypes according to the nature and results of change of job and occupation, the way that this was perceived and its influence on health. The essential factors that placed people in a given subgroup were external circumstances and individual characteristics (age, health, educational attainment, previous work experience, attitudes to place of work and occupation, and so on).

One of the subtypes was crisis entrepreneurship – that is, starting a business because of an employment crisis at the person's main place of work, without any preparatory training for the particular tasks involved and without adequate business start-up resources. Here we encountered some relative success stories, but more often such a change of work activity was not viewed optimistically. Thus, Linar', a male respondent from Kazan' who had joined our panel in 1997 at the age of 27, was the owner of a small business; interviewed in 2005, aged 34, he said:

> I've not been doing what I studied for [at university] or what I was working towards. There was a period when I felt awkward: going from physics and maths into trade. At first I tormented myself: 'Who was I, who did I want to be, and who have I become!' Really, I still feel some remaining regret. If things had been easier materially back then, and if my own occupation [physics] had had prospects, I would have been better to stick to what I had.

In the early 2000s, a gradual change for the better in his business and in life in general had brought him a greater sense of security and durability than he had had in the 1990s.

> When there is money, there is also some peace of mind, some certainty that you will be able to buy medicines, pay for your relations to go into any hospital they need to, come to some arrangement with the specialist.

In our sample, we also encountered less successful examples of entrepreneurial activity, sometimes ending in the collapse of the business. Such respondents, as a rule, fell into the next subgroup to be reviewed.

Change of workplace and usual occupation was one of the most widespread means of adapting to constantly changing employment conditions and to a fall in living standards. It was typical of a significant proportion of male respondents, and for many of them it was the main thing that had undermined their health. For example, it formed part of the life story of Nikolai, a 60-year-old working pensioner from Kazan' (see also Chapters 7 and 9). He said:

> Because of all these reforms, I have had to change my job several times, starting in 1991: I've been a bricklayer, a general labourer, and a watchman. I had to take on any work; since the enterprises were closing, they were letting people go.

This insecurity – complicated by lack of clarity in the rules of the job-hunting game – was the main factor undermining Nikolai's health.

At first glance, the situation of Vitali from Moscow, aged 53, who at the time of his most recent interview was registered as unemployed (following job cuts), seemed similar. The whole story of his changes of job and usual occupation showed a downward trajectory: until the beginning of the reforms, he had been in a technical engineering post in a large Moscow factory, but after redundancy from the factory in the mid-1990s, he re-trained for a blue-collar occupation and changed his place of work several times:

> I have already changed my job about six times over the past ten years. And it isn't because I'm difficult to get on with, but simply because those are the circumstances we are in.

The breakdown of former social and occupational status, this subtype, should be highlighted separately. In our sample, it was represented by the life stories of men who had been skilled specialists (or professionals) with backgrounds of long service in large enterprises, where they had been in fairly high-level posts.

Such a breakdown essentially formed the core of Anatoly's story. Aged 60 and now retired, Anatoly was a doctor of sciences and a former academic at a research institute in the field of space medicine and biology in Moscow. He considered the main aggravating factors in his hereditary diseases to be external, stress-generating, 'macro' ones – the change of situation in Russia (i.e. the overall decline in science) and in his job (the de facto demise of his particular branch of science). His loss of status and of the feeling that his specialism was in demand became a factor in the deterioration of his health and in his claiming disability benefit.

> When I was working, I was a person of some significance, ... at least, my high standing in a particular field of science was recognised all over the world. And suddenly I became nobody – nobody at all! ... Then my subject – space medicine and biology – was no longer needed by anybody. As a science, I mean. And it was roughly around that time that my hereditary diseases all flared up.

Kamil', a 62-year-old male respondent from Kazan', had been a senior professional – an engineer in a scientific and production group of enterprises; he too viewed the breakdown of his occupational status as a loss of security and of a sense of significance and self-respect:

> I used to work in the Science Institute of the Volga Scientific and Production Group. It was a large institute that covered the whole of the Soviet Union. When I worked there, I thought I was really needed. I was someone to be reckoned with there. I lived well. I used to travel on business. I had the chance to enhance my skills. I mastered new technologies: they were always introducing new machines, so I was constantly developing ... I used to be content, I knew that I would always have two secure jobs with high pay. Now there's no such protection, and no kind of respect. Before, because a person was needed at work, he was someone to be reckoned with. Now, that's simply not the case.

For Kamil', the 1990s had been notable for constant changes of job and occupation, arising from the need for some kind of income. This intensive pace of work, which continued after he started drawing his pension, was significant to him because he was driven by the norm of responsibility to provide for his family and his children's education (he had three sons). In striving to maintain a job ('as long as I can walk, and as long as they don't boot me out, I will work'), he neglected to look after his own health.

Life stories of this type were not only characteristic of middle-aged or elderly respondents. However, the fact that they had more adaptive resources meant that younger respondents felt greater equanimity towards the impact of such a breakdown on their social position and psychological state and, consequently, also on their health.

Security in employment, in the context of our research, meant that a respondent accepted the situation that had arisen at his main job, and it was characteristic not only of successful – as a rule, young – respondents, but also of unsuccessful ones (those in poor health whose jobs did not bring them a high income, leaving them living in poverty). Such respondents made up about a quarter of our sample, and, as a rule, they also said that their health had been stable in recent years.

Lack of activity in the area of employment   The number of our respondents who fell into this category was not great, but it is a type that plays a very significant part in understanding the causes of downward social mobility – a type represented by respondents with difficult life circumstances: sickness (disability), retirement with no support, alcoholism, and so on.

One instance was very untypical and even, in its way, unique – because most people in similar situations were women. This was the life story of Sergei from Voronezh, a lone father of two children; aged 50, he was a skilled worker now employed as a repairman (see also the second book in our trilogy and Chapters 6, 7, and 11 of this book). His disabled mother was also dependent on him for a long time. Sergei had changed his place of work several times, and his main difficulty was the need to maintain his children single-handed. In his 2002 interview, he acknowledged:

> A lot of things have gone on at those enterprises ... But basically it's that either they don't need me or there are no jobs. Most often of all, they didn't take me on in the first place, because I didn't make any secret of the fact that I have family problems, I have two children on my hands. That has been the main cause. To be honest, I've also sometimes turned down a job, if it's meant travelling to the ends of the earth. The wages haven't played any special part in it, because those jobs that I have taken have been in State organisations, so 200 roubles more or less hasn't meant much.

Sergei's various employers had never been ready to take into account the complexities of his life: in fact, they had openly made use of them in manipulating him, in particular by imposing poorer working conditions, which also affected his health.

> If they let people go on the basis of their health, that's one thing: I could take them to court for that, and demand a pension for occupational disease from the employer. But if I leave voluntarily, then it's as if nobody made me; I've signed the documents myself. So they force you: they specifically suggest a job with pay that nobody is going to work for, so people leave of their own accord. It's so that they don't have to pay you a pension.

All this had contributed to a deterioration in his health.

Thus our interview materials confirmed our hypothesis about the importance of the influence of men's employment situation on the interrelationship between their living standards and their health. The particular significance of occupational status for men played a special part in the mechanism of this mutual influence, since the breakdown of occupational status – and the impossibility of restoring it – served to exacerbate sickness and a deteriorating living situation, leading them to change their place of work and field of employment in the search for an acceptable replacement for the job they had lost, which only further undermined security and regularity in their lives and merely made their whole situation worse. External limiting and discriminating factors played a major part in creating such circumstances.

Women

According to much research data, the specific feature of women's position in the area of employment is the fact that their labour market position is worse than men's. A number of researchers see one reason for this in the influence of the gender order formed in the Soviet period, which meant that women had to work both in the productive economy and in the household; this forced them out of more economically advantageous, prestige positions within the employment structure, and entrenched their 'secondary' labour market position.

Analysis of interviews with women from our longitudinal research gives a picture of the most typical difficulties – and ways of overcoming these – in the area of employment. Although these situations are generally similar to men's, they combine in a somewhat different way to form a typology of stresses resulting from women's work situations.

An active approach in the area of employment, as in the male subsample, had its own particular, defined 'female' nature.

Entrepreneurial strategies, which represented one of the subtypes of this active approach, were encountered even less often than among men. In our sample, there was only one successful story of a woman entrepreneur – Ludmila, 45, the proprietor of a small food shop in Kazan'. However, she had not founded the business that she headed, but had 'acquired' it in the course of privatisation in Russia: she had created a shareholder company on the basis of the shop where she had been working up to then.

Attempts at entrepreneurship by women in our sample often met with failure, even when supported by the particular skills needed for the business. They made efforts to organise their businesses without any connections or money. A typical example was the life story of Maya from Kazan', a 45-year-old psychologist in a public-sector organisation:

> In 1996, I completed some retraining courses. My first education had been technical, but I retrained to be a psychologist. ... In general, I feel I have 'found myself' in this [job in my new field]. But I would have found myself more if it had been better paid, or if there had been the opportunity to earn more! But to have that opportunity, you need money and connections. My colleagues and I tried for a long time to organise our own consultancy; we went to the Member of Parliament representing our district. We went through all the structures, all the organisations, trying to get some low-rent premises, in order to just get things going. Our MP kept sending us to someone else, despite the fact

that we almost always made it to meetings. And it was only when we understood that it was completely useless that we stopped bothering with it. ...

In trying to start up her own business, Maya had set herself fairly modest aims – not to obtain wealth, but rather to achieve a particular quality of life, allowing her to survive and really support her health and the health of those close to her. But, given the existing restrictions, even this turned out to be unattainable.

> If we had a business – if we had succeeded in achieving that – then we would have been able to provide ourselves with a human way of life. For me, a human way of life would mean being able to go to the sauna, the swimming pool, for a massage, to go away somewhere, to a health resort or somewhere else. To afford clothes of some kind, not just classics that you wear for five years, but something elegant, beautiful ...

Just as in the male subsample, the most widespread subtype of activity in the area of employment was change of workplace and usual occupation. And, as for men, this was most often directed towards obtaining an income to support the family, since a significant proportion of our female respondents were lone mothers responsible for doing so. This also defines a specific feature of this group – that more serious obstacles prevented them from getting attractive jobs.

The group included women of different ages and from various social strata. The very presence of dependants, especially small children, was the first and main factor impeding their ability to find work.

> They just said to me absolutely openly: 'If your child is ill, for example, then aren't you going to take time off sick?' (Tat'yana, 37, economist, Moscow – see above and also Chapter 8)

This kind of attitude became one of the reasons why women had to take any job they could find – meaning 'low-quality', disadvantageous jobs – and, in addition, 'gravitated' directly to certain low-profit workplaces.

> I know some people who are working in four places, just in order to survive somehow. They grab at any job. Single women run around grabbing these bits and pieces, in order to get through life somehow. (Yuliya, 56, an organiser of the Centre for Psychological Support at Kazan' University)

The situation is complicated by the fact that, as a rule, many lone-parent families receive practically no help from ex-husbands. Therefore, after divorce, women mostly have to rely solely on their own efforts.

> My husband doesn't help now. He has money, but no desire to help ... I have no-one to rely on, only myself. (Lilya, 35, lecturer at conservatoire of music, Kazan' – see also Chapter 7)

Responsibility for the family and focus on income from work, without regard to how difficult the job is, were also distinguishing features of the life stories of female respondents who had to take on this responsibility even though they had husbands, because the men were incapable of providing for the family and fulfilling the role of main breadwinner.

Typical of this situation was the life story of Ol'ga, a 43-year-old respondent from Kazan', who had vocational secondary education but was working as a chemical production operative. She had been released by her employer, for whom she had worked as a laboratory technician, during a wave of job cuts across the city in the mid-1990s. Her family circumstances – two daughters to support, and a husband who was drinking – led her to take the whole burden of worrying about the family on herself: she mastered a new occupation and worked in health-adverse conditions.

> I retrained as a machine operator. And now I work as a machine operator at my old factory. The work is heavy – shift work. And it's a health hazard, because it's chemical production. But ... I can't imagine, if I were left without a job again, where I would find one or what it would be. You stick to your job, you're afraid of losing it ... Health has deteriorated over recent years because of the reforms. Things have become worse materially, people have become dependent on employers. You can't show you are dissatisfied with anything, they might sack you.

In women's life stories, breakdown of occupational status (which we noted in the male subsample) was less likely to appear as a factor in the breakdown of their whole lives and so in their health becoming significantly worse. It was apparent in some women's life stories (as a rule, these were specialists with higher education) but, even there, problems with family and children tended to predominate – and these frequently 'softened' the severity and strength of the blow to their career. The problem was also observed in the life stories of professional women who had been in fairly high-status occupations and posts in the pre-reform period and yet found themselves 'flung out into the street' at a moment's notice.

This kind of 'depreciation' mechanism, involving loss of job and professional identity, can be seen, for example, in the life story of Irina, from Moscow, who had been a specialist at an enterprise within the military–industrial complex. In the 1990s, she was on maternity leave looking after her child; after this leave ended, she was released by her employer because of staff cuts. Her health was seriously undermined by these changes ('it was a great blow when we both lost our jobs in 1995') and she went on to disability benefit – in her husband Lev's opinion, 'for her, it was all because of her mental health: it's a common experience' (see also the second book in our trilogy and Chapters 3 and 7 of this book).

In discussing the topic of gender inequality on the labour market, Irina said that women were more likely to find a way out of their employment crisis by devoting themselves to their families. This softens the difficulties of losing their job and occupational status, although it also increases their responsibility for the family's everyday problems.

> Some women I know are not working – recently, in many ways, it's become more comfortable not to work, to spend more time looking after the children and the home. And there should be some work on that basis, with worthwhile earnings, and it's just a matter of waiting a while – so it's better to devote that time to the children; there's such a lot of crime now, you really have to take them to school. And you know they are not going to starve to death with you at home.

Thus, the 'female variant' of the situation in which occupational status breaks down was usually somewhat different in character from the version observed in the male subsample, and so it had a different effect on women's health and, consequently, on their material circumstances.

Lack of activity in the area of employment   was demonstrated by an insignificant number of women; it more often resulted not from the hopelessness of finding work, but from reliance on the household's other resources – primarily, on the support of a working husband who acted as family breadwinner. Most of these women either worked in convenient but low-paid jobs or were housewives who were ready to go out to work if it became necessary.

Lara, 33, from Moscow, was the mother of two children, and had long preferred not to work but to stay at home with her two sons, although she was now making some plans to go out to work. Her previous experience of a job had been unsuccessful because of the low pay, which had made this employment unprofitable from the point of view of the family outgoings:

> ... You didn't have to wait especially long for the wages there ... But I thought that they would be at least 50 per cent higher than they were, and so I would be able to hire a nanny for the children ... Why should I work when my children were starving at home? But now we've reached the limit – I already need to look for something else, because there's no way [that we can survive] on my husband's wages.

So, problem situations in the area of employment during the 1990s took different forms for men and for women, although the economic crisis weighed equally heavily on both. For the majority of men, it was very important, firstly, to fulfil the role of main earner in the household, and, secondly, to maintain their social and occupational status, and this represented a 'double burden' on them as the enterprises in which they worked declined and they struggled on the labour market. The difficulties – often, the sheer impossibility – of shouldering this double burden were stress factors leading to a deterioration in their health. The 'double burden' of women lay elsewhere, yet it also represented a somewhat vicious circle of responsibilities for the everyday problems of the family (frequently without any significant support from their spouse) and ever-narrowing opportunities to improve their situation on the labour market. Paradoxically, women's 'double burden' often alleviated the consequences of losing their job and their occupational identity. Overall then, more intense gender conflict in role norms and in structural limitations for both men and women became

Table 10.3   Men's and women's opinions about contribution to the family budget, by level of welfare, 2006 (%)

Level of welfare (IMD)	Person considered to be main breadwinner	Men	Women	Across the whole sample
Poor	Respondent	80	53	63
	Husband (wife)	12	44	30
	Another member of the family	8	3	7
Badly-off	Respondent	79	47	60
	Husband (wife)	10	39	27
	Another member of the family	11	14	13
Averagely well-off	Respondent	72	23	50
	Husband (wife)	9	61	32
	Another member of the family	19	14	18
Well-off	Respondent	76	27	51
	Husband (wife)	17	63	40
	Another member of the family	7	10	9

Source: Institute of Sociology (2006).

a stressful factor, a driver of the increasingly vicious circle of poverty and ill-health in poor and badly-off sections of Russian society.

Men and Women, Households and Health

Drawing on the data from our research projects, we can distinguish at least two areas of deepening gender inequalities in households – contribution to household welfare and distribution of household duties.

The data we obtained from the representative survey (see Table 10.3) and from the longitudinal survey indicate significant differences in the contributions of women and of men to the family budget. Moreover, the higher the family's level of welfare, the greater the contribution men were making to the budget. This confirms both that the main sources of household income are in the hands of men and that the socio-economic position of women is more vulnerable.

Women's own assessments of the prospects for improving their material circumstances confirm their low level of resources. The difference is marked: overall, 36 per cent of men and 29 per cent of women assess these prospects positively, while women in poor strata are especially pessimistic – only 9 per cent of them give positive assessments of their prospects, as against 23 per cent of men from the same strata.

Women's problems with work–life balance are another significant aspect of the mechanism of gender inequalities that forms within the household. Research into women's health has seen the strain of dual roles as a key issue (Scambler, 2003), citing the consequences for the health of both mother and child that result from delaying having children because of work, the assimilation of 'male work culture', with its smoking and drinking, and stresses that result from women overstretching themselves in the attempt to cope with everything at home and at work.

Russian research has also found this problem to be severe and multi-aspectual. Thus, Tikhonova (2003) lists stresses resulting from the impossibility of effectively combining both social roles – in the family and at work – as one of the negative results of the effect of the reforms on the position of women, especially in poor families. Both Lytkina and Ashvin have shown that, in the 1990s, inconsistency and lack of balance in gender roles within the household played a negative part, leading to both men and women suffering, each in their own way, from the impossibility of fulfilling their own role while reaching a sensible compromise (Ashvin, 2006). The model in which the man provides for the family while the woman worries about everyday issues, handles the money and is responsible for bringing up the children, which is effective in two-parent families and in stable social conditions, becomes unjustified in crisis conditions and with the de facto loss of husband and breadwinner (including instances where he loses this role despite his continued physical presence in the family). Moreover, where a woman has a husband who is not working or is low-paid, or where she has no husband and is herself the head of the household, she is usually forced to economise on her own needs in order to support the family.

Thus, our research confirms the conclusion that the distribution of roles that has developed remains a significant mechanism for the reproduction of gender inequalities, which have become stronger during the period of crisis in Russia.

The Health Behaviour of Men and of Women

Health differences between men and women are often ascribed by researchers to particular features of their self-care behaviour, both at the level of norms and values and at the level of behavioural practices when dealing with health services in regard to their own health (see, for example, Shilova, 2000). Our research also confirmed the existence of these differences.

The first differences related to women's and men's self-rated health. According to data from the Institute of Sociology's 2006 research, women's and men's assessments of their own health were similar overall, with slightly more men giving positive ratings and slightly more women, negative ones. Moreover, the higher their level of welfare, the more equal their ratings. This most probably confirms women's greater objectivity in assessing their own health (i.e. they are not afraid to complain about it); men's striving, despite everything, not to

Table 10.4   Health indicators of women and men, EQ-5D scale, 2005 (%)

Summarised health indicators	Women	Men	Total
0.7 and below (sick)	46	24	40
From 0.71 to 0.74 (unhealthy)	29	16	25
0.75 and above (healthy)	25	60	35

complain about their health is a given of the acceptable 'male' attitude to health behaviour.

In our longitudinal research sample overall, more than half of men and more than half of women rated their health as 'fair', presenting an almost identical picture. At the same time, women were more likely to view their health as 'poor', which was also the case throughout Russia as a whole. The validity of their opinion was confirmed by indicators on the EQ-5D scale. According to this, the health of women in our sample was worse than the health of men (see Table 10.4).

It should be noted that single women were more typically in good health than married women, and married men more typically than single men: more than half of married women were 'sick' according to the EQ-5D method, while more than two-thirds of married men were in the 'healthy' category.[1]

Women were most likely to view difficult material circumstances in their family as the cause of deterioration in their own health, while men cited harmful habits and a generally unhealthy way of life. Other reasons more likely to be given by women were specific misfortunes in the family: death of a husband or child, poor housing conditions, particular illnesses. Men were more likely to mention macro factors: the criminality of the State, staff cuts or even the winding-up of the business where they worked.

Let us now focus attention on particular features of male and female models of health behaviour and how far the formation of these is influenced by attitudes and stereotypes, as well as on declarative and actual practices of seeking care from health services.

The data from our longitudinal survey show that the male model of behaviour in this regard is to a large extent defined by stereotypes that reduce the significance of concern about one's own health. The female model is distinguished by greater flexibility towards changes in conditions. Thus, most women do not agree that those who are too concerned with their own health are 'oddballs', standing out too much from the crowd, while almost a third of men support this statement. Women typically understand concern about one's own health to be characteristic of a modern outlook. They are twice as likely as men to disagree with the statement that constant concern with one's own health shows a person to be egotistical (see Table 10.5).

---

1 Other research is more precise: in families where women make the major decisions, their health is worse than that of the men in the family (see Cubbins, and Szaflarski, 2001).

Table 10.5   Differences in attitudes to maintaining health, by gender (%)

Alternative paired statements	Women	Men	Total
1. I have to economise on health costs because there are other, more urgent needs	36	28	34
2. In no circumstances should you economise on health costs	64	72	66
3. Maintaining good health is vital in order to be successful at work	30	36	32
4. Health is a major value in itself	70	64	68
5. Anyone who is too concerned with their own health stands out from the crowd too much	7	29	13
6. Consistent concern about one's own health is an indicator of a modern outlook	93	71	87
7. Constant concern with your own health shows you are egotistical	10	21	13
8. Constant concern about your own health is vital in the interests of those close to you	90	79	85
9. I have no time to worry about my health, I have too much else to do	54	40	44
10. I am forced to worry about my health in order to cope with everything I have to do	46	60	56

Men's and women's stereotypes of and attitudes towards their own health have been formed under the influence of various factors. Men are influenced to a greater extent by the behaviour of those around them, while, in their opinion, a lesser part is played by family traditions and medical information obtained from the mass media. The set of factors that determines women's attitudes towards their own health is a different one, confirming the greater pragmatism and situational nature of the female behavioural model. Women said that the most significant factors for them were concrete ones – deterioration in their health and fear of possible illness.

The ways that women and men act in relation to their own health were found to have both similarities and differences. Judging from their responses, women are more likely to stick to diets, take medicines regularly and avoid harmful habits; they visit the doctor significantly more often for preventive purposes. Thus, in our sample, smoking was much more typical of men than of women, and men also smoked significantly more.

It is paradoxical that, despite behaviour clearly favouring a healthier way of life, women are much more likely than men to be dissatisfied with their situation in regard to maintaining health. So, over half of women do not think that the efforts they are making are sufficient to maintain their health. Men, however, are more than twice as likely to take the view that they are doing enough to achieve this.

Differences in ways of explaining their own health behaviour are also instructive. Men are much more likely to indicate that they are in no way trying to place any restrictions on their lifestyle; they demonstrate lack of willpower in regard to concern about their health, complaining of lack of time and saying that they are not willing to act. Women worry more about not having the conditions or the money to do anything about their health.

Our research revealed a significant gap between the hypothetical and real actions of men and of women, which provides further evidence of the greater influence on men of the stereotype of a 'male code of behaviour' in regard to health. Thus, one of the most stark differences between men and women was in how they intended to act if they felt unusually ill. Men, for example, were three times more likely not to be prepared to do anything about feeling unwell, preferring to wait for everything to go away by itself.

In general, this model was reproduced on the level of practical action. Thus, when they had health problems, women were significantly more likely to make use of a whole spectrum of channels for possible assistance – ranging from taking advice from those close to them to visiting the doctor. We should add that women were almost twice as likely to have a permanent doctor or to know a doctor to whom they could go if they needed one. There were also some fairly typical responses about reasons for not going to the doctor. Women more often complained about reasons of an everyday nature, such as lacking the necessary money or difficulty getting an appointment with a good specialist. In addition, women were more likely not to trust doctors or modern treatment methods, and were oriented towards obtaining knowledge about their illnesses from other sources and, where possible, towards exercising control over the actions of doctors.

> You already go to the doctor with your own diagnosis. And I ask [them] 'Why are you going all round the houses? What tablets are you going to give me?' And then I read through the instructions on the tablets. So that I'm in the know. (Lara, 33, housewife and mother, Moscow)

Men, in explaining their reasons for not going to the doctor, more often referred to the uselessness of visiting medics, the fact that it was against their principles, the possibility of coping with sickness by other means, or the fact that illness was natural at their age. We also encountered explanations of an economic nature – lack of means or time:

> ... for a person to understand whether he is sick or not, he must go to the doctor, get investigated. And in order to go to the doctor, in our medical system, you need a lot of money or an incredible amount of free time. (Lev, 55, electro-mechanical engineer from Moscow, husband of Irina – see above)

However, in the case of serious illness in the family, whether of the respondent or those close to him (the questionnaire asked people to recall a real instance of this), real behaviour somewhat mitigated such strictly declarative attitudes on the part of men. Although they had actually called the ambulance significantly less often than women in these instances, the number of men and women who had gone to the doctor in this situation was exactly the same, as was the number of those who had treated themselves (about a quarter of men and of women in both cases). However, the picture of what happened with people who had not gone to the doctor was different for men and for women: women were more likely to turn to a broad circle of advisers (relations, acquaintances, friends, neighbours).

Analysis of our interviews also shows that there are differences in the ways that men and women obtain information, and therefore between the bases on which they construct their health strategies. The model of refusing to seek information about health maintenance and going to the doctor only in case of absolute necessity can be described as purely male; whereas the model characterised by a focused and painstaking study of literature, methods of action and places where one can go with health problems (one's own or those of people close to one) is purely female.

Thus, our research confirmed significant differences in the health behaviour of men and of women, even where they have an equal degree of access to health care and are in the same social strata. Women's more responsible attitude towards their own health, which is a generally accepted norm, is strengthened in poor and badly-off households by their greater sense of responsibility for the family's well-being. At the same time, the way in which men maintain attitudes of lack of concern for health not only exacerbates their own health problems, but also frequently leads to a deterioration in their material circumstances and those of their families.

Conclusion

The data from the representative pan-Russian survey demonstrate that inequalities in socioeconomic status result mainly from women's less advantageous position in the employment structure and have a significant, if only mediating, influence on the formation of gender inequalities in health. The insecurity of their position reflects on women's emotional state, which can be defined as fear of their changing situation and a sense of the impossibility of controlling this – it was not without reason that women were more likely to mention stress as a factor in the deterioration of their health.

On this level, women are in a relatively worse situation than men. However, particular features of existing gender roles – in which a woman, even having lost her job, has a sense of her social significance as mother, wife, grandmother, housewife, etc. – mitigate this insecurity for them. Men, on the other hand, get less upset about 'the future', but when they have real problems with work they experience especially severe stress. In addition, the prevalence of defined gender attitudes and of stereotypes about one's own health limits men's concern about health and is making their situation worse.

Taking this point further, we should add that our research also revealed the characteristics of male and female behavioural models in regard to health. The female model is distinguished by greater flexibility and pragmatism about one's own health, both in attitudes and stereotypes and in how people act in real situations. The male model to a greater extent reflects a code of norms prescribing that people should not worry too much about their own health.

The consequence of this is that the most effective models of behaviour in relation to living standards and quality of life – which include the essential element of a strategy for economical preventive measures to care for one's own health – are presented primarily by women. In our longitudinal sample, which consisted mainly of poor and badly-off households, it was precisely such strategies that had more often led to an improvement in the families' material welfare. It may be concluded that, in Russia, in situations where there are few resources and severe structural limitations, the model of health behaviour that is typical of women is more likely to offer favourable prospects for overcoming the closed circle of poverty and ill-health.

Given what has been said above, gender-targeted social policy must be implemented both in the area of employment (first and foremost, equalising men's and women's chances on the labour market) and in the life of the household (social support to lone-parent families, etc.). In addition, a free-standing element of social policy should be a gender-differentiated campaign to promote healthy lifestyles and the formation of new behavioural norms and stereotypes.

Chapter 11
Life Stories of Ten Russian Households: The Sequence of Events over Ten Years of Reform

Nadia Davidova (with linking material by Karen George)

Жизнь прожить не поле перейти
To get through life is not to cross a field

The transition to a market economy in Russia in the 1990s was accompanied by a serious socioeconomic crisis, with falling and stagnating production, rampant inflation and a sharp rise in socioeconomic differentiation. It was far from the case that everyone was in demand in the new market conditions; in addition, the structure of the economy itself, inherited from pre-reform times, scarcely matched the country's new stage of development. Russia successfully escaped large-scale unemployment through the policies of successive Russian governments, which chose to support inefficient production instead of setting in motion mechanisms for controlled bankruptcy; however, placing direct restraints on open unemployment only led to its flourishing in hidden forms. In practice, the labour market crisis – expressed through work stoppages, years of wage delays and sending employees on compulsory unpaid leave – meant circumstances of extreme poverty for those people who were the hidden unemployed, since the State did not recognise them as such.

It was at that time that we first met our respondents, who were suffering from the employment crisis and trying to cope, each in their own way, with the difficult material and psychological situations that had descended on them and their families. Each respondent represented a unique 'sacrifice' to Russia's painful transition to a market economy. Each of them, in their time, experienced what was meant by 'the social cost of the Russian reforms'. Their experiences of surviving a hostile external environment and the need to adjust rapidly to all kinds of cataclysmic upheavals in their lives – with no hope of adequate social support from the State – demonstrate amazing variability and inventiveness in choice of methods of adapting.

Unfortunately, the limits of this book do not allow us to give an account of what happened to all the families we studied; but the stories of ten households, who worked with us more than others (most of them were participants in all three of the research projects we conducted between 1995 and 2005) and whose life circumstances were the most interesting and typical, are presented here.

Irina's Household, Moscow (d.o.b. 1951) – see also the second book in our trilogy

Irina's family was typical of the well-educated 'new poor' in Russia. She herself provided a clear example of someone with a pre-existing disability who entered a downward spiral following redundancy: her disability impeded her job search, the stress of all this had a negative impact on other aspects of her physical and mental health, and she ended by choosing to claim disability pension as her main economic survival strategy. Like many other women, she felt this had some compensations in the support her family gained from her being at home. Although her husband Lev was not our main respondent and so we did not track his health consistently, he seemed to be someone whose essentially good health and previous experience of manual work allowed him to cope reasonably well with the loss of his occupational status; at the same time, he was acutely aware of the impact of the reforms on the health of the whole workforce.

Irina and her family took part in all our research surveys and were interviewed five times in total. In the mid-1990s, Irina and her husband were released, at practically the same time, from the scientific research institute where they worked as communications engineers, because it was being wound up. Their fate was typical of many employees in the Soviet defence industry, who, at the time of transition to a market economy, lost their jobs in extremely disadvantageous circumstances: this couple were both already over 40 years old, which put them in a losing position on the Russian labour market. Particular aspects of their skills also worked more 'against' than 'for' them: it is no secret that, during the Soviet era, there was a distinct surfeit of engineering and technical personnel in Russia. Moreover, they had two dependent children under 18 (a seven-year-old daughter and a student son), whom they had to feed and clothe. Irina said that this was one of the most difficult times in the family's life, since the loss of their jobs led to a sharp deterioration in their living standards, while the impossibility of finding any way out of the situation (the labour exchange where she was officially registered as unemployed was packed with unemployed engineers) made the psychological stress and sense of hopelessness much stronger.

In addition to everything else, Irina was hampered by a stammer, which led employers to refuse to hire her. So, after a year, having been unable to find work through the Employment Service, she made a conscious decision to claim disability pension – on the advice of 'comrades in misfortune, whom I met at the Employment Service'. We should remember that she was only 46 at the time. The grounds for her claim were that unemployment and the various other problems in her life had strongly exacerbated her hypertensive disease, and that humiliating approaches to employers, which customarily meant refusal (in Irina's opinion, exclusively because of her stammer, which became considerably stronger after her redundancy) had led to lack of confidence in herself and persistent depression.

Since then, Irina had never succeeded in returning to permanent work, although she was still sure that she could work in her usual occupation in the field of telecommunications and IT. She only stopped actively seeking a job in the mid-2000s, when she became certain that specialists of her age were not required anywhere. All this time, the family had been mainly supported by her husband Lev, who, practically immediately after being made redundant, had retrained as an electrician (a manual occupation) and worked repairing household appliances. However, as evidence from our observations showed, this did not save the family from existing on the brink of poverty. Lev's employment was distinguished by its insecurity: the small private firms where he worked kept collapsing, and there were interruptions in wage payments. Their incomes were catastrophically insufficient; Irina never refused any temporary additional earnings, and even their son started unregistered work at a young age as a computer programmer. Lev's employment situation normalised only just before our last survey in 2005, when he finally got a permanent job that matched his standard of education and skills, as an electrical engineer in a branch of a major Western firm.

At all stages of observation, the family was stagnating in a state of deprivation, teetering on the brink of poverty. They had problems obtaining and renewing consumer durables, and they constantly restricted their consumption of the most essential items, fearing that there were worse times to come – a lesson learned from their painful experience of trying to survive. In 2000, Irina was very worried about the possible costs of higher education for their daughter, who was leaving school; however, she no longer had the same sense of hopelessness as in the mid-1990s. (Their son had married and moved out of the family home in the early 2000s)

Irina and Lev were typical in having lost the jobs they had had in the Soviet era and in terms of their chosen strategies for adapting to their new conditions: the husband accepted a sharp drop in status in order to obtain any kind of job and was constantly searching for a better one, while the wife claimed disability pension. At the same time, Irina connected the deterioration in her health with the loss of her permanent job and with the material difficulties that the family had encountered when reforms were being implemented in Russia – a typical reaction.

> I felt that my health deteriorated because I lost my job. Although everyone, including the doctors, asks me: 'How and when did this start?', I can never answer sensibly. I began to feel that I wasn't needed, that I was being tossed aside from life; I started to get problems with my heart, my blood pressure went up.

Lev added:

> There are no healthy people now, because our workloads are too heavy. The deterioration in the population's health is because of their working conditions. Before, in the Soviet era, you could just be sitting quietly minding your own business in your scientific research institute or your design office, not thinking about anything and working away quietly, but now you have to be incessantly on the move. Until perestroika, everyone was sitting quietly on their fat salaries; you got your money and you could take a day

off sick at the slightest sneeze, no one would even comment on it; but now you could lose your job for it, and that would simply be that.

In our surveys, Irina consistently rated her own health as 'poor', and she gave health as the main factor limiting her chances on the labour market and reducing the family's standard of living and quality of life. Her indicators on the GHQ scale over the whole period of observation confirmed that she had chronic health problems: in the period when she lost her job, her overall score soared to 58 points; we then observed a fall to 43–44 points; finally, at the time of the most recent survey, her GHQ indicator was again close to 50 points.

Vera's Household, Moscow (d.o.b. 1953) – see also the second book in our trilogy

Like Irina, Vera was never the main breadwinner, yet all her behaviour was motivated by her devotion to her family (in particular to her children's education and future prospects); this included some employment decisions about which she had mixed feelings (compare the account below with her comments in the second book in our trilogy). Her husband Sergei was in many respects typical of the working poor everywhere: though officially above the subsistence minimum, his pay was really too low to maintain his family far above the poverty line, and he was well aware that his wife and children bore the brunt of this situation. At the same time, as Vera's account shows, there were aspects of his circumstances that were especially Russian, and his health had suffered. Ironically, Vera's own health was worse; always poor, it fluctuated with the family's circumstances – but she was one of our many respondents who largely ignored their health problems.

Vera also participated in all our research surveys, having first come into view in 1996 when she was signing on as unemployed at the Employment Service. The construction enterprise where she had worked as a labour planner in Soviet times had undergone a crisis at the very start of the reforms. Striving to adapt to her new situation, she tried to hang on there, even taking a manual job as a workshop quality controller, but in 1995 she decided to leave, since the job did not suit her either materially or emotionally. In addition, at that time the situation in her family changed: her husband Sergei managed to get involved in organising a private construction company.

Vera did not try to hide the fact that she had always wanted to be a housewife and occupy herself with the house and the children. (They had two children: only the younger one, their ten-year-old daughter, was still a child in 1996; their 24-year-old son lived separately from the family and was financially independent – a small businessman 'in a constant whirl', as Vera said) To put it simply, Vera's decision to use the Employment Service was a purely utilitarian one – a way of not working for a while and receiving unemployment benefit (although she did not directly admit this). However, the story of Vera's household was a very instructive example of how there are many circumstances that can destroy a planned course of action in life – and how a person has to seek to escape unexpected problems as fast as they come along. Their prospects, reasonable at the time our observations began, seem to have started to disintegrate in 1997, creating a threat of real poverty and a need to seek other means of survival. Sergei was seriously injured in a car crash and this deprived the family of its main source of income, while troubles with their son's business led him to become dependent on the family again instead of offering additional support.

Vera was faced with the need to go out to work, since the family's material circumstances had deteriorated sharply (her husband's treatment was a significant drain on their resources). She applied to the Employment Service with a specific request – that they should find her a job as a social care worker providing assistance to aged people at home. Her motivations were that this job would give her access to additional social guarantees for herself and her family; the hours and type of activity would suit her; she would not need to take any additional courses of study; the relations of aged or disabled people frequently offer care workers extra money to carry out particular services (night duty, sanitary procedures), which means that the work is potentially very advantageous financially, even though this is on an informal basis. It should also be said that Vera herself had had quite good experiences of the various social services when trying to obtain concessionary benefits and support.

However, although she continued to work for the social services right up to 2004, her earnings did not have any particularly normalising effect on the family's material circumstances – rather, they served the purposes of day-to-day survival. For our whole period of observation, the welfare of this household noticeably 'drifted about', and was strongly dependent on their good or bad fortunes, and frequently simply on chance. Vera herself was working in a low-paid job; Sergei, once restored to health, was able to return to work, but there were periodic crises in his private business (lack of orders, delayed payments, problems with suppliers, and so on). Moreover, expenditure on their children constantly increased: the couple had decided that, come what may, they should give their children an education, which – as the experience of their older child's unsuccessful commercial activity showed – was simply essential in order to achieve success in life. On the other hand, Vera's household was often simply lucky: for example, in the most difficult years, when Sergei was ill, she was lucky enough to receive an inheritance from her sister; their car, which had earlier been stolen, was found; an old lady whom Vera had looked after as a care worker left her a share in her flat as a sign of thanks for her service and care. These factors, each in its own way, had a marked impact on the family's standard of welfare, which, through all these years, 'swung' from troughs – reaching a critical low when the family could feed itself only with the help of relations – to peaks of more or less satisfactory living standards. This is how Vera herself assessed that time.

> That was a troubled time. Most probably, at some time in the future, historians will say that too. The hardest period was in the mid-1990s, when there were difficulties

with employment, with health – in the end, with changing values. It was hard for us to rethink everything, to move away from the mood that there had been, to face something so shocking. And that troubled time, of course, reflected on our health. I can even explain specifically how it came about. My husband really suffered from all that. That is, he suffered as an employee – even now, he doesn't have a copy of his work records. When he was leaving his previous job in order to start his own business (he had to feed the family), they didn't give them to him, they got lost somewhere, and even now I haven't been able to get them back. The records of his whole working life were there, all but the time before he went into the army. Tackling the problem then was actually just impossible; he had no employment protection whatsoever, and it all but cost him a heart attack, he was so worried about his future pension. And although the main responsibility for the family's material welfare lay with him, I didn't so much take on responsibility for the family as take on the suffering.

The example of this family, whose circumstances were affected by problems with work and lack of social protection in the face of loss of income, sickness and other unfortunate life circumstances, was also fairly typical – in that, despite everything, they found it possible to survive and even significantly improve their position. At the time of the most recent survey, in 2005, everything in Vera's household was running relatively smoothly. She had left her permanent job and was helping her son in the firm that he had managed to set up (having finally achieved relevant education), and she had acquired computer skills, of which she was terribly proud. Because of the inheritance they had received, the family had managed to improve their housing conditions and to fund their younger child's expensive but promising – in terms of possible future career – education at the Petrochemical University. (This was despite the fact that Vera had always dreamed of her daughter becoming a professional musician, insisting for many years that she take piano classes at music school, since Vera herself had, in her time, failed to fulfil her own dreams of such a career) Vera's household had always started from whatever the current reality of life in Russia was offering them, and constantly adjusted their strategies in the aim of 'keeping afloat' – which, in general, they managed to do.

This flexibility was reflected in the characteristics of their health, which depended directly on the concrete situation in the family at a given time. At the beginning of our research, Vera's health, as recorded on the GHQ scale, was really very poor – 64 points; however, after just one year, her health had improved to 41 points. As her husband's employment problems worsened in the late 1990s, her GHQ indicators again climbed upwards, reaching 52 points in 2000; they then fell to 45 points in 2005.

Natal'ya, Moscow (d.o.b. 1965) – see also the second book in our trilogy

Over the time we knew her, we saw Natal'ya follow an upward trajectory in material welfare from near-indigence to being averagely well-off. Her general health followed a similar curve, from depression and near-starvation to a strong sense of mental well-being and objective physical good health. To this extent, she was an example of our model of 'better health and better material circumstances', and had a strongly held view of health as an intrinsic value, which – despite having started her life in a conventional medical milieu – she defined very broadly as not just absence of disease. Her life story also demonstrated the importance of social networks and of a sense of job satisfaction and control over one's working life.

Natal'ya was a single middle-aged woman who took part in all our research surveys. The start of the market reforms coincided with her arrival in Moscow from our provincial city, Voronezh, where she had graduated from medical school and qualified as a paediatrician (her parents were also doctors). It was true that she had not completed the required clinical experience that would allow her to begin practising as a doctor, since she had refused to go to Bryansk Province as she was directed after graduation, because of the increased level of radioactivity there following the Chernobyl nuclear power plant disaster. Instead, she simply came to Moscow. At that time, many people gravitated to the capital to try and take advantage of the new possibilities of life there, which were opening up as the Soviet regime crumbled. Rapid growth in commercial relations and trade – and the completely chaotic nature of this process – offered those who were sufficiently entrepreneurial great chances to succeed.

In Moscow, Natal'ya began working as a trader and second-hand dealer, selling souvenirs on Arbat Street. In essence, she was self-employed on a personal basis, and at that time her income was enough to allow her to rent decent accommodation and support a prosperous standard of living, since she mainly received it in foreign currency and unknown to the tax authorities (her souvenirs were usually bought by foreign tourists).

However, in the late 1990s, unorganised private entrepreneurship gradually gave way to more structured business relations, in which Natal'ya did not find a place. In 1994, she was left without work and experienced a serious drama in her personal life (the breakdown of a long-term relationship). This plunged the respondent into prolonged depression. She spent her small savings from her previous activities on rent, which in Moscow is extremely high. In everything else, Natal'ya went without, leading a semi-starved existence.

From time to time, when there were trade exhibitions in Moscow, she did manage to get some unregistered sales work but, in 1996, when she first joined our panel as a de facto unemployed person, her standard of living was extraordinarily low. Once a week, she received a food parcel, brought to her by relations from her native city; she practically never left her flat; she bought nothing. In essence, Natal'ya was experiencing not only a serious psychological crisis, but also a crisis in her personal and professional identity. She could not start work as a doctor because she had no experience and no connections in a strange city.

Until practically the end of the 1990s, Natal'ya experienced constant difficulties with work and suffered from an unsuccessful personal life and a sense of her own lack of worth. We were prompted to enrol her in our second survey in order to track the impact of all this on her material welfare. However, by 2000, she had found the strength to reconsider her view of life: she became keen on alternative medicine and completed courses first in homoeopathy and then in clinical massage using acupressure. Her relations and some friends who had moved to Moscow helped her to pay for these courses. This gave her the opportunity to start a visiting massage practice on a self-employed basis. Her material circumstances gradually improved, although she continued to invest the greater part of her money in increasing her skills, and so she restricted herself in many ways.

In 2005, Natal'ya was working in a medical massage practice on a permanent basis, with a flexible employment schedule. By this time, she had already obtained the necessary certification to work as a paediatrician, but her lack of references and work experience hindered her finding work as a doctor. Nevertheless, her standard of living had risen markedly, and her attitude to life had also significantly changed. She was studying psychoanalysis, and dreamt of becoming a broadly qualified specialist in alternative medicine and then opening her own surgery; she looked back on the earlier period in her life very critically. She was now sticking to a very particular self-care strategy, since she was certain that seeking spiritual self-improvement helps to overcome physical ailments and saves a person from life's setbacks.

> First and foremost, a person must be provided with spiritual health. For me, health is made up of several aspects – it is the health of the physical body, the health of the mind and the health of the spirit. And sickness on any of these levels is, at the very least, unpleasant. I think that the person himself must be aware of this, and say to himself at some point: 'I am sick'. First of all, I have learned to be concerned about my own health myself. While I am maintaining these different levels of health, I can move forward.

In 1996, Natal'ya rated her own health as 'fair', but at the time of the most recent survey, in 2005, she considered it 'good': subjectively, she had felt an improvement. And it was indeed in the 1990s, during the most unfortunate period in Natal'ya's life, that her GHQ scale indicators had reached their maximum (34 points); by 2005, they had fallen to 28 points.

Natal'ya's life story is instructive when applied to the present situation in Russia: very many Russians have had to encounter difficulties involving serious psycho-emotional stress, destroying their life and limiting their prospects. In the new reality, a change in situation and a 'new start' in many ways depend on people's ability and desire to find the strength to overcome crisis.

Valentina's Household, Moscow (d.o.b. 1964) – see also the second book in our trilogy

Valentina was not one of our better educated respondents, yet she was one of the most articulate in expressing how the whole picture of economic reform in Russia has impacted on health. She commented on the hopelessness and apathy around her and the fact that this often arose from poverty, yet she herself had the strength of character to rise above it. Various life events placed Valentina under enormous stress, and her health was objectively poor. She was well aware of this (and at one time had taken medication for depression) – but she was even more aware that poor health could place very significant limitations on opportunities to improve her circumstances; so she had made a conscious decision to ignore these problems and throw herself actively into her children's lives, a new job and a new relationship.

Unlike Natal'ya, whose move to Moscow had been entirely at her own risk, Valentina had arrived in the mid-1980s under a workers' quota scheme – a system of hiring workers for enterprises and construction sites in the capital – that is, as an 'organised migrant'. This move offered the prospect of obtaining accommodation and guaranteed employment at one of the major industrial enterprises, with all social benefits. However, the reforms brought their own adjustments to this essentially favourable 'Soviet scenario'. Valentina was a manual worker (a crane operator) for a goods vehicle manufacturers, but in the 1990s practically the whole of the Russian vehicle industry permanently 'stalled'. This placed Valentina in a position of extreme poverty – living in a room 14 metres square with her two small children, no secure job, and having to cope alone with any difficulties that arose. Valentina had no relatives in Moscow; she was divorced, but her ex-husband had returned home to Georgia and did not help the family.

We met Valentina in 1996 at the Employment Service, where she was seeking work using the computer database on her own initiative. The factory where she was working was at a standstill, and all its employees were on unpaid leave. This situation had lasted for a long time already, but Valentina could not change her job earlier, since if she did she would lose her accommodation and could end up out in the street with two children aged ten and six. It was only in the mid-1990s that it became possible for her to quit her job. However, at that time many factories were idle, and finding work in a manual occupation – especially for a woman with two children – was not easy. In the end, Valentina found a job as a track walker in the Metro, but had to agree to night work and very hard underground working conditions. But even her honest, self-sacrificing labour could not lift her family out of deprivation, although she was constantly striving to improve the situation somehow and provide for her children. This is how Valentina herself, in 1999, described her life.

> A lot of people now have got into a difficult situation, regardless of their education. It's hard for people – and this results from the way life is structured – prices, inflation, wage delays. Both from people I know and from what I see on the television – everyone's talking about the impoverishment of the population ... Poverty means having no tomorrow. In the past we weren't afraid of becoming poor, we could rely on stability (we'll get our wages, we'll buy this now, and wait to buy that). And it was like this – the factory closed, and my children were small, and I was arguing with my neighbours over housing, and my whole nervous system was overtaxed. And although I used to react to things calmly, now a lot of things annoy me; I would like things to be calmer. And sometimes I just want to be on my own for a while, not see anyone or have to

listen to any one. But how can I possibly, when we are living in these conditions?! I'm constantly tense now, constantly on my nerves, so my health is being undermined too.

It was undoubtedly the case that Valentina would have been able to come through her health problems successfully if she had not had constant difficulties with steady paid work, the need to provide for her family single-handed, and housing problems. When an additional room in their communal flat became free, Valentina was dragged into many years of legal dispute with her neighbours. By that time, her children, a boy and a girl, were already 14 and ten years old; Valentina had remarried and this four-person household was continuing to live in the same 14 square metres. Fortunately, her husband was often away for work (he was a conductor on long-distance trains and was at home for only a day or two between trips). In the end, in 2002, the court awarded Valentina the additional, disputed 17-square-metre room, but by now her relationship with her neighbour (who was worse off as a result of the case: she had a grown-up son, with whom she lived in one room) had become practically unbearable. At our last meeting, in 2005, Valentina said that life had started to become easier from a material point of view:

we've got our accommodation, and my son is studying, but he would like to get to the West somehow, simply in order to have his own little corner, where anyone could just drop in, where he could unwind, just for himself.

It was interesting that, at the time our research began, Valentina considered herself completely healthy and rated her health as 'fair' – yet, throughout the whole period of observation, the GHQ scale recorded that she had distinct problems of both a psychological and a somatic nature: her overall scores were 49 points in 1996, at the time she was threatened with unemployment; 61 points (her absolute maximum) in 2000, at the height of the legal case concerning the flat; and 51 points at the end of the period of observation. Thus she provided a typical example of unwillingness to admit, even to oneself, that there is anything wrong, since this was incompatible with her chosen way of life.

The history of Valentina's household shows that the absence of good social policy, including family support policy, exacerbates problems even for those who work honestly and very hard.

Abukhasan's Household, Moscow (d.o.b. 1934)

Abukhasan was another respondent in objectively poor health who did not allow this to compromise his efforts to overcome problems triggered by the reforms and, in his case, compounded by the war in Chechnya. In many ways he was a true Soviet man: educated to a high standard, working far from home in a responsible job (as a cog in the wheel of the old command economy), continuing to believe staunchly in Russia's possibilities for peaceful ethnic and cultural coexistence.

However, this did not lead to a passive mindset: not only did he continually work hard and engage in private enterprise to try and support his family and invest in his children's future, but he had a balanced view of the strengths and weaknesses of the reforms. He made it clear that social policies had had no impact in helping his family out of poverty, yet felt that social trends in general and health policy in particular were starting to improve by the mid-2000s. Sadly, over the period that we observed him, his health declined markedly: he went from being an active working pensioner of 65 to an old man of 70, lacking any significant social capital in Moscow and so having to accept the support of his much younger and less educated wife despite his cultural traditions and personal pride.

Abukhasan was a Chechen, married with two sons (d.o.b. 1986 and 1993). When he joined our research panel in 1999, the children were both under 18, and his wife, who had recently arrived from Chechnya, was not employed (she was 25 years younger than her husband). By then, Abukhasan himself had already reached pension age; however, he was healthy and active, and shouldered the entire burden of concern for his family. A qualified economist, Abukhasan had come to Moscow in 1986 in order to take up the offer of a new job. In the Soviet era, he had been head of an audit section in the markets control department for Chechnya and Ingushetiya; in Moscow he continued in the same type of local government job, and was allocated a one-room flat. At that time, his family lived in Chechnya; he visited and supported them. It should be pointed out that this is still a widespread practice in Russia among people who come from ethnic minority regions.

However, the Chechen conflict interfered with this arrangement, and the family was forced to move to Moscow in 1995. During the years of reform, Abukhasan was mainly engaged in running his own business, but this collapsed after the August 1998 default on public and private debt. Thus, several unfortunate circumstances coincided for this family: financial troubles, being obliged to move a long distance to another city, with four people (including two young children) having to live together in cramped housing conditions. His wife had no occupational training of any kind, so Abukhasan's concern was to come to grips with their accumulated debts and take any opportunity whatsoever to earn money for the family. These 'opportunities' were mainly small-scale trading operations, which did not guarantee a constant income. All this drove the family into poverty; we first met Abukhasan at the social services, where he had applied for a housing subsidy. Here is how he himself described this period in his life.

> In Chechnya in 1995 we were in a really difficult position, absolutely catastrophic. In the most difficult year, because of that – because of the war, we lost everything. When I went down to Chechnya, I saw that nobody was working: you know what it means to go hungry. And then here in Moscow it's turned out to be very difficult, the years have been unlucky. You start to do something, the deal is taking shape, but everything falls through if illness strikes. And not only because of illness. In 1998, there was the financial crisis, everyone lost a lot then; it was hard for everyone, not just me, with the value of savings and possessions falling by almost half. Crooks have stolen everything I managed to earn last year from my business. Now it'll have to go to a settlement.

You know what I mean by 'settlement'. That'll have a big effect on my life and on the state of my nerves. We are undoubtedly living in poverty. We've had no kind of compensation for our house in Chechnya being destroyed. There's no kind of help from the State, only a housing subsidy; we're barely surviving, the children aren't getting enough vitamins. If my age allowed me to, I would be earning. The only way out is for my children to study: they've got the brains, so the main thing is that their health should be up to it.

By the time of the 2005 survey, his circumstances had slightly improved. The children were studying, the eldest to be an economist; in addition, Abukhasan said, 'we have a roof over our head, we can buy clothes and shoes, we can eat properly at least once a day.' However, over the course of time, his health problems became more evident. This was confirmed by the sharply negative dynamic of his indicators on the GHQ scale – 26 points in 1999, but 46 points by the time of the most recent survey. Although he was the head of the family, sickness prevented him from working at full strength, which had a very serious impact on his self-esteem, since in Islamic culture the man should be the breadwinner. By the time of the last research survey, his wife was going out to work as a seamstress, and was doing so mainly because of her husband's deteriorating health.

Abukhasan was certain that the main problem for refugees in Russia now is unemployment: it is impossible for them to earn a living, and there are no social guarantees. Because of this, many of his relations had emigrated to Europe, where there was hope of establishing a more prosperous life. However, Abukhasan did not plan to leave, taking the view that, in Russia,

now – although slowly – life is getting better all the same. And nowadays, if a person wants to do something, then he can live well and contentedly and he isn't just thrown on the rubbish tip, as things still were a few years ago.

At the stage of radical reforms, Abukhasan's family was forced to share the fate of all those Russian citizens who encountered unforeseen misfortunes resulting from escalation of inter-ethnic conflict. In such conditions, it was difficult to arrange one's life as one would have liked: for example, in 1999, Abukhasan said 'if there were no war in Chechnya, I would send the children home: life there isn't so expensive' – but he still believed that he and his children had a future in Russia.

Our country is really great, and if Russian culture is instilled, and all the best things are taken from the Muslim world, then Russia will be unified. There are also negative things in our mutual relations, where everyone is to blame; but we have to instil the good things, and not by violent means, and the good things about Russia too. We have to find the right road: there wasn't such hatred in the Caucasus before they started to put up artificial barriers between the native people and the Russians. Out of a hundred people, maybe ten will be aggressive towards Russians, but not towards Russia as a whole.

Anna's Household, Moscow (d.o.b. 1976) – see also the second book in our trilogy

Anna provided a complete contrast, as she was one of the tiny number of people on our long-term panel who were in 'better health but worse material circumstances' by the end of the observation period. Although she was clearly affected by Russia's economic upheavals, it is probable that she could and would have become similarly dependent on her parents under the Soviet structure, but lived her life unobserved. After all, the circumstances of her family as a whole typified the strengths of traditional Russian self-sufficiency and inclusion in social support networks. Ironically, as her worried parents aged, Anna typified our finding that 'any improvement in our respondents' health over the last few years [was] mainly because of a reduction in their level of anxiety – which, in its turn, has reduced the danger of stress and had a favourable effect on their somatic health'. This can be explained by the fact that, although Anna was passive in relation to social change and the labour market, from the point of view of her health she engaged in active self-care. The measures she took were undoubtedly at the more eccentric end of the possible range but, seen as functioning within a loving family (whom she was considering replacing with a religious community), she fitted our model of 'non-employment, social inclusion and modest preventive health measures'.

Anna took part in all our research surveys from the beginning. Over this time, she was not successful in adapting to the realities of the market economy or finding a place in it. Throughout almost ten years of observation, this young woman never once had permanent employment and for most of the time was not working at all, remaining dependent on her parents, who were pensioners. She first entered the survey as an employee of a Moscow vehicle factory on unpaid leave. Anna had been taken on at this factory, which was already in crisis, on the recommendation of her father, who was then coming up to pension age and had worked there for many years as a specialist test engineer. She was a buildings restorer by training: in practice, this meant working as a painter/decorator and plasterer, which did not suit her, so she never pursued this career. The fact that the factory was planning to close and that this threatened her with impending redundancy had not prevented Anna from taking a job there. Her motivation was clear – to acquire a formal work record and then sign on at the Employment Service in order to receive unemployment benefit. And indeed, that was exactly how things turned out.

Anna's life story presents a typical example of social dependency, voluntary isolation and the gradual destruction of social ties, mainly because of individual psychological traits. She was afraid of the world around her and felt that the external environment was aggressively disposed towards her, and her parents encouraged her in this by allowing her to remain under their wing. This reinforced her infantile outlook and made her even more inadequate.

Over time, it became practically impossible for Anna to return to work. It had ceased to worry her that the family's main income consisted of her parents' pensions, and that her father – who was already coming up to 70 – had to continue to earn more, working as a private carrier, in order to be able to make ends meet, or that their standard of living was falling as there were fewer working people in the household. During the 1990s, the family had just managed to hang on in our 'badly-off' group (although in the Soviet era they had not in any way lived worse than the majority of people around them, so they were probably 'averagely well-off'), but at the time of our most recent survey, in 2005, their living standards showed evidence of growing deprivation. However, Anna did not consider herself or her household to be poor, and was ready to reduce her consumption – most recently, almost to ascetic levels. The family had lived all this time and was still living on periodic help from relations, as well as from their own private plot of land, where they grew vegetables. Here is what Anna herself said about it all.

> Somehow, I've never been able to start work again: I have to help Mum around the house and at the dacha. But I'm getting organised to fix something up. Dad has promised to ask. We're not rich, but we have everything we need. Our situation is still the same, we have enough to live modestly. I don't think anything will change, even if I get a job: I still won't earn very much. I would have preferred not to go out to work, but it didn't seem entirely right.

In 1996–97, Anna rated her own health as 'fair', and in later surveys she stuck to the same assessment; her only concern was for the gradual deterioration in her parents' health. She accepted her new way of life and was noticeably calmer, which led to a sharply positive dynamic in her GHQ indicators: over the course of time, her depression disappeared, she began to feel her social dysfunction less acutely, and her overall score fell from 47 points in 1996 to 15–20 points in recent years.

Anna generally looked after her own health very carefully: for her, self-care sometimes seemed to take the form of an almost paranoid fear of harming her organism with something. She thought that avoiding protein foods, alcohol and contact with electromagnetic radiation, as well as spending time outdoors (mainly at her parents' dacha) would also help her to remain healthy in future. Recently, she had begun to think seriously about throwing in her future lot with religion, even going as far as considering entering a convent.

In Anna's life story, we can observe features of a 'strategy of downward adaptation', similar to that chosen by many Russians who do not know how – or do not want – to live according to the rules that now prevail. These people form a significant subsection of the 'new poor' who have appeared in Russia as a result of the implementation of market reforms.

Household of Vladimir (1948-2002) and his Wife Tat'yana (d.o.b. 1950), Moscow

Tat'yana and her husband Vladimir provided striking examples of the impact of the Russian economic reforms on health. Highly educated specialists, they were essentially thrown on the scrap heap of the Soviet military–industrial complex; they moved into manual work, but later slipped further down the scale to unskilled work, as a result of disabilities from which industrial, social and health policies offered them little or no protection. Tat'yana had a serious progressive disease (situating her squarely in our 'generally worse health' group) and was largely dependent on first her husband and later her son; she continued to work as much as her health allowed, but – like many other respondents – her income was never remotely enough to cover the high costs of all the drugs she needed or the specialist or alternative treatments she would have liked to seek. And, although Vladimir seemed to be 'the healthy one', it was he who died suddenly and unexpectedly from a heart attack brought on by stress – which our research had inevitably found to be 'both a source of and a major factor in disease and deterioration of health'.

In the Soviet era, Vladimir's family had lived prosperously; he was a leading engineer in a scientific defence research institute, and his wife Tat'yana was a draftswoman in the design office at the same institute. The start of the reforms brought abrupt changes to the habitual structure of their life – devaluation of wages and delays in paying them led Vladimir, who had always been the main breadwinner and authority figure in the family, to decide to take a job in a manual occupation at a machine plant, since the family needed money: they had two dependants – their son, who was under 18, and their aged invalid mother. Tat'yana, following her husband, also went to work at the same factory in the early 1990s.

In 1996, at the time of our first research project, Vladimir's family were waiting for wages, which had already been delayed by a total of six months. But they had not lost hope of receiving their money, and continued to work at the factory despite extremely insecure employment, compulsory leave and wage interruptions. In those years the family was already encountering significant material difficulties. Their standard of living fell and, as head of the household, Vladimir felt this very acutely. The situation was further exacerbated when Tat'yana was suddenly struck with a serious chronic disease and had to go on to disability benefit. In 1997, a diagnosis of multiple sclerosis was established, though the disease has been progressing slowly since then.

In 1996–97, Vladimir rated his own health as 'fair'. This corresponded to his GHQ scale indicators – 37 points in 1996, at the time when his employment problems were worsening, and 24 points in 1997, when his employment situation had more or less normalised. However, in the late 1990s, Vladimir had an accident at work and lost four fingers on his right hand, so his health indicators took a sharp turn for the worse.

His disability made it impossible for him to work in the press shop, although by that time the factory had finally started functioning steadily. In this situation, Vladimir tried to use his old connections and return to work as a scientist, but, as Tat'yana later explained:

> In principle, there wasn't any kind of work there: there were some kinds of little jobs, orders, but it was meagre – he was getting kopecks. Then he generally started working

three times a week. And, against the background of this, of course, utter depression ... his heart. ... We were all looking for work for ourselves then. I was also working at the factory and, because they were not paying the wages, I got a job at the Sports Centre, in the men's cloakroom. As a cleaner and cloakroom attendant. Of course, it was hard work – as you know, I was already on disability benefit.

In 2002, Vladimir died suddenly from a massive heart attack. The family was left without a breadwinner, and an avalanche of deprivation ensued. Tat'yana had to go into hospital several times; she completely lost her capacity to work (by 2005, her GHQ indicator was 46 points) and, at the end of 2004, she was released from her job as a cloakroom attendant because the doctors had forbidden her to do anything more than light work at home. Tat'yana lamented that 'working at home – firstly, it brings in just kopecks, and then, you actually have to have some work. And what will I be able to do by way of working at home?' The main burden of supporting the family fell on her 25-year-old son, who had been to university, but was working as a trainer in a sports complex, since this was materially more advantageous. Tat'yana blamed the reforms for what had happened to her and her husband, and was not alone in perceiving them like this – for many people, difficulties surviving reform led to the loss of capacity to work and to deterioration in health.

Household of Mikhail (1956-2001) and his Wife Zoya (d.o.b. 1946), Voronezh – see also the second book in our trilogy

Both Zoya and her husband Mikhail, who died in 2000, also fell clearly into our small 'worse health and worse material circumstances' group – but these were not the only areas of their life that deteriorated inexorably over the period of observation. Mikhail was an alcoholic who contributed little to this (his second) family and was content to be completely financially dependent on his wife, who was almost 60 by the end of the surveys; although we found that alcohol 'was not clearly decisive in health deterioration', in this case it was hard to see it as anything else. However, Zoya also brought many problems with her to the situation – 'a multitude of types of stresses ... led [her] to exhaust [her] reserves of health and exacerbate [her] health problems,' so her own assessment of the inevitability of the outcome for her was probably correct.

Alcohol abuse is frequently mentioned as one of the causes of early male mortality in Russia, and the history of Mikhail's household is instructive in precisely this regard. Mikhail joined our research in 1996 when his employment came to an end. He quit his last job as a qualified hospital doctor voluntarily, citing the fact that the pay didn't suit him. However, it was by then already clear that Mikhail had particular problems with alcohol, which had led to disciplinary problems at work and were also the main reason for his insecure employment throughout the whole period of our observations.

Not long before the start of our research, Mikhail had remarried. His wife had a teenage son, and her life history had been difficult. Zoya had lost her first husband in the early 1990s, when he died suddenly from a heart attack. He had been the head of a major construction group, and the family was very prosperous. This made it even harder for Zoya to adapt to circumstances that were new to her.

Mikhail managed to return to work from time to time (in particular, he worked as a local doctor in a district clinic, and as a security guard in a private firm); but, as a rule, he rapidly lost his job, and in the end he completely stopped trying to look for work, saying:

> Things are different in different families. Where there is the opportunity, wives earn more now, and you'd never guess. I'm sure that, without a wife's earnings, you can't survive now, it's impossible. In reality, husbands are rarely earning enough for the family, that's very rare in practice.

After his brother's death in the late 1990s, Mikhail inherited a flat, which he rented out. However, he directed the greater part of his monetary resources to supporting his previous family, where he had two daughters growing up, and in actual fact he was dependent on his wife. Zoya's pay was low and, in addition, her grown-up son – who had suffered from epilepsy since birth, although his attacks were infrequent – was not working. The family was living in poverty and, if she had not been working in a canteen, which allowed her a steady supply of free foods, Zoya would hardly have been able to feed two adult men.

In 1996–97, Mikhail rated his own health as 'fair', and by 2000 this subjective perception had not changed. However, the GHQ scale recorded that he had definite health problems: he scored 50 points in 1996. In 2000, he died from alcoholism at the age of 45. A year later, Zoya also lost her son, who fell from a fourth-floor balcony during one of his regular epilepsy attacks.

All these misfortunes had a negative impact on her health and, when we met in 2005, she had become disabled and was having extreme psychological difficulties – her overall GHQ indicator by then totalled 58 points. The only relation she had left was her adult daughter, who lived separately and sometimes helped her. Despite having a disability and being over pension age, she continued to work (as a night porter), motivated by lack of money. Zoya connected the deterioration in her own health exclusively with her family misfortunes and material troubles. She considered that her life had ended when her first husband died, and that everything that followed had inevitably been hopeless.

Sergei's Household, Voronezh (d.o.b. 1954) – see also the second book in our trilogy

A difficult life situation that was largely not of his own making interacted with economic reforms and lack of social support to drag Sergei, a lone father, into a spiral of deteriorating health and downward social mobility. His low skills level and his sociodemographic circumstances meant that he started further down the ladder than many of our respondents – so he rapidly reached a level where he spent years on the edge of indigence and social exclusion. Although he demonstrated little activity in the area of employment, he struggled against poor health and discrimination to hang on in work for the sake of his sons; and he was helped in doing so by the persistence of a traditional form of social capital – a sympathetic understanding between local doctors loyal to public-sector medicine and their patients. Despite his best efforts, however, all his disadvantages were exacerbated by social change in Russia and passed on to the next generation in a worse form.

Sergei was the head of a household and the male lone parent of two children under 18, which in itself was an atypical situation. The implementation of the reforms was doubly difficult for him because he lived in a depressed region with a high proportion of defence industries, inherited from the Soviet era, and of uncompetitive civilian enterprises. The regional structure of the economy in many ways predetermined the employment problems there during transition to the market.

What happened to Sergei was in no way an exception to this. He was a driver by trade, so from the very start of the change to a market economy he tried to transfer from a State transport enterprise, where pay was poor, into the private sector. However, his experience of 'working for the owner' (as a driver in a number of commercial organisations) convinced him that it was an extremely unreliable means of achieving security and prosperity: all the businesses where he found work had sprung up quickly, but just as quickly disappeared. In 1996, when we first met him, he had been released when the private enterprise where he had worked as a driver (this time for less than a year) was wound up. At this time, Sergei had definitely decided to apply to the Employment Service for help in finding a steadier job. It was also around this time that he was left with two small children on his hands when his wife, who was receiving psychoneurological treatment, left the family.

After Sergei had caused an accident and lost his professional driving licence for a fixed period, the Employment Service could offer him only jobs at unprofitable industrial enterprises. Since Sergei had to look after the children, who at that time were aged 11 and nine, he agreed to become a general labourer at an agricultural machinery factory located near his home.

He was still working at this enterprise in 2005, as a repairman. However, the factory was in constant turmoil, and Sergei came up against 'a whole bundle' of the kind of problems that accompanied hidden unemployment – insecure employment, long wage delays, low pay. In addition, his household had not been living prosperously even before the reforms: Sergei represented the 'old poor', having been brought up by a lone mother who earned little and had saved nothing during the Soviet era.

For the whole period of observation, the family lived in conditions of the most severe resource deprivation, often without any money at all. The children were growing up without supervision and they had a lot of problems at school; they were both indifferent students, they hung out in the street, and were often involved in pilfering and hooliganism. As Sergei himself said, 'I've simply lost heart, and I don't know what to do.' His job brought him no satisfaction, and his personal life was not turning out well; in addition, in 1999, he was obliged to start caring for his aged mother, who had become paralysed. She was confined to bed up to the time of her death in 2004.

Throughout all our years of observation, the family was living on the borderline of indigence. Their home was in disarray, there were flies and dirt in the one-room flat practically all the time, and consumer durables were not renewed. Although his subjective rating of his own health in 1996–97 was 'fair' and remained the same in 2005, he did notice its deterioration over the years of reform, saying that it was hard for him to work. His GHQ scale indicators over the whole course of our observations recorded that Sergei had serious problems with psychological and somatic health: in the last survey, his indicator was recorded at 46 points, while the most unfavourable period had been the one of worsening employment problems and family breakdown in the mid-1990s, when his indicator was 58 points.

He could not change his job just because he felt bad, and took the view that personal troubles and the situation in the country caused stress that had an impact on his health, including his psychological health: he often shouted at his mother and children, and he looked unhealthy, although this was partly the effect of alcohol. His children's future caused him concern – Sergei had not planned to give them any further education, thinking 'they should be car mechanics, then they'll be in the money'. However, in 2000, when he was 15, his older son said,

> when I leave school I would like to study to be a computer programmer. But you have to study for a long time, I'll have to get help. I think maybe my father will help me, if he's still alive, of course. But my father says that there is no money for my studies.

In the end, by 2005, this young man was neither working nor studying.

Sergei's household was typical of post-reform Russia. It illustrated not only the poverty-stricken existence of many Russian families burdened by characteristic sociodemographic disadvantage (one parent bringing up children alone; having a disabled person in the family), but also the real narrowing of future chances for children from such families.

Sergei's Household, Kazan' (d.o.b. 1969)

Although the impact of the reforms on his family life and prospects was clear – and far from benign – Sergei from Kazan' was both prosperous and healthy. It was not surprising, therefore, that he was one of the 40 per cent of our respondents who 'did not generally mention physiological problems when defining health', and that he looked on it as 'not simply absence of disease, but also overall social well-being, ... as well as moral and material well-being.'

We would like to complete this short account of what happened to our respondents – who had such different experiences of the stage of radical market transformation in Russia – with the story of another Sergei, this time living in Kazan' and in a prosperous family. He had married in the early 1990s, and the beginning of the new couple's life together coincided exactly with a new stage in the country's development. Sergei recalled that time as full of hope.

> When my wife and I got married in the early 1990s, we were both inspired by the fact that life was in front of us, we were young, full of strength, clever and energetic. It seemed to us that everything was turning out in our favour. Practically immediately after leaving university, my wife became a section head in one of the local ministerial departments. We went to the same university, but in different faculties. We were both good students, career-focused. We started writing our postgraduate dissertations together.

However, life soon put everything in its place. The couple realised that it was impossible for both of them to work on their dissertations at the same time, when life was rapidly becoming more expensive. Sergei's wife took on the role of main breadwinner, and her husband concentrated on obtaining his higher degree. However, there were not many 'pros' for Sergei in obtaining a PhD in history, either on the level of a possible career or in terms of material prosperity. A child appeared in the family, and this meant additional efforts were required to maintain an acceptable standard of living. On his wife's insistence, the respondent took a job as a customs clerk, though he found the disappointment of his hopes for a successful academic career very difficult. Sergei did not like his job, and he had to use a computer, which, in his opinion, was detrimental to his health. Be that as it may, he soon left this job, remaining unemployed for a long time (which he was at the time of our first research project in 1996–97).

This was strongly reflected in the family's level of welfare. The wife was forced to take on additional unregistered work all the time; then she actually started working in two full-time staff jobs. Sergei suffered from prolonged depression; he wanted to work only in his true occupation, and in practice this meant working as a teacher in a secondary school, which did not suit him: he tried, but quickly gave it up, although the pay was not bad ('I wanted to find something that was on my intellectual level, and in education, and to be able to support my family. But I couldn't find anything suitable straightaway.'). He evaluated the late 1990s as the most difficult time in his life.

After her maternity leave, Sergei's wife went back to work; her job as a section head had been held open for her. This was important in the constrained material circumstances resulting from her husband's employment problems; the family had feared that another person would have taken over her job and that she – the main breadwinner – would also have problems with work. In the end, in 2005, she had two permanent jobs plus some additional earnings, and Sergei was working in a museum doing repairs and cleaning work. He was not happy with the job (it was not his true occupation and was low-paid) and wanted to change it but, in his own words, 'couldn't find anything'. Sergei had got used to the idea that his wife would always be the main breadwinner in the family, even though this was to the detriment of realising his own plans. He valued this, but did nothing to help her or to share the full range of duties involved in providing for the family, although the household was living in extremely unsatisfactory, overcrowded housing conditions with his parents. In addition, his wife's mother was seriously ill, which entailed significant extra expenditure on her treatment.

Sergei said of his wife, who, like millions of other women in Russia, had taken on herself the main concern for the family's prosperity:

> She works a great deal, and at her work they value that, they are gradually moving her up the service – indeed, the additional work is growing much more than the pay. She also has extra jobs; I understand that she is very busy, but I must say that, despite her employment, she has always been a good wife and mother. Of course, I wanted to help, to support her academic work, but we understood that we could not reduce our standard of living. Indeed, it would mean that my wife had to refuse any extra earnings, she simply couldn't combine the two things, and those additional earnings are very significant for all of us. And also, really you should follow up your academic studies immediately after leaving university; if you have a break, then it's very difficult to get back into the rhythm that you need – the desire to return to academic life falls away. In general, I understand her; she only thinks about how to earn more.

Overall, Sergei had no problems with his health and always thought that it was good. This was fully confirmed by the results of testing on the GHQ scale: his score was no more than 8 points, which is evidence of very good health.

Appendix
Project Methodology

Nadia Davidova

The chief methodological principle underlying our joint project[1] 'Health, health policy and poverty in Russia: the dynamics of the health capacities of the poor and the social policy response (2004–2006)'[2] was a complex approach to data collection and analysis, using both qualitative and quantitative methods. When we originally embarked on the research, we largely tried to focus on the study of a situation in development, since we had at our disposal a unique panel of households that had been running since 1996 (see more below about the principles on which the panel was formed). Given that the research team already had this continuing scientific endeavour in hand, it was decided to base our analysis of the issue of health inequality in Russia on a longitudinal method.

However, on drawing up the main hypotheses of the project, we concluded not only that we would be fully justified in using longitudinal data but also that a combination of qualitative and quantitative methods would be informative in the context of this single piece of research. Although our main aim was to gain an understanding of the essence of the phenomena under study, rather than to measure them precisely, quantitative data could provide a distinctive framework for an in-depth qualitative study of the situation in relation to the health and welfare of the Russian population over the years of reform.

We took the view that large-scale surveys rely on less detailed, more general information, not always penetrating the deepest sociological field, but are nevertheless able to give a picture of scales, trends and patterns in the social processes and phenomena under study. Therefore we felt confident that this combined methodology would allow us to tackle the tasks involved in our research effectively. As a result, the approach we took enabled us to obtain a picture not only of the health situation of our panel respondents (for example, over the life

---

1 Apart from the Russian researchers, specialists from the UK and Finland took part in the project. The overall coordinator of the project was Professor Nick Manning, School of Sociology and Director of the Institute of Mental Health, University of Nottingham; the leader of the Russian side of the project was Professor Nataliya Tikhonova, Director of the Department of Social and Economic Systems and Social Policy at the Higher School of Economics, and Leading Research Fellow in the Institute of Sociology of the Russian Academy of Sciences. The activities of colleagues in Finland were coordinated by Dr Meri Koivusalo, Senior Researcher at STAKES (National Research and Development Centre for Welfare and Health).

2 Ref. INTAS 03-3769.

course of particular households), but also allowed us to observe the approximate distribution of these phenomena on the basis of our broad use of data from large-scale pan-Russian representative surveys.

Thus, this book is based on the results of three independent but methodologically interlinked pieces of sociological research, produced by the same research group between 1996 and 2005. In addition to this research project, they are: 1) 'Restructuring the Welfare State: East and West Compared. Employment and Social Policy in Russia 1995–1998' (Manning, Shkaratan and Tikhonova, 2000) and 2) 'Poverty and Social Exclusion in Russia: Regional, Ethno-national and Socio-cultural Aspects 1999–2001' (Manning and Tikhonova, 2004). All consist of qualitative, in-depth research, carried out by the present research group with the financial support of INTAS. The longitudinal nature of the research, which has lasted nine years in total, has allowed us to track the sequence of events, to observe the dynamics of the situation, and to separate random from repeated or relatively stable phenomena.

In addition, the present research relies on data from major pan-Russian research surveys carried out by the Institute of Sociology of the Russian Academy of Sciences. In particular, in analysing the issues of poverty and health, we made active use of the results of the pan-Russian representative survey 'Social reforms: expectations and reality' (March 2006). We also drew on the database of the Russian Longitudinal Monitoring Survey (RLMS), a major national project, and in particular on the detailed information obtained in the 14th round (the most recent study, conducted in Autumn 2005), which monitored the economic position and the health of Russian households. Indeed we were able to include specific questions of our own in this RLMS round. We also referred to relevant national statistical data.

We shall now give a more detailed description of the information base on which the research drew, and of the methods used in the course of the research.

Research Information Base

Longitudinal Panel Study of Households

The random sample for the main panel survey was formed using a longitudinal method. In deciding this, three circumstances were chiefly important. Firstly, it was essential to conduct a specifically longitudinal study, in order to check the health consequences of particular living situations over various time intervals (as long as seven years in a number of households, in others just three or four years), as well as of the choice of particular models of behaviour in maintaining and restoring health. Secondly, we wanted, on principle, to go back and study the households that had taken part in the previous surveys, which would help us to understand better the dynamics of poverty, standard of living and health across the whole extent of interrelationships between these areas. (In total, participants in our research were surveyed between two and five times over the period from 1996 to 2005) And, finally, for a full picture, it was essential to include cities of various types in our research. Observing all these principles would enable us not only to record changes that arose from the state of health and from the general social and economic situation of people in households with various standards of health, but also to evaluate retrospectively – at least for the urban population in large- and medium-sized cities – the comparative significance of different factors influencing the dynamics of their health, on the one hand, and their level of welfare, on the other.

Thus, the data for the current project is drawn from the results of a panel study of 87 households in three Russian cities – Moscow, Voronezh and Kazan'. The survey took place between November 2004 and the end of January 2005, and was conducted in the families' own homes. The study was based on qualitative, partly pre-coded interviews, lasting no less than two hours, and also on supplementary, tape-recorded open interviews, the duration of which varied from half an hour to one hour. The interviewers, who were the academic staff of the project research team, used a questionnaire. The survey questionnaire included about 100 responses (900 variables), with 15 per cent to 20 per cent of them open and non-pre-coded. However, the closed questions in the questionnaire were complex and flexible in structure, and also contained an alternative open response. Apart from this, respondents were asked seven questions to prompt free discussion in the context of conversation with the interviewer. In total, within the framework of this project, 39 Moscow households were surveyed, 27 in Voronezh and 21 in Kazan'.

We should point out that we were able to maintain the earlier panel in only two cities (Moscow and Voronezh), since Kazan' was not in our first two projects. For Kazan', we formed a random sample that shared the main social and demographic parameters of the existing panel. In addition, our colleagues in Kazan' were able to offer us some data on families included in a 1997 health survey. (We had particularly asked for the Kazan' sample to be formed so that it would include households that had taken part in other qualitative studies at some time.) Having these data allowed us to evaluate a household's standard of living and the health of its family members over that period of time, and to compare these indicators with the results of the 2004 survey.

We must emphasise that, although the sample as a whole was randomised, it did not represent the regional situation – but that this was not one of the objectives of our qualitative, in-depth study. Nevertheless, in forming the sample, the research group consciously tried to observe particular social and demographic proportions and to include different types of households in the survey (by 'types', we mean household structure, age, gender and socioeconomic characteristics).

We should also say a little more about the history and principles of the formation of our main panel in Moscow and Voronezh, although this has already been described in more detail in publications dealing with the results of our previous projects (see Manning, Shkaratan and Tikhonova, 2000; Manning and Tikhonova, 2004). The first survey took place in 1996, in the context of the research project 'Employment and social policy in Russia, 1995 to 1998'. For that study, we selected members of groups affected by the labour market crisis, or 'crisis groups' – that is, people affected by problems in the sphere of employment: registered unemployed; people on unpaid leave; those under notice of redundancy; those who had found work after a period of registered unemployment. The sample was targeted and random; in total, over the whole period of study, 160 heads of households were surveyed. The survey was carried out by members of the research team in the respondents' own homes, using the framework of an extended, partially pre-coded interview. With the aim of tracking the dynamic of the situation in their households (not only with employment, but in their standard of living, how they felt generally, and their view of their own life prospects), the survey was repeated with the same households a year later. Certain technical difficulties arose even at the stage of the first project: since it was vital to ensure participation in subsequent surveys, we had to obtain the respondent's agreement in principle to long-term cooperation. The research interviewers made personal contact with respondents and explained the significance and objectives of the proposed study, in order to minimise the number of future refusals to continue to take part in the research and to increase cooperation and involvement.

The main objective of our next project, 'Poverty and Social Exclusion in Russia: Regional, Ethno-national and Socio-cultural Aspects, 1999–2001', was to obtain a fuller picture of the essential nature of poverty as applied to different types of communities, and also to analyse the issue of the reproduction of poverty in these communities. These surveys were carried out in 1999 and 2000 respectively. Starting from the main objective of the project, the research group tried to include various types of poor households in the survey sample. In constructing the sample, certain social and demographic 'risk' characteristics were taken into account, from the point of view of a particular risk of falling into poverty – the presence in the family of pensioners, disabled people, unemployed people; whether there were a lot of children, whether the children were being brought up by a lone parent, and so on. Naturally, we were interested in including in our study those households which we had identified – according to the results of our previous project on unemployment – as poor. But this fact itself also imposed certain limits on our selection of potential respondents, since by no means all of them were poor. (The relationship between unemployment and poverty in post-reform Russia proved to be far from simple or linear.) However, we succeeded in partially preserving the principle of a continuing panel. In total, ten households from Moscow and nine households from Voronezh that had taken part in the research group's 1996–97 surveys were included in the 1999–2001 study. That is, 19 households in total went on to the second project on the basis of our longitudinal method (described in detail in Manning and Tikhonova, 2004). The total research sample consisted of 104 poor households from Moscow, Voronezh and Vladikavkaz.

Finally, turning to the current project, we felt that it would be extremely significant for the quality of our expected results that we maintain unchanged the composition of the panel established in our earlier surveys. We understood that the most difficult aspect of our idea, on the level of technical feasibility, would be to obtain the respondents' agreement to participate in yet another study. Naturally, the research team had to hand the contact details and addresses of all the Moscow and Voronezh respondents who had ever taken part in previous surveys. But to obtain their agreement for cooperation at the initial stage of implementing the project was far from easy, and here an enormous part was played by the fact that many people knew personally the members of the research team who had talked with them at some time, and their agreement to take part was motivated by trust. At this stage, the significance and objectives of the proposed study were again explained in detail to the respondents. In the end, we managed to achieve full involvement: all the households from Moscow and Voronezh that took part in this project were interviewed on a longitudinal basis (28 households from Moscow that had participated in the 1995–98 INTAS project, plus another 11 families who had taken part in the 1999–2001 INTAS project; for Voronezh, the proportions were 20 and seven households respectively). In total, 14 Russian households (six from Moscow and eight from Voronezh) took part in all five phases of the studies (1996, 1997, 1999, 2000 and 2004).

We should emphasise that throughout all three projects we tried to maintain unified principles in preparing the research instruments (that is, a number of questions had a monitoring nature) and also unified methods of assessing level of welfare. Our respondents' assessments of their own health, given at various stages in the research, relied on a unified five-point scale, in addition to which a somewhat abbreviated version of the General Health Questionnaire (GHQ) was used in all three projects. More detail on the use of these methods will be given below. In the meantime, however, we should look more closely at some of the social and demographic characteristics of the households studied.

Size of Household

In our research, the most widespread type of family consisted of three or four people (there were 45 such families – that is, practically half). However, in Moscow there were slightly more single-person households than in the other cities (seven, as opposed to two in Voronezh and three in Kazan'). When it came to extended families of five or more people, then, taking the regional cross-section, they were roughly equal (six in Moscow and four each in Voronezh and Kazan').

Table A1   Number of family members in households studied (N)

Number in family	Moscow	Voronezh	Kazan'
1	7	2	2
2	7	4	5
3	14	9	6
4	5	8	4
5	3	3	4
6	2	1	-
7	1	-	-

Table A2   Demographic type of households studied (N)

Demographic type of family	Moscow	Voronezh	Kazan'
Pensioner household	3	2	4
Single-person household	4	1	1
Couple without children	10	3	3
Couple with children aged 18–25	9	10	-
Couple with children	9	8	9
Families with specific difficulties (lone-parent families, families with a lot of children)	4	3	4

Demographic Type of Household

Thirty-six of the households surveyed included children under 18 (mostly one child, and only in six cases two children). A further 19 families with children aged 18–25 (as a rule, students) took part in the research. Therefore, 32 households had no children at all, or else their children were already adults. In the regional cross-section, families without children were found primarily in Moscow (17), then came Kazan' (9) and finally Voronezh (6). Eleven households with children were families with specific difficulties – that is, one of the parents was bringing up the children alone, or the family had a large number of children.

Structure of Household

Fifteen families in the study had disabled members, and another 15 included pensioners – who were mostly also disabled. Unemployed people were found in a further 17 families. However, only 12 families had nobody at all in employment. One in four Moscow and Voronezh households had unemployed members, whereas only one family in our whole Kazan' sample included an unemployed person. Our Moscow and Voronezh households were also more likely to include disabled people than those in Kazan' – there were disabled people in 17 families out of 39 in Moscow and in ten families out of 27 in Voronezh, but in only six out of 21 households in Kazan').

Age and Gender Characteristics of Respondents

Overall, the households in the survey were represented by 26 men and 61 women. Twenty-three respondents were aged under 39; 32 aged 39–48, another 16 aged 49–54 – that is, the overwhelming majority of respondents were in the economically active age groups. The average age of Muscovites in the survey was 49, of Voronezh residents, 45, and of Kazan' residents, 44. Across the whole study, the average age was 46.

Table A3   Socioeconomic structure of families (N)

Socioeconomic structure of family	Moscow	Voronezh	Kazan'
Households with pensioners	5	2	8
Households with disabled family members	9	4	2
Households with unemployed family members	9	7	1
Households with high dependency ratio (number of employed people lower than number of non-employed)	10	10	7
Households where everyone is employed	6	4	3

Socioeconomic Status of Head of Household

Despite the gender and age characteristics of the sample, shown above, not all respondents were heads of households. Most often, the person interviewed was the most knowledgeable or the most readily available family member. Nevertheless, out of 87 respondents, 45 were the main breadwinner in their family; another 19 households could not define who was the head of the family, since the contribution of all its members to their welfare was roughly the same. Thus, only 23 representatives of the households taking part in the survey were not the main breadwinner (fewest of these were in Kazan' – four people, and most in Voronezh – ten respondents). However, even in this case such a respondent could be acknowledged by the other members of the family as head of the household (as a rule, women, who – as we shall see later – in this sample more frequently defined their spouse as head of the family, even if they themselves earned more than he did). As a result, only ten households could not be defined as having a head of household (two in Moscow, three in Voronezh and five in Kazan'). The following table will help to give a more detailed picture of who headed the families in our study, by defining the socioeconomic status (occupational status and type of post held) of the head of household.

Correlating the gender of the heads of families revealed a parity between 'male' and 'female' households (38:39, setting aside the ten that were not defined). In addition, no particular differences on this point were observed across the three cities under study: in Moscow, 19 households were headed by men and 18 by women; in Voronezh, ten and 14 respectively; and in Kazan', nine and seven). Notionally, we could take the view that only in Voronezh were there somewhat more families headed by women: nevertheless, the situation was more or less balanced. The average age of men heading the families studied was 48 (minimum 28, maximum 70) and of women, 45 (minimum 22, maximum 87). As far as the skills level of men and women was concerned, there was practically no difference between those doing white-collar work: they included 14 highly-skilled specialists and five 'white-collar workers' as such, although among the men there were slightly more managers. As far as manual work was concerned, among male heads of households, skilled blue-collar workers mainly predominated, while ancillary and service occupations were exclusively the lot of women who were their family breadwinners.

Table A4   Socioeconomic status of heads of households (N)

Occupational status and type of post held by head of household	Moscow	Voronezh	Kazan'
Enterprise manager; running one's own business, employing other people	4	4	4
Specialist with higher education	6	6	4
White-collar office worker	6	1	3
Skilled blue-collar worker	6	6	2
Service staff	3	3	1
Unskilled labourer, ancillary blue-collar worker	2	1	0
Self-employed on a casual or personal basis	2	1	0
Pensioner	6	2	2
Unemployed	2	0	0
Head of household not identified	2	3	5

These were the main sociodemographic parameters of the panel sample. Now we shall turn to a description of the next source of information that we drew on as a basis for this project.

Pan-Russian Representative Research

Since some researchers involved in the current project were simultaneously engaged in carrying out major representative studies at the national scale, which are regularly conducted by the Institute of Sociology of the Russian Academy of Sciences, this allowed us to include a number of questions of interest to us in the questionnaire for the pan-Russian survey 'Social reforms: expectations and reality', carried out in March 2006, and to obtain comparative research instruments which were subsequently actively used in analysing the results.

   In addition, we had a unique opportunity not only to use the database of the RLMS (Russian Longitudinal Monitoring Survey), but also to include a number of questions aimed at comparing our own research with its monitoring of the population's economic position and health in the 14th round of the RLMS longitudinal survey of households (carried out in Autumn 2005). This gave us really priceless empirical material, which allowed us to evaluate the reliability and authenticity of our qualitative data against the background of a broader sociological context, to which the RLMS project has allowed open access across the whole of Russia over a number of years.[3]

---

   3 We would like to express our special thanks to the head of the Russian RLMS project team, Polina Kozyreva, without whose attention, involvement and goodwill the inclusion of our own research instruments in the RLMS questionnaire and the subsequent comparison of our small qualitative sample with the longitudinal aspects and the data of the RLMS (one

We shall now look in more detail at how we used data from these research projects in the INTAS project.

The Pan-Russian Representative Survey 'Social reforms: expectations and reality' was organised and conducted in March 2006 within a framework intended to investigate changes in social policy, the population's perceptions of large-scale social reforms, and the way policies being implemented affect processes of social differentiation in Russian society. The Institute of Sociology of the Russian Academy of Sciences was the body primarily responsible for carrying out this project.

The sociological method of gathering primary data for the research was the individual standardised interview (pre-coded questionnaire). The sample consisted of 1,750 respondents, aged 18 years and upwards, who represented the main sociooccupational groups including the non-employed population (pensioners, students, the unemployed, housewives). Among the employed population, respondents included managers at various levels, entrepreneurs in SMEs, specialists, public servants, white-collar office workers, people working in the commercial and services sector, skilled blue-collar workers, the self-employed and ancillary blue-collar workers.

The survey was carried out in 11 major regions of the Russian Federation, plus the cities of Moscow and St Petersburg, using a two-stage sample. At the first stage, within the framework of the main territorial and economic districts (according to the district zoning used by the Russian Federal State Statistics Service), one province was selected to represent each of the regions. Overall, representatives of 19 Russian provinces, territories and republics took part in the research: the Arkhangelsk, Pskov, Ryazan, Tula, Yaroslavl, Nizhniy Novgorod and Voronezh provinces, the Republic of Tatarstan, the Penza and Rostov provinces, the Stavropol Territory, the Sverdlovsk, Chelyabinsk, Novosibirsk and Kemerovo provinces, the Krasnoyarsk and Khabarovsk territories, and also the cities of Moscow and St Petersburg.

In the second phase, a quota sample was established for these regions, formed observing the sex, age and territorial/local proportions of the general survey population established on the basis of Rosstat data, which guaranteed its essentially representative nature. The results of this survey were, according to expert evaluation, accurate to within plus or minus 3–4 per cent.

It should be noted that all the cities involved in the longitudinal qualitative analysis carried out by the INTAS project (Moscow, Voronezh and Kazan') were represented in the Pan-Russian Representative Survey, which gave us additional opportunities to compare data and clarify the overall regional situation. Those managing and taking part in the current project also drew up the corresponding research instruments for the pan-Russian survey, in such a way that they would be comparable with the earlier in-depth qualitative interviews carried out within

---

of the largest longitudinal household research studies in the world) would not have been possible.

the framework of our longitudinal qualitative research. The main difficulty in achieving our project's objectives through the pan-Russian survey method is the high cost of this type of research. But, in this case, we did not have to carry out free-standing research (which we would not have been able to do anyway within the limits of INTAS funding), and were lucky to be able to attach the block of questions that interested us to some thematically relevant research. This was also made possible by the fact that one of the Russian team taking part in the INTAS project is a member of staff at the Institute of Sociology.

Naturally, because of the particular features of large-scale surveys, we were forced to limit our research instruments, inserting just 11 of our own questions into the 'Social reforms: expectations and reality' study. Nevertheless, we were able to use data from the whole study to look at the population's perceptions of reform in the sphere of health care, since a relevant block of questions had been envisaged for the questionnaire from the outset, and the analysis of this issue was one of the main objectives of the pan-Russian research. Apart from this, the Representative Survey data gave us the opportunity to obtain a picture of the model of the social structure of Russian society and the resources of the Russian population. Also, the research gathered a fair amount of detailed material reflecting Russians' assessments of their own social status and how satisfied they were with various aspects of their life – including the problem of access to high-quality medical care. The results of the pan-Russian survey show with striking clarity the situation of existing inequality in real standards of living, reveal the mechanism by which social inequalities are formed and reproduced in Russia, and also provide unique data on the role of social capital in the process of increasing social differentiation. Thus, we had the additional and very informative opportunity to use representative data in analysing health issues and the potential of the poor to cope in that sphere.

In adding questions to the pan-Russian research, our primary aim was to clarify and supplement the results revealed in the course of our longitudinal qualitative observation. In particular, this related to indicators such as specific features of the views of various strata of the population on health/ill-health, and reasons for their choice of a given way of behaving in maintaining their own health (including how well-informed they were about the possibilities open to them apart from the minimum medical services that the state is obliged to guarantee). Special attention was devoted to the analysis of opinions about attainable social policy in the sphere of health care/health policy and, in particular, the population's attitude to fee-paying medical services, voluntary medical insurance, and their willingness to pay higher taxes in order to preserve free medical care for everyone who needs it. A separate objective was to clarify the state of health of the poor and their possibilities for maintaining it, the situation regarding their access to basic medical services (whether they had experienced refusals of any kind of medical care just because they lacked money), and the alternatives they had if they needed to pay for certain services in order to receive a given type of specialised medical care (whether there is someone they can turn to if a fee-paying operation or expensive treatment is unavoidable, whether they have a permanent doctor or know a doctor they could go to, and so on). In addition, we obtained representative data about the health of various groups in the Russian population, based on the respondents' own ratings on a standard five-point scale that has frequently been used in a great deal of research, both in Russia and internationally.

The Russian Longitudinal Monitoring Survey (RLMS) was the second piece of national representative research that we used in analysing the issues of poverty and health. It is well-known that the RLMS is a major longitudinal sample survey of households, which has been in operation since 1992. The demographic parameters of the sample are representative and completely comparable with the results of the 2002 Nationwide Census (Swafford, 1997). Michael Swafford of the University of North Carolina at Chapel Hill, USA, was the organiser and coordinator and inspired the ideas behind the research. In Russia, the monitoring project is led by specialists from the Institute of Sociology of the Russian Academy of Sciences, the Institute of Nutrition of the Russian Academy of Medical Sciences and a number of other research centres.

> The Russian Longitudinal Monitoring Survey (RLMS) is a series of nationally representative surveys designed to monitor the effects of Russian reforms on the health and economic welfare of households and individuals in the Russian Federation. These effects are measured by a variety of means: detailed monitoring of individuals' health status and dietary intake; precise measurement of household-level expenditures and service utilisation; and collection of relevant community-level data, including region-specific prices and community infrastructure data.[4]

The unique feature of this research lies in the fact that over the course of ten or more years the same families have been monitored, living at the same addresses where they originally joined the sample. Therefore, it may be treated as a panel study, allowing us to track the fate of specific households and individuals (both children and adults) over the period from 1992 to the present. The percentage of dropouts and refusals over the whole period of the study is not very great, in the first instance because the sample is constructed on the basis of existing addresses and not people.

The sociological method used to gather primary data for this research is the standardised extended interview, which is carried out by specially trained interviewers. The survey is conducted exclusively in the household's own home. Respondents are asked to complete three separate survey questionnaires: a family survey questionnaire, where data on all members of the household are collected, both those who are present at the given time and those who are absent; an individual adult questionnaire, and a separate questionnaire for children under 14. As a rule, either the head of the family or the most knowledgeable member of the household takes the role of respondent. However, when completing the individual question-naire, interviewers try to meet each adult family member personally. In total, the size of the sample in the 14th round of the RLMS was 12,237 people (more than

---

4 http://www.cpc.unc.edu/rlms

4,500 households), although we did not count the children under 14 who were included in this sample, since they fall outside the objectives of our own project. Therefore, the size of the sample of adult members of households in the 14th round of the RLMS, which we used in our data analysis, was 10,350 respondents.

Since the RLMS is by definition monitoring research, all the research instruments for use in the field contain an essential block of questions, which is repeated from year to year: detailed information about family composition, standard of living, nature of employment, sources of income and main outgoings of the household, and also about the health of each family member, with detailed information about the respondent's somatic health, whether they have any harmful habits, about access to medical services and frequency of using them, and so on. All this represents a really rich source of sociological information. Therefore, we also viewed it as extremely important and desirable to use RLMS data in the INTAS research on the interrelationship between poverty and health. Many researchers, both in Russia and abroad, use these data, and tens – if not hundreds – of expert academic works have been written on the basis of them. In a word, the reputation of this research is very high, and there is no doubt about the reliability and heuristic significance of its results.

The main difficulty in adding our own questions to the RLMS questionnaire lay in the fact that the research has its own methodology, developed over years, and its own logic of preparing the survey questionnaires, which the specially trained interviewers are very familiar with and can follow clearly. But from one particular angle, we were very lucky that this monitoring focused not only on the socioeconomic position of the population (giving valuable information about the dynamic of this position over the years of reform, people's degree of satisfaction with their material circumstances, the views of the household on its own prospects, and so on), but also on health, which gave us a rare opportunity to measure a number of our own indicators, which we proposed to the organisers of the research for their use.

We consider our main achievement to be that, with the pan-Russian sample and – more especially – with the large-scale RLMS sample, we were able to appraise the widely-known EuroQoL EQ-5D method of evaluating health. We were applying this method in Russia for the first time, and we obtained some very interesting results (more details will be given later). In addition, our proposed questions were accepted for the 14th round of the RLMS: some on the understanding of health (what it means to be healthy or sick), a number relating to how respondents feel psychologically, and also a block of questions on respondents' social capital connected with their health (whether they have a permanent doctor or know someone who is a doctor, how often they go to see them or ask people in their immediate circle for advice, how they think it is best to care for their health and how to treat themselves). In the aim of gaining a fuller understanding of the interrelationship between poverty and health and, in particular, the potential of the poor to cope in this sphere, respondents were also asked about how often they had to cut back their spending on health, what their attitudes were to even thinking about making economies under this heading, whether they could buy medicines that they needed and obtain essential medical care and, if not, then what part lack of money played in this. Apart from that, the RLMS research has made consistent use of a widely-known standard five-point scale for self-rated health, which offered us the additional opportunity of comparing all our data across this indicator.

Experience of Applying Some Western Research Methods in Russia

It is especially necessary to emphasise that the research team was united in the opinion that, in developing the research instruments for our joint project, we must make use of the experience of analogous research in EU countries, in order to ensure comparability of our results and enable us to make international comparisons of the main lines and particular specific features of the guaranteed right of the poor to access to medical care and of their reintegration into society through State social policy measures. Such a comparison could become a significant step on the road to a deeper understanding of the essence of the interrelationship of poor health and poverty in transformation-type societies and might contribute to the creation of more effective social policy in Russia at both national and local levels. In addition, tackling the objective of comparing data from the Russian research with results on health inequality in EU countries may not only contribute to developing proposals for improving attainable social policy, but also, to a certain extent, allow a more accurate assessment of current social policy in Russia and the progress of the Russian reforms in the context of a wider Europe.

Therefore, one of the main methodological aspects of our research was its comparative element. First and foremost, this aimed to produce concise comparative data on the theme of perceptions of one's own health, based on a unified set of Western European research instruments, already used to measure this in many major research projects. Given that the teams taking part in the project on the Western side, from the UK and Finland, were expert in health issues and able to offer authoritative, specialist leadership in preparing the research instruments, we succeeded in overcoming the inevitable difficulties that faced the Russian team members when mastering previously unknown methods.

We can confirm that piloting these methods in Russian conditions yielded interesting and extremely informative results, which are reflected in the corresponding chapters of this book. Nevertheless, we should look here, in brief, at the essential characteristics and indicators of the methods we used.

General Health Questionnaire (GHQ)

The General Health Questionnaire – the GHQ – was developed in the UK and has been used with success not only at national but also at international level. This method can be fairly widely applied, since it enables evaluation not only of the respondent's physical health, but also of how they feel psychologically. The questionnaire is conventionally divided into four subscales, each of which corresponds to a particular block of questions:

Scale A (somatic health)
Scale B (anxiety/insomnia)
Scale C (social dysfunction)
Scale D (serious depression)

On the basis of combining the numerical values of the responses (which vary from 0 to 3 as the expressed intensity becomes worse), an index of health is constructed on each specific subscale. Subsequently, it is possible to create an aggregated index, which is also defined by means of further combining the indicators on the subscales.

It should be pointed out that the project research group had used the GHQ at all stages of its previous research. That is, we have indicators based on the application of this method from the whole period of longitudinal observation – five surveys in all. In the course of all three projects, the respondents' health was defined using both their own assessments and an abbreviated version of the GHQ questionnaire. We should emphasise that ours was the abbreviated version, which numbers 28 questions, whereas the original version consists of 60. However, it is fairly difficult from a technical point of view to include the full version in any interview devoted to tackling certain objectives, and no researchers have really had any success when trying to do so. Rather, use of the full version applies when the specific objective of the study is to obtain the GHQ data. In fact, because of the volume of research instruments used in the large-scale surveys, if we had tried to launch the GHQ-28 version at the pan-Russian level, we would have been largely unsuccessful. As it is, in European research projects, an even more abbreviated version of the survey questionnaire has been used: GHQ-12, for example, has been appraised in French national research on health (French National Health Survey, 2002) and in similar research in the UK (British Household Panel Survey, 2001), Germany (German National Health Examination and Interview Survey, 1998), Italy (Survey of Health Conditions of the Population and the Use of Health Services, 2000) and a number of other countries. In Russia, we were able to use the more extensive GHQ-28 version only because our research is qualitative in nature and relies on a small sample; we therefore applied it only in the context of our longitudinal subsample.

It was Nick Manning who originated the idea of using this method in Russia: in 1997, he suggested using the GHQ to monitor how people with employment problems feel, both psychologically and physically, as there had already been similar research in the UK (Gallie, Marsh and Vogler, 1994). This attempt was fairly successful and provided us with rich data for analysis. Given the fact that most of the Western literature focusing on analysis of health inequality currently puts special emphasis on the psychosocial element of health – particularly the health of the poor, affected by stresses generated by their living environment and conditions of existence (problems especially applicable to Russia) – we obviously needed to carry out another study of our respondents. Overall, we not only gained a unique opportunity to compare Russian data with the results of research carried out in other European countries, but were also able – given the nature of our panel sample – to track the dynamic of health over time according to the GHQ Scale (more details in the relevant chapter of this book).

EuroQoL EQ-5D Scale

In our research, we also used the EuroQoL EQ-5D Scale (scale for self-rated health), which is widely known in Europe and whose scientific and heuristic value has long since been proven. This method came to the fore in 1987 as an alternative approach to assessing health, independent of the diagnostic categories used by doctors. As such, it is a distinctive research instrument that relies on understanding and assessing health not from the point of view of disease but from the point of view of quality of life (Brooks, 1996). EQ-5D was developed by an international research team based in the Netherlands. The group consists of researchers working in the areas of medicine, psychology and economics. Membership of the group is open to all researchers who work with this scale.

Our project offered possibilities for implementing the application of this scale at a national level, since the study was partly based on RLMS data. As we have already said, the sample of adult members of households surveyed in the context of the 14th round of the RLMS – and who, therefore, were tested on the EQ-5D scale – consisted of 10,350 respondents (from more than 4,500 households).

The EuroQoL EQ-5D scale is designed to measure health status and was developed to reflect both self-rated health and degree of concern about health across various strata of the population. The results of previous research projects show that the chief benefit of using this scale is that it reveals the factors influencing people's perceptions of their own health. All these factors are either ascriptive in nature (age), or else directly linked to the respondents' quality of life and socioeconomic status. The latter was especially important to us in relation to the objectives of our project. According to the results of a United Kingdom national questionnaire survey (research carried out in the late 1990s, using a representative random sample of 3,395 respondents aged 18 and over), the main factors influencing people's assessments of their own health were the social class to which the respondent belonged, standard of education, economic welfare, housing conditions and smoking (Kind et al., 1998). Researchers who have used the scale in Germany, Spain and Canada arrived at exactly the same results. We can now state that these were also confirmed in Russia, thanks to our use of the RLMS national sample. Applying the scale only to small samples, of course, would not have allowed us to draw such generalised conclusions.

On the EQ-5D scale, health status is measured according to five indicators:

- Mobility
- Personal care
- Usual activities
- Pain/discomfort
- Anxiety/depression

Within the scale, each indicator has three levels of assessment: 1) no problems; 2) minor problems; 3) serious problems. The short three-page questionnaire form is completed independently by the respondent, and takes only a few minutes. Adding up the points across all three levels of the five measures gives 243 gradations of health in total. In the UK, the validity of the scale and its indicators has been demonstrated through the results of the above-mentioned national questionnaire survey (N=3395). In Russia we now have the RLMS data (N=10350). The EuroQoL EQ-5D scale is accompanied by the standard sociodemographic block of questions, used throughout the RLMS (age, sex, employment status, education, and also information about whether the respondent smokes or drinks and how often, and so on). A regional profile is also easy to work out on the basis of the RLMS data, since the households surveyed have lived at known addresses since 1992.

The application of this method allows calculation of:

1. the level of problems (where there are any) according to each measure;
2. a general rating of the respondent's health status, measured using a 'thermometer' scale, which has divisions from 0 to 100;
3. minimal information about the respondent's life circumstances (this is frequently omitted, since it duplicates information that we have already obtained during the research).

After relevant processing, the EuroQoL EQ-5D scale yielded the following data:

1. a profile defining the level of problems according to each of the five measures;
2. a weighted aggregated index of health (we used a processing matrix taken from 1993 NHS research in the UK).

The standard EuroQoL EQ-5D survey form reads as follows.

For each item on the list below, please indicate which statement best describes your present state of health.

MOBILITY
    1. I have no problems in walking about
    2. I have some problems in walking about
    3. I am confined to bed
PERSONAL CARE
    1. I have no problems with personal care
    2. I have some problems washing and dressing myself

   3. I am unable to wash and dress myself
USUAL ACTIVITIES (e.g. work, study, housework, family or leisure activities)
   1. I have no problems with performing my usual activities
   2. I have some problems with performing my usual activities
   3. I am unable to perform my usual activities
PAIN/DISCOMFORT
   1. I have no pain or discomfort
   2. I have moderate pain or discomfort
   3. I have extreme pain or discomfort
ANXIETY/DEPRESSION
   1. I am not anxious or depressed
   2. I am moderately anxious or depressed
   3. I am extremely anxious or depressed.

Unfortunately, in the context of such a large-scale survey as the RLMS, we did not manage to obtain data on self-rated health, which the respondents should have given on the 'thermometer' scale. The scale is shown graphically and, in preparing the research instruments for launch in the field, it simply was not technically feasible to prepare this and print it off on a large scale. In addition, the organisers of the RLMS themselves opposed the use of an extra research instrument, citing their interviewers' lack of training for this type of work. As we have already said, ratings of people's own health on the 'thermometer' scale are constructed on the basis of their marking the scale independently: it has gradations rather similar to a thermometer's, with the best health corresponding to a figure of 100 and the worst to 0. Depending on how good or bad respondents assess their own health to be over a given period of time, conclusions can subsequently be drawn in the context of the aggregated EQ-5D scale indicators. Taking into account the experience we have of the simultaneous use of the scale and a panel survey, the conclusion may be drawn that a subjective rating of one's own health, as a rule, makes things look much better than the real situation as based on objective scale indicators.

Health Locus of Control Scale (HLC)

We also used the standard version of the Health Locus of Control Scale (HLC), a scale measuring locus of control of health. This scale was developed by Barbara S. Wallston, Kenneth A. Wallston, Gordon D. Kaplan and Shirley A. Maides for the American Psychological Association (Wallston, Kaplan and Maides, 1976). Strictly speaking, the scale was created with the aim of predicting people's behaviour in the sphere of health and their possible reactions to its deterioration. Although similar scales have been very frequently described and presented in the literature (the classic in this regard is Rotter's Locus of Control Scale, conceived in the mid-1950s and subsequently actively developed by the author; Rotter, 1954), they have often become the object of criticism, in particular their application in clinical practice. However, this does not mean that we should reject their use for research in Russia. The application of this kind of scale can represent an important attempt to gain a fuller understanding of the interrelationship of the internal and external locus of control, poverty and health. Almost all methods of constructing scales have their pros and cons; in addition, as in the case of the EQ-5D, this was the first time that this kind of scale had been appraised in Russia – although, it is true, only with a small panel of households, the chief object of analysis in our research.

The scale has very often been used, and continues to be used, in research projects connected with health (Carlisle-Frank, 1991; Strickland, 1978). Many researchers emphasise that the problem with it does not lie in an absence of grounds for the use of a given scale, but in insufficient study of factors determining the locus of control, and they specifically call for future research into these. It was interesting for us to see how the method suggested by our Western partners would work in Russia. The results of our research showed that it really helped us gain to a better understanding of respondents' behaviour in relation to caring for their health.

Now we should turn to a description of the HLC scale itself:

SCALE ITEMS:
- If I take care of myself, I can avoid illness. **Internal**
- Whenever I get sick, it is because of something I've done or not done. **Internal**
- Good health is largely a matter of good fortune. **External**
- No matter what I do, if I am going to get sick, I will get sick. **External**
- Most people do not realise the extent to which their illnesses are controlled by accidental happenings. **External**
- I can only do what my doctor tells me to do. **External**
- There are so many strange diseases around that you can never know how or when you might pick one up. **External**
- When I feel ill, I know it is because I have not been getting the proper exercise or eating right. **Internal**
- People who never get sick are just plain lucky. **External**
- People's ill health results from their own carelessness. **Internal**
- I am directly responsible for my health. **Internal**

Each External item is scored from 1 (strongly disagree) to 6 (strongly agree), with the Internal items reverse scored.

The Social Portrait, or Life Story, Method

In addition – as is demonstrated in the large amount of valuable material in the other sections of this book and in all the previous publications connected with our longitudinal research – we made active use of the so-called 'social portrait', or life story method. Since the research was mainly qualitative and in-depth, it demanded that we pay a high level of attention to concrete life situations. Chapter 11 introduces a number of the most revealing life stories from the households studied, encapsulating the particular nature of their lives over the whole period of observation. Thus, a respondent's real life course can give a better understanding of issues that may otherwise remain hidden behind dry figures.

Methods Developed by the Russian Team and Applied at all Stages of the Longitudinal Study

Apart from the methods described above, we naturally also used'our own methods, developed by us in Russia taking account of experience gained in the previous projects (Manning and Tikhonova, 2004). These methods have already been discussed earlier, both in previous publications, for which references are given, and in the text of this book; but it is certainly necessary to describe them here as well. These methods relate primarily to assessment of our respondents' socio-economic position – or, more precisely, to the degree of their material deprivation – and their use for this has been repeated from one research project to the next. Here we look at them in a little more detail.

Index of Multiple Deprivation (IMD)

The deprivation approach was first established in Russia in 1997 within the framework of Macauley, Mozhina and Ovcharova's research (1998): Russian and Western experts developed a list of 36 restrictions on a generally accepted way of life, on structure of consumption and on social participation. In the course of their research, and on the basis of this preliminary list, they selected 17 of the most significant deprivations characteristic of poverty in Russia. This was the first time that a set of indicators of deprivation, separating poor Russians from the non-poor, had been defined empirically.

As we were carrying out the second stage of our first project 'Employment and Social Policy in Russia 1995–1998' in 1997, but not, in the final event, under any particular influence from Peter Townsend's works, we decided to use the method developed by Macauley, Mozhina and Ovcharova to evaluate the respondents' level of welfare. However, even at that stage, we already felt that the method merited additional development to round it off. At the time of our second project 'Poverty and Social Exclusion in Russia 1999–2000', we wanted to focus especially on how people themselves understand poverty, and therefore decided on further monitoring of the markers that define poverty in Russia. Our respondents were asked 'In your opinion, what are the markers of poverty in Russia at present?' To make this assessment, households were presented with a list of items, goods and services that were habitually present and generally accepted in the everyday lives of most of the population: these were items whose absence, according to the different data, was felt most acutely by the overwhelming majority. Our list includes 26 indicators in total: that is, it is an amended and somewhat broader version of the most significant restrictions on a generally accepted way of life, structure of consumption and social participation, which might be said to characterise poverty in Russia.

Our main objective then became to understand the depth of deprivation experienced by our households, guided by how strongly these people, who were themselves in need, connected a particular suggested marker with poverty. Our analysis of the subjective perception of markers of poverty showed that the less widespread a particular deprivation in everyday life, the greater its weight as 'actual proof' that poverty was a noticeable deviation from generally accepted current living standards.

Some indicators were seen by all respondents as undoubted signs of poverty, and therefore their presence meant extreme need – such families had 'crossed the threshold'. Other indicators were less clearly associated with (especially, extreme) poverty; there was then a gradation towards those that reflected some restrictions on an average way of life in the given community, rather than poverty. Deprivations at the end of the scale furthest from poverty tended to be social, rather than material. Thus, we confirmed that a qualitative 'welfare threshold' really exists, and this in turn led to one of our project's most important conclusions: in any deprivation-based approach to assessing poverty, it is essential to delimit the quantitative and the qualitative aspects of deprivation.

The picture of qualitative deprivation given by our respondents related the indicators to poverty in general and to extreme poverty in particular. It can be divided into four 'bands':

- Band IV deprivation – indigence, when there are not enough resources for normal food (some of the family go hungry; there is almost no fresh meat or fish); the family has cut down on hygiene products, does not replace children's clothing as they grow, does not buy fruit or juice and does not own consumer durables such as a TV or fridge.
- Band III deprivation – severe need (poverty), when there are other deprivations related to the quality of food (restrictions on treats, chocolate, sweets for children, fresh fruit and vegetables for adults) and to lack of clothing and shoes (adult family members cannot afford new); it is difficult to keep the home in good repair, or acquire enough simple everyday furniture; there is difficulty organising ceremonies such as wakes or funerals when necessary; difficulty purchasing vital medicines and medical appliances; there are limited possibilities for inviting people round or visiting.
- Band II deprivation – constrained circumstances (being badly-off), when there are insufficient means for anyone in the family to have delicatessen foods, or to buy presents, newspapers, magazines and books; the quality of leisure is diminished for both adults and children; the family cannot afford a washing machine, or to visit relatives who live at a distance; they cannot afford fee-paying services – in particular, essential medical services.
- Band I deprivation – borderline, characterised by living standards that are close to the average, implying no significant deviations from the way of life generally accepted in Russian society. These families need better housing conditions (because theirs are substandard in some way); they have cut back on expensive, up-to-date consumer durables, fee-paying educational and recreational services, family holidays and entertainment.

The Index of Multiple Deprivation (IMD) is based on an evaluation of the degree of need, and represents the aggregated total of the most significant deprivations present in the households at the time of our surveys. Depending on the index values obtained, depth of impoverishment was then distributed along the scale 'indigent' – 'poor' – 'badly-off' – 'averagely well-off'; this was based not only on quantitative indicators (totals of responses selected), but also on their qualitative characteristics (order of preference) at the various levels of deprivation. As the results of our research projects show, three levels of poverty exist, and it is essential to take this into account when analysing any socioeconomic issues. This was precisely the approach we also adopted to this research on the interrelationship of poverty and health. The IMD was calculated separately at each stage of our longitudinal projects, and this allowed us not only to obtain a picture of a particular household's current living standards, but also to investigate the dynamics of their situation over time.

Overall, the combination of the various research methods used in this project allowed us to make a thorough analysis of the set of issues surrounding poverty and health in Russia, and also to obtain a picture of the dynamics of the position of the households we studied over the course of time.

Bibliography

Abbott, P.A., Turmov, S. and Wallace, C. (2006) Health world views of post-Soviet citizens, *Social Science & Medicine*, 62, 228–38.

Abrahamson, P. (1998) Postmodern Governing of Social Exclusion: Social Integration or Risk Management, *Sociologisk Rapportserie*, No.13, Sociological Instutute of the University of Copenhagen.

Alam, A., Murti, M., Yemstov, R. et al. (2005) *Growth, poverty and inequality. An executive summary*, World Bank.

Alexander, J., Eyerman, R., Giesen, B., Smelser, N. and Sztompka, P. (2004) *Cultural Trauma*, University of California Press, Berkeley.

Andreev, E.M., Nolte, E., Shkolnikov, V.M., Varavikova, E. and McKee, M. (2003) The evolving pattern of avoidable mortality in Russia, *International Journal of Epidemiology*, 32 437-446, DOI:10.1093/ije/dyg085.

Andreev, E., Pridemore, W.A., Shkolnikov, V.M. and Antonova, O.I. (2007) An investigation of the growing number of deaths of unidentified people in Russia., *European Journal of Public Health*, June 2008, 18, 252–57.

Andreyev, E.M., Shkol'nikov, V.N. et al. (2000) *Inequality and mortality in Russia*, Carnegie Centre, Moscow.

Armstrong, L. (2003) *Outline of sociology as applied to medicine*, Arnold, London.

Ashvin, S. (2006) Gender solidarity against economic difficulties? The influence of the Soviet legacy, *Sotsiologicheskiye issledovaniya*, No.5.

Averina, M., Nilssen, O., Brenn, T., Brox, J., Kalinin, A.G. and Arkhipovsky, V.L. (2003) High cardiovascular mortality in Russia cannot be explained by the classical risk factors. The Arkhangelsk study 2000, *European Journal of Epidemiology*, 18, 871–78.

Bartley, M. (2004) *Health inequality: an introduction to theories, concepts, and methods*, Polity Press, Cambridge.

Benzeval, M. and Judge, K. (2001) Income and health: the time dimension, *Social Science and Medicine,* 52, 1371–1390.

Besstremyannaya, G.E. and Shishkin, S.V. (2005) Access to medical care, in Ovcharova, L.N. (ed.), *Incomes and social services: inequality, vulnerability, poverty*, Independent Institute for Social Policy, Moscow.

Blaxter, M. (1990) *Health and Lifestyles*, Routledge (UK).

Bobak M. and Marmot M. (1996) East-West Divide and Potential Explanations, in Hertzman, C., Kelly, S. and Bobak, M. (eds), East-West Life Expectancy Gap in Europe. Environmental and Non-Environmental Determinants, *NATO ASI Series 2: Environment* –Kluwer, Dordrecht, 19, 17–44.

Bobak, M., Pikhart, H., Hertzman, C., Rose, R. and Marmot, M. (1998) Socioeconomic factors, perceived control and self-reported health in Russia: a cross-sectional survey, *Social Science and Medicine*, 47:2, 269–79.

Bobak, M., Gilmore, A., McKee, M., Rose, R. and Marmot, M. (2006) Patterns of smoking prevalence in Russia, *Tobacco Control*, 15, 131–35.

Brainerd, E. (2001) Economic Reform and Mortality in the Former Soviet Union: A Study of the Suicide Epidemic in the 1990s, *European Economic Review*, 45, 1007–1019.

Brainerd, E. and Varavikova, E.A. (2001) *Death and the Market*. October 2001, prepared for the WHO Commission on Macroeconomics and Health http://info.worldbank.org/etools/docs/voddocs/174/357/death.pdf

Brooks, R. with the EuroQol Group (1996) EuroQol: the current state of play, *Health Policy*, 37, 53–72.

Brunner, E. and Marmot, M. (1999) Social organization, stress & health, in Marmot, M. and Wilkinson, R.G. (eds), *Social organization, stress & health*, Oxford University Press, Oxford.

Carlisle-Frank, P. (1991) Examining personal control beliefs as a mediating variable in the health-damaging behavior of substance use: an alternative approach, *Journal of Psychology*, 125:4, 381–97.

Cockerham, W.C. (1997) The Social Determinants of the Decline of Life Expectancy in Russia and Eastern Europe: a Lifestyle Explanation, *Journal of Health and Social Behavior*, 38:2, 117–30.

Cockerham, W.C. (1999) *Health and Social Change in Russia and Eastern Europe*, Routledge, New York/London.

Cockerham, W.C. (2000) Health Lifestyles in Russia, *Social Science and Medicine*, 51, 1313–1324.

Cockerham, W.C., Snead, M., Dewaal C. and Derek, F. (2002) Health lifestyles in Russia and the socialist heritage, *Journal of Health and Social Behavior*, 43:1, 42–55.

Coleman, J.S. (1999; 2000) Social Capital in the Creation of Human Capital, in Partha, D. and Serageldin, I. (eds), *Social Capital: A Multifaceted Perspective*, Washington, DC.

Cornia, G.A. and Paniccià, R. (2000) The Transition Mortality Crisis: Evidence, Interpretation and Policy Responses, in Cornia, G.A. and Paniccià, R. (eds), *The Mortality Crisis in Transitional Economies*, Oxford University Press, Great Britain, 3–37.

Cubbins, L.A. and Szaflarski, M. (2001) Family effects on self-reported health among Russian wives and husbands, *Social Science & Medicine*, 53, 1653–1666.

Davidova, N.M. (2003) A deprivation approach to assessing poverty, *Sotsiologicheskiye issledovaniya*, 6, 88–96.

Davidova, N. (2004) Poverty in Russia, in Manning, N. and Tikhonova, N. (eds), *Poverty and Social Exclusion In the New Russia*, Ashgate, Aldershot.

Deaton, A. (2003) Health, inequality, and economic development, *Journal of Economic Literature*, 41, 113–58.

Din, K. (2000) Methodology as a factor in distorting information about women's health, in *Health and health care in market economy conditions*, Institute of Sociology of the Russian Academy of Sciences, Moscow, 151–53.

ESOMAR (1997) *A System of International Socio-Economic Classification of Respondents to Survey Research*, 10.

Federal Office of the State Statistical Service of Russia (Rosstat) (2004) *The social status and living standards of the population of Russia*, Statistical collection, Moscow.

Federal State Statistics Service, www.gks.ru

Field, M.G. (1995) The Health Crisis in the Former Soviet Union: A Report from the 'Post-war' Zone, *Social Science & Medicine*, 41, 1469–1478.

Fitzpatrick, T., Kwon, H-J., Manning, N., Midgley, J. and Pascall, G. (eds) (2006) *International Encyclopaedia of Social Policy*, Routledge, London, three volumes.

France, M., Ordunez, P., Caballero, B., Granados, J.T., Lazo, M., Bernal, J.L., Guallar, E. and Cooper, R.S. (2007) Impact of energy intake, physical activity and population-wide weight loss on cardiovascular disease and diabetes mortality in Cuba 1980-2005, *American Journal of Epidemiology*, 1–7.

Fuhrer, R., Stansfeld, S.A., Chemali, J. and Shipley, M.J. (1999) Gender, social relations and mental health: prospective findings from an occupational cohort (Whitehall Study II), *Social Science & Medicine*, 48, 77–87.

Gallie, D., Marsh, C. and Vogler, C. (1994) *Social Change and the Experience of Unemployment,* Oxford University Press, Oxford.

Gilmore, A. and McKee, M. (2004a) Moving East: how the transnational tobacco industry gained entry to the emerging markets of the former Soviet Union – part I: establishing cigarette imports, *Tobacco Control*, 13, 143–50.

Gilmore, A. and McKee, M. (2004b) Moving East: how the transnational tobacco industry gained entry to the emerging markets of the former Soviet Union – part II: an overview of priorities and tactics used to establish a manufacturing presence, *Tobacco Control*, 13, 151–60.

Gorshkov, M.K. and Tikhonova, N.E. (eds) (2004) *Russia – the new social reality. Rich. Poor. Middle class*, Nauka, Moscow.

Gorshkov, M.K. and Tikhonova, N.E. (eds) (2006) *Ownership and business in the life and perception of Russians*, Nauka, Moscow.

Gorshkov, M.K. and Tikhonova, N.E. (eds) (2007) *Social inequality and social policy in contemporary Russia*, Nauka, Moscow.

Goskomstat Rossiyi (1997) *Russian Statistical Year Book*, Official publication, Moscow, 222–226.

Grigor'eva, N.P. and Chubarova, T.V. (2001) *The gender approach in health care*, Alpha Print, Moscow.

Growth, poverty and inequality. Eastern Europe and the former Soviet Union (2005) World Bank, 28–31.

Herzlich, C. (1973) *Health and Illness: A Social Psychological Analysis*, Academic Press, London.

Hertzman, C., Kelly, S. and Bobak, M. (eds) (1996) East-West Life Expectancy Gap in Europe. Environmental and Non-Environmental Determinants, *NATO ASI Series 2: Environment*, Kluwer, Dordrecht, 19, 17–44.

Higher School of Economics, Moscow State University (2004), *Russian health care: paying in cash*, Moscow.

Holman, R. (1978) *Poverty: Explanations of Social Deprivation*, Martin Robertson, London.

Independent Institute for Social Policy (2005) *Russia of the regions: what kind of social space are we living in?* Pomatur, Moscow.

Institute for Complex Strategic Studies, Moscow, http://www.icss.ac.ru

International Labour Office (1990) *International Standard Classification of Occupations, ISCO-88*, ILO, Geneva.

Ivanova, A.E. (1992) Health forecast for the adult population of Russia, *Sotsiologicheskiye issledovaniya*, 9, 50–9.

Ivanova, L.Y. (2005) Self-care behaviour and its particular gender features, in *Reforming Russia*, Yearbook, Moscow.

Jowell, R., Curtice, J., Park, A., Thomson, K., Jarvis, L., Bromley, C. and Stratford, N. (eds) (2000) *British Social Attitudes. The 17th Report: focusing on diversity*, Sage, London.

Jukkala, T., Mäkinen, I.H., Kislitsyna, O., Ferlander, S. and Vågerö, D. (2008) Economic strain, social relations, gender, and binge drinking in Moscow, *Social Science & Medicine*, 66, 663–74.

Khakhulina, L. and Tuchek, M. (1995) Income distribution: poor and rich in post-socialist societies (some results of a comparative analysis), in Zaslavskaya, T.I. (ed.), *Where is Russia going?* Aspect Press, Moscow, 166–75.

Kind, P. et al. (1998) Variations in population health status: results from a United Kingdom national questionnaire survey, *British Medical Journal*, 316, 736–41.

Klugman, D. (ed.) (1997) *Poverty in Russia. State policy and the reaction of the population*, World Bank, Washington, 107–40.

Lang, R.E. and Hornburg, S.P. (1998) What is social capital and why is it important to public policy?, *Housing Policy Debate*, No.9.

Lapin, N.I. (2003) The feelings and aspirations of Russians, *Sotsiologicheskiye issledovaniya*, 6, 78–87.

La Stampa, 16 December, 2003 (D. Daniels' interview with Italian Minister of Health Girolamo Sirchia – www.inopressa.ru).

Ledeneva, A. (1998) *Russia's Economy of Favours*, Cambridge University Press.

Leon, D.A., Chenet, L., Shkolnikov, V.M. et al. (1997) Huge variation in Russian mortality rates 1984–1994: artefact, alcohol or what? *Lancet*, 350, 383–88.

Leon, D., Saburova, L., Tomkins, S., Andreev, E., Kiryanov, N., McKee, M. and Shkolnikov, V.M. (2007) Hazardous alcohol drinking and premature mortality in Russia: A population-based case-control study, *Lancet*, 369, 2001–2009.

Lynch, J., Smith, G.D., Harper, S., Hillemeier, M. et al. (2004a) Is income inequality a determinant of population health? Part 1. A Systematic Review, *Milbank Quarterly*, 82:1, 5–99.

Lynch, J., Smith, G.D., Harper, S., Hillemeier, M. et al. (2004b) Is income inequality a determinant of population health? Part 2. US National and regional trends in income inequality and age- and cause-specific mortality, *Milbank Quarterly*, 82:2, 355–400.

Lytkina, T.S. (2004) Domestic labour and the gender division of power in the family, *Sostiologicheskiye issledovaniya*, No.6.

Macauley, A., Mozhina, M. and Ovcharova, L. (1998) *Poverty: alternative approaches to definition and measurement*, Joint monograph, Moscow Carnegie Centre, Moscow (in Russian).

Mack, J. and Lansley, S. (1985) *Poor Britain*, George Allen & Unwin, London.

Makela, P., Valkonen, T. and Martelin, T. (1997) Contribution of deaths related to alcohol use of socioeconomic variation in mortality: register based follow up study, *British Medical Journal*, 315, 211–16.

Maleva, T. (2000) *What Sort of Russia Has the New President Inherited? or Russia's Key Social Problems*. Briefing Papers, 2: 4, April http://pubs.carnegie.ru/russian, and – for comparison with other countries – OECD (1999) *A caring world. The social policy agenda*. Paris.

Manning, N. (2007) Effects of transformation on inequality in Russia, in Lane, D. (ed.) *The Transformation of State Socialism: System Change, Capitalism, or Something Else?* Palgrave Macmillan, London, 161–78.

Manning, N., Shkaratan, O. and Tikhonova, N. (eds) (2000) *Work and Welfare in the New Russia.* Aldershot: Ashgate.

Manning, N. and Tikhonova, N. (eds) (2004) *Poverty and Social Exclusion in the New Russia*, Ashgate, Aldershot.

Marmot, M. (2004) *Status syndrome: How your social standing directly affects your health and life expectancy*, Bloomsbury, London.

Marmot, M. (2006) Health in an unequal world, *Lancet*, 368, December 9, 2081–2094.

Marquez, P.V. (2005) *Dying Too Young – Addressing Premature Mortality and Ill Health Due to Non-Communicable Diseases and Injuries in the Russian Federation*, Washington, World Bank, 9–11.

McKee, M. (1999) Alcohol in Russia, *Alcohol and Alcoholism*, 34:6, 824–29.

McKee, M., Bobak, M., Rose, R., Shkolnikov, V., Chenet, L. and Leon, D. (1998) Patterns of smoking in Russia, *Tobacco Control*, 7, 22–26.

McKee, M., Shkolnikov, V. and Leon, D.A. (2001) Alcohol is implicated in the fluctuations of cardiovascular diseases in Russia since the 1980s, *Ann Epidemiol*, 11, 1–6.

Mellor, J.M. and Milyo, J. (2002) Income inequality and individual health: Evidence from the Current Population Survey, *Journal of Human Resources*, 37:3, 510–39.

Men and women in Russia (2004) Compendium of Statistics, Moscow.

Methods in career counselling of unemployed people with higher education (2001)
    Moscow.
Ministry for Economic Development (2005) www/gsk.ru/wps/portal
Ministry for Health and Social Development of the Russian Federation (2008)
    *Report on the results and main directions for action in forming and delivering
    budget planning for the year 2006, and for the period to 2008.*
Monitoring the health of the population of the Russian Federation (1992-2005)
    (2006) Institute of Sociology of the Russian Academy of Sciences, Institute
    of Nutrition of the Russian Academy of Medical Sciences, DemoSCOPE
    Research Centre, University of North Carolina at Chapel Hill, Moscow.
Mroz, T., Henderson, L. and Popkin, B.M. (2005) *Monitoring Economic Conditions
    in the Russian Federation: Russian Longitudinal Monitoring Survey 1992-
    2004*, Report submitted to the US Agency for International Development,
    Carolina Population Center, University of North Carolina at Chapel Hill, North
    Carolina.
Nazarova, I.B. (1999) Patients' styles of behaviour during illness,
    Zdravookhraneniye, 12, 159–67.
Nazarova, I.B. (2003) The health of the Russian population: factors and
    characteristics (the 1990s), *Sotsiologicheskiye issledovaniya*, 11, 57–69.
Nicholson, A., Bobak, M., Murphy, M., Rosec, R. and Marmot, M. (2005) Socio-
    economic influences on self-rated health in Russian men and women – a life
    course approach, *Social Science & Medicine*, 61, 2345–2354.
Nolte, E., McKee, M. and Gilmore, A. (2004) *Morbidity and mortality in
    transition countries in the European Context*, European Population Forum
    2005: Population Challenges and Policy Responses, Background paper for the
    session on 'Morbidity, mortality and reproductive health: facing challenges in
    transition countries', Geneva, 12–14, January, 2004.
Notzon, F.C., Komarov, Y.M., Ermakov, S.P., Sempos, C.T., Marks, J.S. and
    Sempos, E.V. (1998) Causes of declining life expectancy in Russia. JAMA,
    279:10, 793–800.
Oppenheim, C. and L. Harker (1996) *Poverty: the Facts*, Child Poverty Action
    Group, London.
Ordinance of the Government of the Russian Federation of 6 April 2004, No. 153,
    *Issues of the Ministry of Health Care and Social Development of the Russian
    Federation* (in the version of Ordinances of the Government of the Russian
    Federation of 29 October 2004, No. 586 and of 31 December 2004, No. 904),
    http://prof.consultant.ru/
O'Sullivan, S. and Stakelum, A. (2004) Lay Understandings of Health, in Shaw,
    I. and Kaupinnen, K. (eds), *Constructions of Health and Illness: European
    Perspectives*, Ashgate.
Ovcharova, L.N. (2002) Poverty in the gender perspective in countries with
    transition economies, *Narodonaseleniye*, 3, 26 and 28.

Ovcharova, L.N. (2005) Russia below the poverty line, *Demoscope Weekly*, www.demoscope.ru (electronic version of the journal *Naselenie i obshchestvo*), materials from a seminar of experts held at the Institute for Complex Strategic Studies, Moscow, 23–24 November 2003, http://www.icss.ac.ru.

Palosuo, H. (2003) Health and Well-being in Moscow and Helsinki, *Stakes*, Research Report 129, Saarijärvi Finland.

Palosuo, H., Zhuravleva, I., Uutela, A., Lakomova, N. and Shilova, L. (1995) *Perceived health, health-related habits and attitudes in Helsinki and Moscow: a comparative study of adult populations in 1991, Julkaisija*, Utgivare, Helsinki.

Palosuo, H., Uutela, A., Zhuravleva, I. and Lakomova, N. (1998) Social patterning of ill health in Helsinki and Moscow. Results from a comparative survey in 1991, *Social Science & Medicine*, 45, 1121–136.

Parsons, T. (1958) *An Approach to Psychological Theory in Studies in General Theory*, Koch, S. (ed.), McGraw-Hill, New York.

Parsons, T. (1982) Definitions of health and illness in the light of American values and social structure, *Social Structure and Personality*, 257–92.

Pevalin, J.D. and Rase, D. (2004) *Investigating the links between social capital and health using BHPS*, Working Paper, Institute for Social and Economic Research, University of Essex.

Poduzov, A.A. and Kukushkin, D.K. (2002) Measuring the duration of poverty in Russia, *Problemy prognozirovaniya*, 1, 65–77.

Popova, I.P. (2005) The health dynamics and material welfare of the Russian population (experience from a longitudinal survey), in *Reforming Russia. 2005 Yearbook*, Institute of Sociology, Moscow.

Popova, I.P. (2006) A positive dynamic in the health of the population: behavioural models (from the data of a longitudinal survey), *Sotsiologiya meditsiny*, No 1.

Popova, I.P. (2006) Measuring the dynamic of health using the GHQ: trends and social factors (experience from data analysis of a longitudinal survey), *Health care in the Russian Federation*, No 3.

Pridemore, W.A. (2003) Measuring homicide in Russia: a comparison of estimates from the crime and vital statistics reporting systems, *Social Science and Medicine*, 1343–354.

Putnam, R.D. (1993) *Making Democracy Work: Civic Traditions in Modern Italy*, Princeton University Press, Princeton.

Putnam, R. (2001) Social Capital: Measurement and Consequences, *Canadian Journal of Policy Research*, 2:1.

Results of the 2002 All-Russian Population Census (2004) Rosstat Scientific Research Centre, Moscow.

Reynolds, J.R. (1997) The Effects of Industrial Employment Conditions on Job-Related Distress, *Journal of Health and Social Behavior*, 38 (June), 105–16.

RIA-Novosti, July, 2005.

Rimashevskaya, N.M. (1995) The social cost of the reforms, in *Where is Russia going...?* Moscow, 364–67.

Rimashevskaya, N.M. (2003) *People and the reforms: secrets of survival*, ISEPN, Moscow.

Rimashevskaya, N.M. and Korkhova, I.V. (2001) Poverty and health in Russia, *Narodonaseleniye*, No.4 (14) (October–December), 11–26.

Rose, R. (1993) *Is money the measure of welfare in Russia? How Russians are coping with transition*, Studies in Public Policy, 215 and 216.

Rose, R. (2003) Social shocks, social confidence, and health, in Twigg, J.L. and Schecter, K. (eds) (2003) *Social capital and social cohesion in contemporary Russia*, M.E. Sharpe, Armonk, NY (see also http://www.socialcapital.strath.ac.uk/).

Roshchina, Y.M. (2003) Inequality in access to education: what do we know about it?, in Shishkin, S.V. (ed.), *Issues of access to higher education*, Independent Institute for Social Policy, SIGNAL, Moscow, 102–71.

Rotter, J.B. (1954) *Social Learning and clinical psychology*, Englewood Cliffs, NJ: Prentice-Hall.

Rusinova, N. and Brown, J. (1996) Popular attitudes toward the health system in St. Petersburg, Russia. *Sosiaalilääketieteellinen Aikakauslehti – Journal of Social Medicine*, 33, 355–62.

Rusinova, N. and Brown, J. (1997) Social'no-statusnye gruppy: razlichija v sub"ektivnom zdorov'e, *Peterburgskaja sociologija*, 1, 38–59.

Russia and countries of the world (2006) Compendium of Statistics, Rosstat, Moscow, 107.

Russian Federal State Statistics Service *Analiticheskiy vestnik Soveta Federatsii FC RF (2003)* The issue of poverty in contemporary Russia, No.20.

Russian Institute of Sociology in March (2006).

Scambler, A. (2003) Women and health, in Scambler, G. (ed.), *Sociology as Applied to Medicine*, Fifth Edition, Harcourt Publishers Limited, 125 and 130.

Scambler, G. (ed.) (2003) *Sociology as Applied to Medicine*, Fifth Edition, Harcourt Publishers Limited, 107–23.

Scambler, G. and Blane, D. (2003) Inequality and Social Class, in Scambler, G. (ed.), *Sociology as Applied to Medicine*, Fifth Edition, Harcourt Publishers Limited, 117 and 119.

Scheepers, P., Te Grotenhuis, M. and Gelissen, J. (2002) Welfare states and dimensions of social capital: cross-national comparisons of social contacts in European countries, *European Societies*, 4:2.

Shapiro, J. (1995) The Russian Mortality Crisis and its Causes, in Eslund, A. (ed.), *Economic Reform at Risk*, London, 149–78.

Shi, L. and Starfield, B. (2000) Primary care, income inequality, and self-rated health in the United States: A mixed-level analysis, *International Journal of Health Services*, 30:3, 541–55.

Shilova, L.S. (1999) Changes in self-care behaviour, *Sotsiologicheskiye issledovaniya*, 5, 84–92.

Shilova, L.S. (2000) Change in the female model of self-care behaviour, *Sotsiologicheskiye issledovaniya*, No.11.

Shkolnikov, V.M. and Mesle, F. (1994) The Russian epidemiological crisis as mirrored by mortality trends, in DaVanzo, J. (ed.) *Russia's demographic crisis*, RAND Center for Russian and Eurasian studies, RAND, Santa Monica. Available from: http://www.rand.org/pubs/conf_proceedings/ CF124/cf124. chap4.html. Printed 20.02.2008.

Shkolnikov, V.M., Cornia, G. and Leon, D. (1998) Causes of the Russian Mortality Crisis: Evidence and Interpretations, *Pergamon World Development*, 26:11, 1995–2011.

Shkolnikov, V.M., Leon, D.A., Adamets, S., Andreev, E. and Deev, A. (1998) Educational level and adult mortality in Russia: An analysis of routine data 1979 to 1994, *Social Science & Medicine*, 47, 357–69.

Shkolnikov, V., McKee, M. and Leon, D.A. (2001) Changes in life expectancy in Russia in the mid-1990s, *The Lancet*, 357, March 24.

Shlapentokh, V. (1989) *Public and Private Life of the Soviet People*, Oxford University Press, New York.

Siegrist, J. (2002) Reducing social inequalities in health: work-related strategies, *Scandinavian Journal of Public Health*, 30:59, 49–53.

Simpura, J. and Levin, B.M. (eds) (1997) *Demystifying Russian Drinking: Comparative Studies from the 1990s*, Stakes Research Report No. 85.

Spryskov, D.S. (2000) *Prolonged poverty in Russia*, Materials from the 7th Conference of the Russian School of Economics, 'Transformation of the state sector in the economics of the transition period, Moscow, 13–15 April, http://www.nes.ru.

Standing, G. (1998) Societal impoverishment: the challenge for Russian social policy, *Journal of European Social Policy*, 8:1, 23–42.

Statistical Year Book of Russia (2006) Compendium of Statistics, Rosstat, Moscow, 138 and 188.

Statistics Finland (2007) Leading causes of death in working age people still alcohol related, Press Release 5 November 2007, Statistics Finland: Helsinki. Available: http://www.stat.fi/til/ksyyt/2006/ksyyt_2006_2007-11-05_tie_001_ en.html. Printed 08.04.2008.

Strickland, B.R. (1978) Internal-External expectancies and health-related behaviors, *Journal of Consulting and Clinical Psychology*, 46, 1192–211.

Swafford, M. (1997) *Sample of the Russian Federation. Rounds V, VI, and VII of the Russian Longitudinal Monitoring Survey. Technical Report*, Paragon Research International.

Swafford, M., Kosolapov, M.S. and Kozyreva, P.M. (1999) Russian monitoring of the economic position and health of the Russian population (RLMS): measurement of the welfare of Russians in the 1990s, *Mir Rossiyi*, 3, 153–73.

Tapilina, V.S. (2004) Socio-economic status and the health of the population, *Sotsiologicheskiye issledovaniya*, 3, 126–37.

The demographic situation and state demographic policy in the Russian Federation, Executive Summary of a report of the Minister of Health Care and Social Development of the Russian Federation, M.Y. Zurabov. http://ethnocid. netda.ru/forum/18008.htm

The European Health Report (2002) WHO Regional Publications, European Series, No.97, WHO Regional Office for Europe, Copenhagen.

The Russian population's attitude to health (1993) Institute of Sociology of the Russian Academy of Sciences, Moscow.

The social status and living standards of the population of Russia (2006) Compendium of Statistics, Rosstat, Moscow, 53, 192, 318 and 329.

The St Petersburg Times, 572, 30 May 2000.

Thomson, K. et al. (2001) *British Social Attitudes. 1999 Survey: Technical Report*, National Centre for Social Research, London.

Tikhonova, N.E. (2003) The consequences of reform for women from poor urban families, *Sotsiologicheskiye issledovaniya*, 10, 77.

Tikhonova, N.E. (2003) *The phenomenon of urban poverty in contemporary Russia*, Letnii Sad, Moscow, 372.

Tikhonova, N.E. (forthcoming in 2008) *Social stratification in contemporary Russian society*, Nauka, Moscow.

— Tompson, W. (2007) *Health care reform in Russia. Problems and prospects*, OECD Economics Department Working Papers, No.538, OECD, Paris, 15 Jan 2007, ECO/WKP (2006)66.

Townsend, P. (1979) *Poverty in the United Kingdom*, Penguin, Harmondsworth.

Townsend, P. (1987) Deprivation, *Journal of Social Policy*, 16:2, 125–46.

Townsend, P. (1993) *The International Analysis of Poverty*, Harvester Wheatsheaf, London.

Townsend, P., Davidson, N. and Whitehead, M. (1986) *The Black Report and the Health Divide*, Penguin, Harmondsworth.

Townsend, P., Gordon, D. and Gosschack, B. (1996) *The Poverty Line in Britain Today: What the Population Themselves Say*, Report No.7, Statistical Monitoring Unit, University of Bristol.

Twigg, J.L. and Schecter, K. (eds) (2003) *Social capital and social cohesion in contemporary Russia*, M.E. Sharpe, Armonk, NY.

UNECE at http://w3.unece.org/pxweb/DATABASE/STAT/3-GE/06-Health.asp

Vallin, J. and Meslé, F. (2002) Trends in mortality in Europe since 1950, in Vallin, J., Meslé, F. and Valkonen, T. (eds) *Trends in mortality and differential mortality*, Population Studies No.36, Council of Europe Publishing, Strasbourg, 31–184.

Veit-Wilson, J. (1999) Poverty and the adequacy of social security, in Ditch, J. (ed.), *Introduction to Social Security: Policies, Benefits And Poverty*, Routledge, London.

Wallston, K.A., Kaplan, G.D. and Maides, S.A. (1976) Development and validation of the health locus of control (HLC) scale, *Journal of Consulting and Clinical Psychology*, 44, 580–85.

Walsh, M., Stephens, P. and Moore, S. (2000) *Social Policy and Welfare*, Thornes.

Watson, P. (1995) Explaining Rising Mortality Among Men in Eastern Europe, *Social Science & Medicine*, 41:7, 923–34.

Wilkinson, R.G. (1997) Health inequalities: relative or absolute material standards, *British Medical Journal*, 314, 591–95.

Wilkinson, R.G. (2000) *Mind the Gap: Hierarchies, Health and Human Evolution*, Weidenfeld and Nicolson, London.

Wilkinson, R.G. and Pickett, K.E. (2006) Income inequality and population health: A review and explanation of the evidence, *Social Science & Medicine*, 62, 1768–784.

World Bank (1997) *Poverty in Russia: Public Policy and Private Responses*, Washington, DC.

World Bank (2000) *Making Transition Work for Everyone: Poverty and Inequality in Europe and Central Asia*, Washington, DC.

World Bank (2002) *Health Reform Implementation Project: results of a social evaluation*, Materials from a seminar held in Moscow by the Institute for Comparative Labour Relations Research, 28 March.

World Bank (2005) *Growth, Poverty and Inequality. Eastern Europe and the Former Soviet Union*, Washington, DC, www.Worldbank.org.ru/ ECA/Russia. nsf/ECADocByUnid/3ABAD2CCE2ABBA25C3256E27004863AD

World Bank (2005) *Russian Federation: Reducing Poverty through Growth and Social Policy Reform*. Report No. 28923-RU, www.worldbank.org.ru/ECA/ Russia.nsf/

World Health Organization (2001) *The world health report 2001. Mental health: new understanding, new hope*, Geneva.

World Health Organisation (2008) *List of signatories of the Framework Convention*, available: http://www.who.int/tobacco/framework/countrylist /en/index.html, WHO: Geneva.

Yaroshenko, S. (2001) Gender differences in the employment strategies of Russia's working poor, *Rubyezh*, No.16.

Yaroshenko, S.S. (2005) Local contexts of global issues in the feminisation of poverty, in *Globalisation and gender relations: challenges for post-Soviet countries*, Samara University.

Zaslavskaya, T. (1996) Incomes of social groups and strata: level and dynamic, *Economic and social change*, 2, 7–13.

Zaslavskaya, T.I. (1997) The social structure of Russia: main directions of change, in *Where is Russia going? The general and the particular in contemporary development*, Moscow Higher School of Social and Economic Sciences, Moscow, 168–76.

Zatonski, W.A., McMichael, A.J. and Powles, J.W. (1998) Ecological study of reasons for sharp decline in mortality from ischaemic disease in Poland since 1991, *British Medical Journal*, 316, 1047–1051.

Zatonski, W.A. and Willett, W. (2005) Changes in dietary fat and declining coronary heart disease in Poland: population based study, *British Medical Journal*, 331, 187–89.

Zhuravleva, I.V. (2004) People's attitude to health: methodology and indicators, *Sotsiologiya meditsiny*, 2, 11–17.

Zhuravleva, I.V. (2005) *Attitude to health as a social and cultural phenomenon*, thesis presented for the degree of Doctor in Sociological Sciences, Moscow Institute of Sociology.

Zhuravleva, I.V. (2006) *Otnoshenie k zdorov'ju individa i obchshestva*, Nauka, Moskva.

Zhuravleva, I.V., Shilova, L.S., Lakomova, N.V. and Borzunova, T.I. (1993) The population's way of life and health, in *The population's attitude to health*, Institute of Sociology of the Russian Academy of Sciences, Moscow.

Index

References to illustrations are in **bold**

Abrahamson, Peter 110
achievements, self-assessment 88–9
age, and ill health 155
Albania, poverty 82
alcoholism 6, 10
    Finland 13
    health crisis 13, 14, 15
    men 151, 232
    mortality 27
    and poverty 121–2
    women 151
attitude, and health 57–8

Bartley, Mel 201, 208, 231
birth rate, crisis 3, 6
Blane, D. 208, 216
Blaxter, M. 70
blue-collar workers, ill health 52
bolezn, meanings 17
British Social Attitudes Survey 91–2
budget
    development 3–4
    family, contributions 243
Bulgaria, life expectancy 27

cardiovascular disease 41, 51
    Cuba 11
    decrease, Western Europe 10
    increase 11
    mortality 6, 15, 27
career development, absence of 168
check-up, full 177–8
children, disabled 7
chronic diseases 19, 52
    by age groups **29**
    awareness of 28–30
    and quality of life 30
Chubais, Anatoly 2–3
clinics

need to improve 197
reasons for not visiting 176, 199
see also district clinics
Cockerham, William 149
consumer durables, ownership 85, 86
Cuba
    cardiovascular disease 11
    mortality 11

dental
    clinics 182, 204
    services 182
    treatment 129
deprivation, as measure of poverty 86
disability
    categories xiv-xv
    children 7
    difficulties of registering xv
    and employment 252, 253
    and ill health 44
    pensioners xiv, 207, 223, 252
    pensions xv, 46, 58, 66, 223
    see also social exclusion
disability benefits 31, 37, 38, 46, 49, 265,
      266
    claimants 121, 155, 170, 237, 241
Disability Commission 192
disabled people, numbers xiv
disease, absence of, and health 62, 66, 68,
      70, 72, 73, 74
district clinics
    access problems 185
    staff turnover 185
doctor–patient relationship, improvements
      needed 198
doctors
    accessibility problems 184–5
    home visits, paid for 22
    increase, need for 197–8
    payments to 188
    visits to 22

frequency 174–5
    reluctance, by men 247

Economic Development, Ministry 99, 100
economic growth 2
    consequences 5, 102–3
economic reforms 2
    consequences 97, 119–20, 251
        for men and women 233–4
    and health
        deterioration xiii–xiv, 148, 149,
            152–6
        improvement 155–6
    and poverty 149
economy, informal 4
employment
    changes of 160–1
    and disability 252, 253
    gender inequalities 241–2
    and health 156–70, 236–7
    and ill health 47, 50–1, 122, 124–6, 154
    informal 162
    insecurity 161–2
    life stories 124, 152–4, 236–7, 238,
        239–41, 251–71
    long hours 163–4
    loss of 158–9
    men
        active approach 235–6
        lack of activity 238–9
        life stories 236–7, 238
    multiple 165
    positive factors 169
    secondary 157–8
    and stress 156–7
    types of, and poverty 123–4
    women 239–42
        family responsibilities 240–1
        lack of activity 242–3
    working conditions, and health 166–8
    see also jobs
entrepreneurship
    men 235–6
    women 239–40
EQ-5D health measurement 34–5, 39–40,
        44, 45, 127, 128, 175, 202
    GHQ, comparison 40–1
    three-level scale 41, 43–4, 73, 127

verification 45–52
ESOMAR 19
    definition, social class 96
Estonia, life expectancy 27
EU countries, poverty levels 101
EuroQol
    Group 127, 202
    scale 120
exercise, physical, decrease 151

Finland
    alcoholism 13
    health spending 16
    life expectancy 12
foreign currency reserves 3

GDP
    decrease 2, 7, 15
    increase 3
gender differences
    health behaviour 244–8
    health maintenance 246
gender inequalities
    employment 241–2
    health 23–4, 64–5, 227, 227–9, 231,
        248–9
        behavioural explanation 232
        socioeconomic factors 232
    households 243–4
    life expectancy 227
    mortality 231
    poverty 230, 231
Germany, life expectancy 27
GHQ health measurement 34, 39, 127,
        128, 202, 203
    EQ-5D, comparison 40–1
Gini coefficient 8, 80, 103
Gref, German 2, 100

health
    analysis, models 76
    and attitude 57–8
    attitudes to 210–11
    coping mechanisms 75–6
    decline in 46
    definition, positive/negative 53
    descriptors
        English 17

Russian 17, 20
deterioration, and economic reforms
    148, 149, 152–6
and employment 156–70, 236–7
    changes 161
    interaction of factors 169–70
    poor working conditions 166–8
gender inequalities 23–4, 64–5, 227,
    227–9, 231, 248–9
and harmful habits 151
and hopelessness 92–3
illness, boundary 17
improvement
    and economic reforms 155–6
    and stress reduction 23
    and inequalities 79–96
    of income 79, 84
life stories 120–1
loss of, fear 32
and money 56–7
occupational status groups 49
and poverty 20–1, 119, 131
responsibility for 63–4
self-assessment 95, 152–6
    average 150–1
    and material welfare changes 128
    and social class 95–6
self-care 201
sickness, intermediate state 53–4
and social action 22–4
and social capital 132–40
see also social capital
and social inequalities, models 201–2
and social status 20, 94
and social structure 20–2, 76
as sociocultural phenomenon 63
and stress, absence of 56–7, 62
understanding of 54–5, 59, 63
    absence of
        disease 62, 66, 68, 70, 72, 74
        stress 68, 70, 72
    and educational level 70–1, 72–3
    in RLMS survey 62–5
    and self-rated affluence 72
    vitality 62, 66, 68, 70, 72, 74–5
and vitality 55–6
as well-being 59–61, 62
see also ill health

health behaviour, gender differences 244–8
    see also health dynamics
health behaviour models 216–24
    employment, and self-help measures
        216–21
    unemployment
        and family support 221–2
        social inclusion, and self-help
            measures 222–4
health care
    accessibility 129–32, 181–95
        lack of means 181–4
        organisational problems 184–5
        personal narrative 130–1
        ways to improve 195–6
    changes, and level of material welfare
        196
    costs 9
    credit payment for 179
    establishments, use patterns 174
    funding, and level of material welfare
        196
    inequalities 8–9, 132
    primary 14
    private expenditure 129
    role 14
    Soviet model 131
    spending 14
    system, strains on 147–8
    see also research project
health crisis 9–16
    alcoholism 13, 14, 15
    causal factors 11–12
    lifestyle factors 12–13, 149–50
    origins 10
    psychosocial stress 15
    smoking 13
health dynamics 224–5
    better health group 203–6
        better material circumstances 208
        life stories 205
        unchanged material circumstances
            208
    factors 207–15
        behavioural practices 211–13
        material circumstances 209–11
        occupational activities 213–14
        stress 214–15

worse health group 206–7
    better material circumstances 208
    life stories 206–7
    unchanged material circumstances
        208–9
    see also health behaviour
health indicators
    men/women 245
    respondents aged 14 plus 31–2
    Russia/UK comparison 30–1
    various age groups 33
health inequalities 79–96
health investigation, full 177–8
health maintenance, gender differences 246
health measurement 34–45
    EQ-5D method 34–5, 39–40, 44, 45,
        127, 128, 175, 202
        GHQ method, comparison 40–1
        three-level scale 41, 43–4, 73, 127
    GHQ method 34, 39, 127, 128, 202,
        203
    life stories 45–52, 202
    qualitative/quantitative indicators 74
    subjective assessments 35–7, 40, 41, 48
        examples 38
        material welfare 44
        sick role, adoption 35, 37, 38
Health and Social Development, Ministry 9
    responsibilities 147
health spending
    Finland 16
    Russia 16
    UK 16
herbs, use 187
Herzlich, C. 53
HIV/AIDS 9, 10
homelessness 14
homeopathy 187
homicide rate 15
hopelessness, and health 92–3
hospital stay, paying for 188
hostel dwelling 87
housing inequalities 86–7

Iceland, life expectancy 27
ill health
    and age 155
    blue-collar workers 52

    and disability 44
    and employment 47, 50–1, 122,
        124–6, 154
    fear of 132
    levels 8
    and poverty 46–7, 111, 120, 127–9,
        201
    professionals 52
    social class distribution 52
    and social exclusion 51, 135
    and unemployment 159
    see also sickness
illness
    health, boundary 17
    subjective assessment 43
income, main sources 157
income distribution
    Ivanovo Province 81
    Moscow 81
        per capita 102
    Russian Federation
        1990/2005 81
        per capita, 2000–2005 83
        regional variations 102
    Tatarstan Republic 81
    Voronezh Province 81
income inequalities 8, 79–85
    and health 79
    interfamily transfers 83
    as measure of poverty 83–4, 100
    'shadow' incomes 83, 103
    State's responsibility 93
Index of Multiple Deprivation (IMD)
        291–3
inequalities *see* health inequalities; housing
        inequalities; income inequalities;
        social inequalities
Ingushetiya Republic, per cent below
        subsistence minimum 82
INTAS programme, establishment xiii
International Monetary Fund 2
Ivanovo Province, income distribution 81

job insecurity 161–2
jobs
    additional 66
    changes 160–1
        forced 160

and health 161
loss of, fear 32–4
low-quality 22
jobseeking 160–1

Kudrin, Alexei 2

leave from work
lack of 169
and material welfare 126
life
aspects of, self-assessment 84, 86
positive outlook 42–3
quality of, and chronic diseases 30
satisfaction/dissatisfaction with 21, 48,
156, 161
life expectancy 6, 27
Bulgaria 27
decline 10–11, 15
Estonia 27
Finland 12
Germany 27
Iceland 27
international comparisons 12
male 14
Poland 27
Russia, gender inequalities 227
Spain 27
UK 12, 27
life situations, difficult 178–9
life stories 115–16
employment 124, 152–4, 236–7, 238,
239–41, 251–71
health 45–52, 120–1, 202, 205, 206–7,
251–71
social capital 140–2, 144
unemployment 159
lifestyle factors, health crisis 12–13,
149–50
living standards 1997–2005 115
long hours working 163–4
low pay 162–3

Maleva, Tatyana 5
medical care
accessibility, need to improve 198
better organisation, need for 198
fears about obtaining 21

medical staff, more pay 197
paying for 143–4, 148, 188–93
attitudes to 192–3
seekers, characteristics 176
ways of improving 196–9
medical staff, connections with 138
see also doctors
medicines
payment for 189, 191
problems obtaining 185–7
sources 187
men
alcoholism 151, 232
employment
active approach 235–6
life stories 236–7
entrepreneurship 235–6
smoking 151
money, and health 56–7, 76
see also poverty
morbidity
increase 149, 173
tuberculosis 149
mortality
alcoholism 27
cardiovascular disease 6, 15, 27
Cuba 11
gender inequalities 231
increase 148
infant 149
main causes **28**, 148
male vs female 148–9
Poland 11
Moscow
income distribution 81
per capita 102
per cent below subsistence minimum
82

NOBUS programme 105–6, 108
nutrition, and poverty 113

obesity, increase 151–2
occupational status groups, health 49
OHB household data 105

pain 30, 33
prevalence 19, 34, 42

Parsons, T. 53
patients, types of 179–81
pensioners, employment 30
Poland
    life expectancy 27
    mortality 11
population, decline 6
poverty
    absolute concept 98–101
    Albania 82
    and alcoholism 121–2
    concealment, Soviet era 97
    decrease 98–9, 111
    deprivation as measure of 86
    deprivations 1997–2005 114
    and economic reforms 149
    estimated rates, 1992–2000 98
    estimation
        change 99
        World Bank 99–100
    gender inequalities 230, 231
    and health 20–1, 119, 131
    and ill health 46–7, 111, 120, 127–9,
        201
    income inequalities as measure of
        83–4, 100
    intergenerational effect 104
    invisible 104
    large-scale 20–1
    living standards 1997–2005 115
    markers of 92
    measurement 82
        dissatisfaction with 105–6, 108–9
        material circumstances approach
            112
    models, changing 103
    multivariate approach 109–10
    and nutrition 113
    official views 97–104
        criticisms of 100, 103
    persistence of 113–17, 119
    qualitative analysis 109–17
    relative concept 101–4, 106–7
    and rest 126
    Romania 82
    Russia 82, 104–5, 107–8
    'silent poor' 104
    and social capital 135

    sociological research 104–9
    and types of employment 123–4
    and unemployment 159
    variations 98
    WHO on 131
    see also social exclusion
poverty levels 7–8, 16, 104–6
    children 105
    EU countries 101
    households 1992–2004 108
    reduction 111
        targets 100
    regional variations 102
    rural 7, 104–5
    urban 7, 105
private expenditure, health care 129
professionals, ill health 52
project *see* research project
Putin administration, assessment 4–6
Putin, Vladimir 2, 3, 104

research project 16–18
    aims 18
    data
        pan-Russian surveys 274
        quantitative/qualitative 273
        sources 18
    families, socioeconomic structure 279
    findings 18–24
        health beliefs 19–20
        health and social action 22–4
        health and social structure 20–2
    households
        demographic type 278
        head, socioeconomic status
            279–84
        material circumstances 111–12
        size 277
        structure 278
    Longitudinal Panel Study of
        Households 273, 274–7
    methodology xiii, 273–93
    respondents, age/gender 278
    Russian research methods, application
        291–3
    sociological research 274
    Western research methods, application
        285–90

rest, and poverty 126
RLMS (Russian Longitudinal Monitoring
    Survey) 18, 27, 107–8, 150
  database 274
  household poverty, 1992–2004 108
  understanding of health 62–5
Romania, poverty 82
Rose, Richard 134
Russia
  health spending 16
  poverty 82, 104–5, 107–8
  transformation, 1990s 17
Russian Federation
  income distribution 1990/2005 81
  per cent below subsistence minimum
    82

St Petersburg, per cent below subsistence
    minimum 82
Scambler, Annette 227
Scambler, G. 208, 216
self-care 201
sickness, understanding of 55–6, 62, 63,
    68–9
  and educational level 70
  and self-rated affluence 72
  see also ill health
Sirchia, Girolamo 104
smoking
  health crisis 13
  men 151
  women 151
social action, and health 22–4
social capital 21, 75
  absence of 137–8
  and health 132–40
  Islamic perspective 143
  and level of material welfare 138, **139**
  life stories 140–2, 144
  loyalty to occupational group, model
    144
  mainstream connections 134
  meaning 132–3
  models 140–4
  modern model, example 140–2
  and poverty 135, 139
  quality of 133
  regional variations 140–5

research 134–7
  and social inequalities 144–5
  and social networks 132, 134, 136–7,
    144
  sociocultural contexts 140
  traditional model example 142–3
social class
  ESOMAR definition 96
  and self-assessment of health 95–6
social exclusion xiv, 1, 18, 21, 22, 46,
    110, 145
  consequences 111
  and ill health 51, 135
  see also disability; poverty
social inequalities 83
  attitudes to 91
  and health, models 201–2
  and lack of trust 93
  perceptions 90–6
  and social capital 144–5
  tolerance of 91
social justice, views on 183–4
social networks 21, 23
  function 137–40
  importance of 133
  and poverty 139–40
  and social capital 132, 134, 136–7,
    144
social policy 2
  main aim 22
  stages 1
social problems 5
  responsibility for 194, 195
social reforms 116–17
  consequences 120
social security, model 3
social services, fee-paying, use 87
social State, aspiration 4
social status, and health 20, 94
social structure
  and health 20–2, 76
  Russia/UK, comparison 94, **94**
social support, changes, in Putin
    presidency 195
Soviet model, health care 131
Spain, life expectancy 27
Stabilization Fund 3, 4
standard of living, typical family 89–90

State
  income inequalities, responsibility for
    93
  primacy of 5
stress
  absence of
    and health 56–7, 62, 68, 70, 72,
      73, 75
    and vitality 67, 75
  and employment 156–7
  health dynamics 214–15
  reduction, and health improvement 23
  and unemployment 159–60
subsistence minimum
  calculation 80–1, 99
    shortcomings of 100
  per cent below
    Ingushetiya Republic 82
    Moscow 82
    Russian Federation 82
    St Petersburg 82
    Tatarstan Republic 82
    Voronezh Province 82
  subjective evaluation 101–2

Tatarstan Republic
  income distribution 81
  per cent below subsistence minimum
    82
Tobacco Framework Convention 13
Townsend, Peter 107, 109, 110
  'Black Report' 131
trust, lack of, and social inequalities 93
tuberculosis 9, 10
  morbidity 149

UK
  health spending 16
  life expectancy 12, 27
  Russia
    health indicators, comparison 30–1
    social structure, comparison 94, **94**

unemployment
  benefit payment 158
  health behaviour models 222–4
  hidden 110
  and ill health 159
  life stories 159
  and poverty 159
  rate 158
  and stress 159–60

Veit-Wilson, John 110
vitality
  and absence of stress 67, 75
  and health 55–6, 62, 66, 68, 70, 72,
    73, 74–5
Voronezh Province
  income distribution 81
  per cent below subsistence minimum
    82

wages, non-payment of 166
well-being, health as 59–61, 62
women
  alcoholism 151
  employment 239–42
  family responsibilities 240–1
  employment discrimination 234
  entrepreneurship 239–40
  lack of support, from men 234
  lower status 234
  smoking 151
World Bank 7, 8, 100, 111, 232
  poverty
    estimation method 99–100
    research 104–5, 201
World Health Organisation (WHO) xiv, 201
  on poverty 131
Yeltsin, Boris 2

Zaslavskaya, 109
zdorovyi, meanings 17
Zhuravleva, I.V. 216

DATE DUE

JUN 0 1 2011			